YALE ROMANIC STUDIES

XII

THE *DOLCE STIL NOVO*
ACCORDING TO LORENZO DE' MEDICI

Y0-BSC-605

AMS PRESS
NEW YORK

PREVIOUSLY PUBLISHED IN THE SAME SERIES

THE
DOLCE STIL NOVO

ACCORDING TO LORENZO DE' MEDICI

A STUDY OF HIS POETIC *PRINCIPIO* AS
AN INTERPRETATION OF THE ITALIAN LITERATURE
OF THE PRE-RENAISSANCE PERIOD,
BASED ON HIS *COMENTO*

BY

ANGELO LIPARI

ASSOCIATE PROFESSOR OF ITALIAN
IN YALE UNIVERSITY

NEW HAVEN
YALE UNIVERSITY PRESS
LONDON · HUMPHREY MILFORD · OXFORD UNIVERSITY PRESS
1936

Library of Congress Cataloging in Publication Data

Lipari, Angelo.
    The dolce stil novo according to Lorenzo de' Medici.

    Original ed. issued as v. 12 of Yale Romanic studies.
    1. Medici, Lorenzo de', il Magnifico, 1449-1492.
Comento. 2. Italian poetry--Early to 1400--History and
criticism. I. Title. II. Series: Yale Romanic
studies, 12.
PQ4630.M3C65 1973   851'.2   72-1732
ISBN 0-404-53212-8

From the edition of 1936, New Haven
Reprinted in 1973 by AMS with permission from
Yale University Press
Manufactured in the United States of America

International Standard Book Number:
Complete Series: 0-404-53200-4
Volume 12: 0-404-53212-8

AMS PRESS INC.
NEW YORK, N.Y. 10003

THIS

"FATICA D'AMORE"

IS AFFECTIONATELY DEDICATED

TO

GEORGE LINCOLN HENDRICKSON

COUNSELOR AND FRIEND

HUMANIST AND SPONSOR OF ITALIAN STUDIES

PREFACE

THE character and purpose of this study may be presented best through a short account of its origin and growth. My first interest was the question of Dante's infidelity to Beatrice. It will be remembered that, in the Terrestrial Paradise (cantos XXX and XXXI of *Purgatory*), Beatrice reproaches the poet for his unfaithfulness to her memory, when, soon after her death, he forsook her and "gave himself to others" (*diessi altrui*). The *altrui* is primarily *la donna gentile* or the so-called *donna pietosa,* otherwise known also as "the lady of the window," who, in the *Vita Nuova* (XXXV–XXXVIII) occupies the author's mind to the extent of four sonnets, and who succeeds in consoling him, at least temporarily, for the loss of the *gentilissima.* But the reference is also, no doubt, to *le serene* and the *pargoletta* of *Purgatorio,* XXXI, lines 45 and 59, respectively; indeed, to all the various other ladies of the *Rime,* who, as some Dante scholars think, are probably all related to the said *donna pietosa,* or are the same: namely, Fioretta, Violetta, Pietra, Lisetta, Montanina, and the ones unnamed. Now, in the *Convivio* (II, xv, 3), Dante says definitely and unequivocally, "questa donna è *la Filosofia.*" I wondered, therefore, how the study of philosophy could be said to be antagonistic to his love for Beatrice Portinari, especially after her death. Even if one grants the suggestion of carnal love, which obviously is implied in *le serene* and some of the other "ladies," unless one presumes that the Beatrice of the *Vita Nuova* is also the symbol of a mental activity, how is one to explain this supposed conflict, which did not end with the poet's repentance of his infidelity (cf. chap. xxxix of the *Vita Nuova*), but evidently was resumed and continued throughout the period covered by the *Convivio?* Perhaps, I thought, the Beatrice of the *Vita Nuova,* on the contrary, stands specifically for the intuitive faculty, which, as Croce says, is productive of artistic images, and is akin yet opposed, as it were, to the rational faculty productive of philosophic concepts. Moreover, unless one makes such an assumption, which unwarrantably, to be sure, presupposes Dante's clear anticipation of the modern science of æsthetics, but which, if true, would indicate a natural conflict in the poet between the artist and the philosopher, how is one to reconcile such infidelity with the fact that Beatrice herself later becomes a symbol of philosophy, or, perhaps better, of Christian Revelation, in *Paradiso?* Indeed, the Beatrice of *Paradiso* is no longer merely the Beatrice of the *Vita Nuova,* but a combination or fusion of her previous self with the nature of the *donna pietosa.* Perhaps there she is a personification of the concept of the dual form of human knowledge, and, from the philosophic point of view, she now stands both for the intuitive faculty and for the rational faculty. At any rate, I thought that perhaps this fusion of the two "ladies" previously kept distinct now indicated that the poet at last had reconciled his purely artistic inclination with his philosophic tendency. Thereafter he was definitely the philosophic poet, author of the *Commedia.*

I was pursuing this idea, and had already constructed a well-documented proof, as I thought, of my thesis, when I began to realize that my solution of the riddle rested on the assumption of the allegorical character of the Beatrice of the *Vita Nuova* and on my interpretation of certain quotations from the author's works, which I adduced as evidence of his real thought in support of my argument. This cooled my enthusiasm, for I feared that I should never convince anyone on those grounds, and particularly the so-called positivist critics. At best, I might be stamped as another "symbolist," which would not be flattering. In other words, I found myself involved in the problem of realism and symbolism in the *dolce stil novo,* which always confronts the critic whenever he attempts to detect the esoteric, real intent of the poets of that school. My quandary was all the greater inasmuch as I accepted the ample and adequate proof of the historians relative to the real existence of a Beatrice Portinari.

My problem, therefore, was to solve, if possible, this question first and once for all. But, to do this, I felt that I needed positive, external evidence, on the authority of some reliable critic near those times, of the interrelation between symbolism and realism, both surely present in that style of poetry. Accordingly, I began to inquire into the character of the *donna gentile,* or *donna angelicata* of the primitive poets. Thus, I laid aside my original project, and, widening the scope of my study, I ended by enlarging and altering also its object. The subject now was *la donna gentile.* As I went along, I checked myself by reading numerous opinions on this subject and on the question of realism and symbolism as related to it. But here I found myself in a veritable maze of contradictory, sometimes confused, and, on the whole, inconclusive studies. I was almost forced to discard them all, when I found at last the very critic and the very evidence I had been looking for.

This fortunate discovery was the *Comento del Magnifico Lorenzo de' Medici sopra alcuni de' suoi sonetti*, which I happened to review in connection with my lectures. This little book was now a revelation to me. As soon as my suspicion was aroused with respect to its real character and intent, it seemed to me that Lorenzo answered my questionings clearly, fully, and authoritatively. Indeed, he solved the immediate problem for me, and at the same time he shed such light on the rôle played by the previous Italian poetry in the intellectual and artistic movement of the Renaissance that I decided to scrutinize it very carefully. As the result of this scrutiny, however, I now wished to offer this interpretation as the solution of my immediate problem and of some other questions that the history of the pre-Renaissance period presents. This meant a further expansion of the scope of my study and a further enlargement of my topic. On the other hand, the task itself was now restricted primarily to the critical interpretation of this single work, indeed, for the present, to a small portion of it, or to the first two parts, which the author calls, respectively, the *proemio* to his commentary and the *principio di nuova vita*. The *nuova vita* itself, which is the continued application in practice of the preceding theoretic beginning, and which I need not take up in this volume, comprises the main bulk of the sonnets commented upon, whereas the *principio* consists of the first four sonnets only; but these, in the light of his comments and of the proem, constitute a treatise on the principle of the *dolce stil novo*.

This explains both the title and the subtitle of my study. Moreover, the reader knows now what to expect. If he does not, yet has some knowledge and love of pre-Renaissance Italian literature, let him follow me indulgently through a series of interpretations and discussions, which may not always seem relevant at the time, but which, I assure him, in the end, will be found pertinent to the matter in hand. Owing to the philosophical nature of the subject matter, the reading will naturally be hard at times, and my own exposition, none too fluent, will not, I fear, facilitate it. In fact, my attempt to clarify the meaning and bring out my own points, as well as those of the author, has resulted in a certain "repetitiousness," as kind friends have told me, which perhaps was not entirely avoidable in the treatment of a subject so intricate. But I felt that I, or, better, the Magnificent had something to say, and that my own incapacity should not stand in the way of his message. So, let the kind reader bear with me patiently to the end. I promise him a true conception of the scope, character, and artistic principle of Italian poetry from its inception throughout the Renaissance. Therefore, notwithstanding the imperfection of my exposition, let him follow me closely, attentively, and, may I ask, sympathetically. This is an essential requirement of the very *principio* we shall study. Let us then relive together Lorenzo's own "experience" of this *principio*.

And now, borrowing the close of Egidio Romano's or Archbishop Colonna's preface to his exposition of Guido Cavalcanti's famous canzone, *Donna mi prega . . .*, perhaps I, too, may exclaim:

> "Va, esposizione, sicuramente
> a gente di valore, a cui ti mando,
> e di star con nessun uom ti comando,
> lo qual vuole usar l'occhio per la mente."

ACKNOWLEDGMENTS

To Professor George Lincoln Hendrickson, to whom this study is dedicated, I wish to express here my special gratitude for his kindly criticisms and valuable suggestions. I am grateful also to those who, either in part or in its entirety, have likewise read this work in manuscript and made similar observations: Professors John Milton Berdan, Albert Gabriel Feuillerat, and Karl Young of Yale University; Professor Arrigo Levasti of Florence, Italy; and my associate, Mr. Archibald Thomas MacAllister. My special thanks, however, are due to my colleague, Professor Frederick Bliss Luquiens, and to Lestrois Parish. Without the former's faithful friendship and generous encouragement, and the latter's skilful suggestions of a rhetorical nature, I fear this volume might never have seen the light.

THE COMMENTARY OF
LORENZO THE MAGNIFICENT
ON SOME OF HIS OWN SONNETS

THE PROEM AND THE FIRST FOUR SONNETS

"Tu sai che 'l ciel sempr'è lucente e chiaro,
e quanto in sè non si turba già mai;
ma li nostri occhi per cagioni assai
chiaman la stella talor tenebrosa."

DANTE: *Convivio*, Canzone II, 77–80.

"Dove è piana la lettera,
non far oscura glosa."

JACOPONE DA TODI: *Cantici
morali*, XXXII, 15, 7–8.

CONTENTS

PART I

THE PROEM

PART V

THE *PRINCIPIO:* SONNETS III AND IV

Sonnet III. Translation of the author's own comment. The "gentilesse" of mystic death. The poet's fervor and enthusiasm in the
pursuit of his ideal. The physiological and psychological basis of
the joys and sorrows of the "new life."

Sonnet IV. Translation of the author's own comment. The apparent contradiction and true continuity of Sonnets III and IV. The
labor of love, or the joys and sorrows of the apprentice in the art
of "gentle" poetry. Lorenzo's *gentile passione,* or his poetic avocation.

DEDUCTIONS AND CONCLUSIONS

A glance forward at Lorenzo's *nuova vita.* Final words on the
historico-critical value of Lorenzo's *principio.*

Preamble. Medieval æsthetics: the "privilege of lovers," or the independence of art. The identity of stilnovism and humanism:
seen in the metaphor of Clytie. The influence of Boccaccio.

Concerning the date of the *Raccolta aragonese.*

INTRODUCTION

General Neglect of a Precious Work, and Ignorance of Its Profound Significance in the History of Italian Literature.

ONE of the most valuable documents of Italian literary criticism, the *Commentary of Lorenzo de' Medici on some of his own sonnets,* has lain unevaluated and unappreciated for centuries. Apparently there is no critical study, either ancient or modern, dealing with this work of Lorenzo per se and with the unity of its content. The rich bibliography on the statesman-poet and great patron of the arts contains numerous works on his literary production as a whole, and many special monographs on various aspects of this output relating the author to his contemporaries, dealing with sources and influences, or treating individual works.[1] One comes across articles and essays on details relative to a date, a text, or a historical event connected with the life of the Magnificent, but I have found no work that attempts to reconstruct and interpret the underlying concept which brought forth the *Commentary.*

Thus, examining, for instance, the selected list of special monographs "on the *Commentary,* the amours of the Magnificent, and the *Canzoniere,*" given by Simioni in the Nota just referred to,[2] I find that Neri,[3] Simioni[4] himself, and Del Lungo[5] are all concerned with the less significant question of the historical identity of the ladies sung by Lorenzo. They hardly touch on the nature of

1. Cf. Attilio Simioni, *Saggio bibliografico sulla vita e sulle opere di Lorenzo il Magnifico,* to be found in his Nota to his edition of Lorenzo's *Opere* (Bari, Laterza, 1913–14), II, 365–372; to which I like to add the two most recent and excellent studies; namely, Vittorio Rossi's, contained in a new edition of his *Quattrocento* (Milano, Vallardi, 1933), and J. B. Fletcher's, contained in his *Literature of the Italian Renaissance* (New York, The Macmillan Company, 1934).

2. *Op. cit.,* II, 369–370.

3. A. Neri, "La Simonetta," in *Giornale storico della letteratura italiana,* V (1885), 131.

4. A. Simioni, "Donne ed amori medicei. La Simonetta," in *Nuova Antologia,* June 16, 1908.

5. Isidoro Del Lungo, "Gli amori del magnifico Lorenzo," in *Nuova Antologia,* May 1 and 16, 1913.

the poet's love, which is the important question. It is the real substance of the sonnets of the *Commentary* and the matter for
which the author feels the need of an interpretation. Scarano[6] and
Ferri[7] both deal with Lorenzo's neo-Platonism in general, and
concern themselves more with possible influences (mainly by Ficino) than with his personal understanding of the doctrine of love
and his original contribution to it. Thomas' *Étude*[8] embraces all
the Italian poetry from the Middle Ages to the Renaissance! And
even Flamini,[9] whose subject, one would think, particularly calls
for a special study of this "interpretation" by the author himself,
does not mention it once and barely refers to it indirectly.

In short, it may be said that this precious little work has suf-
fered general neglect, due chiefly to hasty, superficial reading, and
to the prompt recognition of its imitation of Dante and its neo-
Platonic character. For that reason, critics dismiss it with this
simple, now traditional remark, and have not thought it worthy
of a separate and more conscientious study. To be sure, these critics cannot be accused of altogether ignoring it, although they
practically do this. This is evident in Del Lungo and Flamini as
well as in Simioni (who later edited the works of Lorenzo, including the *Commentary*). All of them, as a matter of fact, quote
from it sparingly, but the importance of the work, and its profound significance in the history of Italian literature and Italian
criticism they have entirely missed. This surprises us in a critic of
Flamini's scholarship and acumen, who declares Lorenzo "the
last imitator of the sweet style," devotes to him much more space
than to any other follower of this school, and recognized in him a
continuatore insieme e novatore of the stilnovistic doctrine of love.
Indeed, he even knew that the first four sonnets taken up in the
Commentary, and said to refer to the death of Simonetta Cat-

6. N. Scarano, "Il platonismo nelle poesie di Lorenzo de' Medici," in *Nuova Antologia,* August 15 and September 1, 1893.

7. L. Ferri, "Platonismo di Ficino. Dottrina dell'amore," in *Filosofia delle scuole italiane,* XV (1884), 269; also "Di M. Ficino e delle cause della rinascenza del platonismo
nel Quattrocentro," *idem,* XIV (1883), 181.

8. G. Thomas, *Étude sur l'expression de l'amour platonique dans la poésie italienne
du moyen-age et de la renaissance* (Paris, 1892), p. 51.

9. F. Flamini, "Gli imitatori della lirica di Dante e del 'dolce stil novo,' " in *Studi di
storia letteraria italiana e straniera* (Livorno, Giusti, 1895), p. 59.

taneo, figure among the lyrics of Lorenzo himself, included by him in his famous *Raccolta aragonese*. Apropos of this anthology (and particularly of its introductory letter to Frederick of Aragon), Flamini says that it is "the oldest document, after the *De vulgari eloquentia,* of critical history relative to Italian poetry."[10] It is a mystery just how Flamini, after establishing this connection and making this assertion, could fail to see the close relation between this letter and the *Commentary,* and fail to ascribe to this work at least an equal importance. Still more inconceivable is Simioni's failure to note this relation and to realize the importance of the *Commentary,* when he edited these works, publishing them in the same volume, one directly after the other, and when he shows that he has read Flamini by appropriating this critic's opinion and repeating it almost verbatim.[11] The lack of an adequate critical study on this subject is due, therefore, either to the traditional disregard for this imitative and apparently insignificant work of Lorenzo; or to the natural aversion felt by positivistic critics to admitting and dealing with esoteric meanings, or to mere inadvertence.

The importance of the *Commentary,* as a document of Italian literary history and criticism, second both in time and value only to its Dantean model, will, I trust, become manifest as I proceed with its exposition. I shall translate or summarize the text liberally, and comment on it as I go along.

Structure of the Commentary.

THE text I use is in the new edition of Lorenzo's *Opere,* prepared by Attilio Simioni, and published by Laterza as two volumes of the valuable collection "Scrittori d'Italia." The *Commentary,* as already noted, comes directly after the letter to Frederick of Aragon, son of the King of Naples.[12]

The *Commentary* has three parts, not separated by title or spac-

---

10. Cf. Flamini, *idem,* pp. 59–60; also p. 8.
11. Cf. Lorenzo de' Medici, *Opere* (cited edition), I, 1, 9; II, 353.
12. The text occupies pp. 11 to 141 of Vol. I, published in 1913. In this first volume, the *Commentary* bears the number II. All references to Lorenzo's works will be in this edition.

ing, but distinguished, and even named by the author in the
course of his writing. First comes a *proemio*,[13] or preface, occupy-
ing fourteen and a half pages (from p. 11 to the middle of p. 25);
then a *principio*,[14] also called "argumento dei primi quattro sonetti,"[15] which serves as a sort of unique eight-and-a-half-page introduction (to p. 34); and finally the body of the work, said to
constitute a *nuova vita*,[16] which extends for the remaining 108
pages, and ends abruptly almost in the middle of a sentence.[17]

The *proemio* explains the purpose of the work, gives the author's reasons for his long hesitation and final decision to undertake it, and also defends the appropriateness of the obscure *principio* or "beginning" which he has chosen for his book of "new
life." For in fact, the *principio* consists of four sonnets, which he
declares to have been inspired by the death of a certain lady. They
deal with Death, as he interprets them, explaining fully their
origin and real meaning.[18] Lastly, *questa nuova vita* consists simi-

13. Cf. Text, p. 25, l. 9.

14. Cf. (for one of several instances in which this part is so denominated) Text, p.
23, l. 32.

15. Cf. Text, p. 25, ll. 17–18.   16. Cf. Text, p. 34, l. 6.

17. Cf. Text, p. 141. Simioni does not offer any explanation for this ending, nor does
he comment upon it at all. In his description of the five MSS. containing the *Commentary*, consulted by him, he mars an otherwise full and accurate account by neglecting to
say whether the text ends in precisely the same manner in all the MSS. Nor does he
speak of any apparent or possible mutilation, particularly in connection with R4 (Riccardiano 2726), which he follows chiefly, regarding it the nearest to the lost autograph.
(Cf. Vol. II: p. 329, No. 9; p. 330, Nos. 14 and 18; p. 338, Nos. 41 and 42; and p. 353,
II.) After examining these MSS. myself, I am able to certify that they all end alike, and
that, apparently, there has been no mutilation. I reach a conclusion similar to Simioni's
opinion, who thinks that R4 is a copy of the original autograph and that the others all
derive, directly or indirectly, from another copy (X) of the autograph (cf. *loc. cit.* p.
354). Only one of two conjectures is possible. Either both R4 and X are copies of a
previous copy, and not of the autograph, or the autograph itself ended thus. In the first
case the presumption would then be that the first amanuensis just stopped there abruptly,
since it is not to be supposed that two amanuenses working independently would both
stop accidentally at the identical place; in the second place, the author himself never got
any farther. In any case, be sure that the work in its extant form is not complete, for,
besides stopping in the midst of the last comment, it contains definite references to at
least two other sonnets intended to be included and not found therein. (Cf. Text, p. 63,
ll. 20–21; p. 71, ll. 24–25; and p. 73, ll. 1–3.) Moreover, at the very beginning of the
proem, Lorenzo speaks of "interpretazione e comento de' miei sonetti," which implies all,
and not only *alcuni*, as Simioni justly corrects in view of the circumstances and of the
great many left uninterpreted.

18. As already stated, Flamini observes that these four sonnets figure among the lyrics of

larly of sonnets, here apparently arranged in an intended sequence, and thoroughly explained as to their true significance and the circumstances that gave rise to them. As already observed,[19] this part was clearly intended to include all the love sonnets of the poet, but, since he never finished the book he takes up only thirty-seven additional ones. In all, then, the *Commentary* comprises, explains, and interprets forty-one sonnets out of the 149 ascribed to Lorenzo in Simioni's edition. Just why the author wished to comment only upon his sonnets, and not to include also his other love

Lorenzo himself included by him in his *Raccolta aragonese* (cf. Flamini, *op. cit.*, pp. 65–66). And, in fact, I find them listed in the complete table of contents of the MS. constituting this *Raccolta*, given by Gentile (cf. Luigi Gentile, *I Codici Palatini*, I, 219–232; and, particularly, item XXX, Nos. 1, 2, 10, and 11 on pp. 231–232). Still, Flamini, too, connects them with the death of Simonetta, despite the fact that, according to himself, the date of this anthology is 1466 (cf. Flamini, *idem*, p. 59). Indeed, Simioni dates it back one year, to 1465. In any case, this makes Lorenzo either sixteen or seventeen years old at the time. But the death of Simonetta is said to have occurred in 1476, when Lorenzo was twenty-seven! There is, therefore, a decided historical inconsistency in the opinion of these critics and of all those who relate these sonnets to that event. We shall see later what rôle this lady, or any other, really played in the sonnets themselves. But let us note here that Flamini, who is aware of the inconsistency, rather than reject or even question the supposed source of inspiration, imagines that the four sonnets were possibly inserted later in the anthology, or else were "adapted many years after their composition to lament the passing away of that *gentilissima*" (cf. Flamini, *idem*, pp. 65–66). There is no evidence that this was really the case. No one, so far as I know, has ever seen or heard of an older version of these sonnets differing substantially from the one contained in *Codice Palatino 204*, which Gentile dates back to the beginning of the sixteenth century. In this MS. there is no indication of any such insertion or modification. Consequently, if any occurred, it must have been made before—in the original, or in an older MS. of the *Raccolta*. This is not at all likely, for this extant MS. must be a faithful copy of the original. Otherwise, it seems to me that—if *Palatino 204* had been intended to be a revised edition of the 1465 original—many other lyrics of Lorenzo would certainly have found their way in, and many defects of this anthology (important omissions and errors of attribution, for instance) would probably have been corrected. The fact is, however, that the *Raccolta*—as it appears in this MS.—bears every sign of being the work of a young, though precocious, student. Flamini himself qualifies these sonnets as "youthful," though in the loose, modern sense of the word. Thus I conclude that these sonnets, in the form in which we have them, are really among the earliest of Lorenzo's poems, dating back perhaps to 1465. If, at the time of writing the *Commentary*, the author was actually thinking of Simonetta's death in connection with them, they were "adapted" to this event, not in the sense that they were modified to suit this special death, but in the sense that they were found already fittingly describing his emotions in connection with this death. Surely, they were not inspired by the death of Simonetta, nor written on that occasion. In fact, as we shall see, they are reflections on death in general, and there is absolutely nothing in them that might refer only to Simonetta.

19. Cf. the end of n. 17, p. 4.

poems (five *sestine,* eight *canzoni,* and one ballade), as well as
other verses of similar character, is not known, and is a matter for
critical study and speculation.[20]

Originality and General Character of the Comento.

BEFORE taking up the proem, let us pause for one short consideration. Lorenzo's *Commentary* is a book written in verse and prose,
which, in content and form, immediately reminds one both of
Dante's *Vita Nuova* and of his *Convivio.* Other critics have recognized the relation to the *Vita Nuova.* The nature of the content,
dealing with love, the connecting prose passages which explain
the circumstances leading to the various sonnets, and particularly
the title "nuova vita," are sufficient to indicate, at first glance, this
Dantean source. But this relation is so patent that it becomes somewhat misleading, claiming for itself all the attention of the historian and critic. May I venture to bring out, for the first time, the
Commentary's derivation from the *Convivio* also? In the apologetic *proemio,* there is much that is more reminiscent of the *Convivio* than of the *Vita Nuova.* In justice to Lorenzo's originality,
however, we must observe that there is, in the *principio,* a notable
difference from his two sources. He is conscious of his *principio* as
an innovation, prompted by philosophical considerations.[21] I shall
not treat this innovation here, but must recognize it to be so fundamental and important a change that he accorded it a distinct
treatment and gave it a separate part in his work.

Some preliminary information is necessary also on Lorenzo's
style. I wish to call special attention to a curious, stilnovistic[22]
usage which Lorenzo followed in the form of his allegories. Here,
as in Dante and in all the followers of the school, the body of
Lorenzo's sonnets is not merely the narration, description, or expression of his experience of love; they *are* visibly, tangibly, and

20. Cf. Lorenzo's reasons for the choice of the sonnet form, Text, pp. 22–23; and this
study, pp. 55–56. Also my observations on this point, pp. 57–61.

21. Cf. Text, p. 23, l. 32–p. 25, l. 8.

22. The use of the noun "stilnovist"—coined by the Italian critics to indicate a follower of the school of the *dolce stil novo*—and of the derivatives "stilnovistic" and
"stilnovism," will save frequent circumlocutions.

withal spiritually this new life itself.[23] The first four sonnets, on the consideration of death, do not merely indicate the source of his inspiration, or simply the beginning of his passion, marking the first stages of its development; they *are* the *principio* in its concrete, material, and yet spiritual form. Indeed, as Lorenzo insistently repeats with an apparatus of philosophical reasons and literary examples, death does not merely mark the end of one thing and the beginning of another, but *is* itself this beginning, the source and origin of new life. "E però il principio della vera vita è la morte della vita non vera."[24] For this reason, the four sonnets called "principio" are themselves already "this new life." They are set apart and placed first not merely for chronological reasons, nor so much in order to serve as an introduction to the following, main body of "very different"[25] sonnets, but because they involve the fundamental philosophical principle of the new life. They are at once the first, self-conscious manifestation of his new life, beginning with the realization of the principle in that form and expression. This form of allegory, in which the concrete object *does not stand for* the abstract idea, but *is* the very subject involving and communicating a poetic spirituality—this form is the glory of the *dolce stil novo*. It is not, properly speaking, allegory or symbolism, but psychological realism. The *sovrasenso* or spiritual meaning (purely intellectual, or sentimental, or both) is inherent and implied in the concrete, material expression of it. It hovers above and around the "thing." It permeates, but is not superimposed. It is the soul of the body, and gives it its real existence. Lorenzo follows this style and applies this poetic art in the formative concept of his *principio;* and this he does, not slavishly and unintelligently, but masterfully and originally. It is this that marks him as a stilnovist of no mean value, and, moreover, shows how profoundly he understood the fundamental artistic principle of his school. His originality will become more evident as our discussion proceeds. Meanwhile let us note this example of conscious

23. For this peculiar usage of the terms "nuova vita" and "principio," see p. 4, nn. 14, 15, and 16.

24. Cf. Text, p. 25, ll. 5 and 6. For Lorenzo's argument on this question, read the entire paragraph, which starts on p. 24, and this study, p. 63.

25. Cf. Text, p. 34, l. 2.

conformity to the practice of the school, enlivened with the originality contained in the rich connotations of the title "principio" (which gives to that part of his "nuova vita" the surprise of novelty), and let us note, too, once for all, that Lorenzo does not try to hide his indebtedness, but, on the contrary, frankly avows it. As here, with the title "nuova vita," he always gives the clearest evidence of his borrowings and adaptations.

PART I

THE PROEM

CHAPTER I

Lorenzo's Project, and the Reasons That Had Deterred Him.

OUR author begins by declaring that he has had the preparation of "this interpretation and commentary of *his* sonnets" in mind for some time. But, he says, that whenever he had felt inclined to undertake it, three main reasons had made him so hesitant as to deter him from the execution of the project. These had been: the propriety of commenting on his own verses, the nature of the subject, and the use of the *volgare.* He had feared to appear to think too highly of himself, and (besides not leaving the judgment of his works properly to others) to seem to imply that his readers were incapable of understanding them—all of which might be considered presumption on his part. He knew, moreover, that the subject of his sonnets, being the passion of love, was considered by some not only frivolous but pernicious; not only unsuited for verse but unworthy of the additional honor of a commentary such as one might expect for a theological or philosophical subject. Thus he had feared the censure of wasting his time with such matters—he, in particular, who continually had so many affairs to attend to, both public and private. Finally, it had seemed to him that the *volgare,* or popular mother tongue, was somewhat lowly, even if the subject matter were in itself worthy. And since the *volgare* could not be understood where it was not known, he had even felt that his work and all his efforts might prove entirely in vain. These three difficulties, then, had been the cause of his delay in carrying out a project conceived some time before.[1] Now, however, won over by what seem to him better reasons, he has decided to go on with "this interpretation." But first he must give the better reasons, which completely refute all possible objections, and which are meant to "purge"[2] him of the anticipated "calumnies."

---

1. His precise words are "più tempo fa." Cf. Text, p. 12, l. 8.
2. The Dantesque expressions "purgare" and "purgazione" occur at least twice: on p. 16, l. 23, and on p. 17, l. 24.

The Propriety of Commenting on His Own Verses.

In answer to the first objection, Lorenzo says that it is no presumption to interpret one's own writings. On the contrary, besides saving labor for others, this is no one's business more than that of the author. Indeed, no one can know or determine (*eligere*) the truth of what he really means better than the author himself. This is clearly shown by the confusion that generally results from a variety of comments, in which most generally the commentator follows his own inclination rather than the actual intention of the writer. Moreover, this is no indication of a sense of superiority in himself, nor a denial to others of the right to judge him. Lorenzo believes that it is the duty of every man to work always for the benefit of mankind, whether it be to his personal advantage or to that of others. Since not everyone is born with the capacity to achieve the greatest things, each man should estimate himself, and exercise himself in that capacity in which he can best serve humanity. Not any single occupation can be suitable to the diversity of human talents, or meet the needs of human life—not even the life of contemplation which is, without controversy, considered to be the most excellent.[3] On the other hand, not only many works of genius, but many lowly occupations as well, necessarily concur to the perfection of human life. So, he repeats, it is really the duty of all men to serve humanity in that capacity and to that extent which heaven, or nature, or fortune has determined. He, Lorenzo, would gladly have undertaken greater things, but he hopes to succeed in one direction. Within the scope of his natural talent, and to the extent of his ability, he will not fail at least the few friends who—perhaps more to please him than to gratify themselves— have encouraged him in this task, and whose favor and authority mean much to him. If he cannot otherwise be useful to the readers of his verses, they may at least be pleased to find in him a mind akin and proportionate to their own. If anyone should laugh at his verses, he will be glad to have afforded him that much small enjoyment—especially glad, because in publishing this interpretation he really means to submit himself to the judgment of others. In

---

3. At this point there is a lacuna in the text, but it is apparently short and unimportant. The main idea is not lost. Cf. Text, bottom of p. 12.

fact, if he himself had considered his verses not worth reading, he would have escaped all criticism; while, by publishing and commenting on them, he is actually clearing himself much better of the accusation of presumption in judging himself.

The True Nature of His Subject.

PASSING to the expected "calumnies" of those who may accuse him of wasting his time on such a trifling subject—especially in the midst of his many pressing duties—he admits that he might justly be censured if man were perfect. But, since human nature is not so excellent as to induce all men always to engage in things perfect, since this degree of perfection is allowed to very few, since even these few achieve it but rarely in their lives, it seems to Lorenzo that those things are best in the world through which comes the least evil. Besides, although Lorenzo would not dare affirm it, still he concludes from his judgment of human nature that love in man not only is not reprehensible, but is almost necessary and *a very sure sign of "gentilesse" and excellence of heart.* Above all, it *inspires* men to worthy things, and *prompts* them to exercise those faculties (virtù) that are potentially in the soul. In fact, if we search diligently for the true definition of love, we find that it is nothing else than *an inherent or habitual desire for beauty* (appetito di bellezza). Granting this, all deformed and ugly "things" are necessarily displeasing to him who loves.

Omitting the broader Platonic conception of love, wherein all things achieve their perfection and ultimately rest in the supreme Beauty that is God, Lorenzo limits himself, for the present, to the love of man for human creations only (l'umana creatura). Although man is not that perfection of love called supreme good (sommo bene), still he may be regarded as a good (bene) especially if he has been endowed (ornata—adorned) with the qualifications necessary for a true love. These seem to the author to be two: first that one love a single object, and, second, that he love this object always. These conditions can hardly present themselves unless the object[4] loved be, in comparison with all other human

---

4. Lorenzo says "subietto amato," which implies not only the objectivity (in our modern sense) of the "thing" loved with respect to the lover (that is, its reality apart from

"objects," supremely perfect. The "object" poetically personified, besides possessing the elements of natural beauty, must have also: intelligence to a high degree (ingegno grande), graceful and genuine ways, charming manner and carriage, facility of sweet and accurate speech, and, finally, love, constancy, and faith.

All these attributes, he says, necessarily concur to make love perfect. Even though love originates in the eyes and in beauty, nevertheless those other conditions are necessary for its preservation and for its permanence. In fact, if the face should lose its color, and beauty should fade through illness or age, the other conditions will remain, and they are not less pleasing to the heart and soul than beauty is to the eyes. But even these conditions will not be sufficient unless the lover recognizes fully the value of the intellectual and moral qualities. This presupposes perfect judgment on his part, a quality that he must necessarily possess, because he would not otherwise deserve the object's love, and (presupposing the infallible judgment of the excellent "object" loved) the latter could not feel any love for him.

Accordingly, resuming his main argument, Lorenzo maintains that the portrayal of a true love is equivalent to the proposal of a great perfection—so regarded by the common custom of men—both in the beloved and in the lover. As it happens with all perfect things, he believes that such love has always been very rare in the world—which, however, only proves its excellence. He who loves only one thing, and that always, necessarily has no love for other things, and consequently avoids all the errors and sensual gratification in which men commonly indulge. Moreover, loving an intelligent person, and, seeking to please her,[5] he must try to achieve

the lover's self-consciousness) but also the subjective character and active nature of the "thing" thus objectified. This is, moreover, a generic term like the more material and yet living term "cosa," or thing, that recurs so frequently in this whole passage. Attention is called to this usage, especially with respect to the word "thing," which seems to me very significant. In fact, Lorenzo evidently includes, in his all-embracing generalization, not only woman (the first and most natural object of man's love, the example par excellence), and not only man in general, but all things—beauty in all its forms, physical and spiritual, natural and artificial. Furthermore, all these "things" are vivified by him, indeed personified. And, finally, a current of mutual sympathy and perfect understanding is established between the "thing" subjectified and the lover. To appreciate the poet's stilnovism, it is most important to understand this concept, which is essentially neo-Platonic and stilnovistic, but not devoid of original interpretation and application.

5. The use of the noun "persona"—of feminine gender in Italian—and the clear refer-

merit in all his works, and to excel others. He must engage in worthy tasks (*opere virtuose*) to be properly deserving of her whom he esteems worthy above all others. He must think all the time that, just as *the form of the object loved* is (manifestly and secretly) always present in his heart, so "she" must be present in all his activities, praising or reproaching him like a real witness of his work and his very thoughts. Thus, all such lovers—partly repressing evil through a sense of shame, and partly spurred to good by the stimulus to please the beloved—reach a "good" in the sense of the world, though they fall short of that perfection which they strive after.

Now this, exclaims Lorenzo, *this has been the subject of my verses!* If, in spite of these arguments, he does not succeed in refuting the calumnies of those who would condemn him, at least, in the words of "our" Florentine poet, he

spera trovar pietà, non che perdono

by those who have experienced love,[6] whose judgment is all that

ence throughout this paragraph to a *person* as the source and object of love should not deceive anyone, and lead him to think that Lorenzo is here limiting to woman, or even to mankind alone, the field of activity of his type of love—or that he is contradicting what he has just said. (Cf. n. 4, p. 13, on his generalization of the sources of love.) What he does is to personify the "thing" more obviously now, calling it a person (either man or woman, but evidently meant here to be a woman)—which the "thing" may, indeed, actually be by way of example par excellence. But I believe he does this merely to bring out the subjective character, or agency, of the source of love—which acts and behaves exactly *like a person*, even when it is not a person. In fact, the previous generalization comes out and is maintained in the phrase "the form of the *thing* loved" used in the same paragraph. The whole point is precisely that we react toward all forms of beauty, in nature and in man as well as in his art, as we do toward a perfect woman who inspires us. These innumerable "things" fill us with admiration and respect, inspiring us with true love, exactly as a woman does when she fulfills all the conditions listed by Lorenzo as the factors of perfect love. Thus, they may be personified, or spoken of poetically as such a woman. We have here, then—right in the exposition of the concept of love—merely another example of the realistic allegorism or allegorical realism of the stilnovists. As we see again, it amounts to a simple *sovrasenso* carried by the letter, or, if preferred, to an ordinary metaphor.

6. "Our Florentine poet" is Petrarch, who—in the introductory sonnet to his *Rime sparse* or *canzoniere*—says:

"ove sia chi per prova intenda amore,
spero trovar pietà, non che perdono."

(Cf. Francesco Petrarca, *Le Rime sparse e i Trionfi*, ed. Ezio Chiorboli [Bari, Laterza, 1930], p. 3, ll. 7–8.) Lorenzo's prose translation of the first of these lines is not quite precise, especially if we consider it with respect to the original source of its content (merely he craves. For, if it is true, as Guido the Bolognese says, that "love and 'gentilesse' are convertible and are the same thing"[7]—if this is true—he believes that men may well be satisfied with the praise of the lofty intellects alone, caring little for others, since it is impossible to do anything in this world that all men will praise. Wherefore the elect, or gifted, strive to earn the praise of the noble few who are still worthy of praise, and who care little for the opinion

Dantesque, and common to both Petrarch and Lorenzo), although our author here derives it directly from Petrarch. In fact, if such a line as

> "che 'ntender no la può chi no la prova,"

found in Dante's well-known sonnet beginning "Tanto gentile e tanto onesta pare" is, as I believe, Petrarch's very probable source, Dante's intention is different. Dante does not mean, as Lorenzo puts it "che hanno provato che cosa è amore," that is, who have experienced what love is, or know love by experience, but that love cannot really be *understood* except through experience. (In Dante the antecedent is not love, but amounts to love. This has no bearing on this interpretation.) Petrarch retains Dante's *intender,* but with him the emphasis has already begun to shift to the experience. And with Lorenzo, the emphasis is entirely on the experience. This is due, I believe, not necessarily to any quoting from memory, but rather to the desire—in Petrarch and Lorenzo—to adapt the Dantesque belief to a different context. And it is because of Lorenzo's application that he here follows Petrarch, quoting him instead of Dante, although undoubtedly he was aware of Petrarch's source. In fact, what he copies here, in his Dantesque *nuova vita,* is Petrarch's apology for his *Rime sparse.* The line is quoted more precisely at the end of the paragraph, where it is repeated and again incorporated in his prose. (Cf. Text, p. 18, ll. 5–6.)

7. This quotation is indirect, like the preceding one, but inversely. Here Lorenzo names the original author, but actually quotes his interpreter. For Guido (whom he specifies by the name of his non-Tuscan city, Bologna, in contradistinction to the "our" and "Florentine" Petrarch)—Guido Guinizelli, as he is generally known—never expressed in quite that form the famous concept that was to create a school. Citing from Di Benedetto's edition (*Rimatori del dolce stil novo* [Torino, Utet, 1925]), Guinizelli had said:

> "Al cor gentil repara sempre Amore
> com' a la selva augello 'n la verdura:
> nè fe' Amore anti che gentil core,
> nè gentil core anti ch' Amor, Natura," etc.

And nowhere in his canzone is the identity of Amore with the *cuore gentile* other than implied. Whereas this identity is emphatically asserted by Dante in his sonnet interpretative of his "father's" canzone,

> "Amore e 'l cor gentil sono una cosa,
> sì come il saggio in suo dittare pone," etc.

(Cf. *Vita Nuova,* XX.) So that, obviously, Lorenzo's expression, "amore e gentilezza si convertino e sieno una cosa medesima" (cf. Text, p. 15, bottom), is coined more on Dante's than on Guinizelli's. This does not mean that Lorenzo possibly was not acquainted with the original, for he had included sixteen poems of Guinizelli's in his *Raccolta aragonese* (cf. Flamini, *op. cit.,* p. 62; and Gentile, *loc. cit.*), of which this particular canzone was one. It does not indicate, either, that he is necessarily quoting from memory (as well he may in this case, judging from the external difference between his form and Dante's).

of others. It seems to Lorenzo that what is natural can hardly be censured, and nothing is more natural than the inherent desire to unite with the beautiful object of one's love: a desire ordained to man by nature for the purpose of human propagation, which is very necessary to the preservation of the species. Whence it follows that the true motive by which the desire should be prompted in us is not the consideration of nobility of blood, nor the hope of obtaining possessions, wealth, or any other commodity. We should be ruled by natural selection, not forced in any way, nor influenced by other considerations. Our choice should be caused only by *a certain conformity and proportion* held in common by the object loved and the lover, for the propagation of the human species. Accordingly, those whom the desire moves to love exceedingly "objects" outside the natural order and true purpose set forth by him—those people are most to be condemned. On the other hand, those deserve praise, who, following this purpose, love only one "object" day after day, with firm constancy and faith.[8]

Rather, it means that he follows Guinizelli in Dante's interpretation and modification of his master's concept. This is very significant. Dante's sonnet, cited above, is much more than an explanation or paraphrase. Dante does not merely summarize and demonstrate, but adds and transforms. These changes do not concern us here, but the clarifying and very important addition contained in the last line should be noted in this connection. Dante says: "E simil face in donna omo valente." This is perfectly in line with Lorenzo's much wider generalization, showing that the latter was at least conscious of the innovations introduced in the original concept (even if we are not yet ready to declare him, too, an innovator). In this note we are concerned with his authors. It suffices to observe here that he recalls Guido Guinizelli and Petrarch in the same connection and in the same breath, though he calls the first a foreigner, and the second, fondly "our" poet. This union of the two, established by Lorenzo in relation to his work, confirms what was obvious in the previous note regarding his inclusion of Petrarch among the stilnovists. This he did quite naturally, it seems, and without any suspicion that later generations of critics were to make such a sharp, false distinction between Dante and stilnovism on the one hand, and Petrarchism on the other.

8. One might easily infer from this passage—which smacks of matrimonial regulations, and strangely reminds us of Leon Battista Alberti's different, and yet similar, matrimonial ideal—that Lorenzo is here, surely and only, speaking of man's love for a woman of flesh and blood: a physical, biological love that has nothing to do with the spiritual love of beauty in nature and all things. But if we examine it closely, we shall see that this is not the case. Notice his abandonment of the term "person," and his return to the persistent use of the generic term "thing" or "object" to indicate the beloved. Notice that the fundamental and single requirement of "a certain conformity and proportion" for a natural and ideal union is most unusual—if its application were intended to be limited to human marriage. But it is much more intelligible and perfectly appropriate if it is applied to any sort of marriage—poetically speaking—such as the marriage of Saint Francis to Lady Poverty, or the marriage of any man to his art or profession. And, finally, observe that the

At this point, Lorenzo feels that he has answered fully the objection to the nature of his subject. Granted then that his love is "good," as stated above, he does not think it very necessary to purge[9] himself of that blemish which might seem perhaps more than reprehensible in his case, owing to his sundry public and private occupations. If his love is good, and not sinful—he maintains —it needs no justification. However, if some scrupulous judge should refuse to admit his arguments, let him at least concede this much license to his *youthful and tender age*.[10] When one is young, he says, one is not, it seems, so liable to public judgment and censure. No error seems quite so serious, especially because youth— through lack of experience—is spurred more to deviate from the right path, and can resist less those things to which it is induced by nature and the common custom of others. He says this in case anyone should consider it an error to love much an object which, by its perfection, forces the love of the lover—a love that he does

meaning of the whole passage is couched in such terms that at least nothing prevents, and everything suggests, this esoteric meaning. The choice of a profession, art, or any human activity (as Dante had taught him) should be spontaneous, and determined only by the natural tendency and capacity of the individual, but with an eye fixed on the "true purpose" of mankind as a whole. Accordingly, it is man's duty to love *only one thing* (*his* thing, I add) always, "with firm constancy and faith." This admonition would be naïve, banal, and almost ludicrous in the mouth of a philosopher—especially a man of Lorenzo's reputation—unless it carried such a recondite meaning. Of course, an ideal human marriage is an actual and concrete example of this natural union, furnished by Nature herself, and essential to the propagation and preservation of the species. It is, indeed, a beautiful example, and the most outstanding. But, as Lorenzo might say, quoting Dante:

"fatti non foste a viver come bruti,
ma per seguir virtute e conoscenza."
Inferno, XXVI, 119–120

The purpose of man is not limited to the multiplication of the species, if it is that at all. And Lorenzo distinctly says that the love he refers to is a longing for beauty, which cannot be limited to carnal pleasure, even if this is intended to be included among the beautiful things.

This passage is, then, another example of Lorenzo's conformity to the practice of the stilnovists, taking the love of man for woman as his model for his artistic composition. But, precisely because this love is used by him as a model, the resulting work of art is not a photograph but the expression of a concept derived from that reality, or a lesson which he reads in nature.

9. Cf. n. 2, p. 11.

10. This reference to his age is somewhat puzzling, and can best be discussed in connection with the question of the date of the *Commentary*, which is taken up subsequently in a treatment involving similar references and other related points. (Cf. pp. 35–46.)

not for one moment admit to be an error. But, supposing it were, the reasons given (or the indulgence due to his youth) excuse him. And neither the composition of, nor the commentary on, his verses, *written with this intent,*[11] can be imputed to him as a grave error. Moreover, supposing also that a commentary is unsuitable for such an insignificant subject, he declares that the laborious task of writing this commentary falls very naturally to him, in order that (and this is said with an ironical smile) a more excellent mind may not have to waste time with things so low. If, on the other hand, the subject is lofty and worthy, as he thinks, it is very useful to clarify it and make it plainly intelligible to everyone. And this—for the two reasons just given—he can do with a clear exposition of the true meaning better than anyone else. Furthermore, he is not the first to comment on verses involving *similar amorous themes,*[12] for *Dante himself*[13] commented on some canzoni and other verses of his. He, Lorenzo, has also read the com-

11. This is my understanding of the clause, "nè il comporre nè il comentare miei versi *fatti a questo proposito* mi può essere imputato a grave errore." (Cf. Text, p. 17, ll. 2 and 3.) The *proposito* is the intent that in the preceding sentence is said to signify his sincere and constant love of perfection, and which is here implied to have accompanied both the composition of his sonnets and the writing of the commentary on them. This is important, for he thus testifies, not only to the true implication of his treatise on love, but to the veracity of the original meaning of his sonnets being that explained in the respective comments. This, in turn, may indicate the fear he probably entertained lest he, too, like Dante (in our own times, and perhaps already in his), might be accused of reading philosophical meaning into verses that originally had had none, and had been quite differently inspired. The remarks that follow—relative to the propriety of his commenting on his own verses—confirm these inferences.

12. The original says, "versi importanti simili amorosi subietti" (cf. Text, p. 17, l. 14), with almost equal emphasis on the verbal participle "importanti" and on the partially adverbial adjective "simili." This relative emphasis, with respect to the argument of the main clause, calls attention, it seems to me, to two important points: first, these verses are substantially poetic discourses on love themes; second, they import a "similar," though different, concept of love. Now the point of the passage as a whole is that commentaries like Lorenzo's have been written before. This is the term of comparison on which identity is established. In bringing this out, Lorenzo seems to declare incidentally that the matter treated by the sonnets in his book involves a different, yet similar, concept of love. On one hand, he here admits his derivation from the school with which he identifies himself (as he has already done and will continue to do throughout his *Commentary*), while on the other hand he maintains his own originality, which is repeatedly sustained through the work, and is evident in any case. Furthermore, by that rare usage of the present participle "importanti," he brings out the essential character of the poetry of his school. It at once taught and applied a concept of love implying an ideal of *ars poetica* that was definite and yet susceptible of variations—according to the natural vision and inclination of the

ments of two very excellent philosophers—Egidio Romano and Dino del Garbo—on that "very subtle" canzone of Guido Cavalcanti, beginning "Donna mi prega," etc. In this, comments Lorenzo, a man reputed in his time the best dialectician in the world shows his great merit as an author. This excellence is also shown —outside these verses in *volgare*—by all his other works, but especially by this canzone, which imports nothing other than *the principle whereby love is produced in gentle hearts, and the effects of this love*.[14] If these examples and the above reasons are not sufficient to his *purgation,* then at least compassion should absolve him. Having been much persecuted during his youth both by men and by fortune, he must not be denied the little solace he has found in loving fervently and in composing as well as commenting on his verses. (He adds that he will explain this consolation more clearly when he comes to the exposition of the sonnet beginning, "Se tra gli altri sospir ch' escon di fore.") No one but himself could possibly realize the malignant nature of these persecutions, which have been public and are known to all. No one but himself could possibly understand what a sweet consolation his constant love has been to him in these tribulations. Therefore, even if he had told anyone, it would have been just as impossible for this one to have understood his condition as for him to have told the truth

individual. All of this proves (without the assistance of better evidence coming later) that Lorenzo profoundly understood this poetic art of his school, and that he was consciously, deliberately a "continuatore insieme e novatore" of the *dolce stil novo,* as Flamini would say (cf. *op. cit.,* p. 8). Lorenzo's understanding of his predecessors should be a lesson to us moderns.

13. Here we have the first and most positive evidence (we might call it external, in contradistinction to the internal evidence which we can already recognize throughout the *proemio*) that Dante was Lorenzo's model. In fact, this amounts to a specific and sealing admission on the part of the author himself—at least with regard to his commentary proper, as distinguished from the sonnets therein expounded. But it is also clear, even from this sole reference, that the model, from the very beginning, included the subject of the commentary as well. Lorenzo has just said that he composed these verses with the express intention of commenting on them later (obviously like Dante). Since he also says in this very sentence that the *amorosi subietti* of his predecessors were only similar in character— since he says this—it is again evident that he intends di far *cosa nova*. The influence of Dante on Lorenzo, as I have already said, is no new discovery. But more of this later. For the present, let us note this well-placed reference. Let us observe, especially, Lorenzo's term "himself," or "lui medesimo" in Italian, which expresses the supreme esteem in which the pupil held his *maestro* and *autore*.

14. For a discussion of this, see pp. 22 ff.

about it,[15] and so he repeats the verse of "our" Florentine poet quoted before, saying that he

spera trovar pietà, non che perdono

from those whose understanding of love is through experience.[16] That is—he clarifies in a parenthesis—both *this love he has praised so highly*,[17] and any personal love and charity felt toward him by others.[18]

15. For a discussion of this, see p. 34.
16. Cf. n. 6, p. 15, and compare this text:

"dove sia chi per pruova intenda amore."

17. Notice this careful distinction made in a parenthesis, which—in the original—comes between the two verses of Petrarch. The first is incorporated in the prose, and the second is given as a quotation. Unquestionably, the love sung by Petrarch is for Lorenzo *"this love he has praised so highly."* Otherwise he would not have quoted him as he does in this connection, nor, especially, would he have made this distinction right in the midst of the quotation itself. In fact, it seems to me that he could not have established any more clearly the perfect identity in his mind between his own connotation of the word "love" and Petrarch's. His subject is the same, and the body of his sonnets is like Petrarch's *canzoniere*. This confirms my thesis regarding Petrarch's stilnovism, at least in the opinion of Lorenzo. (Cf. pp. 22 ff., and especially pp. 28–32.)
18. For a discussion of this whole paragraph, see pp. 35 ff.

CHAPTER II

LET us at this point interrupt our broken translation of the text to give way to the consideration of a number of questions either arising from this last paragraph, or now claiming our attention. What I have to say constitutes three digressions. If these prove to be rather long, I beg indulgence, since they are due to my desire to establish my points—text in hand—as we proceed cautiously in this study of a very complex and much-debated matter.

A

Cavalcanti's Canzone, Donna mi prega.

LORENZO calls our attention to the comments of Egidio Romano and Dino del Garbo on Guido Cavalcanti's canzone, *Donna mi prega*. Both of these comments may be found in a Laurentian manuscript of the fifteenth century, containing *rime* by various authors, but primarily by Cavalcanti.[1]

1. This MS. is described by Nicola Arnone on pp. xxxvi and xxxvii of his *Le Rime di Guido Cavalcanti* (Firenze, Sansoni, 1881), and by Pietro Ercole on pp. 174–175 of his *Guido Cavalcanti e le sue rime* (Livorno, Vigo, 1885). Arnone's description is fuller, and apparently more accurate. Yet, transcribing faithfully as he does the defective table of contents found in the MS. itself, he fails to note that the comment by Dino del Garbo is also contained therein. In fact, the very obliging librarian of the Laurenziana, Signor Rostagno, has sent me this precise transcription of the two titles that concern us:

> "Codice Mediceo XLI, 20
> (1)cc. 25ʳ–60ʳ   Comento sopra una chanzona di
>   Ghuido Chavalcanti ec. per Egidio
>   Romano, theologo.
> (2)cc. 60ʳ–95ʳ : Incomincia uno scripto sopra
>   la precedente canzona di Ghuido
>   Chavalcanti fatto per Maestro Dino
>   del Garbo dottore di medicina
>   in latino, e volgharezzato per
>   Ser Jacopo Magatroie notaio e
>   cittadino fiorentino."

It will be noticed that the comment by Dino del Garbo is here said to have been originally written in Latin. And, in fact, this Latin text also exists. For, as Arnone notes (cf. *op. cit.*, p. ix, ll. 18–19, and the note on the same page), the text of Dino's comment, which accompanied the first printed edition of the canzone *Donna mi prega* published in 1498, was in the original Latin. See "Guido de Cavalcantibus, *Natura et motu*, etc., Venet., ap.

An account of these commentators of Cavalcanti's famous canzone is not justified here. Apart from the indications contained in the two titles of their comments (where Egidio Romano is called "theologo" and Dino del Garbo is called "dottore di medicina"),[2] suffice it to say that Egidio Romano is Archbishop Colonna, and to observe that Lorenzo calls them both "eccellentissimi filosofi." Undoubtedly he considered them such, although probably in a broad sense only. His point here is that Cavalcanti's *sottilissima* canzone had been commented upon by no less men than these two grave and highly esteemed scholars. He apparently emphasizes their philosophical qualification because of the philosophical nature of the canzone, which he especially wished to bring out. In other words, he means to say that, if two such men—realizing the deeply philosophical import of this canzone—had deigned to comment upon it and had not considered it a waste of their time—certainly he, too, may comment on his own sonnets, which are on the identical subject of love and which carry a similarly profound significance.

I cannot precisely say just what influence their comments exercised on Lorenzo. Even solely with respect to the idea and form of his commentary, the Dantean influence is so preponderant that it submerges any other. Lorenzo refers to these comments merely as well-known examples of discussions similar to his. But there is no doubt that these commentators must have convinced him of one thing (if, indeed, he needed conviction on this point)—namely,

Oct. Serot., 1498." See also J. E. Shaw, "The Commentary of Dino del Garbo etc.," in *Italica*, Vol. XII, No. 2, pp. 102–105. I have found no similar indication with regard to the comment by Egidio Romano, who apparently used Italian in writing his. At any rate, in this MS., both comments are in *volgare*. This does not have much importance. But it is significant, in view of Lorenzo's discussion of the language question which was as live as ever at that time, that need was felt for the translation of Dino's comment, and that there was sufficient popular interest both in the canzone and the comment to justify it. And it is interesting to know that Lorenzo probably read this comment, too, in the Italian translation. For I suspect (though I cannot affirm it) that the above-mentioned MS. was Lorenzo's copy of Cavalcanti's poems, and that these are precisely the comments to which he refers. In fact, this MS. found in the Laurentian Library, and consisting of two parts, is all of the fifteenth century with respect to the first and main part, which is the one containing the above-mentioned *Rime*, and the two comments read by Lorenzo. The second part, which seems to be of the sixteenth century, and was evidently incorporated later, as an old pagination shows, consists only of "Jacopo Mini's exposition of *Canzone* I," says Ercole.

2. Cf. the preceding note.

that this canzone of Cavalcanti's was of a purely philosophical nature. Otherwise, there would have been no point in his referring
to them as "eccellentissimi filosofi." It should be kept in mind constantly that this defense is against the anticipated criticism that he
has been wasting his precious time with trifles. Thus, while citing
these men apparently only as authors of similar comments, he
really cites them as responsible authorities on the true nature of
Cavalcanti's subject—not forgetting the possible objection to his
work. It may or may not have been through them that he first
learned to understand and appreciate this canzone. I doubt
whether the idea of a commentary first came to him through
them. But the fact is that he presents them at once as examples of
worthy commentators who have preceded him, and as recognized
authorities on the interpretation of the sort of poetry he writes.
Apart from this twofold suggestion, I do not believe there is any
connection between their works and his. In fact, the form of
Dino's comment is so completely Dantean that there was truly no
need for Lorenzo to have had recourse to him rather than to his
vastly more authoritative model. Nevertheless, a careful study of
these comments may be useful. It may reveal some interesting
things with regard to the sort of interpretation attached by the
oldest and most authoritative commentators to such poems of the
first stilnovists as this canzone of Cavalcanti's. It would be interesting, too, to see if their interpretation differed from that derived
by Lorenzo from his direct study of the original—which undoubtedly influenced his own concept of love.[3]

The importance that Lorenzo evidently attached to this canzone
is very great, and highly significant for us. He speaks of it only in-

3. The comment of Dino del Garbo has been available to me in the Yale copy of the
volgarizzamento by Ser Jacopo Mangiatroia (cf. n. 1, p. 22) contained in the *Rime di
Guido Cavalcanti,* ed. Antonio Cicciaporci (Firenze, Carli, 1813), pp. 73–115; and,
since the time I mentioned the advisability of a study of both comments, I have been able
to examine personally the one by Egidio Romano as well, in fact, both of them directly
from the MS. containing them. Although unfortunately this examination had to be cur-
sory, such observations as I was able to make readily—especially with respect to Egidio's,
which I had never seen before—will be of interest here and useful later in the course of my
treatise. They confirm my suspicion relative to the possibly greater merit of this exposition
in comparison with that of Dino del Garbo; and certain things I found there are of the
greatest value as positive, external evidence of both the critical approach and the type of
interpretation current in Cavalcanti's own times. (According to the new *Enciclopedia*

cidentally, as an outstanding example of verse like his own and similarly commented upon. But this particular example, I suspect, was carefully and intentionally chosen for other and more important reasons. These seem to have been: first, the philosophical character of the poem, attested by two such scholars; second, its very special content, fundamental to a true understanding of the stilnovistic concept of love; and, third, the historical importance of this poem in the evolution of this concept, of which Lorenzo is

italiana, Egidio Romano was born approximately in 1246 or 1247 and died in 1316.) These things explain Lorenzo's interest in both comments, while the history of the MS. in which they are found together—a history which is divulged in an accompanying *Notitia*—suggest definitely that they exercised a decided influence on the Magnificent. This applies especially to Egidio's comment.

The said *Notitia,* which, in this *Codice Mediceo* (20° del XLI Pluteo), precedes Cavalcanti's *Rime,* is "di Antonio Manetti a Giovanni di Nicholò Cavalcanti di Guido di M. Cavalcante *suo consorto.*" (The italics are mine.) In it Manetti declares that he undertook this collection of Cavalcanti's poems, including the two comments, not only at the request of the said *consorto,* or descendant relative of Cavalcanti himself, but "etiamdio per satisfare alla exortatione del nostro doctissimo platonico Marsilio Fecino. A quali e per humanita e per molti honesti e intellectuali beneficii io sono grandemente debitore." This is exceedingly interesting, not only because it indicates that the MS., as otherwise known, dates back to the second half of the fifteenth century, but also and especially because it reveals Ficino's great concern in the poems of Cavalcanti and particularly—we may assume —in the two philosophical comments on the latter's most doctrinal canzone. Moreover, in view of Lorenzo's close association with this greatest of the neo-Platonists, we may now infer how he learned about these old comments, indeed, how this MS. came to the Laurentian Library. Most likely, this was at least one of the MSS. consulted by the Magnificent in the course of his literary studies; and the fact that Manetti mentions a third comment by a certain Ugo dal Corno, but does not include it, corroborates this opinion, since Lorenzo obviously recalls only the two he had actually read, presumably in this MS.

Interesting and enlightening as is all this, it is not by far so significant as Egidio's Preface to his comment on the epochal canzone. There, this philosopher and critic imagines that he has a vision, in which he sees two mountains, one higher than the other. On the summit of the lower one are a woman and, kneeling before her, a youth. This youth is none other than Guido Cavalcanti, to whom the woman says, "Tu mi conosci per faccia e per costumi, e sai bene ch'*io sono amore.*" (Again the italics are mine.) She continues: "Io ò mandato al mondo due messaggi, cioè, *Salamone* e *Ovidio nasone.* L'uno mi menoe nel mondo con soavi canti. L'altro fè l'arti com'io dovevo essere condotta. D'allora in qua io non mandai messaggio. Ma quelli che di me hanno dittato, ciò hanno fatto o per loro curiosità o perchè da questo fuocho sono schaldati. Io t'ò electo per mio terzo messaggio, e ciò ho facto ragionevolmente, checchome el primo fu savio divino et l'altro fu poeta perfectissimo, chosì tu se' philosopho di sapienza pieno, e imperoche *non se' dell'amore servo ma se' amicho,* non ti chomando, ma io ti priegho chettu rinovelli al mondo mia memoria et dirai *delle mie proprietadi et conditioni secrete,* le quali non sono tocchate dagli altri dicitori." Then she sends him to two other ladies standing on the summit of the higher mountain, one on each side of a fountain, namely, the fountain of knowledge or wisdom (*sapienza*). These are *"dee philosophiche,* cioè morale e naturale," who, in turn, thus address the youth: "O savio donzello, ascholta da noi questa veritate. Noi non semo contrarie dello amore, ma temperiamolo acciochè non faccia nocimento chome fa l'arte delle chose about to give the latest version. Notice the confused syntax of the sentence in the original Italian[4]—indicative of the complexity of thought seeking to find expression, and of the author's anxiety to include all that is pertinent to his argument. And notice especially the progression from the simple idea of comments similar to his: first, to the philosophical excellence of the commentators; then, to the excellence of the author of the *canzoniere,* of whose works this was the greatest; and, finally, to the profound significance of the *sottilissima canzone* which had occasioned the examples recalled of commentaries like his own. This canzone was nothing less than the philosophic kernel of his own concept of love, or, as he says,

velenose. Onde quelli che non ricorrono annoi perischono in esso *chome nave in tempesta sanza nocchiero.* [Cf. Dante, *Purgatorio,* VI, 77.] Il modo il quale terrai sarà questo: imprimamente farai brieve dittato imperoche quanto meno è sua memoria, tanto al mondo in più salue torna. Anche le tue sentenzie che dirai *le vestirai de' nostri vestimenti,* sicchè non possano venire a saputa di niuno el quale non ha conoscimento di noi dee philosophiche, e questo dicemo perchè l'altre gente non si sanno reggere nello amore." Finally, the vision ends as follows: "Udite queste chose el donzello domandò le donne: chi esponerà el mio detto? E quelle rispuoseno e dissono: esponerallo chi spesse volte soleva venire a bere a questa fonte." The philosopher who will comment properly on the canzone, *Donna mi prega,* is, of course, Egidio himself, who thus later concludes his exposition:

> "Va expositione sichuramente
> agente di valore accui timando
> edistar con nessuno huŏ ticomando
> loqual vuole usar locchio p lamente."

(I give here the diplomatic text of this *commiato,* whereas at the end of my Preface to this study, where I quoted it adopting it as my own *commiato* to my exposition, in turn, of Lorenzo's *Principio,* I modernized the spelling.) I should perhaps add that this manuscript copy of Egidio's comment is signed, "Ego Nicolaus pupiensis transcripsi."

The numerous implications and the great significance of this approach to Cavalcanti's canzone and of the final stilnovistic close with which the comment ends, are, I believe, self-evident, but will be realized more fully in the course of my treatise. Meanwhile, they are surely indicative of the character and scope of this particular comment, and I urge the reader to keep the above quotations in mind throughout my exposition of Lorenzo's *Comento.*

For the benefit of those who now may have become interested in Egidio's interpretation of Cavalcanti's doctrine of love, I may add here finally that his comment may also be found in print, in an edition published by Celso Cittadini in 1602. There is a copy of this publication in the Biblioteca Nazionale of Florence, under the following catalogue reference: "Colonna Egidio: Esposizione sopra la Canzone d'Amore di Guido Cavalcanti, con annotazioni intorno ad essa da Celso Cittadini, con una succinta descrizione della vita, ecc., Siena, S. Marchetti, 1602." There must be other copies in other libraries of the world. I have not yet been able to discover whether or not Egidio's comment was originally written in Latin, like that of Dino del Garbo. I suspect so, but cannot affirm it. In any case, Lorenzo must have read them both in the MS. specified above, where they are given both in Italian.

4. Cf. Text, p. 17, ll. 13–24.

"none other than the principle whereby love is born in gentle hearts, and the effects of this love." In other words, the immediate, manifest purpose of the reference—which was simply to give some examples of similar commentaries—is maintained, and the casualness of the remark remains; but the whole emphasis shifts rapidly, first to the high repute of those critics and the philosophical character of their comments, and then to the importance of the verses—similar to his own—thus commented upon. Finally, the occasion of the reference is almost forgotten, and all the attention is concentrated on the gist of the poem, given in the final, subordinate clause with which the sentence closes. This perhaps is as it should be, since, we must remember, Lorenzo's main object here is the rebuttal of the charge that the subject of his sonnets and commentary is frivolous, puerile, and unworthy of a man in his position.

But there is, I believe, a very significant intention concealed in this brief series of comments relative to the subject of the two works, to which the reader's attention is so forcibly drawn. Lorenzo had real cause for recalling here the merits of Cavalcanti, for exalting this particular canzone of his, and for bringing out so impressively the real substance of the poem. In fact, it was not without reason that this canzone had been honored by the comments of two such "philosophers," and that the one in Latin[5] had been translated into Italian.[6] It was not without reason that this poem of Cavalcanti's was, as Arnone says,[7] apparently the only one remembered for a century after the author's death. It was, too, the favorite topic of the neo-Platonists, continuing to be the subject of infinite discussions and comments up to the beginning of the seventeenth century. And, notwithstanding Lorenzo's inclusion of most of Guido's *canzoniere* in his *Raccolta aragonese*,[8] this was the first and only one published in 1498, in the manner already said. This was the one poem in which Cavalcanti could be said to live completely and eternally, which justified his pensive mood handed down by the chroniclers and Boccaccio, and which contained substantially all his philosophy. It was not so much the

5. Cf. the end of n. 3, above.   6. Cf. n. 1, p. 22.
7. Cf. *op. cit.*, p. ix.   8. Cf. above, pp. 2–3, and n. 18, pp. 4–5.

most popular as the one generally known, admired, and studied. The very loneliness it enjoyed in the midst of the others indicates the preference of Cavalcanti's readers, as well as the importance attached to it by the stilnovists together with the pure neo-Platonic philosophers. Its strictly philosophical title (with which it appeared in print) is proof not only of how it was interpreted but of how commonly this philosophical interpretation was generally accepted by those who made a pretense of understanding it.

Lorenzo's succinct but rich statement regarding this canzone, its author, and its fortune is confirmed by modern historians. But he does not merely repeat here well-known facts and express a generally accepted critical opinion. He chooses this canzone himself from Cavalcanti's complete *canzoniere,* which he knew well. And he chooses it because, in relation to his own subject, it was so significant—both historically and contextually. This is why the emphasis shifts in the sentence and rises to a climax when he finally gives the gist of the canzone. As he writes this defense of "the subject of *his* verse," his mind is filled with the history and true essence of his subject. In a way, this partly intrudes on his present argument, but, in another, it really substantiates it. Thus, in this paragraph of which we are making such a detailed study (the paragraph which begins and ends with the same quotation from Petrarch) he finds occasion to mention, first, Guinizelli (*Guido bolognese*) in his essential significance marked by the poem, "Al cor gentil repara sempre Amore," and then Cavalcanti, also in relation to his most significant poem. He mentions Dante also by name, and if he does not specify any work of his, it is surely because Dante is all-significant for him and because he expects that this author is to be understood in a situation all impregnated with Dantism. Still, he refers to him as Dante "lui medesimo," and is it mere carelessness on his part that he quotes Guinizelli in Dante's interpretative version of Guinizelli's original concept?[9] If these significant recollections (all coming to his mind almost at once) do not indicate the intention of outlining here a history of the *dolce stil novo,* they surely show the presence, in the author's consciousness, of the principal steps marking the origin and develop-

9. Cf. n. 7, pp. 16–17.

ment of the stilnovistic concept of love. Notice that he even includes (in a preceding paragraph) the philosophical basis and
neo-Platonic source of this concept.[10]
But Lorenzo does not limit this incidental suggestion of historical development to the now traditional, famous triad: Guinizelli,
Cavalcanti, Dante. He includes also Petrarch and himself! With

10. Cf. Text, p. 14. My suspicion that the suggestion of an outline—or history of the
dolce stil novo by chapter headings marking the stages of its development—is perhaps involved in the connections established here by the Magnificent, is based on, and confirmed
by, similar "sketches" deducible from certain verses of Dante and Petrarch. In the well-
known meeting between Dante and Guido Guinizelli, which the poet imagines to have
occurred in the seventh cornice of Mount Purgatory, and which he describes in the XXVI
canto of his *Purgatorio*—an episode which ends with the glorification of Arnaut Daniel—
Dante refers to Guinizelli as his literary father, calling him "il padre / mio e de li altri
miei miglior che mai / rime d'amore usar dolci e leggiadre" (cf. *loc. cit.* ll. 97–99); and he
subsequently explains his affection for him on the ground of "li dolci detti vostri, / che,
quanto durerà l'uso moderno, / faranno cari ancora i loro incostri" (*loc. cit.* ll. 112–114).
Guinizelli, on the other hand, points in turn to Arnaut Daniel, declaring modestly that
"questi . . . fu miglior fabbro del parlar materno" (cf. *loc. cit.*, ll. 115–117) than he had
been in the Italian *volgare,* and suggesting thereby that this Provençal poet was, in turn, his
literary father or, at least, a source of inspiration for his poetic ideal. Accordingly, it seems
that, as it is otherwise known, in Dante's opinion as well, the primitive Italian poetry
showed traces of Provençal influence, indeed, of Provençal derivation. At any rate, Dante
points to Arnaut Daniel as a precursor of Guinizelli in the very canto in which he traces
his own literary lineage to the latter poet. With this in mind, if we remember also the even
greater esteem in which Dante held the "first of his friends" (cf. *Vita Nuova,* III, 14), or
Guido Cavalcanti, and especially if we recall the verses in which he compares himself
critically to both these predecessors,

> "Così ha tolto l'uno a l'altro Guido
> la gloria de la lingua; e forse è nato
> chi l'uno e l'altro caccerà del nido."
> *Purgatorio,* XI, 97–99;

there is no doubt, it seems to me, that an outline prepared by him of the origin and development of Italian poetry up to his time would have contained at least the following suggestive chapter headings: Arnaut Daniel, Guido Guinizelli, Guido Cavalcanti, and Dante
himself. This is all the more likely because Petrarch, apparently, has actually left us just
such a sketch implied in one of his least understood canzoni, indeed, one almost identical
to the outline just deduced from Dante's casual and scattered remarks. It will be remembered that in the canzone, "Lasso me!, ch'i' non so in qual parte pieghi" (cf. Petrarca, *Le
Rime sparse e i Trionfi,* a cura di Ezio Chiorboli [Bari, Laterza, 1930], pp. 59–60), Petrarch ends each of the five stanzas with the first line, respectively, of five canzoni by different authors, including one by himself; and that the poets thus recalled and, as it were,
listed there by him are presented in strict chronological order, as well as represented by
what, in his opinion, must have been their most significant canzone, at least for the purpose at hand. In fact, the last line of the first stanza reads "Drez et rayson es qu'ieu ciant
e 'm demori," which, according to Bembo, is the first verse of a canzone by Arnaut Daniel;
the last of the second is, remarkably, the first verse of the same canzone of Cavalcanti's
recalled by Lorenzo, which, in this edition, reads "Donna mi priega, per ch'io voglio dire";
the last of the third is, likewise significantly, the first verse of one of Dante's canzoni for

Petrarch's *canzoniere* in mind, as we have already noted, he begins and ends this important paragraph by recalling the verses:

> ove sia chi per prova intenda amore,
> spero trovar pietà non che perdono.[11]

Petrarch himself was one of those "che hanno provato che cosa è amore," as Lorenzo puts it—namely, the kind of love of which he is precisely talking, "questo amore che io ho tanto laudato."[12] The Petrarchism of Lorenzo is too well-known and admitted for me to dwell on it here. His even greater Dantean stilnovism has been brought out by Flamini.[13] One thing is not realized at all by any critic or historian—it is this intimate relation that Lorenzo establishes here between his famous predecessors, and between himself and them. Their subjects and his are for him one and the same. Just as they did with respect to their immediate predecessors, so

the *Donna Pietra*, which are all deeply philosophical, namely the one beginning "Così nel mio parlar voglio esser aspro"; the last of the fourth reproduces the beginning of a canzone by Cino da Pistoia (Petrarch's literary father), the one commencing "La dolce vista e 'l bel guardo soave"; and, finally, the fifth and last stanza ends with the quotation of the first verse of one of his own canzoni, the one beginning "Nel dolce tempo de la prima etade." Moreover, this canzone by Petrarch himself, thus singled out and intentionally connected by him with the others chosen—no doubt, with a definite criterion in mind—from the *canzonieri* of his predecessors, is the one called "la canzone delle metamorfosi"; it is the one which, according to Bernardino Daniello (cf. *Le Rime di Francesco Petrarca di su gli originali, commentate da Giosuè Carducci e Severino Ferrari* [Firenze, Sansoni, 1924], bottom of p. 101), serves as introduction to the group of three canzoni on Laura's eyes. All this is certainly mysterious and very suspicious. It seems to me to call for acute penetration and the nicest critical analysis of what is implied, for, in view of Dante's clearly manifested historical conception of the stages gone through by the primitive Italian poetry, it is obvious that Petrarch in the said canzone perhaps intended to sketch a similar understanding of the origin and development of the literary ideal now pursued by him. Indeed, if the attribution to Arnaut Daniel of the first canzone recalled is correct, Petrarch's outline, as I call it, of the history of Italian poetry is almost identical with that I have constructed for Dante on the basis of the latter's own remarks. The only difference seems to be that, for some inexplicable reason (can it be that a whole stanza is lacking in the canzone as it has come down to us?), Petrarch omits all reference to Guinizelli's important contribution (important in Dante's opinion, at least), and that, in revising, as it were, such an outline, he, of course, brings it up to date, including now both his own literary father (Cino da Pistoia) and himself. The study of these "outlines" is outside the scope of the present treatise, but the above observations show, I believe, that my suspicion regarding Lorenzo's probable intention of indicating here incidentally at least a similar understanding of the origin and development of the *dolce stil novo*, or—to him—Italian poetry in *volgare*, this suspicion is justified and well-founded.

11. Cf. n. 6, p. 15.   12. Cf. Text, p. 18, ll. 6–7.
13. Cf. above, pp. 2–3.

he, coming after them, marks a stage in the development of the stilnovistic concept of love. Petrarch, for him, is almost as great as Dante, but both of them are—as Flamini might, but does not say —"continuatori insieme e novatori" of the sweet new style. Among these, Lorenzo classes himself *"quinto* tra cotanto senno." Thus, his Petrarchism, like his Dantism, is truly stilnovism, and here he acknowledges this stilnovism to be based on the concept and manner not only of Petrarch and Dante but of the still *eccellentissimo* Cavalcanti, and of the now distant Guinizelli. Indeed, if we may again express his thoughts in the words of Dante (but making them refer to Dante himself, not to Homer), we may say that Lorenzo here presents

> . . . la bella scuola
> di quel signor de l'altissimo canto
> che sovra gli altri com' aquila vola.
>
> *Inferno,* IV, 24–26

Finally, there is one other inference suggested by this reference to Cavalcanti's canzone. I recall again that Lorenzo makes it in connection with his defense of the subject of his verses and of his own commentary on them. We have seen how the examples of Egidio Romano and Dino del Garbo were really stressed here because they gave great authority to Lorenzo's contention about the serious, true nature of Cavalcanti's subject (identical with his own), and perhaps also because their interpretation of this canzone supported or coincided with his.[14] As I have said before, their interpretation of the canzone was the one commonly accepted by the general reading public as well as the neo-Platonists.[15] We cannot be sure that all the intelligent readers—especially those who discussed and commented on it for three centuries—agreed on all points. But there must have been at least one on which they were all absolutely of accord, namely, that the canzone carried a profound philosophical *sovrasenso* which transcended all ordinary

14. Lorenzo found the two commentators authorities supporting the serious nature of his own subject. But they were not, strictly speaking, the most fitting examples to cite in favor of his argument. And they are almost preferred here to his best and perfect example, which was Dante.

15. I believe this is proved by the fact that the poem was printed in 1498, together with the comment of Dino del Garbo, under the title *Natura et motu.* (Cf. n. 1, pp. 22–23.)

meanings of the word "love." It is true that this canzone is one of
the most obviously philosophical in all stilnovistic literature—so
much so that even our modern, positivistic critics admit this. But
here is the point of my argument: Lorenzo cites the canzone here
as an example of lyrics like Dante's, and—note carefully—like his
own—all of which to be correctly understood and fully appreciated require interpretative comments. This, it seems to me, is positive testimony on Lorenzo's part, on two important counts. First,
he fairly declares that this was the spirit with which he personally
approached not only Cavalcanti and Dante, for whom he had
helpful comments, but also Guinizelli, for whom he had at least
Dante's interpretative sonnet, and Petrarch, for whom he had no
comments. Second, he makes us feel that it was generally understood—among a certain élite—that all such poems carried a hidden philosophical meaning. He maintains throughout the *proemio* that this is the character of his own verses. And this is how,
he says, he should be approached, in all fairness to himself and to
his truly lofty subject. He must both be read and be understood in
this way. Since he groups himself with these poets, and declares
his work to be essentially the same in form and in the nature of its
implications, we learn from him that all stilnovistic literature carries an esoteric meaning, poetically and metaphorically concealed
under the veil of the literal sense. This lesson becomes more obvious as we proceed with the study of his commentary.

Lorenzo, unlike his supreme master, nowhere speaks of "menti
grosse." Nor would he limit his readers to "*donne che* hanno *intelletto d'amore*," implying, like Dante, that his subject "non è cosa
da parlarne altrui."[16] We shall see later that he differed from his
predecessors in that the innovations he introduced permit a certain
enlargement of his audience. Perhaps it is precisely because he
does not wish to limit the sphere of his readers, and because he
expects to reach the unsympathetic audience of bigoted critics and
superficial readers—perhaps it is for these reasons that he, too, like
Dante, fears public misunderstanding and consequent blame. Indeed, perhaps he had even more cause to fear on account of his
political position. But this fear on his part does not invalidate his

16. Cf. *Vita Nuova*, XIX, first stanza.

testimony with regard to the true nature of all stilnovistic literature and the correct approach to it. On the contrary, it seems to
me that it strengthens it. If this poetry had not had a philosophical
significance (recognized at least by those who had true intelligence of love), there would have been no occasion to express fear
of misunderstanding. Such verses would either not have been
written at all, or the authors would not have worried about their
reputation. Lorenzo's fear is only with regard to those (intelligent
or not) who might not correctly understand and justly appreciate
his sonnets without a true, authoritative interpretation. This fear
applies especially to the mass of his readers in comparison with
the intellectual élite. This simply proves that in Lorenzo's time, as
in Dante's and as in all times, there were readers without the
qualifications required by Dante for admission to his spiritual
banquet. Lorenzo would perhaps have done well to exclude them
just as mercilessly and scornfully. But he worries about them,
quite as much as Dante, who—after all—had to consider them,
too. Otherwise there would have been no occasion for his *Convivio*. Although the *Convivio* was written ostensibly to clear and
enhance his reputation, I believe that it was really intended much
more to explain and indicate his concept of love in the mind of
the *vulgus* for whose benefit he used the *volgare*.

Without anticipating what properly comes later, we may already ascribe a similar purpose to Lorenzo. Thus (resuming my
argument), Lorenzo guards against all possible censure which he
might be said to anticipate too soon unless, indeed, it had already
been provoked perhaps by a previous, loose publication of his sonnets. We can freely state already, without the additional evidence
that will soon follow, that he does this largely by using Dante's
arguments. But, whether or not this fear was genuine and justified, whether or not he had the noble purpose of bringing his lofty
concept down to the masses, we must conclude that the expression
of fear would have no place here unless he meant to persuade his
readers and critics that his sonnets actually had the deep philosophical significance on which he continually insists for his defense. This shows at least his genuine, critical attitude toward stilnovistic literature. Otherwise, indeed, we must admit that this

proemio is all a fabrication on the model of Dante, and that his sonnets are all a farce—which is unthinkable! Lorenzo is truly a "continuatore insieme e novatore," and his position here is that of a literary critic of the creative type. More of this later. But I may say already that the authority of such a critic—so near those times as to belong to them, and yet so modern as to appreciate our difficulties many centuries later—is extremely valuable to us moderns. He is practically indisputable in a matter so fundamental to the comprehension and appreciation of his own work.

B

Lorenzo's Critical Sincerity.

LET us recall Lorenzo's statement on the sweet consolation of his love during the tribulations of malignant persecutions. He said that, since no one could understand the intensity of the persecutions or the sweet consolation of the love—for this reason (even if he had told anyone), it would have been just as impossible for this one to understand them as for him to tell the truth about them. This is a curious declaration on the part of Lorenzo. We can easily understand that the malignity of his persecutions could be fully realized only by himself, and we can also understand how they affected him in particular. But what "no one but *himself* could possibly realize" applies here also to the sweetness of his consolation found in the experience of love, and he further admits that he himself could not have told the truth about all this. What truth? This "truth" does not refer so much to the nature of the persecutions, which are said to have been very public and generally known, but also and more especially to his experience of love. In other words, I think Lorenzo is saying this: that at the time he both experienced love and composed his sonnets, as a consolation for political troubles, he himself could not have correctly described the feelings connected with his experience, nor fully have explained his concept of love based on this experience; but that now he can, and he does so objectively, like a philosophical critic of his artistic creation. This is important. Taken in connection with his previous contention that no one but the author himself can truthfully interpret his verses,[17] it means two things. First, he, too, like Dante, is

> un, che quando
> Amor *gli* spira, not*a*, e a quel modo
> ch' e' ditta dentro *va* significando[18]

purely subjectively, and without any preoccupations. Second, according to him, the activity of the critic is quite apart and distinct from that of the artist, and comes later. At first he was an artist in the fervor of his creation; now he is a critic of his own work. His theory of art and literary criticism is at once Dantean and very modern. In fact, he strangely reminds us of Francesco De Sanctis and Benedetto Croce.

C

Date of Lorenzo's Commentary.

THIS is perhaps as good a place as any in which to broach a question that I have postponed several times.[19] The approximate date of Lorenzo's *Commentary* is important for us, and it is not known. We ought to know whether we are dealing merely with a precocious youth, or with a mature (though not elderly) man. We want to determine the extent and real character of the author's imitation of previous works, and the degree of seriousness we should attach to this philosophical treatise on love (as Lorenzo insists on declaring it to be). But to do this, we ought first of all to know whether these sonnets and their commentary are a sort of *tesi di laurea* with which a young man made his début in the world of Italian letters and philosophy, or whether they are the result of *lungo studio e grande amore* on the part of a mature scholar and critic, himself a poet. But the MSS. containing this work are apparently silent about its date, and in modern study I find no mention of it anywhere. Vittorio Rossi, for instance, merely says that Lorenzo began "assai per tempo" to compose sonnets and canzoni. This is well known, and is proven by the inclusion of as many as sixteen of his own lyrics in his early *Raccolta aragonese*. But all that Rossi can say with regard to the date of the

17. Cf. above, pp. 12 and 19.   18. Cf. *Purgatorio*, XXIV, 52–54.
19. Cf. n. 18, pp. 4–5; n. 10, p. 18; n. 11, p. 19.

Commentary itself is that the author undertook to arrange his lyrics and to comment on them "più tardi."[20] This is too indefinite for our purpose. Similarly, Flamini, Simioni, and Del Lungo do not concern themselves with the date of the *Commentary*. They merely touch on the probable date of the first four sonnets, which, as we have seen, they connect—rightly or wrongly—with the death of Simonetta Cattaneo in 1476.[21]

From the character of the poems and the explanations furnished, it is quite clear that the composition of the sonnets themselves must have spread over a considerable period of the poet's life. If they were actually suggested by the circumstances which they profess, they were written on different, successive occasions. In fact, the explanations of the particular circumstances frequently hint at events or situations that occurred in different periods of the author's youth and maturity. On the one hand, the fact that the first four sonnets constituting the *principio* were included in the *Raccolta aragonese* shows that Lorenzo began to write very early indeed—at the age of sixteen, at least. But, on the other hand, his apology for "wasting his time with such trifles" (he, a man overburdened with heavy responsibilities, "both public and private") indicates something different. It surely shows that he composed many of his sonnets during the time when he was not only a grave pater familias and political dictator of Florence, but the statesman who held the balance of power in Italian politics. We can often date the various sonnets with some degree of approximation by the help of hints of a personal, biographical nature that are thrown in here and there. At a certain point in our text, Lorenzo declares that to escape the oppressing thought of death the only remedy was to plunge directly into this thought, and he adds that, accordingly, he sought escape "nel freto e tempesta delle civili occupazioni."[22] Considering that the sonnet in connection with this

20. Vittorio Rossi, *Il Quattrocento* (Milano, Vallardi), p. 238. In his new edition of this work (1933), Professor Rossi, influenced—I suppose—by Barbi's arguments in favor of the new date, 1476, proposed by the latter for the *Raccolta aragonese* (cf. this study, pp. 342 ff.), says with respect to the date of the *Comento* "composto, par bene, *dopo il 1476.*" (Cf. this edition, p. 347.) But, irrespective of the validity of the new date assigned to the *Raccolta,* this statement also is too indefinite for our purpose.

21. Cf. above, pp. 1–3, and n. 18, pp. 4–5.

22. Cf. Text, p. 33, ll. 10–11.

remark is the fourth of the first four constituting the *principio,* this accords with what we know from other sources about Lorenzo's very early entrance into political life, and does not discord with the early date of this sonnet confirmed by its presence in the *Raccolta aragonese.* Later,[23] in connection with the sonnet to which he himself refers us toward the end of the important paragraph we are discussing in this digression,[24] he explains the nature of the persecutions for which he sought solace in composing poetry.

E però brevemente diremo: *la persecuzione essere suta gravissima,* perchè li persecutori erano uomini potentissimi, di grande autorità ed ingegno, e in disposizione e proposito fermo della mia intera ruina e desolazione, come mostra l'aver tentato tutte le vie possibili a nuocere ad uno. Io, contro a chi venivano queste cose, *ero giovane privato* e senza alcun consiglio o aiuto, se non quello che dì per dì la divina benignità e clemenzia mi ministrava. Ero ridotto a quello che, essendo ad un medesimo tempo nell'anima con escomunicazione, nelle facultà con rapine, nello Stato con diversi ingegni, nella famiglia e figliuoli con nuovo trattato e macchinazioni, *nella vita con frequenti insidie perseguitato,* mi saria suto non piccola grazia la morte, molto minor male al mio appetito che alcuno di quelli altri.[25]

This reference is obviously to the Pazzi conspiracy. Thus, this sonnet—which is the tenth of the forty-one expounded in the *Commentary*—was apparently written in 1478, and shortly after that attempt on Lorenzo's life. Again, still later,[26] we find a sonnet that is obviously meant to be autobiographical. It marks one of the instances, so frequently alluded to, in which Lorenzo either sought in poetry diversion and consolation from his political worries and family cares, or when these annoyingly distracted him from his poetic art. It is a plaintive poem, expressing his deep regret for a certain long interruption, as well as sorrow that destiny forbids him the beautiful career of poetic art. It reads as follows:

Io *ti lasciai* pur qui *quel lieto giorno*
con Amor e madonna, anima mia:
lei con Amor parlando se ne gia
sì dolcemente, *allor che ti sviorno.*

23. Cf. Text, p. 51.
25. Cf. Text, p. 51, ll. 6–18.
24. Cf. Text, p. 17; and above, p. 20.
26. Cf. Text, p. 75.

Lasso! *or* piangendo e sospirando *torno*
al loco ove da me fuggisti pria;
nè te nè la tua bella compagnia
riveder posso, ovunque miri intorno.
Ben guardo ove la terra è più fiorita,
l'aer fatto più chiar da quella vista
ch' or fa del mondo un' altra parte lieta.
E fra me dico:—Quinci se' fuggita
con Amor e madonna, anima trista,
ma il bel cammino a me mio destin vieta.

I shall cite only one more intimation that the composition of the sonnets apparently spread throughout most of the poet's life. Near the end of his *nuova vita,*[27] he begins the exposition of the last sonnet comprised in the *Commentary,* by saying:

Come molte altre volte accadde, secondo abbiamo detto, ero assai dilungato dalli occhi della donna mia *nel tempo che composi il presente sonetto.*

This is the forty-first of the 149 sonnets that Lorenzo probably intended to include in his commented edition of the hitherto scattered sonnets.[28] If the other two thirds or more had followed, similarly, in fairly chronological and psychological order, their respective dates would gradually have brought us quite close to the author's death. At any rate, we have his word that they were actually prompted by different occasions, and that they were written—frequently at distant intervals—as circumstances permitted. All we know of Lorenzo's busy life as manager of a large estate, as political dictator, as patron of the arts and poet himself—all this certainly concurs with this statement. We may accept it as the true history of the sonnets.

But the point here is not so much the dates of the separate sonnets themselves, as it is the date of the *Commentary* as such, and particularly of the *proemio.* Were the various comments written at the same time or shortly after the sonnets? Or were they written in conjunction with the *proemio?* Lorenzo would have us believe that his history and interpretation of the sonnets is absolutely true, and such as only an author can give. He defends himself for

27. Cf. Text, p. 139.   28. Cf. above, pp. 4–6.

undertaking to comment on his own verses by saying that he is anxious to be correctly and thoroughly understood, and feels that the best commentator of a work is the author himself. But did he make written or mental note of his true meaning at the time of writing each sonnet? Did he intend from the very beginning to comment on them later, as he does in part? The original intention of composing a *canzoniere* on love and of commenting on it later, all with the express purpose of presenting a new treatise on the subject, seems to be implied in his whole *proemio*. This is especially clear, it seems to me, from several remarks made in the paragraph which has occasioned this digression. He insists that "questo . . . è stato il subietto de'versi *suoi*"[29]—that is, his sonnets treat of love in the philosophical sense he has just explained, and constitute a philosophical treatise on love. He tells us elsewhere[30] that these sonnets are "nuova vita." Therefore it follows that they are his philosophical theory applied to life, and actually lived during their composition. In another place,[31] he says that "nè il comporre nè il commentare *suoi* versi fatti a questo proposito *gli* può essere imputato a grave errore." This does not contradict the hypothesis that the composition and commentary went on hand in hand—at least in the form of philosophical meditations and mental registration of the true significance carried by the poems. This hypothesis seems to be confirmed by the synchronism clearly indicated in a later remark made on the same page. There he says that the only consolation he found in the midst of all his troubles was "in amare ferventemente e nella composizione *e commento* de' *suoi* versi,"[32] all of which occurred during his *gioventù*.

Why should we not take Lorenzo's word that he conceived the idea of writing a *canzoniere* and respective commentary quite early, and that his intention (fondly entertained throughout his life) was actually carried out, to the extent we have noted? The youth—who at an early age could show such wide knowledge of the Italian poets, and such critical discernment as Lorenzo evidences in his famous anthology, and especially in the accompanying letter to his royal friend, Prince Frederick of Aragon—could

29. Cf. Text, p. 15, l. 27.
31. Cf. Text, p. 17, ll. 2 and 3.
30. Cf. Text, p. 34, l. 6.
32. Cf. Text, p. 17, ll. 29–30.

well have conceived such a plan. The hypothesis is supported by the fact that—as Flamini notes[33]—more than two thirds of this *Raccolta* is devoted to the poets of the *dolce stil novo,* and by the fact that we find the four sonnets on death (now constituting the *principio*) among Lorenzo's own lyrics included in it. I believe, therefore, that—as a result of his early studies of the Italian poets up to his own times—Lorenzo actually planned a poetic treatise on love like those of his predecessors, following especially Dante's model in the *Vita Nuova* and *Convivio.* Assuming as much, this plan (which, incidentally, shows his approach to, and understanding of, these poets) clearly indicates that the philosophical interpretation attached to his own sonnets was actually intended from the very beginning. The commentary, at least mentally, must have accompanied the composition of the poems.

I say "mentally" because we know of no *zibaldone* of his, and also because the various comments, in the form in which they appear in the *Comento,* were evidently written in conjunction with the *proemio.* Throughout the commentary, the tense used with reference to the time of the occasions that prompted the composition of each sonnet is always the past absolute. And the whole tenor of the *proemio* clearly implies a time now more or less remote. Moreover, this preface—contrary to the usual practice of writers—seems to have been written actually before the comments that follow. The style is consistently the same throughout the work. There is also perfect continuity between the narration of the reasons that finally decided the author to expound his own verses, and the explanations he gives to account for each sonnet, in his orderly exposition of them. In fact, each separate comment is always connected with the preceding one by such a phrase as "come nel precedente sonetto abbiamo detto," or another similar remark that recalls the content of the preceding chapter or chapters. Even the main parts of the work (*proemio, principio,* and *nuova vita*) are so linked together that their division, as we have observed, is not marked by separate titles or spacing. The passage from the *proemio* to the *principio* is not otherwise indicated than by a short paragraph that may be said to be at once the end of the

33. Cf. *op. cit.,* p. 62.

proemio and the beginning of the *principio*.[34] A similar, transitional paragraph marks the passage from the *principio* to the *nuova vita*.[35] Indeed, as I have already remarked,[36] the nature of the *principio* is such that the whole of it is already *nuova vita,* and here the link is really a fusion of the two parts. When we come to the sonnet, "Se fra gli altri sospir ch' escon di fore"[37]—to which our author refers us in the paragraph that we are studying[38]—he begins the exposition by saying: "promettemmo nel proemio." This comment, then, was apparently actually written, in the form we have it, after the *proemio.* Furthermore, Lorenzo refers us at least three times[39] to sonnets surely intended to be expounded and not actually comprised in the *Commentary,* which was left unfinished. If, then, we consider all these indications in connection with the unfinished state of the *Commentary,* we may conclude that the plan did not actually materialize until it was apparently too late to carry it out completely. To be sure, some time must have elapsed between the composition of the last sonnet intended to be included and the time of writing the commentary, and, while the comments were supposedly thought out at the time of each poetic composition, the plan was then only general and vague. At any rate, it appears that when Lorenzo finally decided to execute his youthful project he first outlined his work, arranging his sonnets in some sort of chronological and psychological order, and then proceeded to write, starting with the *proemio.* Certainly one can hardly imagine that a man of Lorenzo's intelligence would intentionally set out to copy Dante's *Convivio* to the extent of reproducing, in his imitation, its imperfections due merely to casual circumstances. I have no doubt that he had Dante's *Vita Nuova* in mind when he first conceived a similar work, and it is also evident that he knew the *Convivio* when he began to execute his early plan. Indeed, when he set out to narrate and explain his poetic *nuova vita,* he must have mused over the strange similarity between the circumstances that accompanied his own literary ef-

34. Cf. Text, p. 25, ll. 9–18.   35. Cf. Text, p. 34, ll. 1–7.
36. Cf. above, p. 7.   37. Cf. Text, p. 50.
38. Cf. Text, p. 17.
39. Cf. Text, p. 63, ll. 20–21; p. 71, ll. 23–25; p. 73, ll. 1–3.

forts and Dante's. At any rate, it must have pleased him to see
how easily he could fashion his own artistic experience after
Dante's model. But I cannot believe that he referred to sonnets not
included, and left the work incomplete, merely to copy Dante.
Since all indications point to the lateness of the *Commentary* as
such, I conclude that death alone or the last annoying interruption
accounts for its incompleteness.

There are other intimations of the lateness of the work, particularly in this important paragraph of the *proemio*. Indeed, this
preface starts with one of them: *"Assai* sono stato dubbioso e
sospeso se dovevo fare la presente interpretazione e comento de'
miei versi."* This, by itself, is rather vague as to the duration of his
hesitation, and does not indicate the period of his life in which it
occurred. But,[40] in the following paragraph he uses the phrase
"più tempo fa," now that he is carrying out the project and refers
to the time when he first conceived it. This indicates that the
above "assai" apparently covered a considerable number of years.
When it is taken in connection with his final decision—made
now, after more mature consideration of the "objections" that
caused his hesitation and delay—it suggests clearly that the author
is now in another and more mature period of his life. In fact, this
is confirmed by the repeated reference here to his "età giovenile e
tenera,"[41] during which the sonnets at least are said to have been
written, and again to his "gioventú,"[42] during which he not only
composed them, but—he now adds—*also commented on them*.
This reference to a time now past, even remote, is a clear intimation to me that at the time of writing the *proemio* he no longer
considers himself "young." But does he mean "young" in our
loose, modern sense? Or—since we find these references in a work
manifestly modeled on the *Vita Nuova* and the *Convivio*—must
we think that he means "young" in the precise Dantean sense of a
period of one's life extending from the age of 25 to 45? This is not
clear. On the one hand, the tenor of Lorenzo's expression clearly
suggests a definite period, and he surely speaks of this period of
his "youth" as a thing of the past. On the other hand, all the in-

40. As we have seen before, on p. 11, n. 1.
41. Cf. Text, p. 16, ll. 28–29.   42. Cf. Text, p. 17, l. 27.

ternal and external evidence tends to prove that "youth" cannot be understood here in the technical medieval sense. When we remember that Lorenzo[43] died at the early age of forty-three, we see that he could at no time have thought of his past "youth" in the strict Dantean sense. Moreover, as I carefully brought out in recalling the second of the above references to his age,[44] he there includes—with some semblance of inconsistency—the writing of the commentary in the same period of his life in which he says that he composed the sonnets. The same thing seems to be implied where he says, a little above, that "o per le ragioni dette o *avuto rispetto all' età,* nè il comporre *nè il comentare* miei versi fatti a questo proposito mi può essere imputato a grave errore."[45] Evidently, then, if he thought at all in Dantean terms, he was conscious of the fact that he was technically still in his "youth" when he was writing this *proemio* and the whole commentary. I conclude that in this respect he does not—for he could not—follow his model strictly.

Still, the Dantean division of life into definite periods was undoubtedly present in his mind. For, in the references above cited,[46] he first calls the same period "età giovenile e *tenera,*" and then "gioventù." This seems to me to be perhaps an attempt on his part to distinguish vaguely between adolescence and youth in the Dantesque sense of these terms. It is clear that he wished to adapt both the theory and actual experience of Dante to his own experience, even though in his case the "new life," starting properly during his "adolescence," extended considerably beyond his twenty-fifth year, into the period of "youth." If this is so, we have here incidentally an indication of Lorenzo's interpretation of Dante's *Vita Nuova* as "vita giovenile" as well as "nuova" in the mystical sense. Thus, I think that when Lorenzo refers to the time of writing his sonnets as "età giovenile e tenera," he is thinking more of his earlier sonnets and of Dante's *Vita Nuova,* although his *nuova vita* comprises also later sonnets. Again when, immediately after, he considers also the varying dates of the later sonnets—especially in connection with the accompanying commentary—he is thinking more of the *Convivio.* Hence the slight confusion, but also the

43. 1449–1492.
44. Cf. n. 42, p. 42.
45. Cf. Text, p. 17, ll. 1–3; and above, n. 11, p. 19.
46. Cf. above, p. 42.

transition from the rather vague term "età giovenile e tenera" to the more definite "gioventù," which was more largely the actual period during which he composed most of the sonnets constituting his *nuova vita*.

His difficulty in conforming to his master's model is due to these reasons: his actual age at the time of writing the commentary; the difference between his age and Dante's during the period of their experience of the new life; and, especially, the fact that he presents a fusion of *Vita Nuova* and *Convivio,* although he calls his work a *nuova vita.* We have here both a proof of Lorenzo's sincerity, and another interesting indication of the history of his work. If we look at the list of Dante's lyrics included by Lorenzo in his *Raccolta aragonese,*[47] we find the entire *Vita Nuova,* but we find only nine other lyrics by Dante (four of which are spurious), and none of these is among those expounded in the unfinished *Convivio.* Now, we remember Lorenzo's persistent declaration that his sonnets were composed with the true, philosophical implication which he now explains, and with the express purpose of constituting all together a treatise on love based on actual experience. We infer from the omission of the *Convivio* in the *Raccolta aragonese* that when he first conceived his project of composing this treatise, and actually wrote the *principio,* he had not read the *Convivio.* On the other hand, the *Raccolta aragonese* includes such significant poems as Guinizelli's *Al cor gentil repara sempre amore* and Cavalcanti's *Donna mi prega,* to which Lorenzo refers especially. Accordingly, it would seem that when the very young Lorenzo thought of imitating the stilnovists, and especially Dante, he had the *Vita Nuova* particularly in mind as a model. This explains the title "nuova vita" given to his own body of sonnets, his emphasis on his age truly "giovenile e tenera" at the time, and perhaps also the conscious novelty of his *principio.* The *Convivio,* with its more profound and exhaustive expositions, and with its first *trattato* on which Lorenzo's *proemio* is modeled, must have come later in his literary life, and when it did, it did not change the original plan, but modified it substantially. More of this later.

---

47. In the form in which this *Raccolta* is found in *Codice Palatino* 204. Cf. Luigi Gentile, *I Codici Palatini,* I, 219–232.

But let us here observe how this attempted historical reconstruction explains both the confusion and the fusion noted above. Let us observe, too, that the introduction of the *Convivio* as a sure and powerful influence on the author of the *Comento* tends to make the *Comento* a rather late work. It is in the *Convivio*[48] that Dante divides human life into four periods. It is almost inconceivable that, in a work so permeated with elements of the *Convivio*, the author should repeatedly refer to his age in such Dantean manner without being conscious of Dante's implication.

Accordingly, I conclude that Lorenzo does what he can, without being able to conform in all respects to the theory and experience of his master. Having decided to write a commentary on his *nuova vita* (which began in his adolescence and continued in his youth), wishing to do so in the manner of Dante, and being technically still in his youth, he anticipates, as it were, his *senettute*, and throws his experience all into the more or less remote past absolute. It is entirely possible that he at least *felt* old in some respects. Certainly, his life was such that he actually could be old—that is, mentally mature and experienced—at the age of forty or so. At any rate, with Dante's concept in mind, Lorenzo could not speak of his youth as a thing of the past unless he was at least approaching the age of forty-five. Since the work was probably interrupted by his death, it may very well be that he began it shortly before his death, in 1490 or 1491.

I repeat that the *Commentary* at least is a late work. If this is so, then we are not dealing with a mere youth and his *tesi di laurea*, but with a mature man, philosopher, and poet. His treatise on love is actually a severe, critical study of a profound and philosophical subject. It is the serious exposition of a grand concept that commands our respect and scrutiny. We should remember this when we consider Lorenzo's authoritativeness on the subject of love (technically understood), and we should bear it in mind when we weigh the importance we should attach to his critical interpretation and general understanding of his predecessors.

48. Cf. *Convivio*, IV, 24.

CHAPTER III

Lorenzo's Use of the Volgare.

LET us now return to the text, and resume our translation of the *Comento*. Having refuted the first and second of the three objections that he suspects may be raised against his *Commentary*, Lorenzo now proceeds to reply to the third and last. This is that he writes in the vulgar tongue, or Italian language—which some people consider neither capable nor worthy of being the vehicle of expression in treating of any excellent subject matter. And his answer is as follows.

The fact that anything is more common than any other does not make it any less worthy. On the contrary, the greater diffusibility and universality of any "good" shows that it is all the better in proportion—as is by nature what is called "supreme good." This would not be supreme if it were not infinite, and nothing can be said to be "infinite" if it is not common to all things. Therefore, it does not seem to Lorenzo that the quality of being common to all Italy detracts in any way from the worthiness of his mother tongue. What should rather be considered is the perfection or imperfection of the language.

Now, considering the requisites (condizioni) that lend dignity and perfection to a given tongue or language—these seem to him to be four. But only one of them, or at the most two, may be said to be real, praiseworthy qualities of the language itself. The others actually depend on the habits and opinions of men, or are the results of good fortune.

The one praiseworthy quality of a language is its richness and copiousness—its ability to express well the apprehensions and concepts of the mind. For this reason Greek is considered more perfect than Latin, and Latin more than Hebrew, because the one language rather than the other expresses better the mind of the speaker and writer.[1] The second requisite that most dignifies a

---

1. It is interesting to note this development of the language question in Italy. Dante had had very little to say about Greek, which he did not know directly. But, by Lorenzo's

language is its sweetness and harmoniousness, as compared to other tongues. But, it seems to Lorenzo, this sweetness is more a matter of opinion than an established fact. Although harmony is natural in man and proportionate to the harmony of body and soul, yet there is a wide variety of human intellects not all well proportioned and perfect. And those things that are judged according as they please or not, are judged more by opinion than by sound reasoning. The pleasure or displeasure is proved by no other reason than the desire for them. Notwithstanding these objections, Lorenzo will not affirm that sweetness and harmoniousness may not be an inherent, praiseworthy quality of a language. Harmony being, as he has said, proportionally an attribute of human nature, it may be inferred that the judgment regarding its sweetness properly falls on those who are similarly well proportioned to receive it. And the judgment of these should be accepted as good, even though they be few in number. The sentences and judgments of men are things to be pondered upon, not to be counted.[2]

Another condition through which a language may attain a higher degree of excellence is the profound and important nature of the content of the works written in that language—a content necessary to human life, both for the edification of the mind, and

times, Greek studies had progressed so far as to permit this pupil of Ficino and patron of Poliziano to express perhaps a personal opinion, at least with respect to Greek and Latin. He dares to express also a similarly common opinion with regard to Hebrew. But this, probably, is not based on personal impression. I suspect that he mentions Hebrew—relegating it to the last place—merely because Dante had referred to it too, though he was not better informed. It is evident that when Lorenzo attempted to solve his own language question and to study this matter for himself, he had in mind Dante's *De vulgari eloquentia* as well as the *Convivio*. Throughout his argument let us note not only his evident Dantean sources, but also his originality, or, at least, his personally accepted opinion. It is the result of study, and frequently involves the introduction of new points in favor of Italian.

2. In other words, the sweetness and harmoniousness of a given language is, in itself, indeed, a matter of opinion. It depends on how the language sounds to the speakers and listeners, and on what the latter love to hear, desire, or expect. This quality is not, then, strictly speaking, inherent in the language. It results from, and is proportionate to, the degree of musicalness with which the individual speakers and listeners are naturally endowed. A language may be more or less harmonious according to the harmony reigning in the poet's soul. The latter's poem will be found more or less harmonious according to the harmony reigning in the soul of the critic. Therefore this matter can really be decided only by the critics best qualified by nature to express an authoritative opinion—however few these may be.

its usefulness to man in the care of his body. This is the case, for instance, with the Hebrew language, which is so rich in wonderful mysteries suited to—and, indeed, necessary to—the infallible truth of our faith. And the same may be said of the Greek language in which many of the sciences very necessary to mankind are written: the metaphysical, the natural, and the moral. But, whenever this happens, it must be admitted that the merit belongs to the subject rather than to the language. The end is the subject, and the language is only a means to it. In such cases, the language cannot be said to be more perfect in itself. In fact, those who have written on theological, metaphysical, natural, and moral subjects —in thus dignifying the language in which they have written— seem to reserve the praise more for the subject matter and to consider the language only an instrument. The latter is good or bad according to the end.

Finally, there is a fourth condition that gives repute to a language. This holds true whenever, by good fortune, that which naturally and properly pertained to a city or single province becomes universal and almost common to all the world. However, this can more readily be said to constitute a blessedness and a prosperity due to fortune than a real and praiseworthy quality of the language itself. In this case, the value attached to the language and its high renown in the world correspond to the opinion of those who prize it and esteem it highly. But what depends on others rather than on oneself cannot be called one's own, true quality. In fact, those very persons who value a given language highly may easily change their minds and depreciate it. Or the circumstances may change, whereby—with the cause failing—the dignity and merit of the language will also end. A very good example of this kind of worthiness (resulting from an appraisal based on the fortunate occurrence of favorable circumstances) is furnished by the Latin language, which the spreading of the Roman Empire made not only common but necessary throughout the world.[3] Therefore, Lorenzo concludes, these external merits

3. This merit of the Latin language—due to fortunate, external circumstances that gave it great renown until very recent times—now hardly holds true any longer. This proves the truth of Lorenzo's acute argument. In fact Latin—losing in "the opinion of others," as Lorenzo would put it—has lost ground since the end of the Italian Renaissance. Now its

of a language—depending on good fortune or the opinion of others—are not inherent, praiseworthy qualities of it. Accordingly, if we wish to prove the worthiness of the Italian language, we must insist only on the first requisite, namely, that the Italian *volgare* expresses easily any concept of the mind. For this, no better proof can be adduced than experience.[4]

Our Florentine poets—Dante, Petrarch, and Boccaccio—(continues Lorenzo) have clearly shown in their profound and very sweet verses that any meaning can be expressed in Italian with great facility. In fact, anyone reading Dante's *Commedia* will find expressed therein, with great skill and ease, many a theological and scientific concept. And he will also find that the author uses

renown due to universal usage is practically extinct. Indeed, the Latinists have been forced to retreat to the stronger trenches of merit due to the content of the works written in Latin. But, as Lorenzo maintains, even this merit is dependent—in the last analysis—on "the opinion of others." The content of a given literature may be superseded, and even the harmoniousness of the language be surpassed by the greater sweetness of another. And this, indeed, is precisely what has happened in respect to Latin and Italian. Therefore, it is extremely interesting to find Lorenzo apparently already conscious of the superiority of Italian to Latin—at least in respect to its great harmoniousness. It is no mean credit, it seems to me, that Lorenzo acquires as a literary critic by the acumen he shows in this original argument in favor of Italian.

I might add, in this connection, that if Lorenzo were writing today, he would have now almost no end of examples to illustrate this particular point. Take French, which for a long time has been the diplomatic language of the world, and only now is gradually being supplanted by English in this respect. Take German, which is studied primarily "for scientific purposes," until this opinion has made it a necessity, as well as the real merit of the works written in it. And take, finally, Spanish, which enjoys a similar renown as a "commercial language." Such merits, says Lorenzo, are external and circumstantial, but not intrinsic and lasting.

4. It will be noticed that none of the points here discussed by Lorenzo is in Dante, although Dante was also greatly preoccupied with the language question, and the use of the *volgare* was one of the *macule* of which he, too, had to clear his *Convivio* in the apologetic first book. The language question, started by Dante, continued to be a real and lively one for a long time after him, and it was still a cause of sincere preoccupation in Lorenzo's time. Indeed, as it is well known, the Italian *volgare* had to fight a long and strenuous battle against Latin all through the Humanistic period. When this battle was won, a sort of internal strife started that has only barely finished now. Thus, besides finding the question in Dante, Lorenzo undoubtedly felt it as a real difficulty to be surmounted. He had good reason for anticipating criticism along these lines, and defends his dear *volgare* with all his might. Whether or not his arguments are entirely original and valid is beside the point. The point here is that his approach to the question and his treatment of it are entirely different from Dante's. He had one weapon that Dante could not have—experience. It is on this—the experience of Dante, Petrarch, and Boccaccio, chiefly—that he will base his defense and praise of the *volgare*. Again we see, therefore, that Lorenzo does not precisely copy his Dantean model. He knows it, adapts it to his case, and—as it were—brings the *Convivio* up to date.

CHAPTER III

51

very aptly the three kinds of style that orators praise, namely, the humble, medium, and lofty. Indeed, Dante—combining all three —has accomplished in a single style what it took a number of Greek and Latin authors to do in their various styles.[5] Who can deny that in Petrarch we find a grave, jovial, and sweet[6] style, and that *this subject of love* (queste cose amorose) is treated by him with such gravity and gracefulness as is certainly not found in Ovid, Tibullus, Catullus, Propertius, or any other Latin writer? The *canzoni* and sonnets of Dante are so grave, subtle, and elaborate[6] that they have almost no equal in prose and diction. Anyone who has read Boccaccio (a man of very profound learning and great facility of expression) will easily conclude that not only his originality but also his copiousness and eloquence are singular and unique in the world. And if he consider the varied subject matter of his *Decameron*—now grave, now medium, and now light[6] —involving all the perturbations of the soul of man (in his love and hatred, fear and hope), and containing also many new examples of craftiness and ingeniousness—if he consider that the author had to give expression to all existing natures and passions of man—he will conclude without discussion that no language is any better fitted for expression than Italian. Finally, take Guido Cavalcanti, who has already been mentioned. It would be impossible, declares Lorenzo, to say how nicely he has combined gravity with sweetness—as the previously mentioned *canzone,* as well as some of his sonnets, and his very sweet ballades, all show.[7]

5. The Dantean terms for these various styles are, respectively, the elegiac, comic, and tragic. In the *Comedy,* these may truly be said to be more combined than fused—in the superb manner of Dante that permits him to be, according to the situation, now "tragic" or supremely lofty, now "elegiac" or light and humble, but generally "comic." The comic style is a happy medium, more close to the tragic than to the elegiac. His work is properly called *Commedia* more for this reason than because it begins unhappily and ends happily. Lorenzo's mention of these three styles here is another indication of Dantean influence, implying also knowledge of the *De vulgari eloquentia.*

6. Cf. the preceding note. These are other ways of indicating the use of the same three styles also by Petrarch, Boccaccio, and even Cavalcanti.

7. Again I feel that I must call attention to Lorenzo's critical acumen all through this valuation of the great Italian authors who have preceded him. And I must do this for two reasons. First, I must correct—by adding to it—Flamini's remark (repeated by Simioni: cf. Text, II, 353, ll. 4–5) that Lorenzo's *Raccolta aragonese,* together with his introductory letter to Frederick, is "dopo il *De vulgari eloquentia,* il più antico documento di storia critica della nostra poesia" (cf. Flamini, *op. cit.,* p. 60, ll. 4–6). Second, I must point out the truly great, critical value of the *Comento* which was written by the same (though more

Many other writers could be mentioned here, who are at once serious and elegant. But, in order not to be prolix, and not because they are unworthy, he will not speak of them.[8] And thus he con-

mature) author of the letter that is now confirmed and surpassed. Flamini's failure to re-call Lorenzo's *Comento* in making the above-quoted remark cannot be a wilful omission. It is inexplicable to me, except as the result of the traditional opinion that the *Comento* is merely a neo-Platonic work of Dantean imitation. If we consider it profoundly rather than superficially, we will find it infinitely more than that. We will see, indeed, that it is quite an original work of greater importance than the said letter for the history of Italian lit-erary criticism. Notice here Lorenzo's significant addition of Cavalcanti to the great trium-virate early recognized by others (but not by all) in his time. Notice that he finds the three classical styles perfectly combined in all four of these great examples of Italian writing. Notice that his nice discrimination between Latin and Italian authors, and his remarkably acute criticism of the latter, are undoubtedly the result of profound personal study on his part. His conclusions are largely original with him. And notice, finally, a most significant little detail: Petrarch, for him, is the author of a *canzoniere* treating *these* same *cose amorose* that constitute the subject of his own verses and commentary. Moreover, Boccaccio is not only grouped with the other three, but given *magna pars* in the splendid use of the three styles. For this reason, I repeat that, in my opinion, there can be no doubt as to Lorenzo's clear, critical understanding of the history of Italian literature up to his time (including his own literary production). Undoubtedly, this history seemed to him the origin and development of a certain philosophical concept of love, involving a great lit-erary and artistic ideal. Naturally, this had undergone certain modifications at the hands of time and of various authors. But it seemed to him to be essentially the same conceptual aspiration throughout the two centuries of its glorious struggle for expression. This history is equivalent to the history of Italian pre-Renaissance, as the contemporary Lorenzo saw it with his keen, critical insight. The significant chapters of it bear, for him, the titles of Guinizelli, Cavalcanti, Dante, Petrarch, Boccaccio, and now Lorenzo himself. (Cf. n. 10 on pp. 29 ff.) If this is so, and he is right,—then we must study better not only Petrarch but also Boccaccio!

8. One may wonder whom he has in mind especially. The *Raccolta aragonese* makes it rather easy for us to surmise whom he might have mentioned in addition. This anthology is valuable, for it furnishes a definite clue to his early reading and preference. There is nothing absolute in this clue, for it goes on the supposition that the reading of an author indicates interest in his style and subjects. We must remember that this anthology was made when Lorenzo was very young, and is therefore no indication of the wide number of Italian authors he must have read by the time he had reached his forties. The poems in the anthology are sometimes wrongly ascribed, and the number of poems there included from each author is no sure indication of his preference even at that time. He may have assembled simply what he read or could obtain easily. But the anthology is a valuable piece of evidence. Therefore, Flamini is right in attributing "singolare importanza" to this anthology, "poichè è certo," he adds, "ch' egli [Lorenzo] formò il suo stile poetico su di essa e sul Petrarca" (cf. Flamini, *op. cit.*, p. 59). Now, it is significant, as Flamini also notes (cf. *idem*, p. 62; and above, p. 40) that more than two thirds of this volume is de-voted to the stilnovists. It is even more significant, I add, that the Notary and Guittone and Bonagiunta, who remained "di qua dal dolce stil novo" (cf. Dante, *Purgatorio*, XXIV, 55–57), fare rather badly at the hands of Lorenzo. In fact, while he may not have known more than three poems by Giacomo da Lentino, he surely must have read more than four lyrics by Bonagiunta Orbicciani. Only Dantean contempt, it seems to me, made him include so few as three *canzoni* by the great *caposcuola* Guittone d'Arezzo. On the contrary—besides Guido Guinizelli, represented by sixteen poems; Guido Cavalcanti, represented by forty (two of which are spurious); and Dante, primarily by his *Vita Nuova*—we find there as

cludes that—rather than the men and the subject matter lacking a language—it is the Italian *volgare* that has lacked men willing to cultivate it. Indeed, for anyone who has become accustomed to it and uses it somewhat habitually, the sweetness and harmoniousness of the language is very great and profoundly emotional.

These praiseworthy qualities of a language (copiousness, harmoniousness, and effectiveness), which seem to many people to be inherent, appear to Lorenzo to abound in Italian. Owing to the content of Dante's work, in especial, it seems to him both useful and necessary that this poet be read for the profound effect that he has. Consider the numerous commentaries that have been written on his *Commedia* by very learned and famous men, and the frequent citations made from it all the time (ogni dì) by godly and superior men in their public orations.[9] With prophetic intuition and stanch faith in the glorious future of Italian literature, Lorenzo adds: perhaps other profound and important subjects, worthy to be read, will still be written in this language! Until now, it may be said to have been in its adolescence, and every day it becomes more elegant and "gentle."[10] During its youth and mature age, it may easily achieve a higher degree of perfection. This will be likely if concomitant circumstances favor it, and if the Florentine sphere of influence spreads. This is, indeed, not only to be hoped for, but striven toward by every good citizen with all his might and intellect. But—since this rests with Fortune, and is subject to the will of God, whose wisdom is infallible—it can neither

many as eighty-seven lyrics of Cino da Pistoia, eighteen of Dino Frescobaldi, eighty-eight of Franco Sacchetti, fifty-eight of Cino Rinuccini, and thirty of Bonnaccorso da Montemagno. (Some of these poems are genuine, and some spurious.) Last, but not least, he includes himself with as many as sixteen poems(!), probably all he had written till then. These last-mentioned poets are, I imagine, most probably the ones he has especially in mind here. The others included in the anthology are each represented by a very small number of poems.

9. This is unquestionable testimony, it seems to me, that Petrarch did not reign alone over the world of Italian letters during the Quattrocento. He undoubtedly enjoyed a wide popularity, and exercised a tremendous influence on his followers, the Petrarchists. But in Italy, at least, his glory never obscured that of Dante—who was not only read and studied with greater veneration, but similarly memorized, indeed quoted like the Bible. Dante penetrated deeper into the hearts and minds of men, and his work, called modestly *Commedia,* was qualified as *divina.* But Petrarch, after all, remained simply *il cantore di Laura.* And let us remember that this testimony is from a generally (too generally) recognized Petrarchist, who in this connection does not even mention Petrarch!

10. Cf. n. 13, p. 55.

be properly asserted, nor should it be given up.[11] Suffice it for the present to conclude that Italian is very richly endowed with those praiseworthy qualities that are inherent in a language. Therefore all complaint against it is unjustified. And, for this reason, no one can reproach him for having written in the language to which he was born and in which he was brought up. In their time, Hebrew, Greek, and Latin were also natural, mother tongues. Only, they were spoken or written more accurately (according to well-established rules) by those who are held in honor and esteem than by the common people.[12]

LORENZO feels that he has now quite sufficiently proved that the Italian language is not inferior to any. In thus refuting the last of the three feared objections, he has also completed his refutation of all anticipated criticism of his *Commentary*. These are his "better" reasons for having finally resolved—after long hesitation and more mature consideration—to resume his youthful project, and actually undertake to write out in this form his understanding and experience of love. One might well expect him to end his *proemio* here. But he discusses two additional points. Before passing on to the *principio,* Lorenzo feels that he ought to explain his choice of the sonnet form for his versification, and also to apologize for the rather strange *principio* which is to follow. The discussion of the three verse forms—the sonnet, the tercet, and the *canzone*—constitutes a sort of appendix to his treatment of the question of language, and, therefore, I include it properly in this chapter. The ex-

11. Patriotic Lorenzo, how unjustly you are frequently judged! For this sincere and spontaneous expression of your faith in the destiny of Italy, and for your efforts to raise and spread the prestige of your native country, you deserve a place beside your fellow-citizen, Machiavelli.

12. Of course, this last argument is entirely Dantean—derived both from the *Convivio* and the *De vulgari eloquentia.* Moreover, it is appended here as an afterthought, added for good measure to the preceding reasoning. Perhaps Lorenzo recalled it suddenly, as—coming to the end of his refutation of the third and last expected objection to his work—he probably reviewed in his mind all the arguments he knew in favor of Italian. Or he may have thought that this was a suitable place in which to mention this very good reason for using and naturally preferring his native language. In any case, two things are evident from this curious sort of interpolation. First, he undoubtedly recalled those works of Dante in adding this final argument. Second, he used his sources most discreetly. In fact—here, and all through his defense of Italian—he does not allow them to interfere with his originality, but only takes from his authorities what he himself accepts with discernment.

planation of the nature of his *principio* involves an important point which must be understood for a fair appreciation of his work, and for an actual comprehension of his artistic and philosophical concept. It is, therefore, a part of the *proemio,* but its treatment calls for a separate chapter. In the author's original text, however, the reader passes almost imperceptibly from this consideration to the *principio* (and thus into the body of the treatise) without the slightest break in the continuity of the narration.

Lorenzo's Choice of the Sonnet Form.

Now that he has demonstrated the perfection of the Italian language, Lorenzo thinks he ought to pass from the general to the particular. Since his primary object is the interpretation of his sonnets, he will limit these considerations to an attempt to show that (among the various verse forms used customarily by the Italian writers) the sonnet is not inferior to the tercet, the *canzone,* or any other kind of versification in *volgare.* And he will base his argument on the difficulty of the sonnet, for *virtù*—according to the philosophers—involves difficulty.

It is the opinion of Plato, he begins, that terse and lucid narration not only seems marvelous but almost divine. And the brevity of the sonnet does not permit that a single word be vain. Therefore the proper subject matter for sonnets must be some pointed and *gentle*[13] thought, that can be expressed aptly in a few concise verses, without obscurity or harshness. This manner of writing is similar in import and form to the epigram, as regards the acumen of the matter treated and the cleverness of the style. But the sonnet is both capable and worthy of embodying and expressing weightier matters. Therefore it becomes all the more difficult. He admits that the tercet involves a loftier and grander style, very similar to the heroic. But it is not any more difficult for all that, since the tercet has a wider range, which permits the writer to amplify (without prejudice to himself) any thought that cannot be encompassed within two or three lines. As to the *canzone,* this verse

---

13. We should study most carefully the connotations of the adjective *gentile,* which recurs so frequently in Lorenzo and all the stilnovists. Regarding Lorenzo's meaning of it, we should naturally follow his own philological explanation of the term, given on p. 57 of the Text. This explanation will be taken up later. Cf. this study, pp. 111–113.

form seems to him very similar to the Latin elegy. But this similarity may be due either to a peculiarity of this Italian style, or to the custom of those who have so far written canzoni. At any rate, he thinks that the style of the canzone admits of the treatment (not without decency) of subjects that are not only light and vain, but entirely too soft and lascivious. All of these, in Latin, are generally found written in the style of the elegy. Furthermore, since the canzone, like the tercet, has a wider scope than the sonnet, he does not consider it so difficult as the latter. This, he says, may be proved easily by experience. In fact, anyone who has ever composed sonnets (and, in so doing, has confined himself to a subtle, definite subject) has always experienced the greatest difficulty in escaping obscurity and harshness of style. He adds—with caustic, but just, criticism—that there is a great difference between the composition of sonnets so that the rhymes compel the subject matter, and their composition so that the subject forces the rhymes. Besides the natural division into feet, the Italian verse requires that one preserve the additional difficulty of the rhyme scheme. And this, as anybody knows, disturbs many a beautiful thought, and does not permit the narration to proceed clearly and easily. He remarks incidentally that for this reason Latin prosody affords greater freedom than does the Italian. If anyone doubts that Italian verse involves a natural division into feet, Lorenzo proves it to him by remarking that one could easily write any number of hendecasyllables that do not sound like verses, or otherwise differ from prose. He concludes that Italian versification is very difficult and that the sonnet is the most difficult of its forms. Of course, he does not mean that in his own sonnets he has attained the degree of perfection that he claims for this style of verse. But he is satisfied at least to have tried his hand at the most excellent verse in Italian. If he has not quite succeeded in driving, to perfection, this chariot of the sun (he says, recalling Ovid's account of Phaethon's experience), he must at least be credited with having dared to try as much, even though—perhaps through his own fault—his strength has proved unequal to so great an enterprise.

ONCE more we must pause awhile, and—without actually digressing—allow what we have said on the question of language and on Lorenzo's verse form to lead us into another discussion.

Lorenzo's Sonettiere *Viewed Critically as a Continuation and an Innovation in Form.*

I HAVE indicated in various notes[14] that the discussion of the question of language (just preceding this brief consideration of Italian versification) is properly one of those elements that justify the qualification of the *Commentary* as Dantean. The consideration and rebuttal of this third objection (which is decidedly a Dantean *macula* of which Lorenzo also must "purge" his work) leads one to feel that surely now there can be no doubt that Lorenzo knew the *Convivio,* indeed his Dante *tutto quanto.* For the *proemio* at least, Dante was his *maestro* and his *autore.* But we have also observed,[15] in reading Lorenzo's defense of the Italian language, that his arguments are neither precisely nor solely the ones advanced by Dante. We can see that Lorenzo's treatment, although unquestionably Dantean, evinces considerable originality. Whether or not he was influenced by other sources, there is no doubt that his fresh argumentation was the result of personal study. His warm, sincere defense indicates a positive conviction on his part. If he took up the question of language in his *Commentary,* it was not exactly because he found it discussed in his obvious model, but primarily because (as I have noted before)[16] it was still timely in his own day. It was perhaps more timely, and truly vital as a result of the rise and spread of humanism. Still the influence of the Dantean model cannot be denied. While giving Lorenzo just credit for his original and modern treatment of the question, we must conclude that —throughout his defense of his dear *volgare*—he undoubtedly recalled both the *Convivio* and the *De vulgari eloquentia.*

But another question arises now, in connection with the appendix that follows Lorenzo's defense of the Italian language. Is a similar discussion of Italian versification to be found also in Dante? It is. The entire second book of the *De vulgari eloquentia*

14. Cf. n. 1, p. 47; n. 4, p. 50; nn. 5 and 7, p. 51; and n. 12, p. 54.
15. Cf. n. 1, p. 47; n. 4, p. 50; n. 7, p. 51.
16. Cf. particularly n. 4, p. 50.

(as far as the work goes in its unfinished state) is, as everybody knows, all devoted to a study of Italian prosody, particularly of the *canzone*. And what is interesting for us is that Dante is mainly concerned with *three* verse forms, of which he exalts one above the others. They are the ballade, the sonnet, and the canzone. The one preferred is the canzone, which he therefore takes up first, studying it in great detail—without exhausting the subject, and without ever getting to the fourth book in which he "intended" to take up similarly the sonnet and the ballade.[17] This is unfortunate for us. But we know definitely from the reference that for him the canzone was a nobler form than the sonnet, and the noblest of the three in question. On this point, then, there is a decided divergence of opinion between Dante and Lorenzo. The latter places the sonnet far above the canzone, which—as a matter of fact—he considers the lowest of the three forms that he, in turn, takes into consideration. But what is even more interesting to note is that Dante's third form—the ballade—is not even mentioned by Lorenzo, while its place in his list is, numerically, taken by the tercet. The lists of each, in the order of merit, are: for Dante, the canzone, the sonnet, and the ballade; for Lorenzo, the sonnet, the tercet, and the canzone. The reasons for this remarkable divergence of opinion may perhaps be obvious. But they are not, for all that, any less significant for the history of Italian poetry and prosody, and particularly for our judgment of Lorenzo as a literary critic, and independent thinker, poet, and artist. It is obvious that Dante did not intend to include the tercet in his study, for the simple reason that apparently he had not invented it at the time of writing the *De vulgari eloquentia*. (This, incidentally, is an argument in favor of an earlier date for this work than has sometimes been assigned to it.) And Lorenzo, also obviously, neglected to mention the ballade perhaps for the simple reason that, by this time, this verse form had become fused and confused with the *canzone a ballo*. But this remarkable substitution of the tercet for the ballade in Lorenzo's list, and his almost reverse order of the three styles—these tell us a great deal regarding the vicissitudes of the various styles of Italian poetry in two centuries of history.

17. Cf. *De vulgari eloquentia*, II, iv, 1.

They show that Lorenzo was not a blind and slavish imitator of his great master, but knew his Italian literature exceedingly well, judged it with the nicest independent discernment, and was perfectly aware of his purpose and ability. This great similarity in the treatment of an identical subject—particularly here, in this *proemio,* or Laurentian version of the first book of the *Convivio*—undoubtedly proves once more how profoundly Lorenzo was influenced by Dante. But, at the same time, his widely divergent opinion on the character, scope, and merit of the various forms prevalent in his own time proves the originality of his study based on direct contemporary evidence. And it shows the independence of his judgment, regardless of any authority, even Dante.

I believe that if Dante had written his *De vulgari eloquentia* after he had invented the tercet and adopted it definitely for the *Commedia,* he would have surely placed it above the canzone, without necessarily detracting from the glory of the latter. But he still would have considered the canzone a nobler form than the sonnet. If he had lived again in Lorenzo's times, I believe that he would almost surely have agreed with him on the latter's *constatation* relative to the use made of the various forms prevalent in those times, and of the relative merits of each. This is a positive, historical speculation, based on two centuries of *cammino* that the Italian *ars poetica* had covered in the meantime. But why does Lorenzo have such a striking regard for the sonnet, and how does he come to have such a lofty concept of it?

The answer is very simple and very obvious, it seems to me. He comes after Petrarch, and is decidedly a Petrarchist, besides being a stilnovist. In fact, it does not even occur to him that anyone might make the false and absurd distinction between the two connotations, as modern critics generally do. Although, of course, he uses neither term, the two are identical for him. For him, Petrarch is a *continuatore* quite as much as a *novatore* of the sweet new style. Indeed, this school is no longer *a* school for him (and perhaps for all in his day) but already *the* school—or, better, no "school" at all, but Italian literature! Guinizelli, Cavalcanti, Dante, Petrarch, and scores of so-called Petrarchists (including Boccaccio, and none of them rising above the masters)—these are his predecessors. This is for him, as it should be for us, the only Italian literature there was up to his times. It is no wonder, then, that taking cognizance of this history and of the *ars poetica* current in his time—it is no wonder, I say, that—wishing to follow in the footsteps of the great masters, and yet *far cosa nova*—he prefers the sonnet, and feels the need of explaining and defending his usage. His *Commentary* will be found to contain only sonnets. His is not the usual *canzoniere,* but exclusively a *sonettiere* (if I may be permitted the connotation as well as the pun). And it is, indeed, a novelty and a departure from tradition which he needed to justify here on good grounds. He has them, and here they are. The sonnet—now carried (by Petrarch especially) to a height of perfection that had not been achieved even by Dante—was justly popular. But the canzone had truly degenerated—even in Petrarch—from the lofty concept that the first stilnovists, especially Dante, had originally had of it. Moreover, the sonnet had now acquired a definiteness of noble purpose and beautiful form. This was eminently suited to the use that Lorenzo intended to make of it for his analytical study of the subject of stilnovistic love—based on his actual personal experience, and presented in a series of poetic incarnations of his thoughts and feelings during each successive stage of this experience. But the canzone, as it was now conceived, would not have been at all suitable to this purpose. It would have involved the writing of larger chapters than he intended, in accordance with his manner of treating the subject. And the rather light and lascivious character of the canzone now (let us recall especially the *canzone a ballo*) would perhaps have forced him to adopt a lighter vein in his writing, and would certainly have exposed him more than ever to the danger of being misunderstood as to the seriousness and real nature of his subject. Finally, the technique involved in composing a fine sonnet as conceived by Petrarch and which Lorenzo now thoroughly understood and appreciated, was infinitely more difficult and complex than that of the canzone. And this was no mean reason for choosing this style in presenting a subject so serious and profound as the stilnovistic concept of love. It was fitting that this most difficult and noble topic be treated in the noblest and most difficult style;

Lorenzo feels that his work gains thereby in both dignity and seriousness. These, therefore, are his reasons for departing in this respect, from the traditional practice of all his great predecessors. With respect to form he is a *continuatore insieme e novatore*.

In a subsequent consideration we shall see how he is this also with respect to the content of his work. Meanwhile, let us note here the clear consciousness that Lorenzo has both of his art and his innovations. This consciousness proves, in the first place, his intelligent, direct derivation from the predecessors whom he exalts so significantly. And it shows in the second place (which is much more important) his profound and thorough understanding of their art, which he emulates with a lively spirit of independence, and the feeling perhaps of advancing beyond them. Lorenzo thereby shows himself to be a truly excellent critic and an author of considerable originality, to say the least. And, incidentally, we see through his poetic and critical activity the progressive march of the Italian artistic genius.

CHAPTER IV

Lorenzo's Apology for His Strange Principio.

LET us now return to the *Comento,* and resume our reading of the text. At this point, Lorenzo passes to the second (and last) of his additional prefatory remarks. He makes another apology before he begins the *Commentary* proper. Before he prefixes to the narration of his amorous passion the very *principio* of this experience, he hesitates. Perhaps, he says, this *principio* will appear to some little suited to his book of verses. And he feels that he is introducing here a truly radical deviation from the customary practice of his predecessors. He begins in a manner that does not conform to the practice of those who have written similar verses up to his day. He even reverses the apparent order of nature, by presenting first what usually comes at the end of human experience. The *first four sonnets* now commented upon, he declares, were composed by him on the occasion of the death of one ("per la morte di una")[1] who wrested these sonnets from him and generally forced tears to be shed by all men and women who knew anything of her. But he insists that death seems to him a most fitting beginning, notwithstanding the apparent incongruity of such a beginning. This he proceeds to explain.

1. Cf. n. 18, pp. 4–5. It should be added here that at the time of writing this *proemio* Lorenzo may have been thinking of Simonetta Cattaneo, and may have considered her death a better concrete example of the incarnation of mystical death. But the point here is not the death of any person in particular, but the phenomenon of death in general. The crux of the matter is that these sonnets are *on* death, or deal with death. Therefore they may seem out of place at the very beginning of his collection. The personality of the lady does not really count for the value of the argument, and is—at most—a side issue. Otherwise, there would be no point to the whole discussion on the mystic death, following immediately, and the absurdity of such a beginning in a book of "new life" would not follow logically. Lorenzo's innovation, which is the essence of his remarks, consists solely in commencing his exposition of the experience of love with mystical death. Almost any example of physical death would have served equally well as a point of departure or source of poetic inspiration. In fact (as we have seen) the death of Simonetta Cattaneo was not and could not have been the first cause of the sonnets, whatever Lorenzo may have read into them later. Moreover, let us note here that men *and women* alike weep for this lady—whoever she may be, if she is anyone at all. Certainly, this whole account smacks of the mystical *sovrasenso* that follows immediately, and the indefiniteness of the *una* is not the least reason for suspecting an esoteric meaning.

Good philosophers hold that the corruption of one thing means the creation of another. The achievement and termination of one evil is a step toward and the beginning of another. This is necessarily so, because, since form and species are immortal—according to the philosophers—one (the creative spirit) is always prompted by matter. From this perpetual motion results necessarily a continuous generation of new things. These, following each other without the slightest intermission, remain in any given quality or form for the briefest period of time. Therefore it follows logically that the termination of any one thing is the beginning of another. According to Aristotle, privation is the origin of all things (necessity is the mother of invention?). Therefore Lorenzo concludes that, in all human things, end and beginning are identical. Of course, he does not refer to the end and beginning of the same thing; rather, he repeats, that the termination of any one thing is at once (immediate) the commencement of another. If this is so, then death is a most fitting beginning for this work of his. This is all the more suitable, for a closer examination of the question will reveal that the life of love springs from death. He who lives a life of love (chi vive *ad* amore) dies first to all else. Truly, if love implies the perfection he has said it does, it is impossible to achieve such perfection without first dying to all less perfect things. Homer, Virgil, and Dante all apparently followed this same maxim. Homer sends Ulysses to the lower regions; Virgil, Aeneas; and Dante goes down in person—to explain the inferno. And they all do this with the purpose of showing that mystical death is the way to perfection. After acquiring a knowledge of imperfect things, it is necessary to die with respect to them. In fact, after Aeneas has reached the Elysian Fields, and Dante has been taken to Paradise, neither of them ever remembers the inferno any more. Similarly, Orpheus would have taken Eurydice out of the lower world and brought her back among the living, if only he had not looked back. This may be interpreted to mean (says Lorenzo) that Orpheus was not truly dead. For this reason he did not achieve his perfection, namely, the possession of his dear Eurydice. Lorenzo insists then that the beginning of the true life is conditioned upon the death of the false life. And again he concludes

that he was justified in placing death at the beginning of his
verses.

THIS interesting discourse leads us to another discussion, where we
shall ponder on the fact that Lorenzo read a philosophical *sovrasenso* into all the poetry of his school. We shall see how he once
again perceives the most absolute conformity in the poetry of
Dante and Petrarch, and how his discussion of his strange *principio* is really nothing other than his profound study of the philosophical significance of "mystical death" in the works of his
predecessors. This concept of "death" becomes so transformed, in
Lorenzo, that his work is in *content,* both a continuation and an
innovation of the writings of the *dolce stil novo.* His introduction
of a new *form* contains his understanding and is his concrete exemplification of the difficult *ars poetica* of the school.

Our discussion will show us, too, that, since Lorenzo found an
esoteric meaning in the works of Virgil and Homer, there may be
a strong stilnovistic *sovrasenso* in the works of the purest Italian
humanists of the Quattrocento!

Lorenzo's Principio *Viewed Critically as a Continuation and an Innovation in Content.*

LET us note (in this discussion of "mystical death") the remarkable explanation that Lorenzo gives of the true nature and fitting-
ness of the *principio* in this work, and his stanch defense against
any possible criticism of the innovation he thereby introduces into
the type of literary works with which his own *sonettiere* should be
classed. This explanation and this defense amount to a veritable
revelation for us moderns—both with regard to the attitude that
we should assume toward this particular work of Lorenzo, and
with regard to his own attitude, in turn, toward similar works of
his predecessors. Observe the clear consciousness of his poetic art
revealed here by this would-be apology for his *principio.* Observe,
particularly, his conscious departure from established custom—
wilfully and intentionally made with the idea not merely of introducing an innovation but of adopting a new principle signifying
(in his opinion) a step forward in the clarification of the stilnovis-

tic concept of love and its more logical poetic manifestation. This critical approach to the poetry of his predecessors and this conscious departure from their practice prove two things to us definitely, with regard to Lorenzo. First, they reveal to us that he was a consummate literary critic, and—at least by intention—an original artist. And they also imply on his part a perfect understanding and thorough appreciation of his masters—those great poets who had preceded him in the art of singing the mystical love, those poets whom he emulates here with a spirit of respectful independence and the definite sense of improving on them. For no one can even pretend to improve on his predecessors who does not feel that he has thoroughly mastered their art.

We must take stock of Lorenzo's absolute confidence in his mastery of the meaning of previous Italian literature, or better, his feeling that he has correctly and thoroughly understood both the theory and practice of his great predecessors. This is of supreme importance for a correct reconstruction of Italian literary history up to his time, and especially for a correct understanding of the stilnovistic movement. This confidence, on the part of such a critic and artist, makes him in our eyes an authority of the first order in our attempt to understand the *stil novo*. His *principio di nuova vita,* he tells us in his way, is at once *cosa vecchia* and *cosa nova.* It is a *cosa vecchia* that obviously testifies to an approach to the poets emulated. This understanding of his predecessors is indisputably correct in Lorenzo's opinion and apparently in that of his readers, for no criticism is feared on this ground. It is a *cosa nova* that brings out the author's originality. We must infer that it suggests a modified form of the old concept of love, which is now perhaps beginning to assert itself over the old, and which is possibly already held by the neo-Platonists of Lorenzo's circle. Of one thing we can be positive. Evidently, in Lorenzo's time, not only was Virgil read allegorically (as he had always been variously interpreted throughout the Middle Ages), but now also Homer, in the height of humanism. Not only was Dante similarly understood in his *sovrasenso,* but Petrarch as well must have been generally understood to imply a *sovrasenso* in his lyrics—like Cavalcanti, like Guinizelli, and like all the poets that the author of the

Commentary here exalts and follows. Otherwise there would be no point, in a paragraph which explains philosophically the concept of the mystic death, to his mention of Homer, Virgil, and Dante as providing examples of this death in their works. In his opinion, Ulysses, Aeneas, and Dante are all understood to have died mystically in their metaphorical descent to the lower regions, indeed, Homer, Virgil, and Dante all implied as much "per mostrare che alla perfezione si va per queste vie." He even adds that Orpheus would have achieved his perfection, personified by his Eurydice, if he had not turned around toward the inferno: "che si può interpretare Orfeo non essere veramente morto," mystically of course. Lorenzo's coupling here of Dante with Virgil and Homer, in this respect, is most significant, as is also the fact that these poets are said to have implied an esoteric meaning, in their verses, in a *proemio* which is all impregnated not only with Dantism but also Petrarchism—indeed, with general stilnovism. I repeat that such reading of a *sovrasenso* in the poetry of the various authors imitated—including Petrarch—is not even questioned by Lorenzo. Apparently, this went without saying, for in this respect he does not fear any criticism. This was not a *macula* of which he had to "purge" his commentary. In any case, Lorenzo must naturally have read Petrarch as he now expects his readers to read his sonnets. To be sure, his preoccupation and insistence that he, in turn, be correctly understood in his *sovrasenso* (as explained here and throughout his *Commentary*) indicates that there were "literal" interpreters in his day also. He well knows that this serious annoyance disturbs the proper approach to his treatment of the subject. It not only applies to the reading of all the poets in question—including Homer, Virgil, and Dante—but has been disposed of definitely by him in his rebuttal of the objection to the nature of his subject wrongly considered light and vain. There is no question in his own mind as to the implication of a *sovrasenso* by all his predecessors, who have written *"simili versi."* It has already been brought out, and will be seen better anon, that Lorenzo undoubtedly included Petrarch. For Lorenzo—as previously for Dante and the first stilnovists, indeed, for most of the Italian poets throughout the Renaissance at least—those "literal" readers and superficial thinkers constituted *la gente grossa,* opposed to *gl'intelletti sani* and to all those who had *intelletto d'amore*.[2] As a matter of fact, his commentary—though not intended precisely for them—was certainly meant for them also, provided they were willing to accept this implication of the *sovrasenso* that he explains.

But Lorenzo does not have them in mind here at all. His justification (on the strictest philosophical grounds) of the strange *principio* constituting his great innovation and radical departure from the traditional practice of similar poets is directed to the *intelletti sani* of his day. Perhaps because they also had *intelletto d'amore,* and perhaps practiced this theory, they might easily misunderstand his motive and censure his innovation unless he thoroughly explained both. It is in this explanation that the inclusion of Petrarch among the stilnovists—or poets with a *sovrasenso*—becomes absolutely manifest. For what is Lorenzo's departure from tradition in this connection? It consists merely in not doing something that only Dante and Petrarch (of all the previous poets) had done in an obvious and outstanding manner, and with evident—if mysterious—intention, as we now learn from Lorenzo. His innovation consists in beginning his poetical treatise on love with *morte.* That is, he commences his *nuova vita d'amore* by writing four sonnets on death (or dealing with death), which constitute the *principio* or actual beginning of his new life, and which also involve a new principle in the stilnovistic concept of love. This last connotation of the word *principio* is not the least important. But how is this a clear departure from established practice? Lorenzo must be thinking especially of Dante and Petrarch. Each of them, like the other poets, had celebrated his lady while she was still alive, and after her death. But, unlike the others, they had

2. Cf. Francisci Petrarchae, *Africa,* IX, 100–101, quoted by Corradini in his notes on this book, and compared by him to Dante's famous tercet from *Inferno,* IX, ll. 61–63. A better parallel would have been the very first verse of the canzone, *Donne ch'avete intelletto d'amore,* or the first paragraph of the *Convivio.* Moreover, as my colleague, Professor G. L. Hendrickson, informs me, other parallels may be found in Boccaccio's *Eclogues.* Indeed, the practice of hiding a *sovrasenso* "sotto il velame de li versi strani" was pretty general, and with this went the expectation of being understood only by the highly cultured. The principle of addressing oneself only to these seems to be based on a theory which might be called theory of the aristocracy of the intellect. In Europe, and especially in Italy, such a theory, though no longer propounded very vigorously, is still alive.

manifestly arranged these poems systematically in two distinct
groups:*"in vita"* and *"in morte* di madonna." Dante does this in his
Vita Nuova, and Petrarch's *Rime* are similarly distinguishable; in
fact, they were so divided in the sixteenth century. Thus, these
works both consist of two distinct parts, the first leading gradually
to the lady's death, the second beginning with a gradual transfiguration of *madonna.* How well Lorenzo knew his Dante and
his Petrarch! As everybody knows, the *Vita Nuova* culminates in
the *mirabile visione* of Beatrice in Heaven. And, as another excellent critic, Francesco De Sanctis, was to discover for us centuries
later, Laura actually becomes "transfigured" after her death.[3]

Lorenzo does not follow Dante and Petrarch in their grouping.
He has no poems *"in vita* di madonna," but only *"in morte,"* and
this is his departure from custom. What is more, he does not wish to
have any such poems *in vita* in his collection. This is because of a
new, philosophical principle he has conceived. Therefore, his
nuova vita does not merely begin with the lady's death, but with
his own death to the false life as well, occurring coincidently with
the lady's death. In other words, he believes that the true life of
perfect love implies both the mystic death of the lover and the real
or mystic death of the beloved. The spirit only must live in both.
And this is the principle constituting the substance of his innovation. Therefore (in perfect stilnovistic manner) he applies his
slightly new theory in practice. He introduces first a *principio*
which is both the philosophical *principle* on which his new treatise of love is based, and the actual *beginning* of his amorous passion. Finally, I might add that he evidently feels that the original
stilnovistic understanding of the life of love is somewhat outgrown, and surpassed by a clearer and more definite concept replacing the old. He feels that, in presenting this new modernized
treatise on the subject of love—which partly discards the old doctrine—he does no more than apply the same, natural principle of
deriving the new from the old. This consciousness of a conceptual
ideal that inevitably changes and develops is truly marvelous in
Lorenzo. One feels, in this discussion, the fermentation in his
mind of the Renaissance spirit. And—what is even more valuable

3. Cf. F. De Sanctis: *Saggio critico sul Petrarca* (Napoli, Morano), chaps. ix and x.

for us—he makes us see where and when this spirit originated, and how it grew.

There cannot be any doubt that he is here perfectly conscious of following a movement—a movement that he found incarnated in the philosophical and poetic activity of the stilnovists. And how can it be doubted that in the *bella schiera* he included also Petrarch, when here we find him clearly marking a departure from his master? No one man, not even a Dante, can be said to constitute the *custom* of many (di quelli che insino a qui hanno scritto simili versi). And who, better than Petrarch, had followed the custom that Lorenzo here breaks? Who, besides Dante and Petrarch, had written "similar verses" arranged in a manner that Lorenzo decides not to follow? I repeat this, and insist on this apparently unimportant detail because I take it as an unsuspected, external proof of the falseness of the traditional idea that a sort of gulf existed between Dante and Petrarch, and between the first stilnovists and the poets of the Renaissance. Lorenzo here proves that no such gulf really ever existed. A continuity is found between the first stilnovists and the later poets of the Quattrocento, and even the Cinquecento, much as one is seen between the first primitive painters and the later masters of the Italian Renaissance. Dante himself saw this continuity in his own time, and foresaw it for the coming generations when he wrote:

> Credette Cimabue ne la pintura
> tener lo campo, e ora ha Giotto il grido,
> sì che la fama di colui è scura.
> Così ha tolto l'uno a l'altro Guido
> la gloria de la lingua; e forse è nato
> chi l'uno e l'altro caccerà del nido.[4]

The process, according to the circumstances, continued. Changes there were, no doubt, but no break in the chain. And the Italian literary chain is that indicated by Lorenzo, with Petrarch as important a link in this chain as Dante himself, but a link nevertheless.

Let us return to Lorenzo's *principio* for one or two more considerations. Evidently, this striking division or distinction (in both

4. *Purgatorio,* XI, 94–99.

the *Vita Nuova* and the *Rime*) of poems *in vita* and poems *in morte* of the respective ladies had a deep, philosophical significance for our critic. He had therefore applied himself to study it most carefully—so carefully, in fact, that he had ended by deriving from it a slightly modified concept of the principle involved. But Lorenzo must have read originally some *sovrasenso* in the phenomenon of death, which he interpreted to be the philosophical meaning attached to it by Dante and Petrarch. Otherwise we could not explain here his modification of something or other—a modification that constitutes his innovation. Therefore, we must conclude that, for Lorenzo, the real or supposed deaths of Beatrice and Laura had a philosophical *sovrasenso* at least akin to the significance he now attaches to *morte* in his own *principio*. It would be premature to discuss now the difference, however slight it may be, in the connotation of the word according to each poet. The point here is that Lorenzo undoubtedly recognized a *sovrasenso* in the death of those ladies, corresponding to the philosophical opinion of the respective poets. He, too, had a similar, yet different, connotation for the same phenomenon.

Morte is one of the most mysterious and most frequently recurring words in all stilnovistic literature, with the possible precedence of *gentile* and *amore* itself. It is very significant that Lorenzo centers his attention primarily on these words, in his study of previous literature. We have already seen that a large portion of this *proemio* is devoted to an explanation of the true nature of his subject. This is intended to give to the readers a correct understanding of his strictly technical use of the term "love," involving a deeply philosophical concept and a scientific principle. In fact it will be remembered that at the very beginning of his defense of his subject matter, he promptly defined love as *appetito di bellezza*.[5] Later, in connection with the twelfth sonnet, he will explain[6] the very precise, technical meaning of the adjective *gentile*. Here he takes up the term *morte*. And his discussion of this strange *principio* is really a profound study of the philosophical significance of death in the works of the poets who have pre-

5. Cf. Text, p. 14, l. 9; and this study, p. 13.
6. Cf. Text, pp. 57–58; and this study, pp. 111–113.

ceded him. There can be no doubt, I say, as to his attaching a *sovrasenso* to this recurring phenomenon in previous literature, and as to the connotation carried by the word *morte* (in his opinion), which must have been very similar to his own. For he certainly feels that he is advancing beyond his predecessors. And, if this advance is not precisely in a more profound and true understanding of the mystic death, it is certainly in the direction of a logical consequence following from it. In fact, if what really counts is the new life coming after the mystic death, what is the use of the poems *in vita di madonna?* They may as well be omitted. Lorenzo may be right or wrong, but this is his line of reasoning. His advance, then, may not amount to much. But this will come out in our study of his actual treatise on love. Here I suspect that it may be a question more of method than of substance. Therefore we may have here a true, clear echo of the technical *sovrasenso* generally attached to the word *morte* in stilnovistic literature (at least by those who had *intelletto d'amore* in Lorenzo's time, and certainly by Lorenzo himself). Then we must modify our understanding of the so-called humanism of the day, and recognize its relation to, if not its origin in the *stil novo.* Otherwise we could not explain Lorenzo's coupling here of Dante with Virgil and Homer, and of all the ancient classical literature with the modern Italian classics. Nor could we appreciate this reading of a *sovrasenso* in Virgil and Homer on the part of such a humanist as Lorenzo undoubtedly was.

But what is the meaning of *morte* according to Lorenzo? We need not dwell on its mystical aspect, for this is most obvious from his own discussion. We should concentrate, rather, on its real, philosophical significance for our author. This is of the nature of a fundamental principle, philosophically speaking, and of the nature of a method, didactically speaking. In other words, it all seems to me a matter of psychology. Let us recall once more Lorenzo's definition of love. We may say, before studying his treatise, that his God or *summum bonum* is the god of his Renaissance times— *artistic beauty.* This means beauty in all *things,* as we have seen he says. It is not only physical beauty, but "virtual" beauty (in the Latin sense of the word *virtus*)—spiritual or moral beauty, and the beauty of grace, refinement, and culture in general. This includes the beauty of nature, the beauty of ideas, the beauty of all artistic creations, the physical and spiritual beauty of all cultured individuals, both men and women. This is the substance of his understanding of the adjective *gentile* explained later on, and this is the substance of perfect love in his sense of the word. Therefore the perfection of love is the ideal beauty that animates all things and persons and emanates from them in perfect correspondence with their potential *virtus,* and as a complete or perfect expression of this virtue. Thus, the life of love or *passione d'amore* is the veritable "suffering" that accompanies the pursuit of this beauty: in the things about us, in an attempt to extract from them their true form and essence; and in ourselves, in an attempt to achieve our own perfection. This perfection is equivalent to the complete manifestation of ourselves, or the gradual working out of our various destinies on the basis of our natural *gentilezza.* All of this, of course, is pure neo-Platonism, or better, pure Dantean stilnovism. But the point here is not from whom and to what extent Lorenzo drew his concept. It is rather that he used such a concept for the proper understanding of his predecessors, as he did in composing his own sonnets. And the point here is not that this concept was old in itself, but that Lorenzo understands it better (as he thinks) than his predecessors, and modernizes it. This will become more evident later, in our special study of his *nuova vita d'amore.*

Returning to the meaning of *morte,* it is clear that man must spiritualize himself and the world about him in order to achieve this perfection of love. In other words, both lover and beloved must die mystically in the flesh, in order to remain only pure spirit or form. And this is how the beginning of the true life (equivalent to the pursuit of this beauty) coincides necessarily with the end, or death, of the false life (which is any life that does not pursue this true objective). Thus, also, this beginning of the new life is substantially a conformity with the basic principle of nature, whereby life is a continuous emanation of form from matter, or a perpetual transformation of the old into the new. Whoever pursues this true, natural course—abandoning perforce the false one

—will certainly attain his goal or true perfection of love, with respect to the complete manifestation of all his personal *gentilezza*. But it should not be forgotten (Lorenzo seems to say) that the very objective of the lover must be the possession of this beauty, or the grasp of the pure form in things. Therefore the lady, or other *thing,* must also die, mystically if not in reality. This is in order that she live only as pure form in the mind of the lover. For, as long as the lady is *in vita* (that is, incarnated in a definitely fixed form) her soul, or form, is bound in that body and not free to move. In other words, she may be said to be in reality *dead,* and not *truly* alive. But her *true life* really begins when she, in turn, dies physically, or at least mystically, in the mind of the lover. Furthermore, as long as she is *in vita,* her physical self is always going to be a disturbing element in the mind of the lover, who is trying to live his own *true life.* And, for all these reasons, while *in vita,* she is not really that absolutely perfect thing that the true, perfect lover must love. In our language, this simply means that the perfect lover, according to Lorenzo, must (in his consideration of all things) always discard the perishable and fleeting, to concentrate on the eternal reality of form in its manifold and ever new manifestations. This is the only *true life* making for progress in the natural evolution of matter and form.

Form, it seems to me, is the keyword to Lorenzo's philosophy and art: form in thought, and form in art. A new concept—like this one of his *principio*—is for him a new form proceeding necessarily from a previous concept. In this case it is a concept of Dante, if, indeed, one by Petrarch did not intervene between Dante's and his own now. And a new image in art—we may infer—is for him necessarily a new intuition based on a new form that is born out of the eternal and continuous changing of all things about us. Therefore the true poet and artist, or the perfect lover in general, does not only bring out his own *gentilezza* in the course of his *true life,* but grasps the form, or extracts the *gentilezza* out of all things about him.

This is why he insists on the mystic death of both lover and beloved in this *ars poetica* of his. This is his understanding of the term *morte* in stilnovistic literature, as well as his own connotation of the word in his *Commentary*. This is why he perhaps differed slightly from his predecessors. At any rate, this is why he logically decided to omit or not to write any poems *in vita di madonna*. For his *nuova vita* is going to be merely the narration of his experience of the amorous passion which began with the realization of the principle enunciated here. Whatever preceded his mystic death, he thinks, is neither important nor really appropriate in his treatise. And, therefore, he departs from the custom established especially by Dante and Petrarch.

There is one final remark I should like to append to this long elucidation. The matter is really incidental here. It is apropos of what Lorenzo says about Orpheus' failure to save his Eurydice. If Orpheus had not looked back, he would have succeeded in taking Eurydice out of Hell, and brought her back among the living. And this, Lorenzo adds, may be interpreted to mean that he was not *truly dead* mystically. I wonder if his friend Poliziano thought so, too, when he composed his famous *Orfeo*. It seems to me that, if Lorenzo thus interpreted the Greek myth, Poliziano also very likely did. Otherwise, I doubt whether Lorenzo would have thus interpreted it without the slightest compunction, especially when we consider that he did not really need this additional example for his argument. In fact, it rather intrudes. It seems to be added because he felt that this apparent contradiction would occur to others as well as to himself. Therefore he hastens to show how this apparent exception really proves his rule. At any rate, it seems to me probable, in view of Lorenzo's sure interpretation of the myth of Orpheus, that Poliziano interpreted it similarly. And, if he did, it means that those who have regarded Poliziano's *Orfeo* as implying an allegory are very probably right. Moreover, if this work is allegorical, it means that it should be considered also stilnovistic. And we may end by finding the *umanistissimo* Poliziano another downright stilnovist, precisely like his patron!

Lorenzo's Apology for the Prolixity of this Proemio.

LET us return to our reading of the *Commentary*. Here the *proemio* really ends finally. But the author now feels that he must still apologize for its length before passing definitely to the exposi-

tion of the *principio*—which, as a matter of fact, he has already begun by giving us the preceding philosophical basis for his innovation, consisting precisely in the true nature and character of *morte,*
with which it deals. As I said before, then, these two parts of his
work, *proemio* and *principio* (like the second and third, or *nuova
vita,* later) are welded together in such a way that there is not the
slightest break in the continuity of the narration. Nor is there any
break in the logical and psychological presentation of his subject
matter, involving—as it does—his actual experience of the amorous passion, and being equivalent to his conscious practical application of the theory he expounds.

Perhaps, says Lorenzo, this *proemio* has been much too prolix,
and a greater preparation than the purpose warranted. But it
seems to him that its copiousness was quite necessary. He makes a
remark here with apparent modesty, but in reality with pungent
sarcasm. He says that, considering the slightness (inezia) of these
verses of his, they seemed to need a little embellishment, such as
becomes things naturally unadorned. Moreover, he could not have
exculpated himself otherwise of the faults that might have been
attributed to him. Having thus accomplished this part, however,
he says in closing, let us pass to the exposition of the sonnets. "But
first we must discuss somewhat the first four sonnets, for this
seems necessary."

Notice how this last sentence especially makes the *principio* at
once a part of the *proemio* and an indissoluble part of the *nuova
vita* or body of his sonnets. This insistence of mine on an apparently insignificant fact may seem strange. I insist on the perfect
continuity of Lorenzo's *Commentary* for several reasons. It
strengthens my contention that it is a late work, and the result of
long, profound meditation and planning on the part of the author. Then, too, this perfect, artistic unity is a proof of Lorenzo's
consummate stilnovism in the manner of Dante. Finally, this
unity seems to me to be his way of impressing the reader with his
sincerity, and of proving to him that this amorous passion was an
actual experience of his mind and heart—all occurring when,
where, and how he is about to say. Let us remark a certain parallel. In the first place, in perfect stilnovistic manner, his first four

sonnets here *are* the philosophic principle incarnated, and *are* at once the theory and the actual, personal experience of the truth of this concept. In the second place, the other sonnets anon will similarly be both the exposition of his concept of the *true life* and his actual, personal experience of this new life exemplified in those sonnets or *nuova vita* of his. Then, in the third place, the *Commentary* as a whole—including the *proemio*—is intended to be at once both the theory he holds and the art he practices following this theory. This theory both animates and is derived from his actual experience. Therefore the experience is real, actual, and true in every respect. It constitutes the author's indisputable testimony as to the veracity of the facts involved and his psychological interpretation of them—*for these facts, thus interpreted, are the scientific basis of his theory*. Therefore, unless we presuppose that all this is a fanciful fabrication—which is unthinkable and untenable—we must accept his own testimony with regard to his sincerity and absolute truthfulness. If we do not, then his theory tumbles, his actual *ars poetica* is contradicted, and he is not a Petrarchist, nor a stilnovist, nor anything but a fraud in our conception. Whereas, if we do, we follow him perfectly in his understanding of Italian literature up to, and including, himself. We understand better than we ever have before the philosophical and artistic movement in which he participates so nobly. And, finally, we can place him intelligently in his proper position in the history of Italian literary art and criticism.

Before we ourselves pass on to the study of the *principio,* we must now make our deductions from the preceding study of the *proemio,* and indicate our expectations from the further study of the *Commentary* as a whole.

CHAPTER V

A Glance Backward and Forward; Deductions and Expectations.

IN the course of this paraphrase of Lorenzo's Preface to his *Co-mento*, a number of significant questions have naturally arisen. I have tried to solve these with a certain broadness of view, but with especial relation to the particular point involved. Now let us gather up these threads to see at what general and more definite conclusions we may arrive, and also what we may expect from our further study of this most interesting, though neglected, work.

First, let us consider the question of sources and influences. That this *Comento* is Dantean and neo-Platonic, as generally said by those who have glanced at it, is true enough. But, on the basis of our findings, we may now correct, specify, and amplify this general, and yet narrow, statement. The Dantean sources of Lorenzo's *Commentary* are not limited to the *Vita Nuova,* but—as we have seen—include also the *Convivio* and the *De vulgari eloquentia,* especially for the *proemio.* In fact, we may say already (on the basis of certain hints he has already given us, and in anticipation of what he leads us to expect) that he draws from all of Dante's works, including the *Commedia,* and that Dante's influence radiates over him like the light from a single sun, not like rays coming from distinct and unrelated stars symbolizing his works separately. Moreover, the neo-Platonism undoubtedly evinced by this work is not merely, or so much the philosophy of a Ficino and his circle, as it is the neo-Platonism that forms the soul of the *dolce stil novo.* Indeed, it could not even be called precisely Dantean neo-Platonism, but should be termed, more broadly, stilnovistic neo-Platonism. While this neo-Platonism may be said to be the philosophic basis of the *stil novo,* the latter is much more than a philosophical principle—it is the translation of this principle into a complete *ars poetica.* And what Lorenzo evinces in his *Commentary* is not so much an interest in neo-Platonism pure and simple, as a decided and lively interest in the *ars poetica* derived from it. Thus, it seems to me much more correct and precise to call his philosophy and style merely (if more broadly) stilnovistic!

This conclusion naturally leads us to a broader consideration of this same question of sources and influences. What other sources had Lorenzo for this work, and what other influences operated on him? The answer given by Lorenzo himself definitely establishes his stilnovism, and confirms this conclusion. His authorities are not the neo-Platonists as such—none of whom is even mentioned, as a matter of fact—and are not by any means limited to Dante. His authorities, as we have seen, are—in a clear, orderly, and definite manner—stated by him. They are primarily: Guinizelli, Cavalcanti, Dante, Petrarch and Boccaccio. This is the school he now joins and follows faithfully, even if he has minor reservations and a certain independence. They are essentially poets and artists, not pure philosophers. Furthermore, they are substantially the best authors of Italian literature up to his time. They are, indeed, *the* Italian literature that really counted for him. With the exception of Petrarch and Boccaccio, they are the stilnovists, par excellence, generally recognized by every critic and historian as the main promoters of, and principal contributors to, this essentially literary movement.

As I have repeatedly pointed out, the significant thing is that Lorenzo undoubtedly includes Petrarch among his authorities, and thereby recognizes him as a member of this literary school, and a *magna pars* in this movement. Indeed, he clearly indicates in his discussion of the question of language that he also included even Boccaccio, although, for obvious reasons, he did not apparently draw on him for this treatise on the subject of mystic love. This leads us to the next important question—Lorenzo's own authority for us as an historian and literary critic. But before we proceed with this consideration, we need to remind ourselves of the approximate and probable date we have assigned to this work. After a long and careful study of the evidence—mostly internal— we came to the conclusion that this *Commentary* must be a late work. While we grant that it was conceived and planned quite early, yet it must have been actually undertaken after Lorenzo had written most, if not all, of his sonnets. We concluded that it was probably interrupted by his death. This permits us to infer that he meditated over this subject of his sonnets, on and off, for over twenty years: that is, from the time when he probably first conceived the project of this work in connection with his *Raccolta aragonese,* to shortly before his death, which occurred in 1492. Accordingly, the *Commentary* reflects long study, and apparently represents for us Lorenzo's mature judgment regarding all the matters treated in it. Furthermore, this means that our author is not the mere youth, however precocious, who collected that anthology, and even wrote the famous letter that went with it: he is Lorenzo, the humanist, great friend of Poliziano; Lorenzo, the great patron of the arts and letters; Lorenzo, a great poet himself. In a word, Lorenzo the Magnificent! This makes a great difference, it seems to me, in our regard for his knowledge of things, for his judgment of them, and especially for his general outlook on literary and artistic matters. And our regard is greatly enhanced when, in reading him we find him evincing such fine and thorough comprehension of the authors that had preceded him, such nice discernment, critical acumen, and exquisite taste. In fact, we feel that a man with such endowment, who was so near to that earlier time as to be profoundly influenced by its most important movement to the extent of wishing to participate in it, should be precisely our main authority for the correct understanding of that movement. Of course, we must use discretion. An intelligent participant in a movement (and Lorenzo was such a one) is likely to show considerable originality. To this question I now come.

Lorenzo has, indeed, a certain originality of his own, or at least he strives for it. We saw this in his explanation and defense of his peculiar *principio,* and may well expect to see it much better in our subsequent study of his sonnets and his comments on them. We must be careful to distinguish in his *Commentary* the *cosa nova* from the *cosa vecchia,* and must guard against the interpretation of the old in terms of the new. But I wish to defend Lorenzo's originality, which is generally denied, especially with respect to his *Commentary.* We have seen that, while the *proemio* which we have just read is undoubtedly inspired in content and form by the first book of Dante's *Convivio,* it is in no sense a slav-

ish imitation of it, but—at most—an adaptation of it to a similar
work. Especially with regard to the content, Lorenzo's *proemio* is
an original and modern treatment of the same and similar questions that confronted him as they had confronted Dante. His is, in
fact, a highly original, critical study of the preceding Italian literature in its most important phase, and in its most significant authors. This study, of course, includes Dante himself and authors
whom Dante could not have treated, since they came after him.
And Lorenzo's critical judgment is based on his own, personal,
direct study of his predecessors in their original works. There is no
critic of Italian literature before Lorenzo. Even Dante's scope was
necessarily very limited. And Lorenzo, in this respect, *fa invero
cosa nova.* Therefore, I repeat (modifying radically Flamini's
quoted remark) that

dopo il "De Vulgari Eloquentia," *non solo* la lettera accompagnante la
preziosa silloge, *ma, con essa e più importante di essa, questo "Proemio"
dello stesso Magnifico al suo preziosissimo "Comento"* è il più antico documento di storia critica della nostra poesia.

   Lorenzo's grouping of his distant and immediate predecessors in
the *bella scuola* of which he declares himself a member is historically correct. His profound understanding, nice discrimination,
and just valuation of the various authors and their works is also
critically correct. And his approach to them, I may now say, is,
therefore, scientifically sound—following as it does the traditional
method he undoubtedly used. We may, indeed, accept him with
confidence as our greatest, if not sole authority, on the preceding
Italian literature, and especially on this very puzzling matter of
the *dolce stil novo.* This *proemio* promises a new, modernized,
and partly original version of the old concept involving the entire
ars poetica of the stilnovists up to, and including, Lorenzo himself. The *Commentary* as a source is therefore a most precious discovery for the history of Italian literature and literary criticism.
Let us approach it guardedly, but also trustingly—guardedly, because we must not expect it to be quite the open sesame to the
mysterious *dolce stil novo,* but also trustingly, with the hope of
finding in Lorenzo's divulgence of his philosophic faith and artis-

tic secret some light that may illumine for us the obscurity of his predecessors as well. Lorenzo will be found to speak more or less our modern language in his expository prose. At any rate, he seems to realize the main difficulties in reading the ancient poets, and even seems to anticipate our greater difficulty in this respect, after so many more centuries. It is entirely possible that we may find in his explanation of "some of his own sonnets" not only the key to those sonnets but a key that (used with discretion and intelligence) may actually open for us the doors of some of the treasure chests whose contents were apparently familiar to him.

This approach to the *stil novo,* through Lorenzo and under his guidance, seems to me logical and scientific. It may seem like going backward instead of going forward, and—as Lorenzo says of his *principio*—"come pare *prima facie,* pervertendo quasi l'ordine della natura." But I trust that this apparent reverse order will be productive of good results, and will give us at least some light, where we now have all but total obscurity.

PART II

THE *PRINCIPIO:* SONNET I

CHAPTER I

The Four Sonnets Called Principio: *Text and General Observations; an Experiment in Reading Stilnovistic Verse.*

LORENZO'S *principio,* as we recall, constitutes the second part of his *Commentary,* following the *proemio* and preceding the *nuova vita.* There are no absolute lines of demarcation in the continuous, expository narrative of his doctrine and experience of love. In our study of the *principio,* we must constantly keep in mind the triple sense in which our author (consistently and emphatically) uses the term. *Principio,* for him, means: first, a basic philosophic *principle;* second, the actual *beginning* of his "new life"; and, third, the *introduction* to the body of sonnets constituting the essence and experience of this "new life."

The four sonnets, which (on Lorenzo's own authority) embody all this, are the following:

I

O chiara stella, che co' raggi tuoi
togli alle tue vicine stelle il lume,
perchè splendi assai più che 'l tuo costume?
perchè con Febo ancor contender vuoi?

Forse i begli occhi, quali ha tolti a noi
Morte crudel, ch'omai troppo presume,
accolti hai in te: adorna del lor lume,
il suo bel carro a Febo chieder puoi.

O questa o nuova stella che tu sia,
che di splendor novello adorni il cielo,
chiamata esaudi, o nume, i voti nostri:

leva dello splendor tuo tanto via,
che agli occhi, c'han d'eterno pianto zelo,
sanz'altra offension lieta ti mostri.

II

Quando il sol giù dall'orizzonte scende,
rimiro Clizia pallida nel volto,

e piango la sua sorte che li ha tolto
la vista di colui che ad altri splende.
    Poi quando di novella fiamma accende
l'erbe, le piante e' fior Febo a noi vòlto,
l'altro orizzonte allor ringrazio molto
e la benigna aurora che gliel tolse.
    Ma lasso! io non so già qual nuova aurora
renda al mondo il suo sole: ah, dura sorte,
che noi vestir d'eterna notte volse!
    O Clizia, indarno speri vederl'ora:
tien' gli occhi fissi infin li chiuda morte
all'orizzonte estremo che tel tolse.

III

    Di vita il dolce lume fuggirei
a quella vita, ch'altri "morte" appella;
ma morte è sì gentile oggi e sì bella,
ch'io credo che morir vorran gli dèi.
    Morte è gentil, poich'è stata in colei
ch'è or del ciel la più lucente stella;
io, che gustar non vo' dolce, poich'ella
è morta, seguirò quest'anni rei.
    Piangeran sempre gli occhi, e 'l tristo core
sospirerà del suo bel sol l'occaso,
lor di lui privi, e 'l cor d'ogni sua speme.
    Piangerà meco dolcemente Amore,
le Grazie e le sorelle di Parnaso;
e chi non piangerà con questi insieme?

IV

    In qual parte andrò io ch'io non ti truovi,
trista memoria? in quale oscuro speco
fuggirò io, che sempre non sie meco,
trista memoria, che al mio mal sol giovi?
    Se in prato, lo qual germini fior nuovi,
se all'ombra d'arbuscei verdi m'arreco,
veggo un corrente rivo, io piango seco:
che cosa è, ch'e' miei pianti non rinnuovi?
    S'io torno all' infelice patrio nido,
tra mille cure questa in mezzo siede
del cor che, come suo, consuma e rode.
    Che debb'io far omai? a che mi fido?
Lasso! che sol sperar posso merzede
da morte, che oramai troppo tardi ode.

The order of these sonnets is not that in which they appear in the *Raccolta aragonese,* where they were all included. But it is the order in which they appear in the *Commentary.* Among Lorenzo's own sixteen lyrics, with which the *Raccolta* ends, they are respectively numbers 11, 10, 2, and 1. Which was the actual, chronological order in which they were composed? The question cannot be answered positively. But, if the author's own testimony, so persistently insisted upon in the *Commentary,* is correct—they were written in the reverse order from that in the *Raccolta.* And they were written before any other of the poet's lyrics in the *Raccolta,* in fact before any other of his poetic compositions on the subject of love. He tells us that his experience of the passion of love—equivalent to his poetic "new life"—began precisely with the consideration of the philosophic principle involved in these four sonnets. And he is ready to expound them as four consecutive chapters of his doctrine, corresponding to four consecutive moments of his experience of love. Then we must conclude that they were actually his first love sonnets, and that the order of the *Commentary* represents the true chronology of composition. There may be, of course, objections to this view. Perhaps, in the course of his study of the doctrine as a whole, he first conceived the four parts all together, but then did not actually write out the chapters or sonnets in the order suggested by the plan. Perhaps—while he was engaged in this task, with his poetic life already begun—he had other inspirations that demanded a more immediate execution and embodiment in some of his other early lyrics. In this case, the order of his poems included in the *Raccolta* may be more strictly chronological. But this conjecture is hardly supported by the sonnets themselves. On the contrary, the lack of all chronological order in the *Raccolta* as a whole (even with respect to the authors included) indicates no more than a casual, or some other intended, order for these sonnets as well. We have absolutely no reason for disbelieving the author of the *Commentary* on this point. In fact, the presence of these sonnets in the *Raccolta* strongly supports his contention. We know definitely that these sonnets must have been among his earliest compositions, and were probably his very first, as he intimates. At any rate, this is what he would have us believe in the *Commentary,* whether for purposes of doctrinal exposition or through historical fidelity, but primarily, I believe, as evidence of the perfect conformity of his theory to his personal experience. For throughout his work, and especially in the *principio,* we can see the intention of proving his theory by his actual experience. Indeed, he wishes to give the impression that his doctrine is derived from his practical experience and entirely based upon it. This should be carefully remembered, since it will be found to be a point of capital importance in the poetic art of the stilnovists. Lorenzo here wishes to demonstrate thus both the scientific attitude of this school of poets toward the truth, and its requirement of utter sincerity. This is also the essence of the realism of this school: theory and practice must conform absolutely, or the theory is false. The *verbum* must always be incarnate, or true sincerity is not achieved. In the example given by Lorenzo in his *principio,* of an extreme desire to establish the historical veracity of his experience, we have both his critical understanding of his predecessors, and the desire to demonstrate the truth of their doctrine by the verification afforded by his own experience. Once more, therefore, his critical study of his own experience is of immense value to us in understanding both his poetry and the art of the school he follows.

I have taken these sonnets out of the expository context that the author later embroidered about them in his *Commentary,* and reproduce them here in the original Italian according to Simioni's text,[1] for obvious reasons of convenience in referring to them. But, frankly, this study is intended to have a secondary purpose, besides the primary one of understanding them both in themselves and in connection with Lorenzo's avowed theory. This secondary purpose is to demonstrate how inadequate and incomplete, if not entirely wrong, the study of a *canzoniere* like Lorenzo's can be, when incorrectly approached. And when I say this, I mean approached only with our modern mentality, without a good knowledge of those times, or even without the assistance of such aids as the poet himself may have left. So frequently it happens that we base our critical judgment of an author or a school of poets largely on our fancies resulting from the reading of single, disconnected

1. Text, pp. 25–33.

poems, and from our first impressions of them! Then it is no wonder that we misinterpret them, and build castles in the air about an epoch or a literary movement. Since the main purpose of this study of Lorenzo's *Commentary* is to correct such an error (both with regard to himself and the school of poets he follows) it is not amiss here to perform an interesting experiment. Thereby, perhaps, we shall see how and why our usual, modern concept of the *dolce stil novo* is largely wrong, or, at least, inadequate. And this will familiarize us with these sonnets, serving as an introduction to our study of their full and true exposition according to the author himself.

Accordingly, I propose first to take them up only in a general, normal way, without any deeper penetration of their poetic *sovrasenso,* than is fairly obvious to the uninitiated. I invite the reader to approach them without any other assistance than a good knowledge of the Italian language coupled with a little familiarity with Italian poetry, and some literary appreciation. On the other hand, I advise him to read them very attentively, as many times as may be necessary for him to feel that he understands them thoroughly or at least finds them intelligible. This is in order that he may later compare his own understanding of them (based solely on such a study) with the author's avowed meaning, when I shall give it to him in my free but faithful rendering of Lorenzo's exposition of the text. By thus approaching these poems first, I believe that we shall appreciate fully the author's real and serious preoccupation lest he be misunderstood or not understood at all. We shall all, then, agree with him that a commentary on his verses was not only useful, but necessary, especially for us moderns, and, smiling perhaps at our own shortcomings, we shall agree with him that the only true expounder (if not the sole judge) of a work is the author himself.

Literal Meaning of the Principio, *and Its Obvious Implication of a* Sovrasenso.

UPON first impression, these sonnets appear to be perfectly intelligible and quite simple. They do not seem, at a glance, to require any special commentary to reveal their whole obvious meaning.

In the first sonnet the poet is gazing romantically at a certain brilliant star whose splendor obscures the light of all the other stars near by. He apostrophizes it, wondering why it shines more than its wont; why, indeed, it wishes to vie with Phoebus. Perhaps, he thinks, this is because the star has taken to itself certain beautiful eyes that cruel Death, now become altogether too presumptuous, has taken from the world; and thus adorned with their light, it may well ask Phoebus to lend his chariot. However this be (the apostrophe continues),

whether thou be this, or a new star that with new splendor adorns the sky, we beg thee, o god, to grant our wish: remove enough of thy splendor that our eyes, longing to weep forever, may see thy gladness without other harm to thee than this.

In the second sonnet, the scene shifts. The poet is now discovered contemplating Clytie, the *tornalsole.*[2] He says:

When the sun goes down on the horizon, I observe Clytie, pale-cheeked, and I weep over her fate that has deprived her of the sight of him who now shines on others. Then, when Phoebus, to us returned, enflames anew the grass and plants and flowers, I render liberal thanks to the other horizon and to the gracious dawn that took him from her. But alas, I know not what new dawn will ever give back its sun to the world! O dire fate that willed to clothe us with eternal night! O Clytie, vainly thou hopest to see it now: Keep thine eyes fixed upon the distant horizon that robbed thee of it, until death doth close them.

A similar shift of thought (and apparent change of subject)

2. The *tornalsole* contemplated by our poet is a "sunflower," but not of the large American variety called in Italian *girasole.* The common species of large-size heliotrope, such as the marigold, is an American plant which was not therefore known in Europe until after Columbus' discovery. On the contrary Lorenzo's *tornalsole* is a *"picciol* fiore . . . di colore pallido, perchè è giallo e bianco." (Cf. Text, p. 27, l. 30, and p. 28, l. 1.) With the kind assistance of Professor A. W. Evans, Curator of the Eaton Herbarium in Yale University, I have been able to identify this "little" sunflower with the *Heliotropium Europaeum,* which vulgarly is also called *porraja* or *porricella* in Italian, while in French it is called precisely *tournesol,* and in English "turnsole." In fact, Hegi describes it as a little flower having a "Krone weiss bis etwas bläulichweiss, im Schlund gelb." (Cf. Gustav Hegi, *Illustrierte Flora von Mittel-Europa,* III, 2132–2133, under No. 2295.) And Willkomm, less precisely, also says that it has a "corolla parva alba." (Cf. Mauritio Willkomm et Joanni Lange, *Prodromus florae hispanicae,* II, 513.) It is well to note now for reference later, that, according to these authorities, this European species of heliotrope is decidedly *a summer flower,* like the American. The *tornalsole* blooms in Germany during July and August, and in Spain from June to September. It follows that in Italy, too, and particularly in Tuscany, April would be entirely too early for it.

characterizes the third sonnet. This is all a lamentation. The poet exclaims:

From this life's sweet light would I escape to that life that others call "death." But death is so gentle now, and so beautiful, that I believe the gods themselves will [*sic*] wish to die. Gentle is death, since it has come to her who is now the brightest star in heaven. But I, who wish not to taste of sweetness—since she is dead—shall follow out the course of my wretched life. My eyes shall weep forever, and my sad heart lament continually the setting of its beautiful sun,—now that the eyes are deprived of their sun, and the heart of all its hope. And with me Love will sweetly weep, and the Graces, and the sisters dwelling in Parnassus; aye who would[3] not weep with these?

The fourth sonnet seems to be somewhat more intimately connected, at least with the preceding one. But this also introduces certain new elements that seem to detach it from the rest. Now, apparently, the previous discouragement has become utter despair. The poet cries out:

Whither shall I go that I do not find thee, wretched memory? Into what dark recess of woods or mountain shall I flee where thou art not always with me, O wretched memory, that availest only mine evil? If I betake myself to the field, where new flowers grow, or to the shade of green trees,—there, at the sight of a running brook, I weep with it. Is there anything that does not renew my grief? And if I return to my father's once happy home,—there, in the midst of a thousand cares, I find her (memoria) seated at my heart's core, gnawing and consuming, as if my heart belonged to her. What am I to do now? In what can I place my trust? Alas, my only hope of help is from death, who now heeds but too late.

This is the result of our first reading. If we now consider these poems somewhat critically, but accepting only face values, what do we find? First of all a question confronts us. Are these a group of sonnets intimately connected by the nature of a single subject; or are they detached thoughts born separately and independently at various times, and later grouped artificially to constitute a series? Then, do they actually develop a theme in four progressive movements? If they do, what is this theme? In other words, is there any unity and coherence in these sonnets? Let us remember,

3. *Palatino 204* and *Vaticano 3219* read *piangeria* in place of *piangerà* found in the other MSS. and preferred by Simioni.

in our answer, that we are not at present supposed to be enlight-
ened by the author's own comments on them, but are judging
these verses *per se,* knowing only that they are said to constitute a
principio di nuova vita.

Our very doubt, thus expressed, seems to condemn them as a
single composition. To be sure, we see more than the germ of a
common idea embodied and developed in them, but this imper-
fectly. This idea, apparently, is not precisely "death" in the abstract, but the effects produced on the poet by the death of someone, some lady. It is obvious that in the first sonnet he compares
the brightness of her beautiful eyes to the splendor of the most
brilliant star in heaven. He speaks metaphorically of her splendid
soul as this star or a new star illuminating the heavens like a new
sun. To this star, as to a god, he prays that it dazzle him not, but
—dimming its splendor just enough—allow him to gaze lovingly
at it, without otherwise losing of its beauty. In the second sonnet
the death of this lady is viewed poetically as the setting of the
"new sun" she presumably was in life. The poet now compares
himself to Clytie, meditating sadly over his worse fate that may
never permit his sun to rise again. He, and the whole world with
him, can have only the recollection of the last vision of this de-
parted lady. The third sonnet is obvíously a development of this
same theme, namely, the lady's death. But what a strange and
mysterious development! Death, formerly cruel, is now ennobled
by having taken this gentle lady. Disconsolate, the poet would
gladly die; but he will have none of sweetness, and will not taste
the sweetness of death. His sun has set in the previous sonnet, and
it was then but vain hope that it would ever rise again. But here
this lady is still (or again) the brightest star in heaven! At the
same time his eyes and heart will both regret for the remaining
years of his wretched existence the setting of his beautiful sun.
Finally, there seems to be another contradiction. On the one hand,
now that Death is made noble, the gods themselves will wish to
die, but, on the other hand, Love and the Graces and the Muses
will all weep sweetly with him and all the world. All this creates
considerable confusion in our minds, but vagueness is perhaps a
privilege of the poets. The fact is that there is development and

progression here, and therefore a certain unity. And the same may be said for the fourth sonnet, in which the poet tries every means to escape the memory of this lady—after promising himself to keep his eyes fixed upon the last vision of her, and after deciding that he will seek no solace, but will weep and sorrow all his life! Here, indeed, he not only hopes to find solace in many ways, but his one, final hope is the very death which he has just rejected! Unquestionably there is, or seems to be some lack of coherence here, too, as in the composition of the whole group of sonnets. But we are satisfied that they all deal with the single subject of a certain lady whose death has profoundly affected the poet. And we are satisfied that there is a certain progressive movement from one to the other, which leads to a certain climax at the end of the last sonnet. Furthermore, it is evident that this developing content is not on the surface, but constitutes the very soul of these sonnets. We conclude, therefore, that they must have been conceived all together from the very beginning as four consecutive parts of a single composition.

The flaws we have noted are so mysterious that, as I have hinted, they may be more apparent than real. Let us say for the present that they are probably due to youthful inexpertness in the art of writing—since we cannot well impute such blemishes, indeed, faults in poetic composition, to the mature Lorenzo. This is in accord with the author's claim, and our own previous findings, regarding the very early date of these poems. Besides, they are youthful in other respects as well. We have seen how simple they truly are, both in form and content. The phraseology and syntax, and the numerous metaphors, are all quite usual and simple. In fact, there is a certain naïveté about them that is as juvenile as it is pleasing. A deep, sentimental idealism, which is pure romanticism, pervades them all. Indeed, tears and sighs abound. Sadness, discouragement, and hopelessness verge on despair. Enthusiasm is mingled with dejection. There is a rise and fall of all the emotional elements. And, while it may be said that these factors are neither uncalled for by the nature of the subject, nor restricted to youth—still such extravagance in the use of them can hardly be attributed to a notorious realist in his maturity. The thing, however, which gives these poems all the evidence of being a youthful composition, is perhaps the character of their being obviously studied—too studied, in fact. They bear all the signs of a sheer imitation from beginning to end. And certainly it does not require a very profound knowledge of Italian literature to see where all the concepts and metaphors, all the phraseology and style, the very sentiments and this romantic attitude, the subject itself—where all these come from. If, in keeping with the experiment proposed above, I may now call this small knowledge slightly and momentarily into play, we realize immediately that all this is Dantean and Petrarchan: that is, pure stilnovism, according to Lorenzo. In fact, the idea of celebrating the lady's death is, as Lorenzo himself has intimated in the proem, the common practice of his predecessors. The metaphor of the star and sun is not only common property to all the earlier Italian poets, but classical, and as old as poetry itself. The concept of the gentle lady ennobling Death by her decease is primarily Dantean, as is the rest of the third sonnet in which it occurs. The fourth, with its idea of escape to a life of solitude in the midst of beautiful and mysterious nature, is, of course, entirely Petrarchan in concept, phraseology, and style. Indeed, all the *concettismo* of these lyrics, all the wailing and sighing, and the inconsistency of love and despair, are especially Petrarchan. Petrarch, Dante, and classical literature are the author's sources of influence in this composition that is all influence. Of Lorenzo there is hardly anything, except perhaps the arrangement in a new adaptation obviously artificial. This makes these poems insincere, at least with regard to the reality and spontaneity of the sentiments expressed in them. And it clearly suggests a purely mental activity and an intellectual effort to express a mere emotional idealism, or the concept of this idealism.

This conclusion, reached without the aid of the *Commentary,* is very important, and should be remembered later, when we turn to the latter for verification of our findings. Meanwhile, let us continue our direct study of these sonnets, and note here (in the midst of so much destructive criticism) certain merits which they undoubtedly have. For these lyrics, though imitative and so largely borrowed, have true merit, which grows in our estimation when we consider the youth of the author. The poet's idealistic attitude is certainly sincere. His aspiration, whatever it be, is truly felt. And his agony for the loss of something, his hopeless reaching after it —these at least seem real. One feels that he actually gazes at the heavens, in mute contemplation and veneration of his beautiful star which is, as it were, the splendid "soul" of his lady who in life was a dazzling "sun." His loving observation of the *tornalsole* is very poetic; and his sad meditation over its daily experience and his own worse fate is also realistic. Even his resignation to this fate, his suffering in the company of Love, the Graces, and the Muses, and his contradictory feelings (with that final, desperate appeal to Death), are all realistically expressed. There is a certain delightful vagueness and youthful ardor which cannot be denied, and which is very beautiful, despite the imitation and artificiality of the composition. The very romanticism, which accompanies all this vague and mysterious *concettismo,* does not seem extravagant in a precocious youth. Moreover, the verses are smooth, easy flowing, and melodious. And the young poet reaches surprising heights of poetry and style, even in his sheer imitations: as in his Dantean prayer to his star in the first sonnet, or in his pathetic resignation to his fate in the second (which is also reminiscent of Dante). Poetic accents, impulses, and motives are not lacking, and, if the phraseology and style are borrowed, they are well adapted to a partly or wholly new context. Indeed, we are pleased to think of the boy Lorenzo as the author of such really estimable verses, and we admire his noble (though vague) sort of poetic aspiration manifested so early.

But now that we have thoroughly analyzed these sonnets and estimated them critically, now that we think we understand them fully without the need of any extraneous explanation (not even the author's)—let us pause. Before we turn to the *Commentary* in a spirit of scrupulous but—we feel—needless verification, let us first apply our own intelligence to the detection of the *sovrasenso* obviously implied, and see if we have really no doubts concerning their significance. Are they as perfectly clear to us as we think? Perhaps the best way to inquire into this will be to ask a series of questions. These poems were ostensibly all prompted by the death

of a certain lady. But who is she, and why is there a whole progressive series? We are told absolutely nothing about her, except
that she had had beautiful eyes—and this we learn only indirectly.
Indeed, the only identification that she was a woman is an indefinite *colei* and the remark *poich'ella / è morta,* both found in
the third sonnet (cf. ll. 5 and 7–8). We do not learn any of her
qualities and virtues; we do not know how she looked; we do not
even know whether she was young or old. It may be answered
that all this, and even the question of personality, is irrelevant in
a poetic composition. But, if these poems were on the death of some
specific person, should we not expect some sort of encomium in
which at least some of these things would be referred to or suggested? As it is, we can merely *infer* that this "she" must have
been beautiful. And, on the other hand, we have four progressive
sonnets in which the whole and only subject is the poet himself—
his reactions and his state of being due to *the fact that she is now
dead* and become a star. Besides, the whole third sonnet is really
on Death, or that "life" that others call death, and on the conditions or nature of this "life."[4] And the fourth sonnet, in which he
would drink of the waters of Lethe, is all a struggle to forget the
past, and a longing to achieve this "death"! It is not at all obvious
that *"trista* memoria"—the subject of this last sonnet—refers to the
colei; and, in fact, this would be inconsistent and unnatural. Indeed, the *colei* does not enter in at all—even in the third sonnet,
where this pronoun occurs—except as a point of departure, an in-
centive for the poet's death to the past and resurrection to a new
life. So we conclude that the real subject of these poems is not the
death of the mysterious, unknown lady that possibly prompted
them, but Death—a peculiar, mysterious type of death. This we do
not understand.

Still another question arises. Why are the "beautiful eyes" the
only personal characteristic singled out to represent this lady? Possibly, it may be answered, because—as Dante says—the eyes are the
windows of the soul. I agree. But then it follows that the soul is
what matters in this *colei*—the soul and not the physical character-

---

4. Observe that, while *Morte* (with the capital *m*) has become *gentile* "poich'è stata in
colei," and the poet will not taste even the sweetness of death "poich'*ella* è morta," the
subject of this sonnet is *not* the death of *colei,* but *Morte* now become *gentile.*

istics or anything else. This is obvious and natural. But, again, we are not really told anything about this soul, either. A poetic simile likens the "light" of these eyes to the splendor of a star, and this soul is metaphorically represented as a new Phoebus. But all we learn about this soul is that it is now the brightest star in heaven. Furthermore, this lady, who in life was so brilliant, is now like a sun that has set, not for the poet alone, but for the entire "world." Finally, the poet first prays to this soul, *as to a god,* that he may realize all its beauty without being dazzled by its splendor, or bewildered; and then he despairs of the return of this vision. He keeps his eyes steadily fixed on the point of its disappearance, and at the same time wishes to die in order to enter "that life which others call death."

Without injury to our experiment, that is, without the assistance of the author's *Commentary,* may I ask: Are these indications of a real, physical death on the part of anyone? Can all this be explained as a hyperbole and a mere rhetorical figure? Surely, these are clear signs of an ideal now past, the embodiment of an ideal once realized and now lamented as the passing away of a beautiful person. Otherwise, what would be the appropriateness of the comparison between the fate of the *tornalsole* and the present condition of this new Clytie, namely, the poet and the whole *world* with him? Especially, what would be the appropriateness of the exclamation at this point: "O dire fate that willed to clothe *us* with *eternal night!"*—that is, the world in our times? Why the admonition to this new Clytie to keep her eyes fixed on the horizon where this glory went down? Furthermore, should we not think logically that the poet's longing for the mystical death is also the desire of this new Clytie, who is the embodiment of all the world of idealists living in darkness? And is not this, therefore, all an appeal to the poets and artists of his day to recall a splendid and glorious ideal now past and gone; is not this an exhortation to join with him in a noble, supreme effort to resume it and perhaps to achieve it again?

Certainly, from this point of view, the whole third sonnet, and especially the last tercet—with its assurance of participation by Love, the Graces, the Muses, and (in fact) everyone—assumes a natural significance that is as obvious now as before it seemed inappropriate and mysterious. We also understand now how and why death might be said to be "altogether too presumptuous" in causing the eclipse of a splendid ideal; and yet be a most noble thing as the abandonment of an ignoble life for the pursuit and realization of this same ideal! We understand how the poet might well represent this ideal as a god, to be venerated, and to be asked to mitigate its dazzling brightness in revealing its beauty. All this seems to fit so well into the general poetic allegory, and the unity and coherence of the whole composition is so enhanced by this interpretation—that we feel justified in advancing it. But what has become of the lady now? She seems to be a myth. And what is this ideal apparently symbolized by the *lume* of her beautiful eyes? This soul we do not know, except that it constitutes the object of the poet's lofty aspiration, and the real *raison d'être* or subject of these and all his poems of love. These questions we cannot answer without the author's own commentary, which is fortunately at our disposal.

Meanwhile we are perhaps convinced that the experiment we have tried in connection with this preliminary study of Lorenzo's *principio* has proved successful. The foregoing is, I believe, just about all that one can reasonably expect to derive from a direct study of the verses alone, and without the assistance of outside information. Indeed, my indiscreet anticipations make it considerably more than the ordinary modern student, coming casually upon these sonnets and reading them probably at random (if not superficially), would find in them. Yet we have seen how inadequate even this careful study appears to be. How many first impressions we have had to revise already! How many questions still remain unsolved! We see that this type of poetry cannot really be approached with any expectation of arriving at the true intention of the author unless we have the latter's assistance when it is available. Perhaps this is, in itself, a grave fault. But that is beside the point here. The question here is how to read and interpret this esoteric poetry. Lorenzo had every reason to expect a more or less complete misunderstanding on the part of all his readers, except his most intimate friends and the initiates in this "new style" of verse (which in this respect may not seem at all "sweet" to us). And if he greatly feared this general misunderstanding in his own times, how much more surely is it to be expected five centuries later! Wishing to guard against this real danger, and possibly also to initiate all his readers into the school of poetry he himself understood and loved so well as to make himself its continuator and expounder, Lorenzo prepared a commentary to his amorous verse. But now, as probably then, few of those who read him at all ever read this valuable exposition. Let us not expostulate, but turn now to his *Commentary* to find the true, complete light on these sonnets, to see how far we have arrived at the actual intention of the author, and especially to discover the answer to our most puzzling question: how are these poems a philosophic principle?

Throughout our study of the author's own exposition of these sonnets, we must remember that (according to our findings) the *Commentary* was written some twenty years later. To be fully understood, it frequently requires (as we have experienced in the proem) much critical and interpretative analysis. In consequence, a mere translation, or a superficial reading of the original text, is not always sufficient, and we must add our own reflections and explanations as we go along, interspersing them wherever it seems best.

CHAPTER II

Esoteric Meaning of Sonnet I: Identification of the
Lady Mentioned in the Comment.

LORENZO begins the exposition of the first sonnet by recalling
the occasion that had prompted it. As he has just said[1] in
explaining the nature of this *principio,* a lady had died in
Florence, whose passing away had profoundly moved the entire
population. This lady is not named now, nor later, any more than
she had been named before in the sonnets when they were composed. The only possible means of identification, now furnished
us by the *Commentary,* are certain apparently peculiar circumstances attending her funeral as described in the comment on Sonnet I.[2] Otherwise, a thick veil of mystery continues to surround
her identity. Even the apparent wealth of information now added
in this comment, regarding her person and her life,[3] is of such a
nature that, instead of helping us to solve the mystery, it clouds it
still more. Obviously, neither the poet before, nor the commentator now, wished to divulge this secret. Whatever may be the reason
for this secrecy, or whatever the purpose of giving this impression,
the fact is that Lorenzo does not seem at all concerned with the
actual, historical identity of this lady. Instead, he is very much
concerned with explaining the reasons for the general sorrow
caused by her death. And what he says about her person and her
life is ostensibly more with the intention of explaining the circumstances attending her funeral, than with any direct intention to
establish her identity. If these statements give us an idea of the
personage, and help us to surmise who she might be, it is only incidentally. As in the sonnet, the subject of the comment on it now
is not the lady, but strictly her death. The fact that her actual
identity is neither established nor seems to matter—this, I say, suggests that perhaps the real subject is not even her death, so much

1. Text, p. 24, ll. 2–3; and this study, p. 62.
2. Cf. Text, p. 26, ll. 1–11; and this study, p. 102.
3. Cf. Text, p. 25, ll. 19 ff.; and this study, p. 101.

as the phenomenon of death exemplified in her demise. We remember the author's contention in the proem, that "molto convenientemente la *morte* è principio a questa *sua* opera,"[4] and recall also our own findings independent of the *Commentary*,[5] and are satisfied that this tentative conclusion accords with both.

Perhaps, then, before we can settle this question of the lady's identity, we need to consider what the commentator either chooses or has occasion to tell us about her—in explanation of the general sympathy aroused by her death and of the peculiar incidents mentioned above as marking her funeral. The tone and character of the introductory remarks lead one to expect a full account of a well-known personage. Instead, we are given only a few indefinite qualities easily applicable to any number of famous ladies of the time. The single concrete detail regarding the funeral is not by itself sufficient to mark this particular lady.

First we are merely told that she excelled in "beauty and human gentilesse."[6] And then we are informed that these excellent qualities (possessed by her in as high a degree as any woman that had ever lived before) were not what marked her out particularly.

Among her other excellent gifts, her manner was so sweet and attractive that all who had any intimate knowledge of her (qualche domestica notizia) thought they were immensely loved by her,—women as well, and girls of like age with her. Indeed, the women not only were not in the least envious of this, her most excellent virtue of all, but they highly praised and exalted her beauty and "gentilesse." So that it seemed impossible to believe that so many men could love her without any jealousy of each other, and so many women praise her without any feeling of envy.

This sweet, loving disposition and most charming manner, that captured all (both men and women alike), was the virtue in which she excelled especially, and the quality which distinguished her particularly. To be sure,

while her life in these exceedingly dignified conditions greatly endeared her to all, the pity of her death, too,—owing to her tender age, and to her

4. Cf. Text, p. 24, ll. 23–24.   5. Cf. this study, pp. 95–98.
6. *Bellezza e gentilezza umana* (cf. Text, p. 25, ll. 21–22). "Gentilesse" is my rendering of *gentilezza*, signifying the quality of being *gentile* as explained and defined by Lorenzo. Cf. Text, bottom of p. 56 to middle of p. 58; and this study, pp. 111–113.

beauty which even in her state of death surpassed that of any lady alive,—
left in everyone a most ardent desire for her.

But the reason why everybody went to her funeral, and wept so
copiously, was not primarily either this beauty or her youth. But it
was because of her wonderful personality and immense popularity, and especially because of the amazing, incredible fact that
she loved all and all could love her without either jealousy or envy
on the part of anybody, man or woman alike! This seemed absolutely miraculous.

And a sort of miracle actually takes place at her funeral, in confirmation of this supreme, unique virtue of hers. Since, owing to
her importance and popularity, she was in accordance with Florentine usage carried with face uncovered in the funeral procession
(to do her especial honor, and afford everybody a last opportunity
to admire her), her charm operated as never before. In her death,
she appeared even more beautiful than she had been in life, and
this new cause of amazement drew new lovers to her, besides in-
tensifying the love of her old admirers! Says the Text:

Those who previously had any knowledge of her (alcuna notizia), now—
besides feeling pity—marveled at the discovery that she in death excelled
her own beauty, that very beauty which while she was alive had seemed un-
surpassable. Moreover, those who previously had no knowledge of her, now
were grieved and almost remorseful not to have known so beautiful a
"thing" (cosa) before they were to be entirely deprived of her. Indeed, the
latter reflected on the irony of fate that had permitted them to know her
then—as it seemed, in order that ever after they might grieve over her
death. Verily, she bore out the truth of the observation of our Petrarch,

"Morte bella parea nel suo bel viso."[7]

All this is extremely puzzling, and the impressive tone in which
it is said does not diminish our wonder. We become aware that an
air of mystery surrounds this remarkable lady of almost miraculous beauty and charm; and it would seem that this is the effect
which our author means to convey. We are reminded at once of
la donna angelicata of the stilnovists. But before we discuss this aspect of the author's description, let us resume our consideration of
the lady's identity, and dispose of this question first.

7. Cf. Petrarch, *Trionfo della morte,* l. 172.

No identity is established by the specific remarks which our author makes about certain qualities of the lady, qualities that are in themselves vague and indefinite (superior beauty and human "gentilesse," a sweet and most attractive personality, and youth). Her identity is not established by her immense popularity alone, nor by the rare circumstance of her being carried *scoperta* to her final resting place. Taken separately, these vague indications remain at best mere hints. But all together they may and actually do seem to point to a definite person. The name of this person has already several times come into the course of this study;[8] for it was necessary to anticipate a partial discussion of this hypothesis, in connection with the date of these four sonnets (found included in the *Raccolta aragonese*), and in connection with the author's first reference to this lady, in the proem. She is believed to have been Simonetta Cattaneo, wife of a certain Marco Vespucci, reputed mistress of Lorenzo's brother (Giuliano de' Medici), and especially famous as the subject of Botticelli's *Primavera* and Poliziano's *Stanze*.

Without repeating the arguments I have previously advanced against this hypothesis, I now recall merely our conclusion, before presenting the positive side of the question. We concluded that, chronologically, Lorenzo could not possibly have been inspired by Simonetta's death, which occurred in 1476, for the composition of these sonnets which were written at least as early as the date marking the compilation of the famous anthology.[9] (Observe that I say *sonnets,* not *commentary.*) As we have previously concluded, the commentary was written, approximately, a quarter of a century later, and this comment on the first sonnet may therefore be an embellishment of the actual history of the sonnet itself. In truth, it is.

Simioni recalls the historical fact that when the beautiful, charming, and extremely popular Simonetta died (at the age of twenty-three, in the month of April, 1476) she, too—like the young lady of the sonnets we are discussing—was carried *scoperta,* with a large attendance of sympathetic people, to the solemn

8. Cf. this study, p. 2; n. 18, p. 4; n. 1, p. 62.
9. For the date of the *Raccolta aragonese,* see this study, pp. 342 ff.

peace of the Church of All Saints in Florence.[10] This fact, together with the whole personality of this famous lady, accords so well with Lorenzo's account of the notable event and with his description of the subject of his sonnet, that one can hardly escape the suspicion that the two are one and the same person. This does not, however, strictly constitute a proof. The proof, it seems to me, lies in a letter of Sforza Bettini to Lorenzo, also quoted by Simioni. This letter, dated April 27, 1476, contains the following account of Simonetta's death:

La benedetta anima della Simonetta se ne andò a paradiso, come so harette inteso: puossi ben dire che sia stato il secondo *trionpho della morte,* che veramente havendola voi vista così morta come la era, non vi saria parsa manco bella e vezzosa che si fusse in vita: requiescat in pace.[11]

Inasmuch as Lorenzo, in his comment, also recalls Petrarch's *Triumph of Death* in an identical connection and in the same manner, this most striking coincidence confirms all the others, and together they leave absolutely no room for doubt. The commentator is here thinking certainly of *la bella Simonetta,* and referring to her funeral.

But how does this conclusion, no less precise and authoritative, accord with our previous one, so diametrically opposed? The contradiction is only apparent, for it will be observed that we are here dealing with the commentator, and not with the poet. This distinction, here and above, removes the inconsistency. As a matter of fact, the two conclusions complement each other in the process of tracing the true history of these sonnets and their commentary. The influences that determined the foregoing comment were obviously not the same that originally inspired this first sonnet and the entire *principio.* We do not learn from this comment what the original source of inspiration really was, and wonder why the author consciously makes this false connection. But we do know that the death of Simonetta Cattaneo had nothing to do with it, and we are curious to discover the reason that prompted the false explanation.

10. Cf. A. Simioni, "Donne ed amori medicei. La Simonetta," in *Nuova Antologia,* June 16, 1908, p. 691.
11. Cf. *idem,* p. 689.

Let us examine the evidence further. As Simioni points out, Lorenzo obviously was not in Florence on the date of Simonetta's death, and was not himself present at her funeral—since Sforza Bettini thought fit to inform him and send him this account of the event. Accordingly, he was not directly inspired by this event, either—not even for the above comment. In fact, this is clearly not original with him, and its paternity must now be assigned to his obscure correspondent. The record of the impression on the by-standers made by Simonetta's beauty (though she was dead), and especially the reference to Petrarch, are in Bettini's letter. And these are, we may say, the only poetic touches that lend significance to the whole account. The rest is mere elaboration and embellishment. But is there absolutely nothing by our author, besides this elaboration? Yes, indeed! There is the choice of this notable event, and its careful adaptation, to explain some old sonnets of his—sonnets which are ostensibly on the philosophic principle of the mystical death. Probably many years later, while working on his *Commentary,* he recalled this vivid account of what must have seemed to him an excellent and suitable concrete instance of the physical death, in which to incarnate his *verbum* of the mystical death. He appropriated it, adapting it to his purpose. There can be no other, more plausible, or more obvious explanation, it seems to me, than this, to justify an absolute falsification that is as patently intentional as it would be uncalled for otherwise. In fact, what reason could he have had for thus falsifying his source of inspiration for these sonnets? The desire—continues the Text—himself to be one of those to sing the praises of this lady, and be one of *"tutti i fiorentini ingegni* who, as was befitting in such a public misfortune, lamented this bitter death, either in verse or in prose, according to their talents"—could this have been his reason? This is most unlikely, not only because (after all) the death of Simonetta Cattaneo did not constitute a *pubblica iattura* in any serious sense of the word; but because Lorenzo, had he actually thought this and really meant to emulate the other Florentine talents on this occasion, could and would have certainly written new and more suitable verses for her. If Lorenzo had really wished to join with the others in paying tribute to La Simonetta, he would have composed verses more obviously in praise of her, rather than to take a group of old sonnets and merely change their attribution.

No, the truth here is quite the contrary of what has been held heretofore. The sonnets of this *principio* were not inspired by Simonetta's death, nor even adapted to this event. On the contrary, some account of her death described by another was enlarged, embellished, and otherwise adjusted as if to explain the none too obvious character of these poems written many years before. In other words, the comment as given by Lorenzo is entirely artificial—consciously so and not without intention.

This conclusion is important, for one thing, because it definitely disposes of Simonetta Cattaneo as a true source of inspiration for the *principio,* and to this extent at least it corrects the imagined history of these verses (falsified by the author himself). But an even greater value is that the inferences it permits give us a true insight into the real character of these poems and into the author's method of procedure. This method, in turn, will verify his contentions in the proem, and reveal to us a fundamental point in the poetic art of the stilnovists.

We are now ready to return, without any false, preconceived notions, to Lorenzo's description of the lady in his comment. He does not actually say that the lady in question was the famous Simonetta, although the inference might falsely be that for those who knew her and recalled her death, and although our reconstruction of the history of this comment proves that the discussion was verily inspired by an account of her death. It is evident now that his consciousness of this intentional falsification must have been at least one of the reasons for not identifying his lady any more definitely. Furthermore, he nowhere commits himself. He does not declare, for instance (as he might have declared), that he was personally present at this particular funeral, or that he was directly inspired by this particular death. One looks in vain even for such an implication. Instead, the comparison of his account with that of Sforza Bettini reveals an honest derivation for a purpose. His whole account savors of a common report, which he could have legitimately drawn from any and all sources. It is obvious that he has simply taken Bettini's account as representative of the general impression produced by Simonetta's death. Lorenzo has used this report as a perfectly proper source of inspiration. The only special suggestion he owes to Bettini is the reference to Petrarch. This must have been the spark that kindled the fire of his imagination and made him decide to choose this particular case of death as the most excellent with which to explain his philosophic *principio*. Possibly, the tenets of his art demanded that a concrete example be presented as the actual source of inspiration for these sonnets. But there is no poetic or critical insincerity in all this—if the true concept originally embodied in these lyrics could best be revealed and made plain in such a historical dress. After all, now that we have discarded Simonetta, and perhaps have begun to suspect that no special or particular case of death ever actually inspired these verses—the only sincerity that concerns us here is the truthfulness of his implication that these sonnets were originally all that they now purport to be. If a new (and possibly better) instance of the incarnation of his philosophic principle, involved in them, now presents itself to him, the poet-critic (Lorenzo) can hardly be censured for indulging in a bit of fanciful, creative criticism that does no harm and apparently helps him in his exposition. The fact is that (for his purpose) Lorenzo is essentially sincere in the above comment, and, since his purpose here is obviously the fabrication of an elaborate and suitable *milieu* for the birth of his philosophical sonnets, the falsification proves that the character of these poems was really conceptual from the very start. Moreover, it is a strong indication that very probably there never was any real woman involved at all in this whole concept.

CHAPTER III

*Esoteric Meaning of Sonnet I: the True Nature of This Lady,
as Seen from Her Qualities.*

THIS is precisely the conclusion we are tempted to draw, as
soon as we begin to consider the character of the few qualities noted by the commentator with respect to the supposed
lady of his *principio*—as soon as we consider her very singular
virtue, together with the sort of miracle she works at death.

As we recall, her primary qualities are only "beauty and human
gentilesse" (bellezza e gentilezza umana), surpassed by the single,
supreme gift of "a sweet and charming manner" (dolce ed attrat-
tiva maniera). Her specific and unique virtue, consisting in the
power and apparent disposition to enamor all, is a concomitant of
the latter. It is especially remarkable only in so far as it operates
without arousing either jealousy or envy. And finally, upon her
death, she amazes all by appearing more beautiful than in life,
and making new admirers of those who had not known her before. These characteristics, few in number, strike us immediately
by their apparent definiteness and actual vagueness, and by their
extraordinary effect. We are particularly impressed by the strange
miracle operated by death. As already noted, the above qualities
are too generic to individualize anyone in particular. And now
their absolute superlative degree hardly makes them applicable to
any ordinary human being of flesh and blood. Furthermore, the
singular virtue, distinguishing this superwoman, is actually supernatural. A veil of mystery envelops both her being and her activity. Her absolute beauty is undefined; her human "gentilesse,"
likewise; and her peculiar charm comes merely from a manner
not otherwise specified than as "sweet" and "attractive." Gener-
ality and absoluteness characterize—we may say—all her qualities,
while the actions and reactions accompanying her life and death
are (as I have said) supernatural. So we conclude that, from this
point of view as well, she cannot be, is not intended to be, and is

not any actual woman! The type and character of the few qualities chosen to describe her, and particularly the supernatural behavior ascribed to her, absolutely preclude any such hypothesis.

Then, what is she? And why is this "what" thus presented? Obviously, she is a personification, and this rhetorical device must be used for poetic and artistic convenience. She is primarily the personification of those same qualities attributed to her in their generic abstract sense, and absolute superlative degree. She *is* those qualities. She is an abstraction, or the author's concept of an ideal embodying those qualities in their full, true essence and highest degree. Then, she is also the embodiment of a potential, spiritual force possessed by those qualities: a natural force emanating love, and generating love. These qualities willingly and gladly give themselves over, as it were, to anyone who is at all intimately acquainted with them[1]—enamoring all alike, men and women, young and old. And this occurs irresistibly, without causing either jealousy or envy. Finally, in her death is exemplified the mystic death. The abstraction of these qualities from her physical self representing a concrete personality, is what is meant by her mystical death. It is the act of extracting the pure form from the concrete material object incarnating it, or the return to heaven (as it were) of the Platonic idea after its temporal and material existence on earth. It is a process of purification and elevation to the state of absolute perfection. Therefore, both the beauty of this lady (embracing all her qualities), and her prestige, are increased by this death. For, in the mystical death, they have achieved absolute perfection. And the realization of this fact (or comprehension by the bystanders of the pure form of this absolute, superlative beauty) fills everyone who grasps it with awe and admiration, with sorrow not to have perceived it before; and with longing to rise to this perfection now. Therefore it might truly be said that death on her lovely visage itself seemed fair,

Morte bella parea nel suo bel viso.

1. Not for nothing does Lorenzo use here the apparently strange and inappropriate phrase, now significant—*qualche domestica notizia,* which he repeats shortly after in the form *alcuna notizia.* Cf. Text, p. 25, l. 25, and p. 26, l. 4; and this study, pp. 101 and 102.

For, from this point of view (regarded as the mystic death), death is truly a good thing, and its association with the perfect and absolute *gentilezza* of this lady may well be said poetically to have made it, too, *gentile*—as the poet says in the third sonnet. And now we also appreciate, finally, the commentator's striking use of the term *cosa* with reference to the increased beauty of this lady after her mystic death. She is hardly a person; she is a concept, an abstraction—a mere *thing,* or undefinable *being.*

We now understand that we are evidently dealing with an ideal, or, better, with the concept of an ideal. This concept of an ideal is apparently dead, although still recalled by a few who perhaps strove to preserve it; but it is generally realized too late even by those who understand it now. But the precise content of this ideal escapes us almost entirely. To apprehend it fully, we feel that we need to examine more fully than hitherto the essence of the qualities constituting it—and especially the exact meanings of the terms *bellezza* and *gentilezza umana.* Fortunately for us, we have the authority of the commentator himself for these meanings, so that we may proceed surely and confidently.

Indirectly, the term *bellezza* has already been fully defined by the author in connection with his stanch defense of the true meaning and real subject of his verses.[2] There, defining love as *appetito di bellezza,* he had occasion to discuss at some length the nature of this beauty, as the object and subject of love. We may therefore derive from his discussion the full and precise connotation of the word, according to him. Let us sum up the essential points of this discussion, and thus refresh our memory preparatory to our own considerations. The beauty Lorenzo there discusses is not simply the natural or artistic beauty that strikes our physical eye and draws us to it. It is primarily the beauty, or value, of intellectual and moral qualities, which is manifested by the metaphorical eyes (or intellectual *lume*) of this metaphorical lady, and which spurs the *gentle* heart to love it and desire it. It is interesting and significant that he there also limits his subject to the love of (and for) human beings (l'umana creatura). But, postponing this consideration, we note that the object and subject of his love is identified by

2. Cf. Text, pp. 14–15; and this study, pp. 13–15.

him naturally with the supreme beauty of supreme good that is God, according to Plato. His "beauty," therefore, is essentially *goodness,* human goodness—a *bene,* though not the *sommo bene.* But it is goodness in the broad, philosophical sense of *perfection,* of the same nature as the absolute, divine perfection. Accordingly, this perfection proposed by human love is limited and relative. But it is of the same divine nature; that is, it is perfection in aim, scope, and achievement. This is *bellezza.* In other words, Lorenzo's *bellezza* is at once both divine and human: divine in nature, and human in conception, realization, and attainment. It is the beauty of lofty ideals, of high intellectual and moral values, and of perfect, artistic execution in any field of human endeavor. It does not exclude the physical beauty of nature; but nature (for our author) includes the spirituality of man, as well as his external physical aspect and behavior. Indeed, this is paramount in the nature of man.

Passing to the second quality of *gentilezza umana,* we need to consider this phrase in its two distinct elements, in order to interpret it correctly. And, as for the first, we must anticipate a portion of the comment on the twelfth sonnet (the eighth of the *nuova vita*), in which Lorenzo defines the term *gentilezza.*[3] I have already referred to this explanation before,[4] but now I must take it up, for we can no longer continue without it. In this comment, the author (voicing our disquiet and his own regarding the connotation of the tantalizing adjective *gentile* and its derivative *gentilezza*—both of which recur so frequently in this text and in the preceding Italian poetry) finally decides to work out a definition of these terms, according to his own opinion, and thus to settle the question of their meaning once for all, at least in his verses. His short study of this very important point is a marvel of lucidity and penetration, a study which does great credit to his critical acumen and historico-philological insight. For us it amounts to a veritable revelation, and constitutes a most valuable authoritative opinion, for which we feel very grateful. Lorenzo starts by noting that the term, "in the sense in which it is used, is an entirely new word,

3. Cf. Text, p. 56, l. 35 to p. 58, l. 11.
4. Cf. this study, n. 13, p. 55; n. 6, p. 70; pp. 71–72.

and one strictly Italian" (vocabulo nuovo ed al tutto vulgare).[5]
Dante—he says—in his *canzone* on *gentilezza*,[6] confined himself
to the definition of this quality with respect to man, declaring it
to be *quasi nobiltà*. But Lorenzo finds it generally applied to almost all things. And, since—with respect to its *new, Italian* connotation—no certain "propriety" or sphere of usage can be assigned
to it on the authority of the "Ancients," either by any definition of
theirs or usage followed by them, he himself undertakes to study
the probable origin of its new connotation.

It seems to *him* that the word *gentile* must have come from those who were
called *gentili,* namely the Romans, whom the Hebrew and Christian theolo-
gians called first *gente* (by antonomasia of the phrase *gens romana*), and
later *gentili.* . . . Inasmuch as these *gentili,* or Romans, had the reputation
of being most excellent in those things that the world honors and prizes, *he*
believes that anything in any way excellent in comparison with others began
to be called *gentile*—as if to say: "made by the *gentili,*" or befitting their
excellence. Later, usage widened the meaning, until now its definition has
become very difficult.

This is, or seems to be, naïve etymologizing, but he arrives at a
very admirable definition of *gentile* and *gentilezza* as used in the
current language of his time.

Thus—continues Lorenzo—in the way of example, ivory may be said to
be *gentile,* and likewise ebony,—according as the first is the more beautiful
the whiter it is, and the second, the blacker it is the more it is prized. These
are contrary things expressed by the same word. Accordingly, he will say
that anything is *gentile* if it is well fitted and disposed to answer perfectly
the purpose for which it is naturally suited, and if it carries with it grace,
which is a gift of God. (Diremo adunque "gentile" essere quella cosa, la
quale è bene atta e disposta a fare perfettamente l'ufficio che a lei si conviene, accompagnata da grazia, la quale è dono di Dio.)

To illustrate this, he gives a long, detailed description of a *"gentile
cavallo corridore"* (or fine *race* horse)—adding that anyone who
would praise a *war* horse on the same counts, would err grossly,
since the latter has a very different *function*. And he concludes by
saying that, accordingly, *"gentilezza è quasi una distinzione iudi-*

5. Cf. Text, p. 57, ll. 8–9. Of course, by *vulgare* he means "Italian."
6. *Convivio,* IV.

ciale di tutte le cose"; or, *gentilezza* is a predicate applied to the distinctive excellence of all things *as a result of previous, nice discrimination.* In other words, for Lorenzo, the *gentilezza* of anything is its distinction, or the particular quality that characterizes it, and by virtue of which it excels, all *in our judgment.* With respect to any particular object under consideration, it is the "excellence" of that "thing," or its particular superior *virtus* (in the Latin sense of the word) accompanied by divine grace; but, with respect to the judge of this excellence, it is the result of a critical process. In fact, observe that, in his definition—which we might qualify as itself *gentilissima*—the word *distinzione* retains, by virtue of the qualification *iudiciale,* both its active meaning of "act of distinguishing" and its passive meaning of "result of distinguishing." As we shall see better later on, it is precisely this double process of detaching, as it were, the *virtus* from "things" and of incarnating it in "things" that, according to the Magnificent, characterized the life of the Roman people and accounted primarily for their own "excellence" or *gentilezza.*

The light that this definition sheds on all stilnovistic literature is perhaps as obvious as it is great. Its value, especially in connection with the proper interpretation of the author's amorous verses, can hardly be overestimated. And the significance of this small point, with reference to Lorenzo as a literary critic and authority on such questions, is also evident. But we must not digress.

We shall now take up the qualification *umana* applied to this "gentilesse" or, I may now say, *quasi Romanità.* It is clear that (although by his time usage had extended the applicability of the qualification *gentile* to all things animate and inanimate) the author here wishes to confine his discourse to the *gentilezza* of man: that is, to the particular distinction that characterizes man, or the natural *virtus* in which he may gracefully excel. And, since Lorenzo's metaphorical lady is said to possess this condition or prerequisite in a supreme degree, it is also clear that he refers to the supreme distinction or excellence of man. In other words, just as above we found him limiting his subject to the love of and for *l'umana creatura* (and there his definition of *bellezza* as the object and subject of this love, implied the beauty of lofty ideals, of high intellectual and moral values, and of perfect, artistic execution—all conceived, realized, and achieved by man)—so here he confines himself to "human gentilesse" in its highest degree. There is a most intimate relation between his *bellezza* and his *gentilezza:* the first is the divine element in man, and the second his human potentiality. The former is the spark of divine genius in man, his mental, moral, and artistic vision; the latter his natural and characteristic "*vir*tus," or physical and spiritual capacity by means of which he attains and carries out his highest conceptions. Lorenzo's subject is therefore MAN, and the object of his love is man's highest achievements within the limitations of his vast human scope and superb possibilities. We shall return to this presently.

Here, it is appropriate to note first that, in thus confining himself to "gentilezza *umana,*" he follows the example of Dante, whose limitation of subject in the same connection he recalls.[7] This is significant, not merely as another indication of how closely this imitator followed in the footsteps of his master, but especially because here it is perhaps more obvious than usually that he followed him with veneration, yet critically. He, too, is interested particularly in *human* "gentilesse," but notes critically the significant fact that, in his time at least (and presumably also in the time of Dante) the qualification *gentile* was equally applicable to things animate and inanimate. He does not contradict Dante's explanation of *gentilezza* as *quasi nobiltà.* Indeed, he apparently accepts it. But it is obvious that he is not content with this explanation. He must have studied the fourth book of the *Convivio*—as well as Guinizelli's and Cavalcanti's *canzoni* previously recalled by him; and he was undoubtedly convinced that *gentilezza* was not *nobiltà di sangue*—not an inheritable quality, nor anything else his masters taught him it was not. But all the negative and positive statements made by these poets, while most illuminating in other respects, did not furnish him with any clue as to why this quality was called *gentilezza.* *Nobiltà* perhaps gave him a certain connotation, but, besides itself calling for an interpretation, it did not explain the inherent applicability of the word *gentilezza* to

7. Cf. Text, p. 57; *Convivio,* IV; and this study, p. 112.

connote this quality. Lorenzo was interested in tracing the derivation of the word, and in seeing its natural implication as well as
original application. Consequently, he is not satisfied with his
masters' mere explanation of the connotation of the term, and
goes further than any of them had gone—proceeding along a
purely philological line. Evidently he did not know when the adjective *gentile* began to be applicable to the excellence inherent in
anything. But the origin of this connotation, according to his derivation, implies that there was no reason why its general applicability should ever have been limited from the moment the new
significance was introduced. On the contrary, his explanation of
the derivation as "quasi *opera* fatta da' gentili o che alla eccel-
lenzia loro convenissi" proves that, in his opinion, the qualification must have been applicable, at least equally (if not exclusively), to inanimate objects from the very beginning. What is the
import of this? Why does he bring out the general applicability
of the adjective in its Italian connotation apparently from the time
the latter was first attributed to it? The reason cannot be a purely
philological interest—for the implication of his research (as well
as the results obtained) is that the derivation of the modern connotation of the word explains both its source and true original import now as before. Lorenzo is seeking the original concept that
naturally brought about the development of this new *significazione,* which, in turn, relegated the old Latin adjective *gentilis* to
the Latin language, and made its modern cognate appear to be a
"vocabulo *nuovo* ed al tutto *vulgare.*" He means to interpret scientifically the full connotation of the Italian adjective *gentile,* according to Dante and all the other poets who ever dealt with *gentilezza,* including himself. And, even more than this, he means
(however fancifully) to trace to its original source the birth of an
ideal, which, according to him, was purely and exclusively Italian!

Thus, his reason is primarily critical, and perhaps patriotic.
There stood in all its splendor, before his dazzled eyes a whole
glorious literature in the Italian *volgare,* depending for its proper
comprehension and thorough appreciation on the correct interpretation of this keyword—this keyword which implied an ideal
and a strictly Italian contribution to the advancement of mankind.

There stood this ideal of *gentilezza umana*—sprung from Roman sources, due to Roman excellence and influence, and conceived by the Italians—awaiting an interpreter and a popularizer. And there was Lorenzo, the creative critic, the *continuatore insieme e novatore!* The conclusion cannot be escaped: with this derivation, Lorenzo undoubtedly meant to trace the fundamental concept of the *dolce stil novo.* It follows, not only that his sonnets are stilnovistic in form and content, and not only that they constitute a modern, personal version of this ideal, but also that his whole *Commentary* is intended to serve as a guide in reading both his own amorous verses and *those of his predecessors.* Incidentally, he appears even to touch on the history of this idealistic literary movement, tracing its origin back to an unconscious beginning marked by the emergence of the concept of *gentilezza.* His derivation of the adjective *gentile* is philologically unsound, or, better, inexact, but I call attention once more to the fact that he does not trace the formation of the *word* so much as the origin of the new *significazione.* He was not interested in the Latin adjective *gentilis;* he was deeply concerned with the meaning of the Italian *gentile.*[8]

8. His Excellency Giulio Bertoni, member of the Reale Accademia d'Italia and professor of Romance Philology at the University of Rome, whom I consulted on the accuracy of Lorenzo's derivation of *gentile* and on the relation of this word to the old-Italian adjective *gente,* has kindly sent me the following comprehensive reply: " 'Gentile' nel sec. XIII in Italia ebbe il senso di 'nobile'; e 'gentilezza' ebbe il senso di 'nobiltà.' L'origine ne è il lat. *gentilis* (detto di una classe di persone nel medio evo) derivato da *gens, gentis.* Altra cosa è l'ant. ital. *gente* ('bello, leggiadro') che è di derivazione provenzale: *gent* (*genitus* probabilmente). Dall'ital. *gentile,* che non va dunque appaiato con *gente,* venne il francese *gentil.* Ha dunque ragione il Magnifico quando deriva da *gente* la voce *gentile,* ma ha torto quando dice che 'è vocabulo nuovo,' perchè nel senso di 'nobile' fu usato nel medio evo. In età romana, il senso di *gentilis* era diverso, come si sa; e questo senso, che diremo dotto, non è mai scomparso presso gli scrittori colti, allato al nuovo significato di 'nobile' assunto dal vocabolo. Per me non v'ha dubbio che quando il Magnifico dice 'vulgare' alluda all'italiano, esclusivamente all'italiano." I am very grateful for this authoritative opinion, which confirms my own and, in the main, supports our author's contention; but, with all respect to my *maestro,* I wish to add one or two remarks for the purpose of further clarifying Lorenzo's position in this debatable question, and of justifying to some extent his qualification of the *vocabulo* as *nuovo* besides *al tutto vulgare.* As I say in my exposition, Lorenzo's derivation of the word concerns its *significazione* current in *his* time, although he implies that this meaning was then substantially the meaning *gentile* had had all along since its introduction in the Italian *volgare.* But, as we have noted, he disagreed with Dante on the latter's limited definition of the word as *quasi nobiltà,* applied, moreover, only to man. His point is that the term was applicable to all "things," both animate and inanimate, as an indication of the superior excellence of any "thing," accompanied by grace. Therefore, I suspect that his understanding of both the connotation and the usage

Whether or not his thesis is historically sound, however, the fact remains that it is for our purposes authoritative: it is the opinion of a stilnovist, and it was intended not only to enlighten the general reader but also to persuade his fellow initiates of the true connotation of the term *gentilezza*. And the fact finally remains that this origin of the word, together with the revelation of its natural implication and general applicability, constitute the most intelligent and most valuable contribution ever made to the comprehension and history of the school of the sweet new style!

After this discussion of Lorenzo's evident dissatisfaction with Dante's simple connotation of the word *gentilezza* (apparently implying a restriction of its application to human beings only, whereas our author found this contrary to current usage), let us resume our study of the adjective *umana* in the phrase *gentilezza umana*. After all, this is the *gentilezza* with which our author, too, is primarily concerned. Although we have taken his definition out of its immediate context in relation to a later sonnet, his discussion of it may seem contradictory. On the one hand, he insists on the general applicability of the quality; and on the other, he himself limits his reference here to human "gentilesse." There is a reason for this. As a restrictive adjective, we have seen that *umana* simply limits the reference to the *gentilezza* (as above defined) peculiar to man, or with respect to man. We understand that by *gentilezza umana* is meant first the characteristic inherent *virtus* that distinguishes man from all other *things,* and at the same time a high degree of this *virtus,* sufficient to permit him to excel even among men. It consists first of all of his distinctive and exclusive human faculties, or manliness; and then of an excelling amount, quality, or degree of this manliness. It is man's particular function

of the word shows a slight but significant modification of its original "modern" meaning —a further modification due perhaps to the influence of more recent, humanistic studies. And I believe that his interpretation as well as his derivation is colored by his own concept of the origin and character of the Italian poetic ideal, derived by him from the literary production of his great masters. This will become clearer in the course of my treatise, but, meanwhile, I may say that his own interpretation of the word is the connotation for which he claims both novelty and Italian exclusiveness. Moreover, in my opinion, the exclusiveness he claims for the Italian *gentile* sounds the same patriotic note that he voiced in the proem in connection with his hopes regarding the future of Italian literature. (Cf. Text, p. 21, ll. 25–35; and this study, pp. 53–54.)

(*uffizio*) in life, determined by his general potentiality as man, and by his special talent, or capacity, or inclination, as an individual. If he excels as man, and as an individual, in any manner— he is *gentile*. Therefore we have already noted that man's *gentilezza* is marked by his genius, by his intellectual and moral forces, by his artistic disposition, and consequently by his great achievements in any and all fields of strictly *human* activity and *human* possibility. Indeed, we may now add, his peculiar faculty of speech, his sensory system, his idealism, his loving and aspiring disposition, and his natural tendency toward refinement and civilization, are all included.

Thus we now understand fully, as well as correctly, the author's previous, strange enumeration of the qualities implied by the *grande perfezione* proposed by a *vero amore*. In his explanation and defense of the subject of his verses,[9] he had said that the two conditions of a true love (namely, the loving of one object only, and constancy in this love) cannot be fulfilled

se il subietto amato non ha in sè, *a proporzione dell'altre cose umane, somma perfezione,* e che *oltre alle naturali bellezze* non concorra nella cosa amata *ingegno grande, modi e costumi ornati e onesti, maniera e gesti eleganti, destrezza d'accorte e dolci parole, amore, constanzia e fede.*[10]

This concept of *gentilezza umana* as the sole and constant object of true, human love, is—I believe—the ideal of the *dolce stil novo* according to the Magnificent. And this ideal of human perfection is certainly the great aspiration and glorious achievement of the Italian poets before and after Lorenzo. We see here the germination, growth, and flowering of the *vocabulo nuovo ed al tutto vulgare*. And, although the great harvest of the Italian Renaissance is still to come, the early fruits, the *primizie,* have already matured. For the stupendous works of the great Italian literary trio aim at, and attain, precisely this ideal of culture and refinement. A lofty idealism characterizes these works, great geniuses conceive them, and these geniuses have one faith, one great and constant love: strictly human perfection in conception and execution, in refinement of manners and customs, in accuracy of

9. Cf. Text, p. 14.
10. Cf. translation of this text, on pp. 13–14 of this study.

thought and sweetness of expression. This is humanism pure and simple: humanism already in full swing with the early Italian poets, humanism that is the very essence of *gentilezza,* and, therefore, of the *stil novo.* Finally, our authority for this identification is a humanist and stilnovist himself, one who makes this attainment of human perfection his own ideal.

My own enthusiasm for this ideal—thus traced by Lorenzo to its Roman source and new, Italian conception—has again diverted me from our immediate task. We were saying, then, that (as a restrictive term) the adjective *umana* simply determines the type of *gentilezza* ascribed by the author to his metaphorical lady. It means simply that he is dealing with *human* "gentilesse." But as a qualifying word of the noun *gentilezza,* this adjective may, and does carry a connotation of its own, that is thus extended to the noun. It implies that the *gentilezza* is human, which is not quite the same as saying that it is the *gentilezza* peculiar to man. This is saying that *gentilezza* is essentially a human prerogative, a human conception, or a human product. In fact, by definition, it is a "judicial distinction" that only man (of all *things*) can make by virtue of his particular *gentilezza* which gives him this intellectual power of discrimination. By derivation (as Lorenzo fancies), it is historically the excellence conceived, aimed at, and attained by the ancient Romans by virtue of their very excellence in human qualities. Consequently, the concept of *gentilezza,* the distinction of this *gentilezza* in all things, and the aspiration to (as well as the attainment of) excellence—these are all a human product, and precisely the highest distinguishing mark of human perfection. In *things* in general, this is a sort of human trait communicated to them, or read into them by man, who thus humanizes them, as it were. And in man, it is his real, maximum distinction—his *"humanitas"* par excellence. It follows that the two terms of the phrase *gentilezza umana* are identical and in a sense convertible. *Gentilezza* equals *humanitas.* And we may properly speak of either *gentilezza umana* or *gentile umanità.* This is pure *concettismo* of stilnovistic brand, but also pure humanism—philosophically speaking—and this in the very heart of the *stil novo!* These ideals, found indissolubly bound together—indeed, fused in Lorenzo's derivation and definition of the term *gentilezza*—are not two, but one for our author. And this single ideal—visualized by the first stilnovists, and divinely attained and perfectly realized, especially by Dante and Petrarch—is the humanistic ideal of the Italian Renaissance![11]

We may now recapitulate our findings without any superfluous repetition. This concept we have explained is the full and proper significance of the two qualities ascribed by the author to his metaphorical lady in a supreme degree. And this is, therefore, the substance of his ideal—an ideal not original with him, and already realized before, fully and perfectly (in fact now passed away)— but one entirely and exclusively Italian, he implies, both in conception and first realization. It is the greatest Italian contribution to the progress of civilization. It is the ideal of strictly human perfection, human in scope and potentiality, but divine in nature; the ideal embodied in the personification of *la donna gentile;* the ideal visualized by the first stilnovists, and fully attained especially by Dante and Petrarch. Finally, it is the ideal incorporated in, and (in the field of letters) carried out to perfection by the Italian literature before Lorenzo. This ideal, called a *"bene,* though not the *sommo bene,"* is the supreme *gentilezza* of man, or his divine *humanitas.* It is his divine aspiration toward the highest possible achievements in all fields of strictly human activity and peculiarly human excellence. And therefore it includes not only the field of letters but all the arts and sciences, and all the thought of man, through which man performs his most distinctive human function, achieves his individual and generic perfection, and ascends from the human to the divine. This ideal is the program of the Italian Renaissance, and this is the lady that has now died, or rather appeared dead, and, in a sense, might be said actually to be dead in Lorenzo's time. In fact, that first glorious period of Italian arts and letters was now over. Although the movement had only entered on a new phase, and the Renaissance was already in full swing, neither Lorenzo nor anyone else in his time could tell exactly what the future had in store for Italy. An air of optimism

11. In this connection, it is interesting to read a brief study by Rudolf Pfeiffer, entitled *Humanitas erasmiana* (Leipzig and Berlin, B. G. Teubner, 1931).

undoubtedly prevailed, and this is even implied in Lorenzo's own attempt to resurrect and carry on this old ideal. But everybody must have felt that that first glory was now definitely passed, and probably Lorenzo saw no one around him either aspiring to, or equal to, that first incarnation of human perfection. At any rate, this was the supreme *bellezza e gentilezza umana* that in life had had the unique virtue of such an exceedingly "sweet and charming manner that all who had *any intimate knowledge of her* thought they were supremely loved by her." This was the lady who in life had enamored all alike, without distinction, and without either jealousy or envy; who in death now seemed even more beautiful than she had in life, and now caused even those who had not known her alive to love her; whose death, finally, had stirred all the Florentine population, could properly be called a *pubblica iattura,* and had inspired "tutti i fiorentini *ingegni*" to sing her praises. Lorenzo is thinking of the supreme beauty of the Italian poetry during this first period—of its essentially human character, human range, and perfect human execution, incarnating the very concept of *gentilezza umana,* and he is demonstrating it at the same time. This is his *donna gentile,* indeed, *gentilissima,* fashioned by him, traditionally and in true stilnovistic manner. For us now the strangeness of this miraculous life and death disappears as if by magic. The slight and generic character of the qualities distinguishing this lady now seem adequate and suitable. Her supreme and general charm is entirely explicable, is found entirely natural. Her greater beauty after death is intelligible. Even the inappropriateness of the exaggerated phraseology used—had the account referred to a real woman and to a case of real death—is now discovered to be most appropriate. In fact, the whole account, which before had seemed mysterious, inadequate, and inappropriate, is now perfectly clear, full, and convenient!

CHAPTER IV

*Lorenzo's Metaphorical Method as the Result of his
Understanding of Stilnovistic* Gentilezza.

THIS is well. But we must not forget the philosophic nature of the *principio* we are studying. We must also bear in mind the fact that Lorenzo's account of his inspiration (taken literally) is a historical falsification. We have concluded that this pseudo-historical account of the occasion that prompted these sonnets was, as a matter of fact, a borrowed account—elaborated and artificially adapted to serve as the true source of inspiration. And now we have just concluded that the author was all the time referring to the passing away of the great ideal of human perfection, conceived and realized by the first Italian poets. Moreover, we know that this is his critical opinion, corresponding to his understanding or concept of the previous Italian literature. The question still remains why first, as poet, he chose to incarnate this concept of his in a human personification; and why, later, as commentator, he presented this allegorical lady as a physical reality (to the extent of adapting to her metaphorical death the true account of the real death of a well-known and easily recognizable woman). The question still remains how and why the philosophical concept of the mystic death is also incarnated in this case of real, physical death—in which death itself appears personified. In other words, what is the explanation of this desire or sort of requirement to personify all concepts and to personify them realistically, even historically? The suggestion offered above—that this is naturally accounted for by artistic, poetic convenience, and also probably by traditional, common usage—is not entirely convincing, and does not suffice here. For this simple—too simple—explanation, besides not explaining either the convenience here of this rhetorical device, or the origin of this custom among the first Italian poets, does not account at all for the great need of an actual model apparently felt here by our author. He obviously goes out of his way to find as perfect an example as he can of a real personage and a real death to explain his sonnets properly. Granting the naturalness of employing such rhetorical figures in poetry, and granting also the influence of tradition, the proper justification for such precise, historical identification, must be more profound.

I believe that, in fact, it is due to the application of a theoretic principle apprehended by Lorenzo in the course of his investigation and critical penetration of the stilnovistic principle of *gentilezza*, which, as we have seen, he follows consciously and with the clearest understanding of its essential import. As we know from his derivation of the word, *gentilezza* is a generalized, human concept. It is derived—he holds—from the Roman ideal and attainment of excellence in conformity with their superior *virtus* and highly developed *humanitas*. It is a concept further based on the direct observation of the particular, natural *virtus* by which all things are distinguished and in which they excel. Moreover, historically, this concept was due to an original Roman influence of an educative character, so that it may be said that the Roman ideal of natural beauty and human excellence itself carried this influential and educative character. Indeed, presumably, the Romans themselves were subject to this influence, which accounts for their superior culture and civilization. Finally, as we have also seen, the very essence of *gentilezza* has been defined as the supremely human function of exercising discrimination in our apprehension of the excellent *virtus* in every *thing*. This "judicial distinction" on our part, corresponding to the excellence of the *things,* becomes their influential, instructive element—and they thus become humanized. Accordingly, the very principle of *gentilezza* is human in character, human in scope, and human in function. *Gentilezza* is itself a personified concept to begin with; and this by nature, as well as by virtue of its active influence on man himself. It follows, then, that this mode of conceiving poetically is suggested by the very nature of *gentilezza*. That is, the exercise of human "gentilesse" on the part of the poet-critic himself suggests to him the employment of the rhetorical figure called personification, or, for that matter, of metaphors in general. Just as the "judicial distinction," which gives him the *virtus* of a given "thing," is a process of detaching, as it were, the "soul" from the "body" of that "thing," so his personification of any concept of his is, reversely, the act of incarnating a "soul" into a "body." Naturally, the more real or realistic is the "person" found, either incarnating already, or capable of incarnating his concept, the better it will be for the poet, whose artistic creation then will be more or less perfect, and in conformity with nature, in proportion to its realism. I maintain, then, that the concept of *gentilezza* itself suggests a theoretic principle of poetic art, which is in perfect conformity with it and almost a natural consequence of the exercise of this supreme human function. Inasmuch as this principle is axiomatic of the whole philosophy of the sweet new style, the inference naturally is that it was derived directly from it.

So much for the personification of concepts. Now for the natural example par excellence, or for the personal identity that invariably accompanies this personification. Since this humanized or personified excellence of any *thing* is its distinguishing natural *virtus* by which it becomes known to man; and since this knowledge is acquired by him only through direct observation (or through intimate contact with the *thing* in its most distinctive and essential nature); it follows that the apprehension of this *virtus* is equivalent to the acquisition by him of a strictly scientific truth. His subjection thereby to the beneficent influence emanating from it amounts to a process of self-education. Conversely, it follows that true knowledge is acquired by man through his "judicial distinction" of *gentilezza* in "things," and that the truth of any concept can be verified by the concrete evidence presented by the "things" themselves. From this comes the need, or natural desire, to accompany the concept with its material incarnation. Hence, we might say, follows this practical identification of the *virtus* of the "thing" with the "thing" itself, or its example par excellence. This is the same thing as saying that, once more, the principle of *gentilezza* itself suggests the metaphor and the allegory.

We are here reminded of Dante's justification for his personification of the concept *amore,* given in his *Vita Nuova;*[1] of his various discourses on the subject of allegory, found especially in the

---

1. Cf. *Vita Nuova,* chap. xxv.

Convivio,[2] and in the letter to Can Grande;[3] and particularly of his specific declaration: "Vostra apprensiva da esser *verace/* tragge intenzione," found in the *Commedia.*[4] And there is no doubt that, in this respect as well, Lorenzo both adheres to the theory and follows the common practice of the stilnovists. But, judging from the above consideration of his significant investigation and scientific study of the term *gentilezza,* there is more than mere adherence to this poetic art in his practice. There is his critical, scholarly opinion regarding the true nature and full import of the fundamental principle involved in the poetry of the stilnovists; and there is his authoritative interpretation of this allegorical poetry, based on, and justified by, this research of his. As we have seen, this allegorical lady of his is his concept or understanding of the first Italian literature. She implies not only the most thorough and exact comprehension of the esoteric meaning of this poetry but—inasmuch as she is his ideal—also the acceptance of the philosophical principle involved. And now this principle reveals itself in our analysis as a principle of human education—carrying, as it were, its own scientific method for its proper application in learning and teaching. In fact, as we have observed, Lorenzo's understanding of *gentilezza* implies precisely such a principle; and our inference is based on his derivation, connotation, and application of the word. *Natura docet,* he seems to say; and if, in order to make this process perfectly clear, I may expatiate upon it, this is how she teaches. First man, by virtue of his natural and supremely human *gentilezza,* detects both the particular *gentilezza* that distinguishes, respectively, the innumerable "things" and his own generic and individual *gentilezza.* Then this human, judicial distinction or excellence of "things" (including human perfection) exercises a beneficent influence over him: instructing him, as it were, concerning the true facts of nature in general, and educating or developing his own self along the lines of strictly human perfection—that is, intellectually, morally, and artistically. Accordingly, for Lorenzo, *gentilezza* in any form and any being—whether animate or inanimate—is an educative factor, an ennobling influence, or a

2. Cf. *Convivio,* II.   3. Cf. *loc. cit.,* secs. 20–22.
4. Cf. *Purgatorio,* XVIII, 22–23.

humanizing agent. *Gentilezza,* we may say, is a teacher and a humanist in the true sense of the word. This is how he must have explained to himself the personification of *la donna gentile* in all stilnovistic literature. Undoubtedly she stood (in his opinion) for the particular ideal or concept of human perfection held by the various poets according to their individual, natural disposition. And this is why, consequently, he also personified his own ideal. Moreover, since we have concluded that his own *gentilissima* is none other than the great realization of the ideal of human perfection incorporated in the supreme literary achievements of his glorious predecessors, we now gather that he conceived this Italian literature as a magnificent, humanistic educator and a most powerful force for the advancement of mankind! He was absolutely right. For, without quibbling over the æsthetic problem of whether or not art should teach, and whether or not literature should be moralistic, the fact is that this first, great Italian literature does teach, and was meant to teach. And the Italian Renaissance is there to testify with its magnificent achievements in all fields of human endeavor to the quality and effectiveness of this teaching. At any rate, we now understand clearly that *gentilezza,* for our author, is a scientific principle of humanistic education, and a true, natural factor of human culture and civilization. We understand through him both the nature and the force of the miraculousness attributed to the *donna gentile* by all the stilnovists, including himself. Perhaps we are also convinced by now that stilnovism is for him synonymous with humanism in the sense of the word as we have defined it.

At the risk of appearing unnecessarily prolix in this matter, I feel that we must investigate further this concept of a natural and humanized, educative function of *gentilezza.* This is in order to realize the scientific, philosophical basis on which this principle of human education purports to rest—for the purpose of understanding and appreciating the peculiar mode of conceiving poetically evolved by the stilnovists.

It is now obvious that Lorenzo—presumably like his predecessors—was most concerned with the scientific acquisition of human knowledge, which is the natural and most essential requirement for the achievement of human perfection. Therefore, his and their question must have been: What is knowledge, what constitutes the truth of anything, and how can this true knowledge be ascertained as well as acquired scientifically? The problem was eminently philosophical, and naturally led to scientific speculation. But also, naturally, it was scientifically solvable only on the basis of the philosophy held by the poets who conceived the principle of *gentilezza*. This principle proved its veracity by the poets themselves achieving human perfection, precisely by their "gentilesse," and through the "gentilesse" of their works in which they at once expounded the doctrine and demonstrated its exactness by a most successful application. What was their doctrine? It is generally assumed that it was entirely neo-Platonic in character and substance, and undoubtedly it had elements of neo-Platonism in it. But Lorenzo's single, incidental reference to Plato (none to Aristotle, nor to Oriental mysticism), and, especially, once more, his derivation and definition of *gentilezza,* prove that—at least in his opinion, and whatever influences may have been at play—the concept of human "gentilesse," and particularly the realization of its constituting a scientific principle of human education, were new and original with the stilnovists. Accordingly, in Lorenzo's opinion, if the doctrine of the stilnovists was neo-Platonic at all, it was a very special brand of neo-Platonism. It was *stilnovistic* neo-Platonism; and his Ficinian neo-Platonism seems to have had very little to do with his understanding of this doctrine.

In any case, basing our inferences purely on the nature and results of his original research—as well as on the practice of himself and all the stilnovists—this philosophy seems to be a sort of conceptualism with all the elements of both idealism and realism combined. We must not imagine, however, that it is an eclectic system aiming to settle the dispute between realists and nominalists. The conceptualism of the stilnovists aims at indisputable truth established scientifically, and is based on an axiom that precludes all philosophical speculation. In fact, its basis and point of departure is the substantial *reality* of the "gentilesse" of "things." This, as we know, is the essential and natural virtue of any given "thing," and is therefore a concrete, directly observable fact, and an undeniable truth. So that, to this extent, and in this respect, their philosophy is realism of the purest brand. But there are two important points to be remembered in connection with this realism. First, the "thing" is, to be sure, a substantial and concrete object, but this object may be purely *conceptual* as well as material, and *animate* as well as *inanimate*. Second, the *gentilezza* of any "thing" (corresponding as it does to the excellence of its *virtus*) is a judicial, human distinction, and therefore itself a *concept* to start with. This gives to this philosophy all the character of the purest idealism. In fact, it is, accordingly, a fundamental axiom that all reality is by nature conceptual—since, I reiterate, not only the "thing" may itself be merely a concept (incarnate, but a concept), or a conceiving, animate being; but (even when this object is material and inanimate) man's knowledge of its *virtus* is an abstraction, or merely a mental concept of this physical reality. Only, this idealism is obviously just as real, and indisputable in its naturalness and scientific findings, as the realism of the concrete observable *virtus* of "things." For we well remember that the faculty of judicial distinction is the *virtus* par excellence of the "thing" called man, and is itself, therefore, not only an undeniable, natural, and active factor of human knowledge but also man's only criterion for arriving at truth scientifically. In other words, while it is an axiom that true knowledge comes to man only through his senses, it is also an axiom that this knowledge comes to him only in the form of concepts. But, at the same time, while this knowledge amounts to the notice he takes of the particular *virtus* distinguishing one "thing" from another—this consciousness in the form of a concept is the immediate result of his direct observation and presumably infallible judgment of this *virtus*. (For, if this judgment is false, it is the individual's own *virtus* that is at fault or deficient.) This makes the two axioms really one, since the one implies the other.

The one resulting axiom is: knowledge is by nature conceptual —but true, scientific knowledge (as far as achievable by man) is the result of his correct judgment based only on the direct observation of the essence of things. Thus, the philosophy of the stilnovists, according to Lorenzo, seems to be (as I have called it) a sort of conceptualism, which we may now qualify as realistic. It is a philosophy springing naturally from the original concept of *gentilezza,* and evolved in perfect conformity with this axiomatic principle. More than mere neo-Platonism, it seems to me a worthy attempt (perhaps a successful one) to reconcile the medieval, deductive method with the new, inductive method which now asserted itself as the scientific method of investigation and search after truth.

The concept of *gentilezza* may, indeed, mark the birth of this modern, scientific method. At any rate, this philosophical belief explains both the aim and the *style* of the stilnovists. Their aim is to comprehend and divulge the essence of human perfection, as well as to achieve it themselves in the way most commensurate with their own particular *virtus.* Their peculiar mode is to conceive poetically as they proceed to realize their aim. Since the coexistence of the *virtus* and the corresponding concept in any form of *gentilezza* amounted for them to a virtual identity, the allegorical personification was naturally and logically the rhetorical figure best suited to express both this identity and the active influence emanating from *gentilezza.* And, since the preoccupation was both to ascertain and to prove the scientific truth of the *gentilezza* proposed and contended for, the custom also developed naturally of presenting as evidence either a personification of the "thing" itself, or the example par excellence which illustrated and demonstrated actually the poet's contention. Thus (as we have already seen) in this very *principio* the two main concepts involved are presented as two such personifications. First, the author's concept of the preceding Italian literature is identified with an allegorical lady embodying the supreme beauty and human "gentilesse" of this literature (together with its ineffable, fascinating charm, and its beneficent, miraculous influence on the development of human character for the achievement of human perfection), and then, in the second place, his concept of the mystic death is similarly personified. The first is, as it were, a self-proved *gentilezza,* evident to anyone who is "at all acquainted with it" and has personally come under its charm. The second, on the other hand, is demonstrated by the common experience in any case of physical death—and especially at the death of a person dear to us, whom we admired supremely. In fact, who can deny that the sight of the face of such a person dead, reveals to the "gentle" heart a sort of glorified image of the virtues of that person? As we gaze upon it fondly, we abstract and spiritualize these virtues. And this calm, peaceful, supernatural beauty lifts itself, as it were, from the flesh—hovering above it, and forming a sort of halo around her body. This is the mystic death of that person. It is the process of detaching her *gentilezza,* or our judicial distinction of the *virtus* in which she excelled. And who can deny that, especially in the case of the death of a personage supremely *gentile,* we ourselves, the by-standers, are uplifted, and live, as it were, only in the spirit (provided we ourselves have a "gentle" heart)? This is *our* mystic death, as long as the condition exists. Finally, who can deny that the consideration of the passing away of a lofty ideal—the supreme and most grandiose of all ideals, that of human perfection itself—will have the same physical and spiritual effect on either *donna* or *omo valente,* as Dante might say? And this is the mystic death of which Lorenzo speaks here.

Accordingly, the result poetically was the allegorical incarnation, in any case of excellence, of the respective ideal of perfection best exemplified by a given "thing": a sort of *verbum factum caro.* In practice, the desire to achieve human perfection—in oneself, in mankind as a whole, and in nature beautified by the artistic genius of man—led to the scientific study of man and nature according to the following apparent procedure or methodology. First came the direct study of "things" in their respective, essential *virtus,* followed immediately by a generalized concept of the particular *virtus* (best illustrated by a perfect, outstanding example of this *virtus*); or else the study of a single, concrete existence, likewise followed by a concept embodying the spiritual reality of this being, severed from its physical consistency. Then came the humanization or personification of the spiritual influence exercised by this concept. And, finally, came the identification of this concept, or ideal, with the "thing" itself or its best exemplification. Of course, the process was reversible. That is, the concept might be borrowed, or perhaps vaguely rush to the fore, and thus precede the analytical process of direct examination. In this case, the task would be to verify the concept by comparing it with the concrete evidence furnished by the actual facts, or to find the example par excellence capable of demonstrating perfectly and palpably the veracity of this concept. But, in any case, concept and actual *virtus* had to correspond exactly and be practically identical, or the concept would not be scientifically true. In other words, it seems to me that this method of research and this peculiar mode of conceiving poetically—excogitated by the stilnovists in conformity with their philosophical principle, and strictly adhered to by them to accomplish their noble purpose—implies a critical attitude, an earnest desire to apprehend and present only the established fact. It also implies the observance of a scientific procedure which, being at once both analytic and synthetic, assures the penetration of the essence of things without destroying the natural unity of their constituent elements.

So far as I know, this is our ideal of scientific research today— whenever we, too, perhaps strive to contribute our part to the achievement of human perfection. There is no doubt, however, that this is the way the Magnificent interpreted Dante's definition of the sweet new style, already quoted:

> I' mi son un, che quando
> Amor mi spira, noto, e a quel modo
> ch'e' ditta dentro vo significando.[5]

As Dante, too, had previously said, quoting Guinizelli,

> Amore e 'l cor gentil sono una cosa.[6]

Accordingly—in view of the above explanation of Lorenzo's interpretation of the term *gentilezza*—there can be no doubt that, for Lorenzo, what inspired Dante was the spirit of *gentilezza*, as he, Lorenzo, understood this concept and principle. Indeed, remembering that Dante had defined love as the natural inclination of the soul toward anything that stirs it pleasantly,[7] we may practically reconstruct his (Lorenzo's) probable paraphrase of the above

---

5. *Purgatorio*, XXIV, 52–54. Cf. above, p. 35.
6. *Vita Nuova*, XX, first line of sonnet.   7. *Purgatorio*, XVIII, 19–27.

verses. This must have been as precise as a mathematical formula, and must have sounded like one. Therefore, for the sake of clearness, I may perhaps put it crudely as follows. Love equals gentle heart, equals natural propensity of Dante's "gentilesse" toward the "thing" that stirred his soul most pleasantly. This "thing" was his ideal of human perfection conceived by his "gentilesse" in perfect conformity with the nature and principle of "gentilesse" itself. Therefore, what he meant by the above lines might be expressed as follows: "I, Dante, am simply one who, endowed with the required 'gentilesse' to perceive the supreme 'gentilesse' of the ideal of human perfection, and therefore naturally disposed to love or respond to this supreme 'gentilesse'; whenever this love prompts me to penetrate the real essence and excellence of human perfection—I merely observe, distinguish judicially, and *note down,* precisely as it reveals itself to me, the essence of this 'gentilesse' manifested in the life and works of the most excellent men. Then I merely proceed to reproduce faithfully, or just to present, this identical concept formed by 'my gentilesse'—conforming myself perfectly to *the manner* used by Love himself in communicating it to me. That is, in my own life and works, I strive to achieve human perfection, so that, in conformity with the natural mode of 'gentilesse' itself, my life and works may exercise on others the same charm and efficacy that the supreme achievements of other men have exercised on me."

In other words, I believe that, for the Magnificent, this mysterious elucidation of the *dolce stil novo* implied the firm belief in the moral value and cultural efficacy of all great human achievements. And it implied the strictest adherence in all the arts to the philosophic concept of "gentilesse" with its inherent principle of human education. For him, this theory was not intended to be limited to literary art, but it extended to all the arts, and to all forms of human conception and expression. So that (again I remark) for him the *dolce stil novo* was merely humanism. Indeed, not only the content of this style was humanistic, but the form as well; while the products had the virtue of educating, or *humanizing,* as it were. Otherwise, he would not have made the life of love and verses of the stilnovists, and especially Dante's and Petrarch's, his own ideal of a perfect, poetic life, explaining this ideal as he does. Otherwise, his own performance, *mutatis mutandis,* would not have been of exactly this character, and avowedly so.

In connection with the verses quoted above, Lorenzo must have thought especially of the supremely humanistic character and tremendous efficacy of the *Divine Comedy* for human development.[8] This is in contradistinction to modern Dantists, who are wont to restrict arbitrarily the application of this definition to the poet's *Rime* and to the verses of the first stilnovists. Modern critics also usually interpret Dante's extremely accurate and dramatic exposition of the *dolce stil novo,* in a vague and superficial manner. They declare that it merely implies sincerity and spontaneity in art. But for Lorenzo (indeed, for anyone at all familiar with stilnovistic literature—except the said critics in the act of exercising their function!) this art is anything but sincere and spontaneous. Sincerity and spontaneity are understood, yes; but not in the art of expression, and not in the sense of a casual, perhaps fanciful, inspiration expressed at random. Rather, sincerity and spontaneity occur in aim, and in the effort to accomplish this purpose. Sincerity occurs in the sense of full consciousness, on the part of the author, of his particular *gentilezza* or special talent, as well as of his natural limitations. Sincerity also occurs in the sense of a thorough comprehension of, and absolute faith in, the principle of *gentilezza,* evolved by these poets, and in the sense of the strictest adherence to this principle in practice. And spontaneity occurs in the sense of a natural disposition to love and to practice "gentilesse." Spontaneity is also found in the choice of the special field of human activity best suited to one's natural potentiality. And there is spontaneity perhaps also in the sense of the poet's not forcing his attention and care on any particular objective falling within this field. But there the spontaneity and sincerity cease. The rest is pure science, artifice, and skill. It is the anxious pursuit of true knowledge; the conscientious, scientific study of self, humanity, and nature in general; a strenuous effort to detect, absorb, and convey to others the *gentilezza* of any and all things. Finally, it is all ingenuity and contrivance to produce a work that, in its

8. Cf., in fact, Text, p. 20, and especially p. 21; or this study, pp. 50, and 53.

conceptual character, will have the same charm and efficacy as the original *cosa gentile.* That is, it must be a work that will itself be a *cosa gentile,* and be practically that identical "thing" in which lay its real essence and distinctive character; so that it may well be said that the "gentilesse" of this work is actually the "gentilesse" of the "thing" itself. And this was all the art, but, at the same time, the really difficult art of the stilnovists. It was a *conscious* art, and an art aiming to produce *living* concepts of living realities. It had no rules, and no other precepts than this one—to adhere to essential reality and to imitate nature.

To be sure, the most successful contrivances to produce this effect soon became the rules of this art, replacing among mediocre men the art itself. Petrarchism, for instance, soon developed out of Petrarch's ingenuity and marvelous skill. The pseudo-stilnovists, or Petrarchists, took the means for the purpose, and, forgetting the cause, made the effect their end. So the humanists forgot the real *humanitas* of the stilnovists, and gradually degenerated into fanatics of Roman antiquity; became slavish, superficial imitators of the language, customs, and "gentilesse" of classical Rome; or merely turned out to be hunters of manuscripts and book collectors. So, too, the *bellezza* or divine *goodness* of the ideal of human perfection was soon misunderstood, or understood superficially. The failure to penetrate the real essence of the new style was, I believe, largely responsible for the origin of such false, æsthetic principles as: art is beauty, or art should teach, and the like. Indeed, the *concettismo* of the seventeenth century was not of a different character.

But the stilnovists themselves had no such mistaken notions; they merely strove to conform themselves to their simple concept and scientific principle of *gentilezza.* And so Lorenzo understood the *stil novo,* as it will become more and more evident in our study of this *principio.*

CHAPTER V

Esoteric Meaning of Lorenzo's Account of the
Composition of Sonnet I.

AFTER this long digression, in which, however, we have
touched on a great many pertinent points (which, finding
confirmation in Lorenzo's *Commentary,* will meanwhile
help us greatly to understand the comments themselves on this
and the other sonnets of the *principio*), we may now resume our
reading and study of the comment on this first sonnet.[1]

We now know the true nature and real importance of the
"quasi personality" that had passed away. We know the character
of this death, and the kind of miracle it operated. We understand,
too, how this event could well be considered a public calamity;
and why at the same time the best Florentine minds should all
have been inspired by it to celebrate her past glory and even
greater beauty now, in prose and verse. Finally, we understand
perfectly Lorenzo's natural and youthful desire to join with them
in this praise. Was he not, as it is very probable, engaged right
then in preparing an anthology of Italian verse for his royal
friend? What a wonderful gloss is this new life and commentary
of his upon that *Raccolta* with its prefatory letter! How well the
spirit with which that collection was made is now confirmed by
the spirit animating him in this love life of his! And what a close
relation exists between these two works—the first anticipating the
second, each explaining the other, and both prompted by the desire to exalt the first great period of Italian literature! We may
well speculate on whom he especially designated with the expression *fiorentini ingegni.* But, whoever they were,[2] it is obvious that
he and they all considered the first period—characterized by an
inspiring ideal and a magnificent execution—now closed and past.
This is extremely significant for us, since it is equivalent to the

1. Cf. Text, pp. 26 and 27.
2. Probably his so-called neo-Platonic circle of friends.

most eloquent testimony on the part of our author relative to an authoritative, critical opinion then current. And this is also his own critical opinion, supported by an analysis and a living synthesis of the *dolce stil novo,* that fully and definitely establish him as the first Italian literary critic, and a creative critic at that.

It was night [he says,] and I and a very dear friend of mine[3] were talking together of this common misfortune (*commune iattura*). The sky was very serene, and, as we spoke, our eyes were turned on a very clear star visible *toward the west.* So great was its splendor *certainly,* that it not only surpassed *by far* the other stars, but was indeed so bright that *bodies* intercepting the light cast some shadow. As at first we wondered at this, I turned to my friend and said: "This is not to be wondered at, since the soul of that *gentilissima* is now either transformed into this *new* star, or else it has *united* with it. And, if this is so, this splendor does not seem marvelous. Therefore, just as our eyes found great comfort in her beauty while she was alive, let us now comfort them with the *vision* of this very bright star. And, if our sight is weak and frail for such a flood of light, let us pray the deity (that is, her *divinity*) to fortify it by diminishing in some degree such splendor, that we may contemplate it awhile without injury to our eyes. Moreover, adorned as it is with the beauty of her (*colei*), it is surely no presumption on its part to wish to outdo in splendor the other stars. Indeed, it might contend even with Phoebus, and ask him for his chariot to be itself the cause of the light of day (*autrice del giorno*). And, if it is a fact that this star can do this without presumption, it follows that death has been extremely presumptuous in laying hands on such a surpassing beauty and *virtù.*"

The tenor, language, and whole style of this conversation would puzzle us here, if we were not now familiar with the poet's ideal and the peculiar mentality of the stilnovists. But, remembering our findings with respect to his ideal of *bellezza e gentilezza umana* (and recalling the preceding exposition of the principle of "gentilesse," which is the formative principle of the new sweet style), we sense immediately its inner meaning, and we do not find unnatural its consistently allegorical form. The commentator

---

3. One wonders who this *carissimo amico* may have been, and the thought naturally runs immediately to Poliziano. This, if it were established, would throw a flood of new light on the works of Poliziano. But it need not have been he, nor any of Lorenzo's actual literary associates. In fact, I doubt the historicity of this particular conversation. For, although it must be thought that not once, but probably many times, this subject was the topic of conversation in Lorenzo's neo-Platonic circle, the reference here savors too much of Dantean reminiscence. Cf. *Vita Nuova,* close of chap. iii. More of this friend later.

reports it as the actual, immediate cause that produced this first sonnet in its present form. That is, after accounting for the occasion and source of inspiration for all four sonnets of the *principio,* he now means to explain particularly the first. He goes so far as to reconstruct the whole scene and trend of thought that led precisely to this content and form. But, as a matter of fact, not only does the whole account savor of artificial stage setting, but it is also clearly an argumentation in defense of the concepts and statements already contained in the sonnet. In fact, it is really a soliloquy and a one-sided discussion, rather than a conversation. For the friend does not participate in it at all, except as a silent, and, presumably, assenting listener. So that, even if we did not know that this comment was written many years after the sonnet—and this alone might invalidate the historicity of the account—we should doubt the validity of the reconstruction. We could not fail to doubt it on the ground of the obvious contrast there is here between the commentator's ostensible desire to account for his concepts in the sonnet, and his actual defense of these concepts as if he had assumed a questionable position in the sonnet. Undoubtedly, this reconstruction is historically false, just as the previous adaptation of Simonetta's death to the metaphorical death of his metaphorical lady was entirely artificial.

On the other hand, just as above we found him true to his art in the choice of a concrete, convenient model to convey his concept, and found him also essentially—if only theoretically—sincere in the expression of the actions and reactions produced by the living reality hidden under the allegorical veil, so here we find him similarly truthful and sincere. In fact here one is inclined to believe that not one but many such conversations must actually have taken place between himself and some friend of his. For we now know that he is talking of his and the current Italian ideal of arts and letters—founded on the theory and glorious practice of the preceding Italian literature. And nothing could be more plausible than precisely this type and style of conversation actually taking place innumerable times among the literary men of his day discussing this ideal. Consequently, the author may well record here the actual discussion that led to this sonnet, or recall such a one that serves his purpose equally well. This purpose undoubtedly was the preceptive realism of his conceptual art. But, incidentally, this requirement to be sincere and spontaneous reveals to us what must have been the history of more than one poetic composition in the new style, shows us the procedure of the stilnovists in arriving at and selecting their metaphors, and gives us an insight into their poetic life, or *nuova vita d'amore.* What this life was exactly we can now begin to infer directly from this real or realistic history of the first sonnet, which (precisely as Lorenzo maintains) is not only the first of the series involving his philosophical principle, but marks also the beginning of his life of love. But let us not digress or anticipate. Let us first present the evidence by turning now to the content of this account offered as the explanation of the sonnet.

Taken literally, this explanation does not really demonstrate anything. It merely paraphrases the concepts and phraseology involved in the sonnet, and pretends to justify them, all in a language that is as highly figurative as the language of the sonnet itself. In fact, this paraphrase for the most part merely repeats, using the same words, what anyone can gather from a first reading of the sonnet. But we get from it an additional point of information, and a most important identification. We are given the position of the *chiarissima stella,* as being in the *western* sky; and the *begli occhi,* which even before could be said to be identical with the bright star, are now definitely identified with the *soul* of that *gentilissima* who had passed away. These two facts suffice to throw a flood of light on the rest of the exposition, and, consequently, on the sonnet as a whole. For, remembering the true essence of the "lady" (whom the commentator now calls *gentilissima* —precisely as Dante had done—and *eccellentissima bellezza e virtù*—as he interpreted her) we now know that her soul is his concept of the supreme *gentilezza* of Italian literature. Her soul is equal to its excellence or distinction, which, in turn, consists in its human perfection—having due regard to human "gentilesse," human scope, and human potentiality. We know that this critical concept of the literary ideal and achievement of his great predecessors is also his own ideal now. And we know that, in his opinion, this ideal is the most splendid in all *western* Europe. Consequently what he gives us here is really a wonderful page of the most valuable literary criticism. What he reports here, as the source and subject of his sonnet, is a humanistic, literary discussion pure and simple.

In fact, what is the purport of this discussion? What the commentator clearly means is, first of all, that his ideal of Italian arts and letters (symbolized by the brightest star *visible in the west,* and corresponding to that of the best Florentine minds of his day) is not only *superior by far* to any other conceived and pursued in western Europe, but is ideally perfect in itself. And then he also means that this current Italian ideal (shared especially—it is to be presumed—by this assenting, dearest friend of his) is largely and substantially the ideal found incorporated in, and superbly carried out by the preceding Italian literature. In other words, he compares critically the Italian ideal with the French, the Provençal, and possibly the Spanish—because it is not to be imagined that he knew anything about the still primitive literatures of the other peoples of Europe—and finds it immensely more splendid than any of them. In fact, he finds it so absolutely and perfectly splendid that it is a veritable *sun* in comparison with these other *stars.* Moreover, it is so idealistic or conceptual in character that the intellectual light emanating from this spiritual, Italian "sun" actually causes all "materialistic aims" (*quelli corpi che a tale luce si opponevono*) to cast a sort of shadow by contrast with its pure spirituality—just as the light of the real sun causes any *body* confronting it to cast a shadow. But how does it happen, why is it so? Because—says Lorenzo—"the soul of that *gentilissima* is now either transformed into this new star, or else it has united with it." That is, the same concept now animates the current, Italian ideal of arts and letters, that had animated the ideal of the previous Italian poets and artists. The same spirit is present in the current forms of Italian art (not necessarily limited to literature), that had animated a Guinizelli, a Cavalcanti, or a Giotto, and had produced the great literary achievements of Dante especially, surely Petrarch, and apparently also Boccaccio. Or else—he also adds— the old ideal of the stilnovists has become fused with the new, current ideal, and is now one with it. But, in any case, the present ideal is so splendid because it is, or contains, the old. Substantially, it is entirely or practically the old ideal. And it is perfect because the old was perfect: that is, derived from the perfect concept of human "gentilesse" (which, in turn, is based on the unquestionably sound principle that the very nature of things dictates). In other words, through this enthusiastic and fully justified praise of the Italian ideal, Lorenzo testifies, in effect, that the humanistic ideal of his times was essentially and substantially the stilnovistic ideal—even if it appeared somewhat transformed. He testifies, too, that the poets and artists of his day believed profoundly in the fundamental principle of stilnovistic art (considering it philosophically sound, and absolutely perfect), and that (striving to impress their works with the same character) they sought inspiration and guidance in the perfect works of the old masters. This was so, as the subsequent history of Italian literature proves.

It is indeed really remarkable how clearly the Magnificent saw the program of Italian humanism that was to result in the glorious Renaissance of arts, letters, and science throughout Europe. The true, scientific principle of *gentilezza* actually performed a miracle. It taught, it inspired, it humanized and civilized.

> Fatti non foste a viver come bruti,
> ma per seguir virtute e conoscenza.[4]

The Italian ideal of a renaissance to a *nuova vita d'amore* was a veritable sun radiating intellectual light. It could indeed be considered as a new or another Phoebus illuminating all mankind spiritually. And it was embodied, like a *verbum incarnatum,* in that body of Italian literature which it had first produced, almost as evidence of its divine potentiality and divine perfection in character, scope, and purpose. What truer and nobler ideal could be conceived? And what human achievement could be greater than the achievement of human perfection through the realization of the principle of human "gentilesse," and in the presentation of this concept as the supreme, human ideal par excellence? This body of Italian literature was, indeed, not only immensely superior to any other literature of western Europe, but was, as it is, truly divine. (That is, of course, divine in the sense in which Dante's *Commedia* especially came to be called *divina.*) And

4. *Inferno,* XXVI, 119–120.

rightly does Lorenzo call it metaphorically a god, meaning by this, as he himself explains, precisely this *divinità sua*.

As we have already observed, this first period of Italian literature was now over. The great triumvirate, especially, was no more. And in 1465,[5] or thereabout, the real, the great Renaissance of arts, letters, and science had not yet commenced. The noble tradition was, to be sure, maintained by the numerous Petrarchists (so called), neo-Platonists, humanists, and what not. But no really great works were being produced, not of that first supreme grandeur and profound significance. The young poet, as later the mature critic, felt such a deep and sincere sorrow that "his eyes would fain weep forever." And, truly, the stupendous concept with its scientific principle was only an ideal now. But what an ideal! It carried with it the full, divine spirit of the previous literature. Only slightly transformed, perhaps, in appearance, it had substantially the identical character, scope, and purpose. And the Italian literature had only died a mystic death, and was destined to continue its stilnovism, in theory and in practice, in the new forms of art and scientific inquiry that were even then beginning to come into being. The author strikes a note of the greatest optimism in the midst of his regret, and we sense the fermentation of the spirit that—renewing the old *vita d'amore*—was to produce the great achievements of the high Renaissance. In fact, Lorenzo suggests to his friend that, just as they have refreshed their souls in the contemplation of this divine, living beauty (reading and studying the works of the great masters), they now seek consolation in the consideration of this most splendid and clear ideal. Only, he fears that they may be confounded by its profound import, unless they approach it humbly and simply—considering at first its simple elements, so that they may enable themselves gradually to understand its full implication. For the light that radiates from this ideal,

> luce intellettual, piena d'amore;
> amor di vero ben, pien di letizia;
> letizia che trascende ogni dolzore,[6]

5. The traditional date of the *Raccolta aragonese* comprising Lorenzo's *principio*. For this date, see this study, pp. 342 ff.

6. *Paradiso*, XXX, 40–42.

this light is so brilliant, or profound, that it dazzles, that is, it confuses at first. It must be mitigated until the human mind has been made strong enough, by the study and practice of this ideal, to comprehend fully its import. Then alone it becomes really a possession, and an attempt may be made to carry out its dictates. Therefore they turn confidently to this literature, knowing that they will obtain from its study the necessary knowledge and practice to "fortify" them for the contemplation and eventual accomplishment of this ideal in themselves and in their works. And, poetically, they pray to this deity: that is, they hope to derive from it guidance and inspiration.

It may seem presumptuous—Lorenzo continues to imply—to make this great claim for the Italian ideal of cultural art. Or better, as he puts it, the ideal itself may seem presumptuous in claiming for itself this immense superiority, indeed supremacy, over the other concepts of art. But this affirmation, he explains, is no presumption at all; because it is a fact that the Italian ideal is "adorned with the beauty of *colei,*" or of that *gentilissima* Italian literature produced by the natural "gentilesse" of man following the natural principle of "gentilesse." That is, the supreme splendor and perfection of the Italian ideal derives from the divine beauty of the concept of human perfection (evolved by human "gentilesse" in the normal exercise of its natural function), which is incarnated in Italian literature with sublime grace and (through this last quality) is also a "gift of God."[7] Therefore, this claim of the Italian ideal amounts to a mere statement of its natural *gentilezza,* or distinction, or excellence—made without the slightest implication of arrogance. It is equivalent to declaring merely the inherent *eccellentissima bellezza e virtù* of Italian literature, which is a fact. In the same way it is an undeniable fact that this spiritual sun, risen in Italy, radiates intellectual light upon humanity—precisely as the material sun sheds physical light upon the earth. It is, therefore, actually another Phoebus capable of contending in importance with the physical Phoebus. There is surely no presumption in affirming that which the "thing" really is.

Indeed—the commentator declares with an obvious but nice

7. Cf. above, p. 112.

conceit—if there is any presumption anywhere in all this, it is Death that has been most presumptuous (Death, who had decreed the close of this first, most glorious period of Italian literature; Death, who had laid hands on *tanta eccellentissima bellezza e virtù,* modifying and transforming somewhat its perfect content and form). In fact, as Lorenzo implies, and as we have already pointed out, the current works of Italian literature had neither the vast scope, nor the deep significance, nor the artistic beauty of the previous masterpieces. And, if it could correctly be said that the present ideal was the creator of intellectual daylight in the human mind, what a pity that the great, original conception—capable of producing such perfect masterpieces—had ceased to be a reality to become merely an ideal! What a pity that there were now no Dantes, no Petrarchs, nor even Boccaccios! And what a pity that the original ideal, though slightly, had been modified at all! On the other hand, this was perhaps only natural. For, as Lorenzo has thoroughly explained at the end of the proem—where he discusses the meaning of death—"since form and species are immortal, . . . the creative spirit is always prompted by matter; . . . the termination of any one thing is at once the commencement of another; . . . *and* the life of love springs from death."[8] In other words, the concept and principle of *gentilezza* are the immortal form derived from the material nature of "things." It is but natural that different "things" should originate new, concrete forms in art, while the generic form remains identical. The love life of the stilnovists is precisely this continuous derivation of form from matter. This, as we now know, implies: first, a certain "gentilesse" of the lover; second, his free or spontaneous inclination (in accordance with this "gentilesse") toward *any* subject of love relatively perfect; and, third, absolute sincerity or fidelity in rendering conceptually the "gentilesse" of the particular "thing" thus *freely chosen.*[9] The life of love was a purely spiritual life devoted to the qualified study of *any and all "gentle things,"* at choice, though one at a time. It was a life, we might say, devoted to artistic, creative criticism in any field of "gentle" nature, though in the particular field of human activity for which the critic-artist was best

8. Cf. Text, p. 24; and above, p. 63.   9. Cf. above, p. 118, and pp. 133–134.

fitted by his own "gentilesse." Hence, it was but natural that, in a sense, certain fields of investigation should become exhausted. Naturally, then, a given subject of love, having attained its fullest expression in a perfect work of art, died a mystic death,—remaining eternally fixed in that work in its perfect, conceptual form, like a veritable *verbum incarnatum.* In Lorenzo's opinion, and perhaps in ours, Dante, Petrarch, and Boccaccio had said the last word on their respective subjects of love, and had achieved human perfection in this respect, giving a superb manifestation of their particular *gentilezza.* Consequently, it was but natural that the *gentilezza* of their works (themselves constituting a "thing," and undergoing the mystic death) should now live in the form of an ideal derived from the true concept resulting from their study. Moreover, new "gentle hearts" were being born all the time. They were men endowed with a more or less different type of natural *virtus* or "gentilesse" and consequently inclined toward other subjects of love (in the boundless extent of human interests and human activities) through which they hoped to achieve their relative or commensurate human perfection. These poets, these artists, these scholars—all humanists—were naturally deriving new forms and species from matter.

The principle alone remained steadfast, of course: the principle of "gentilesse" making for human progress toward human perfection in any of its ramifications and manifold manifestations. Accordingly, the commentator—who, in a way, sincerely regretted the passing away of the previous literature with its lofty aim (primarily moral and artistic) and rightly decried poetically the *grandissima presunzione* of Death in causing it—this commentator at the same time recognizes the naturalness of the process in the normal course of the love life itself. By the very principle of "gentilesse," death is not only inevitable, but necessary—for it assures the continuation and continuity of the life of love. Moreover, it is the very passage of the material *virtus* of any "gentle thing" in its conceptual form into the mind of the conceiver, who then expresses it accordingly. It is by this means that new forms are continually derived from "matter," and the course of the life of love is thus made possible. The love life itself is nothing but the spiritual process of distinguishing "gentilesses," and every new concept of any "gentilesse" means automatically a new form with a perfectly consonant expression. Therefore, the poet will tell us in the third sonnet that, indeed, death itself was made *gentile* by the passing away of that *gentilissima*—since, in fact, his critical conception of the supreme "gentilesse" of Italian literature implied the mystic death of this metaphorical lady—which, in turn, itself imported the similar idealization of the phenomenon of mystic death.

This is my interpretation of the first sonnet and comment relative to it, made in the light of the author's own exposition with the veil of allegory removed. It is a much longer study than I myself had anticipated, and the complexity of the subject (as well as the innumerable, debatable points to settle) have caused me, I fear, to be prolix without obtaining perfect coherence in my exposition. But, whatever its defects, I am confident that my interpretation is sufficiently clear to bring out at least the full justification of the author's own final remark in his comment on this sonnet. In true Dantean style, Lorenzo ends his comment by saying: "As all this *reasoning* seemed to me very good material for a sonnet, I left my friend, and retired to compose this sonnet, in which I address myself to the aforesaid star." If it were not perhaps presumptuous on my part, I should now advise the reader to keep this interpretation in mind and read again the words of the Magnificent in his first sonnet:

> O chiara stella, che co' raggi tuoi
> togli alle tue vicine stelle il lume,
> perchè splendi assai più che 'l tuo costume?
> perchè con Febo ancor contender vuoi?
>   Forse i begli occhi, quali ha tolti a noi
> Morte crudel, ch'omai troppo presume,
> accolti hai in te: adorna del lor lume,
> il suo bel carro a Febo chieder puoi.
>   O questa o nuova stella che tu sia,
> che di splendor novello adorni il cielo,
> chiamata esaudi, o nume, i voti nostri:
>   leva dello splendor tuo tanto via,
> che agli occhi, c'han d'eterno pianto zelo,
> sanz'altra offension lieta ti mostri.

PART III

THE *PRINCIPIO:* SONNET II

CHAPTER I

Literal Translation of the Comment on Sonnet II.

THE second sonnet, to which the reader is now referred,[1] is thus expounded by the author:

This most excellent lady died *in the month of April,* at which time of the year the earth is wont to clothe itself with a variety of flowers very pleasing to the eyes and quite refreshing to the soul. Prompted to enjoy this pleasure, I was walking pensively and alone through certain meadows of mine exceedingly charming, and, *all engrossed in the thought and memory of her, I seemed to reduce all things into terms of her* (a suo proposito). Thus, regarding and distinguishing flower from flower (guardando tra fiore e fiore), I noticed in their midst that little flower which is vulgarly called the *tornalsole,* and in Latin is called *clitia*—after the name of a certain nymph, Clytie, who, according to Ovid, was transformed into this flower, and who loved the sun with such vehemence and ardor that even thus converted into a flower she turns continually toward the sun, following her lover with longing gaze. As I was, then, looking attentively at this amorous flower, which is *pallid as lovers naturally are*—and because this flower is actually pale in color, being yellow and white—I was moved to pity her lot. For the evening was nigh, and I reflected that she would soon lose the very sweet vision of her beloved. In fact, the sun was then approaching the horizon, which deprived Clytie of her beloved sight. Her grief was all the greater—I thought —as what was denied to her would be enjoyed by many others (era comune a molti altri): that is, by the eyes of those who are called "antipodes," on whom the sun shines when we are deprived of it, and whose night is daylight to us. This thought led to another. I reflected that, although Clytie did lose her beloved vision for a night, at least on the following morning she was allowed to behold it again. In fact, while the western horizon deprives her of it, the eastern horizon restores it to her, and the benign dawn, pitying her love, shows it to her again. Indeed, I thank the eastern horizon for restoring it to her, because *it is very natural and human to feel compassion for all sufferers,* especially those whose affliction is somewhat similar to our own. Then this diverse and alternate fate of Clytie made me consider how much harder and more unjust is the lot of him who longs to see a thing

1. Cf. this study, p. 151; also pp. 85–86; and the whole section entitled "Literal meaning of the *principio,*" pp. 89–99, especially pp. 90, 92, and 97. Also, Text, p. 27, l. 24–p. 30, l. 10.

the sight of which is necessarily denied to him, not for one night, but for ever. I see the dawn that gives Clytie back her sun, but know not what other dawn may restore to the world this other sun, namely, the eyes of this lady (colei). If this sun cannot return, it follows that to the eyes of those who have no other light it must perforce be night for ever—since night is merely the absence of the sun's light. Therefore, direst is indeed the fate of him who longs expectantly for that which he cannot have. He can have no other comfort than that afforded by *the memory and mental gaze of what he has loved most and has been dearest to him*. Because precisely like Clytie, as I believe—who in the evening remains with her face turned toward the western horizon (namely, that which has deprived her of the sight of the sun) until, the following morning, the sun makes her face the east again; so *this new Clytie* cannot experience greater comfort than by holding his mind and thoughts fixed on *the last impressions and dearest things of "his sun."* These, like a western horizon, have deprived him of his beloved vision.

It may also be said [the commentator continues] that *by this last horizon is meant the death of this "gentilissima"*—since "horizon" merely means the extreme limit beyond which human eyes cannot see. In fact, when the sun sets, that is what we call the last place beyond which it is no longer visible, and when it rises, that is what we call the place where it first appears. Therefore, it is proper to call death that horizon which deprived us of the sight of her eyes. And there is where this new Clytie—namely the lover of her eyes—should hold his [mental] eyes firmly fixed: reflecting that *every mortal thing,* although beautiful and most excellent, *dies necessarily.* Such a consideration is usually a great and efficacious remedy for the consolation of every grief and to show men that mortal things should be *loved as finite things* subject to the inevitableness of death. Moreover, whoever considers this fact with respect to others will easily realize this condition and necessity with respect to himself: adhering to that wisest of sayings inscribed in the temple of Apollo, *Nosce te ipsum,* and persevering in this thought until death does come. *Death will return his sun to this new Clytie, just as the dawn returns it to Clytie turned flower.* For then his soul, freed of the body, will be able to consider the beauty of the soul of this lady (costei) [and he will find it] much more beautiful than that formerly visible to his eyes—since the light of human eyes is like shade in comparison with the light of the soul. Thus, *just as the death of "colei" was a [western] horizon to the setting of the sun of her eyes, so the death of this new Clytie*—with reference to the eastern horizon that will return him his sun— *will be like the dawn returning it to Clytie already converted into a flower.*

As this thought [concludes the author] seemed to me very suitable material to put into verse, I composed the following sonnet:

Quando il sol giù dall'orizzonte scende,
rimiro Clizia pallida nel volto,
e piango la sua sorte che li ha tolto
la vista di colui che ad altri splende.
Poi quando di novella fiamma accende
l'erbe, le piante e' fior Febo a noi volto,
l'altro orizzonte allor ringrazio molto
e la benigna aurora che gliel rende.[2]
Ma lasso! io non so già qual nuova aurora
renda al mondo il suo sole: ah, dura sorte,
che noi vestir d'eterna notte volse!
O Clizia, indarno speri venderl'ora:
tien' gli occhi fissi infin li chiuda morte
all'orizzonte estremo che tel tolse.

I give a preliminary version of this comment here in full, at the
beginning of the section dealing with it, because I fear it is going
to give rise to another series of long discussions concerning now a
part of it and now the whole of it. Therefore, it is well to have the
subject of these discussions where it may easily be referred to, and
where the reader may also find it conveniently whenever he may
need to refresh his memory or wish to see the bearing of my discussion on the context from which they rise.

By way of introduction and transition, I may also say that,
while the first sonnet of Lorenzo's *Principio* might be entitled
"Initial Stage of the Mystic Death of Lady and Poet" or "Lorenzo's
Poetical Ideal," a suitable title for this second sonnet might be
"Indispensableness and Simultaneousness of This Common Mystic Death" or "The First Requisite To Achieve This Ideal." In
fact, this is the subject, as we shall see, of the sonnet and of the
comment we are about to study. And the reader will see that the
progressive development we noted in the subject matter of the
Principio while discussing its literal meaning,[3] now becomes
clearer and more obvious as we apprehend the esoteric meaning of
each sonnet in turn. Moreover, with the help of the author him-

2. In Simioni's edition, based on *Riccardiano 2726*, the text here reads *tolse* in place of
rende. But the variant *rende*, found in *Palatino 204*, *Vaticano 3218*, and *Vaticano 3219*, is
obviously the better reading, both for the sense and the rhyme.
3. Cf. this study, pp. 89–99, and especially pp. 92–95.

self, we shall see how all four sonnets come to constitute a veritable philosophical principle, an ideal theory of poetic art, and the commencement of his personal *nuova vita d'amore.* I believe I have fully substantiated the title I have just proposed for the first sonnet, and shall now proceed to do likewise regarding the title I suggest for the second.

The Date of the Lady's Death and Its Mysterious Significance.

BEFORE I begin this exposition, let us observe how inappropriate is this sonnet, too, to consecrate the death of Simonetta Cattaneo. A mere glance at the author's own introduction and explanation suffices to make us discard once more this hypothesis, which we have rejected already on other grounds.[4] In fact, the presumed comparison of that mundane lady to the sun that daily sets and again rises the next morning for the ancient, mythological Clytie, is utterly absurd; and the comparison of the author to the *tornalsole* with respect to her, as "this new Clytie," absolutely precludes any such supposition. Furthermore, the tenor of the whole comment, with its obscure, philosophical content, and especially the obvious application of this philosophy to the author himself for his comfort and edification, surely indicate that there is not the remotest connection between this sonnet and the death of Simonetta. Yet this lady intrudes once more into our study, and we must accord her one last consideration.

It will be remembered that Sforza Bettini's letter to Lorenzo, containing his account of Simonetta's funeral, was dated April 27, 1476.[5] Presumably, then, this lady died very shortly before this date. For, despite the fact that the phrase *come so harette inteso* implies a certain lapse of time between the date of decease and the date of the letter, it is more likely that Bettini composed his warm and enthusiastic account of the impressive ceremony while he was still under the emotion produced by her demise on himself and all those present at the funeral; that is, not more than a day or two later, if not on the very day of the funeral. In any case, Simonetta must have died within the month of April, which is the point here. For now we learn from the above comment that the "lady" of the *Principio* also died in the month of April. This coincidence has apparently definitely convinced the historians that the lady alluded to by the poet here *is* Simonetta Cattaneo.[6] Indeed, it may be observed that Lorenzo does not specify the day of the month, any more than Bettini had specified it in his letter. Which strengthens this conclusion, inasmuch as apparently then, the reason why the commentator does not specify the day is probably because this element was lacking in his source of information. But, apart from the fact that Lorenzo does not give the year either, and that, if he did not recall the precise date of Simonetta's death, he could have easily ascertained it from other sources, what does the coincidence really prove? It merely proves that the commentator, mind you, and not the young author of these sonnets, having once decided[7] to avail himself of this particular, concrete example of physical death *for his exposition* of the mystic death of his metaphorical lady, simply took, for reasons of his own, this additional realistic element from the *esser verace* constituting his "model." At best, then, he is merely consistent with his previous falsification, and the confirmation here that his model for the artistic portrayal of his concept was the death of Simonetta does not invalidate at all the arguments against the thesis that this lady inspired the *principio* of his "new life."

On the contrary, this confirmation of the identity of the model now makes us wonder why the critic-artist chose to bring out this particular detail, to the exclusion or neglect of the precise date in full. If these sonnets had been merely *versi d'occasione,* and the person referred to were actually Simonetta, should we not expect here the date of her death *in full*? Indeed, in an "exposition" of such verses, should we not expect the "commentator" to have come out with her name as well, long before this? Such omissions are not in keeping with the idea of an expository comment, even if we grant to the poet his customary secrecy and vagueness. More-

6. Cf., for instance, Simioni, "Donne ed amori medicei. La Simonetta," already cited.
7. Cf. above, p. 106.

over, it is certainly inconsistent with the purpose of an implied identification to be both specific and indefinite at the same time. Accordingly, I conclude that the above-noted coincidence is no confirmation at all of an identification, which, it is now obvious, was never intended.

The most that may perhaps be said is that the stilnovist commentator of this *principio* was undoubtedly pleased to find in his model this additional historical fact, which further enriched the historical background for this realistic portrayal of the mystic death. I should not go so far as to say that he chose this particular model primarily for this reason; although, remembering the realistic requirement of the new style, I might say that if this coincidence had not actually occurred, he would have had to fabricate one perhaps after the manner of Dante or Petrarch. But the fact remains that the death of Simonetta Cattaneo in 1476 cannot have inspired this and the other sonnets of the *principio* written about 1465.[8] In other words, it was not the date of Simonetta's death that determined the date of the *lady's* death in April, but, once more, it was the model that happily fitted the picture within the framework of the commentary. It was not that the poems were in any way altered and "adapted" to commemorate the death of *la bella Simonetta,* but it was this model that was most advisedly chosen for the stilnovistic incarnation of their content. (Need I point out the fact that this specification of the month of April is, of course, in the comment and not in the sonnet, which merely suggests spring?)

It follows, I believe, that this specific remark, made at the outset of a philosophical comment, is, to say the least, suspicious. The commentator begins his exposition sharply, saying unequivocally, "Morì questa eccellentissima donna del mese d'aprile." And this salient remark, which introduces the history of the sonnet, at first seems purely casual and natural. But I ask, why did he not choose to give this information before, and properly in connection with the full account of her death, at the beginning of his comment on the first sonnet? And what leads him now to accept the April element in the date of Simonetta's death, to the exclu-

---

8. Cf. Appendix B on the date of the *Raccolta aragonese,* pp. 342 ff.

sion, as we have observed, of the other two, namely the year and the day of the month? Moreover, he immediately follows this sort of formal statement, which brings us back to the first account, with an explanatory clause, "nel quale tempo la terra si suole vestire di diversi fiori molto vaghi agli occhi e di grande recreazione all'animo." This destroys all the casualness and naturalness of the initial remark, and plunges us into a philosophical meditation; because it seems to say, very strangely, that the month of April was *for this reason* a very appropriate and natural "season" for the occurrence of this demise. In fact, observe that the writer does not say *nel* but *del mese d'aprile:* which does not mean *"in the* month of April" of a given year not specified, but *"of a* or *on a* month of April" pure and simple. This calls for no further specification because obviously the phrase is not so much intended to *date* the occurrence as to bring out the *character* of the season of the year, in which, as the qualifying clause indicates, it was suitable, perhaps natural, that this death should have occurred. In other words, the author here does not date the death of his lady as much as he characterizes, for reasons of his own, the "time" of the year in which it occurred. In view of this and of the esoteric meaning which, as we have now begun to realize, permeates this entire *principio,* we are therefore justified in suspecting this indication, and we scent already a *sovrasenso.* In any case, we surmise that the "time" or season of the year marked for the *lady's* death may be significant; perhaps it is theoretic.

Accordingly, let us now collate this "time" with our previous conclusions relative to the esoteric meaning of the poet's "lady." If we were here dealing with a "date," we should now infer that logically this statement carried the following implication: "the literary ideal conceived and achieved by the great Italian poets of the thirteenth and fourteenth centuries just spent itself abruptly in the month of April of an unspecified year." Which would be pointless in so far as the expected date is not actually given; and would be absurd, inasmuch as, of course, artistic ideals and literary periods do not end, as it were, overnight. Moreover, even if we supposed that for this reason, or no reason at all, the indication of the year had been carelessly omitted, surely no one, and least of all the Magnificent, would seriously imply that any one year, not to say month, marked the time in which it might be said that the ideal of the sweet new style became extinct, or that the poets of this school were all found to have died out. Finally, historically it could not possibly be said that this occurred, in any case, in the author's lifetime.

As we have seen, we are not dealing with a definite date of the lady's death, but with a mere characterization of the month of the year mysteriously suited to what obviously now must be merely the "mystic" death of this metaphorical lady. It follows that the suspected significance of the remark must actually be of a theoretic nature; and, since the propitiousness of the season cannot plausibly be referred to the "lady" *per se,* this suitableness must be with respect to the poet himself. Presumably, then, the meaning is that *the stilnovistic ideal was fully or definitely realized by "this new Clytie" on a month of April;* and this properly, in accordance with a theory that smacks of "naturalness." If it were shown that the young Lorenzo actually compiled his famous anthology *in the spring* of 1465, or of whatever year he was studying the early poets for this purpose, this would be an illuminating gloss to this passage of the *Comento* and to the realism of the stilnovists. Recall the spirit of proud display with which this *Raccolta* was made, and the historical, critical value of the prefatory letter. But, whether or not the above date is historical, there is a definite import in this indication and characterization of the month of April. This must be the theory, or belief, that the spring of the year, and particularly the month of April, was, as it were, the biblical "acceptable time" for such a spiritual realization as that of the whole scope, character, and ideal of the first Italian literature exemplified by the selections in the said anthology.

It behooves us, therefore, to investigate this appropriateness of the lady's mystic death with respect to the poet's own mystic death and commencement of his *nuova vita.* But before we attempt to detect stilnovistically the peculiar virtue, excellence, or "gentilesse" of the month April, that we may realize its natural *ufficio,* or function, and therefore fitness here as a condition for this double mystic death, let us follow the commentator closely in

his careful reconstruction of the poetic experience which resulted
in his personal spiritual elevation, simultaneously with his realization of the philosophical concept and artistic ideal personified by
his lady.[9]

9. The reader is here invited to read the comment on the second sonnet over again, in
order to refresh his memory, and to note especially the phrases I have italicized. Cf. Text,
pp. 27–29; and my version, above, pp. 149–150.

CHAPTER II

Clytie, the Tornalsole, *Symbol of the Mystic Death.*

IT was in April, and the earth, as usual in Italy at this time of
the year, was all abloom. The air was fresh and invigorating,
the sky clear and pure, and the country around all a variety of
colors in the midst of a luxuriant vegetation. Thus nature rejuve-
nated itself and entered upon a new period of vigorous, fertile life.
The young man, probably feeling within himself the same natural
urge to expand, grow, and produce, was prompted by this condition to go out in his garden and enjoy the pleasure offered by
beautiful nature. His eyes feasted on the variety of flowers, and his
spirit, too, was recreated by the glorious surroundings. But he
was sad and pensive withal. His lady was dead, and he was engrossed in the thought and memory of her. As he walked along
the paths, everything about him seemed to speak of her, or better,
to bespeak her essence and his condition. Indeed, it was he himself
who "seemed to reduce all things *a suo proposito.*" In other words,
the various flowers of his charming garden all seemed to him to
incarnate her spirit and to represent his own spiritual state with
respect to her, dead. One flower in particular seemed to do this
best. As he regarded the various flowers, and distinguished one
from the other, considering the special virtue and "gentilesse" of
each *with reference to their natural aptness to embody his concept
of the present situation,* he noticed the little *tornalsole,*[1] which immediately seemed to him to serve the purpose perfectly. This
flower, mythologized by the ancients, had been named *clitia* to
immortalize and typify the idealism of the nymph Clytie, supreme
example of eternal love for the intellectual light. As this flower
turns continually toward the sun, and is actually pale yellow in
color, or "pallid as lovers are by nature," it had served this purpose
well in antiquity, and now served his own even better, indeed perfectly, thus mythologized. Inasmuch as his *eccellentissima donna,*

1. Cf. above, n. 2, p. 90.

personifying the modern Italian literature in *volgare* and endowed with supreme *bellezza e gentilezza umana,* was undoubtedly that Sun of intellectual light which the ancient Clytie had adored and, transformed into flower, still follows with her loving gaze; and inasmuch as this *donna,* or modern "nymph," was also called *gentilissima* precisely because she was both of Roman derivation and worthy of ancient Rome: therefore, owing to the setting of this new "Sun," he, her passionate modern lover, could well call himself "this new Clytie," and thus represent perfectly with this mythological flower the whole situation, both with respect to himself and to his lady dead.

This was why this particular metaphor was chosen, and how he came to compare himself to the ancient Clytie. Then, as he gazed at this amorous flower, studying its natural characteristics, and marveling perhaps over its distinctive virtue, excellence, or "gentilesse" to typify eternally the constant lover of the human ideal, the natural object and the rhetorical figure became fused, though not confused, in his mind. He was moved to pity the lot of the little *tornalsole,* which, with the approaching night, would lose the sweet vision of the sun, and the lot of any lover of intellectual light, who at times is similarly deprived of this light while it undoubtedly illuminates other intellects in other parts of the world. Indeed, the grief of such a one seemed to him all the greater precisely for this reason; namely, because what was denied to this lover in his part of the world was common to many others on the other side. This curious conceit led to another thought. He reflected that, although Clytie (both the flower and the symbol) does lose her beloved vision periodically, at least there is always a benevolent dawn (literally and figuratively speaking) that restores it to her. This was indeed comforting, and he rejoiced over this good fortune of Clytie "because it is very *natural and human* to feel compassion for all sufferers, *especially those whose affliction is somewhat similar to our own."*

"*Qualche similitudine,*" says the text now. In fact, at this point the absolute correspondence found between the essence and fate of the *tornalsole* and the nymph Clytie on the one hand, and himself on the other, as "this new Clytie," ceases to be perfect. There was a difference between the ancient and the modern Clytie. Reflecting over "this *diverse and alternate* fate of Clytie," the poet then observed "how much harder and more unjust is the lot of him who longs to see a *thing* the sight of which is *necessarily* denied to him, not for one night, but *forever*." This was the lot of the new Clytie. This was *he,* who saw the daily return of the sun to the *tornalsole* at dawn, and also, it seems, realized the natural periodic return of intellectual light to all lovers of it, *"but knew not what dawn might restore to the world this other sun, namely the eyes of this lady."* The vision of supreme *bellezza e gentilezza umana,* embodied in the splendid Italian literature of the Dugento and Trecento, seemed to Lorenzo, as we have already deduced, to have spent itself by this time. The literary ideal and humanistic scope of the sweet new style had apparently been lost to view. Especially, the great trio that had given to the movement a most powerful impetus, and by theory and example had elevated it to a height of stupendous vision, this trio was no more. And with them seemed also to have gone the spirit that had guided them, shaping their love lives and informing their splendid works. In fact, as I have observed before, for nearly a century after the death of Petrarch and Boccaccio, there had been no poets of their magnitude, and the originality of their humanistic *ars poetica* appeared to have degenerated into sheer imitation without either the acumen or the scope and purpose of the first literature in *volgare.* Perhaps the great stilnovistic principle was no longer understood, and therefore remained infecund. At any rate, it seemed to "this new Clytie" that the *gentilissima* was verily dead by this time. Obviously, he regarded that first period of Italian literature as definitely closed, and consigned to history forever. He regretted this exceedingly, particularly the apparent cessation of all truly ennobling activity in the field of the creative, cultural arts. It seemed to him that, without the spiritual elevation exemplified and effected by that literature, there could be no further human progress, and that, without its enlightenment, Italy and all western Europe, *which had no other source of intellectual light and artistic inspiration,* remained in utter darkness. Accordingly, he longed for the revival of that glorious period of lofty thinking and artistic creation, but knew withal, or at least thought, that this was not possible. Not possible as long as that literature was not understood beyond its literal meaning, especially with respect to its basic, stil-novistic principle, and not until its spirit were caught up again. Therefore, with special reference to himself, he felt that "direst in-deed is the fate of him who longs expectantly for that which he cannot have." The young poet perhaps knew his limitations, or felt at this early stage of his poetic "new life" that the profound and vast scope of that literature and the real secret of that literary art were beyond his reach. At any rate, he felt unequal to the task of eliciting and producing this revival within himself.

Such a one, he thought, "can have no other comfort than that afforded by the memory and mental gaze of what he has loved most and has been dearest to him." He, Lorenzo, would continue to cherish and study the works of Dante, Petrarch, and Boccaccio, and all the literary "flowers" or gems of the old stilnovists. And, once more, precisely like the ancient Clytie, who at night remains with her face turned toward the western horizon, "this new Cly-tie" would "hold his mind and thoughts fixed on the last *impres-sions* and *dearest things* of *his* Sun." Those literary works em-bodied the loftiest human vision. They were the "most precious," highest achievements of the *gentilissima,* or ideal of Italian letters, now dead. And the disappearance of this ideal, directly after these "last impressions" had been made, marked the farthest point reached by that enlightening literature, *"l'ultimo termine,* beyond which human eyes cannot see." Therefore, in the absence of this enlightenment now, or obscurity of the stilnovistic principle due to the general, and his own, incomprehension of it, he could not experience greater comfort than that afforded by constant medita-tion over those works.

Accordingly, "this last horizon," or *ultimo termine* of human insight, could well stand for the death of this *gentilissima.* This had deprived him of his beloved vision. Indeed, every "lover of her eyes" was thereby deprived of "the sight of her eyes."[2] And all there was left were those works bearing the impress of the great-

---

2. The commentator here introduces a *ne* equal to *ci,* obviously wishing to generalize the effect of this metaphorical sunset.

est minds. So "there is where this new Clytie—namely, the lover of her eyes [Lorenzo or any other]—should hold his [mental] eyes firmly fixed." He should meditate on those works, and extract their profound significance. He should deduce from them the principle of those authors' poetic art, and realize it fully, definitely. However, at the same time,[3] he should reflect that "every mortal thing, although beautiful and most excellent, dies necessarily." Those men were mortal, and human their conception. Their intellectual and artistic activity necessarily had to come to an end, and their creations, however splendid and supremely excellent, could not but be *"cose finite e sottoposte alla necessità della morte."*[4] That is, they were "things done, *finished*," which were definitely and finally *fixed* for all time. And so far as these were concerned, the spiritual activity of their authors had ceased the moment they were finished. They carried death with them. They were respectively objective products of a mind, which at that moment had severed itself from them, and perhaps turned its attention to other "things" in the making. Indeed, as such, distinct and separate from the creative mind that had produced them, they were truly "dead" right there and then, the moment they were "finished." For the life of the spirit is one continuous act of transforming old "things" and creating new ones. Or, as the commentator had said in the proem, *"il fine d'una cosa è principio d'un'altra."*[5] This *fine* is its death and the commencement of the life of another. Therefore, the critic maintains, one should love those works as "finite things subject to the inevitableness of death." They are things accomplished which may be expected to originate and give rise to others. This is why this whole consideration was for him, as usual for all in similar circumstances, "a great and efficacious remedy" to console him for the death of "this lady."

Moreover, how had those poets arrived at their marvelous poetic creations? By means of their own mystic death. By rising above the material to the spiritual sphere of thought and art. By holding their mental eyes firmly fixed on the ideal of individual and uni-

---

3. Here the commentator makes another of those transitions, which lift and broaden the tenor of his discourse, transforming the historical account into a critical, philosophical discussion.

4. Cf. Text, p. 29.   5. Cf. Text, p. 24; and this study, p. 63.

versal human perfection, *and at the same time examining their ego*. *"Nosce te ipsum"* was inscribed in the temple of Apollo. And those poets had fully observed that very wise saying. They had first of all successfully endeavored to detect their personal, potential virtue, their natural capacity and inclination, their special talent and possible excellence, in a word, their "gentilesse" of heart. And then, with their longing eyes fixed on the ideal of *bellezza e gentilezza umana* derived from the ancients (philosophers and poets) and conceived as a *donna gentile,* they had merely given free scope to their own *gentilezza.*

> I' mi son un, che quando
> Amor mi spira, noto, e a quel modo
> ch'e' ditta dentro vo significando.

As already explained,[6] this was all the sincerity and spontaneity demanded by the new style. This was perhaps the point that Bonagiunta da Lucca, and Guittone, and the Notary had failed to grasp.[7] And now this also explains the great difference in the works of Dante, Petrarch, and Boccaccio, although they were all "followers" of the same school. Indeed, Boccaccio's artistic production especially, with its great variety of *genres,* and at the same time his unquestionable place in this school (according to Lorenzo), cannot be explained otherwise, and depends on this single, simple, but basic requirement of the new style. Every poet must find himself, make his own style, and create his own *genres.* With his eyes fixed on the ideal personified by the *gentilissima,* he should await her inspirations, and then merely express these conceptions faithfully, in accordance with his own artistic talent and "gentilesse." This was how those great poets had realized and attained their lofty, personal ideals. This was how they had achieved their full measure of personal human perfection, their distinction, and their excellence. This was how they had contributed to the progress of human civilization, raising the standard of intellectual and artistic life to new heights. And, finally, this was how, artistically, they had adhered to the sole, true principle of art, and maintained their remarkable originality.

6. Cf. this study, pp. 131–134.   7. Cf. Dante: *Purgatorio,* XXIV, 49–62.

Accordingly, this was how this new, or any other modern Clytie, should now, as it were, work out his own salvation, attain the state of mystic death, and enter upon his own new life of love. If he realizes the necessity of the mystic death (as above explained) with respect to those poets and their works, he "will easily realize this condition and necessity with respect to himself"; that is, he will realize the necessity of his own mystic death, or conscious spirituality necessary to his poetic, creative genius. Therefore, let him, too, adhere to the principle implied in the saying *"Nosce te ipsum,"* and persevere in this thought until death shall come. "Death (the mystic death) will return his sun to this new Clytie, just as the dawn returns it to Clytie turned flower." In other words, the hidden significance or implied ideal of that body of literature will actually "dawn" upon him when he himself shall have attained a state of pure spirituality. "For then *his soul,* freed of the body, will be able to consider the beauty of *the soul of this lady,* [which is] much more beautiful than that formerly visible to his eyes." And this because "the perception (luce) by the human eyes is as dark as shade in comparison with the light perceived by the soul." That is, the spiritual eye perceives much more clearly. Finally, the clear comprehension of this esoteric meaning, coincident with his own spiritual elevation, will remove the veil of the literal meaning, and the glorious ideal, principle and all, will stand revealed before his loving, mental gaze.

This death, therefore, will actually be like the "dawn" of a new day for the modern Clytie. And the comparison is now complete, the simile perfect. *Just as the literal expression of the ideal embodied in the literature of that first period was a definite poetic conception, which, once fixed in those artistic creations, remained a series of "finite things" subject to change* (inasmuch as creative art is one continuous renewal of old forms);[8] *and just as this veil of fiction obscuring that ideal, needed to be pierced by a spiritual penetration of the recondite, true significance of the literal expression, in order that the ideal itself might stand revealed; so the spiritual elevation of this new lover of that poetic ideal, which will*

8. *Il principio dell'amorosa vita procede dalla morte,* or "the life of love springs from death." Cf. Text, p. 24; and this study, p. 63.

permit him to raise or tear away the said veil, will be literally the dawning on him of this very ideal. This will be his intellectual, artistic birth, the commencement of his similarly original poetic production, in which only the principle of his art and the humanistic ideal pursued by him will be derived from his beloved predecessors and great authorities on the new life of love.

In this sense, and in this manner only, the critic implies, could the much needed and longed-for revival of Italian letters be brought about. At least, this is my modest interpretation of this difficult, complex comment, with respect to its historico-critical import.[9]

Postponing for the present a number of questions that arise from it, and the various inferences that immediately suggest themselves, largely in confirmation of our previous deductions; let us now return to the mysterious appropriateness of the month of April to designate theoretically the most suitable, natural season of the year, through which both "lady" and poet become, as it were, spiritualized simultaneously, and the new Clytie is initiated into the "new life."

9. Remembering my interpretation of "the brightest star visible in the west" (made in a previous chapter, cf. pp. 139–140) as the Italian literary ideal of Lorenzo's own time, the reader may think that there is contradiction here, between what I said then and what I say now with respect to this revival of Italian letters. The latter appears here to be only *hoped for,* whereas there it seemed to be already *present.* But, if he will also recall the content of the following pages (141–142), where I brought out the still *idealistic* stage of this revival then, and will remember, too, that between the date of the sonnets and the date of the commentary there is a span of over twenty years, he will see that, instead of contradiction, there is confirmation here of the two deductions independently made. In fact, if "the dearest friend" of Dantean flavor, who silently assents to his discussion of the matter there, and whom he apparently draws into the preparation necessary for the *wish* to become a realization, is, as I suspect and there suggested (n. 3, p. 136), none other than Poliziano; and if "the best Florentine minds" of his day are, as I also imagine, his circle of neo-Platonic, literary friends: we may well conclude that we have there a sure indication of the conscious beginning of a definite movement to *revive,* as I say, the previous ideal of Italian letters; a movement in which the young Lorenzo and Poliziano must have had the *magna pars.* (Cf. pp. 137–138.) On the other hand, it is also likely that, inasmuch as when the Magnificent wrote his commentary this revival was already in full swing, and his own as well as his friend's literary productions were already accomplished facts, the commentator now confuses slightly the previous hope with the present realization. But, I repeat, with the possible exception of this apparent, slight confusion, due, in this case, to the late date of the commentary with respect to the sonnets, there is no contradiction here. On the contrary, the two separate deductions drawn from the two separate, distinct passages, confirm each other, and I feel that substantially my interpretation, here as well as there, is correct.

CHAPTER III

Lorenzo's Understanding of the Concept of Mystic Death
in Relation to His Method of Literary Research.

TO sum up and fix the points made so far: we concluded above that the apparent date of the "lady's" death was not a date at all, and that, in any case, this vague indication could not possibly refer to the presumed extinction of the literary ideal thus personified. Consequently, we inferred that the sole mention of the month could merely mark the propitious "season" of an unspecified year, when probably the poet himself realized this "concept" in full, or definitely; and, in view of the implied appropriateness of the said season for such a realization, we also decided that the significance mysteriously attached to the month of April presumably involved a theory. Finally, the preceding interpretation of the whole comment, made in the light of the esoteric meaning of Sonnet I, has given us an inkling of the philosophic "naturalness" of this time of the year for such an occurrence, and also, I believe, a fairly clear idea of the sort of death the author is talking about.[1]

This elucidation of the mystic death, made incidentally and on occasion in the course of the said interpretation, now also needs to be recapitulated and brought home, in order to apprehend clearly the supposed theory.

We are now convinced that, as the commentator maintains in the proem, this *principio* of his actually deals with the "principle" of the mystic death; to which we may now add of "lady" and poet conjointly, and especially of himself as the author of these sonnets and all the following *nuova vita*. Of course, he himself never prefixes the adjective "mystic" to this philosophical term of medieval origin, and if I do, it is merely for want of a better epithet with which to distinguish properly for the modern reader its exact con-

---

1. Recall here also my previous elucidation of the term *morte* made in the course of my interpretation and discussion of the proem, on p. 63, and pp. 64–74.

notation in the figurative sense in which it is used here from its literal meaning of physical death. But there is nothing strictly mystical, religious, or transcendental implied here in his understanding and use of the old conception. Lorenzo was not concerned with the contemplative life of the mystics, and probably there was no room in his realistic philosophy for their mental speculations of a purely theological character. Indeed, we may recall that in the proem he explicitly limits his present subject to *quello amore che s'estende solamente ad amare l'umana creatura*.[2] And now we know from his subsequent development of this theme that the object of his "single and constant love," or the "human creations" in which he was chiefly concerned, were the highest, artistic products of the human genius: primarily and specifically, those poetic works in which he found incarnated the ideal of human perfection itself and the very principle of the "new life of love." Consequently, all he means by *morte* as the principle and commencement of his poetic "new life," is merely the sort of spiritual elevation I suggested above, in my interpretation of this second comment: the spiritualization of both "lady" and poet, in order that, on the one hand, the true essence of that literature, its artistic principle, and its humanistic purpose may stand out; and, on the other, in order that the poet himself may be in the proper frame of mind and spiritual mood to penetrate, realize, and appreciate all this. Lover and beloved die, as it were, in the flesh (he with respect to his physical self and the material world about him, and she with respect to the literal meaning of the fiction, or artificial "body" in which she is incarnated), and their souls, rising out of their bodies, enter the world of pure spirit, where communion of mind and heart is perfect. As the author puts it in his figurative language, then the *soul* of this new Clytie is able to consider the beauty of the *soul* of this "lady," which is much more beautiful than that formerly visible to his eyes. Or, as we may specify again, more clearly in words devoid of all *sovrasenso*: with respect to himself, the poet puts aside worldly cares and interests, pays no attention to his functional being beyond the bare necessities of physical life, disregards particularly all pleasures of the

2. Cf. Text, p. 14; and this study, p. 13.

senses, and, rising above the consideration of things simply from their material aspect, elevates his mind and heart to a plane of spiritual fervor and lofty thinking only; and at the same time, with respect to his "lady," or personification of the ideal embodied in those "finite things" he loved so well, he merely applies himself to a zealous, intensive study of that literature, assumes a favorable attitude, sharpens his wits, and strives with all his intellectual might to understand it thoroughly.

This is why *morte* is truly the first, absolute requisite for a proper initiation into the "new life." And this is why it will be called *sì gentile oggi e sì bella* in the next sonnet.[3] For, itself thus divested of its external, physical character (or spiritualized with respect to its real essence), its *virtus* and excellence, or qualification to typify the spiritual rebirth, have been brought out, and its "gentilesse" in this connection has become manifest.

As we see, then, there is nothing mysterious or extraordinary in this sort of poetic mysticism. The above connotation of the "mystic death," as I call it, merely implies an ordinary metaphorical usage of the phenomenon of death, especially common in the Middle Ages, to signify mental absorption in philosophical or scientific problems. Inasmuch as the true, *human* life is spiritual activity, anyone who does not exercise this distinctive human faculty of the intellect may properly be called dead, metaphorically speaking.[4]

Moreover, here the author uses this metaphor merely to signify the spiritual and psychological state of mind necessary to engage profitably in a serious, profound study of the said literature, preparatory to his own or anyone else's poetic activity along the same humanistic lines and following the same artistic principle. His implication, which is all of a critical and methodical nature, therefore regards chiefly *the proper approach,* in his opinion, to that body of literature. He clearly implies that those poetic works conceal in the fictitious meaning of the literal expression, which is their "body," a true esoteric meaning of vast and profound hu-

3. Cf. Text, p. 31, sonnet, l. 3; or this study, p. 86, Sonnet III, l. 3.
4. Cf., for instance, the anecdote of Guido Cavalcanti in the graveyard, in Boccaccio's *Decamerone*, Giornata VI, Novella 9.

manistic importance, which is their "soul"; and that the study necessary to penetrate and appreciate this real significance requires the deepest concentration of the mind and the highest, purest devotion to the implied ideal. No one, he seems to say, can expect to become imbued with the real spirit of those authors who has not first understood them thoroughly, and no one can arrive at this true, complete understanding by a hasty, superficial, and supercilious reading of their works, or without a sincere, spontaneous, and deep love of the ideal embodied therein. In other words, as I said when this technical term first came up for discussion in the course of interpreting the proem, it all seems to me a matter of psychology.[5] Nothing else is implied by it here than the suggestion of an ordinary, *intelligent method of procedure* for the study of those particular authors especially.

On the other hand, the implication also is that this approach is by no means easy, as I have just said. In fact, two more sonnets will be devoted to signifying the extreme difficulty of extracting and perceiving the soul of that literature, before the poet may be said to have finished his formal initiation into the new life, and may finally proceed with his own *versi importanti simili amorosi subietti.*[6] The spiritual agony he must endure as student and critic of this literature, the pangs and throes of death he must actually go through, in order to graduate, as it were, from this apprenticeship, and receive a figurative diploma entitling him to "commence" his own *nuova vita,* this will all properly be described in connection with the interpretation of the comments on those sonnets.

But here we need already some idea at least of the nature of the difficulty, or better, of the exact method of procedure he proposes to attain the end desired—in order that we may have precise and complete knowledge of the kind of experience called "death," for which the month of April is supposed to be particularly and naturally suitable. This elucidation now will also tell us how the "lady" in turn "dies" in the mind of the critic, or precisely by what system the modern initiate into the "new life" comes to a full realization of the ideal and principle of his predecessors.

5. Cf. this study, p. 71.   6. Cf. Text, p. 17; and this study, n. 12, p. 19.

This system is none other than the stilnovistic method, with which, I trust, we are now familiar, after the long discussion of it in a previous chapter.[7] Indeed, we ourselves have used it in order to arrive at a clear and true understanding of the author's own concept of *bellezza e gentilezza umana* following in his own footsteps.[8] It is the *natural,* scientific method of research, suggested by his very definition of "human gentilesse,"[9] which in turn, is the result of a would-be strictly historical and philological study, and itself the nicest example of the normal exercise of this "supremely human function of judicious discrimination." As I have repeatedly said for purpose of clarification and emphasis, it is the truly *humanistic* method of critical investigation, whereby the self-educator, exercising his distinctive human prerogative of critical judgment, strives to detect the essence of "things," brings out their particular, individual *virtus,* and, by comparison with other "things" of the same species, passes judgment on its excellence and "gentilesse." Finally, it is the method, at once *analytic and synthetic,* whereby the critic dissects, as it were, the "thing" under consideration, only to put it together again in a reorganized concept of his own, after he has distinguished and valued its formative elements, and the very "soul" of the "thing," thus brought out, has become the "soul" of his own, new artistic recreation of the original "thing." In other words, it is the modern method of literary criticism called "creative," which Francesco De Sanctis practiced, and Benedetto Croce has defined theoretically.

Examples of this Laurentian theory and practice, of unquestionable stilnovistic brand and derivation, are not lacking in this very *principio.* Indeed, this whole *principio* in itself, theoretic, demonstrative, experimental, and experiential in character, is perhaps the most outstanding and typical of his general procedure. But, to limit myself to smaller ones already studied, I recall again in this connection his just-mentioned illuminating research on the real connotation of the term *gentile,* which culminates in his acute definition of *gentilezza umana,* a veritable, unexpected revelation. I recall also again his nice discernment of the real, essential quality

---

7. Cf. this study, Pt. II, chap. iv.   8. *Idem,* chap. iii.
9. Cf. Text, pp. 56–58, and above, pp. 111–113.

of the physical death, which is the basis of his critical judgment of the "gentilesse" of the mystic death. And now I shall add another, taken from this very comment on the second sonnet. I wish to show just why and how he *really* came to compare himself to the ancient Clytie; which explanation, besides serving as another demonstration of his creative criticism, will give us the *real* origin of this sonnet.

Choice of the Metaphor of Clytie.

To understand what the commentator is actually saying here, in this stilnovistic (that is, realistic and esoteric) reconstruction of the history of this sonnet; and especially to realize what took place in the mind of the poet, now critic of his own composition; we must reconsider for a moment the first part of his comment in the light of my critical interpretation of the whole.[10] The reader should not imagine, as indeed he is artfully led to believe, that the poet, necessarily, actually went in his garden to enjoy the beauty of nature in April, and thus apparently consoled himself for the death of his lady; which death, if you please, occurred conveniently during this particularly suitable season of the year, natural for her demise and propitious to his edification, as he promptly proceeded to console himself! This would not make sense, or would be absurd in itself, inasmuch as such an action on his part, accompanied by such an intention, if taken literally, would hardly be either commendatory to him or complimentary to her memory. That is, it would not be consistent with his deep sorrow, for him to seek enjoyment and thus console himself for the death of his lady, nor in keeping with his high regard for her, to wish to do so, indeed, to proceed promptly to do so, with this precise intention. Besides, that is not what the text, studied in its careful syntax, actually says. As we observed before, the text merely says, or at least clearly implies, that April, or early spring, was simply the "character" of the season marking the lady's death. And now we should observe that what ostensibly "prompted" (*mosse*) the poet to go out and recreate his soul in the midst of

10. Cf. Text, p. 27; and above, pp. 149, 158–165.

such delightful, varied bloom, was not primarily this condition of the earth and character of the season *per se,* but all this *with reference to his lady's death.* For her death was his chief, indeed, sole preoccupation at the moment; and, in fact, what did delight his eyes and actually did recreate his soul, was his *mental activity,* whereby, "tutto occupato nel pensiero e memoria di colei, pareva che tutte le cose reducessi a suo proposito." Knowing, as we now do, the real essence of this "lady" and the exact nature of her "death," both with respect to herself and with respect to him, it is obvious that what he was really doing was investigating or considering this complex concept; carrying his study, stilnovistically, into a would-be scientific verification of the veracity of the concept. This he established by comparison with the proof offered by nature (nature literally and figuratively understood, as we shall see). It is not so obvious, perhaps, but nevertheless a fact that he was really engaged in a comparative, critical study of other "examples" of the poetic mystic death. This he did in order that, first of all, he himself might realize this principle by detecting and comparing the essential *virtus* of each as such; and then, also in order that by a "judicious distinction" of their respective nicety, excellence, and "gentilesse" to typify this principle, he, too, might perhaps discover or invent a similar "example," which, besides having the same essential quality, would incarnate best his own reconception, and fit perfectly his own particular case. In other words, as a modern initiate into the "new life," he was seeking the "example" par excellence that would signify perfectly the present state of Italian poetry and his own spiritual condition, with respect to the literary ideal now spent, of poet longing for its revival. And this was why he went out in the garden. This was why as soon as he perceived the already mythologized *tornalsole* among the other flowers, he was especially captivated by it. For, although the other flowers, too, seemed to him to illustrate the mystic death, conforming to this principle, and demonstrating the veracity of this concept, it was, I say, the already established mythological character of the *tornalsole,* typifying eternal love for the intellectual light and signifying the longing for the return of this light, that seemed to him to incarnate perfectly the concept he was then revolving in his poetic mind. It was this *literal* "gentilesse" of the mythologized *tornalsole,* of literally Roman brand or adoption at least, and typically Roman in the excellence of its poetic fancy, that distinguished it from the others, and now constituted its special distinction here, and particular excellence to embody his new conception. Wherefore,[11] it was immediately adopted. That is, this myth, or *Clitia* with the capital *C,* and not so much the original, physical *tornalsole;* this myth, I say, was immediately adapted as a simile to represent the present spiritual condition and experience of "this new Clytie." Therefore, it was much more likely that, instead of going to his garden, he actually went to his library; where, in fact, it was more plausible and natural that he would find the various "flowers" he meant to examine. There were, indeed, the manuscripts from which very probably, he was even then compiling his anthology of "stilnovistic" literature. There were, especially, his great, favorite authors and absolute authorities on the principle of the "new life." And there undoubtedly were at least the main Latin classics, which he well knew had inspired the authors of the new Italian literature, and thus passed on to them the literary ideal now molding this modern *gentilissima.*[12] So that, I maintain, especially in view of the task he meant to perform, it was infinitely more likely that "the future commentator of his own verses" in reality went to his library. This immediate task was, as commentator, to explain incidentally the origin of his simile of Clytie and, as creative critic of the school of the *stil novo,* primarily to reproduce his whole experience realistically. His task was to synthesize now in the form of an experiential reconstruction what before he had analyzed as student-critic of that literature, or had perhaps only vaguely been conscious of in the fervor of his poetic intuition. Moreover, as a stilnovist, or *humanist,* his task was not only to reconstruct his personal experience of the mystic death, but to demonstrate to others how they, too, might

11. The text introduces this discovery with the connective *E però,* which indicates the process of critical examination in the course of which this particular flower was first noticed among the others, then considered, and finally chosen, immediately.

12. The list of these authors, besides Virgil, of course, would certainly include Ovid, Tibullus, Catullus, and Propertius, recalled in the proem. Cf. Text, p. 20, and this study, p. 51.

achieve it. In other words, he meant to philosophize, as he does, on this humanistic principle, to generalize it, and to teach it to others, in order that this *principio* of his might perhaps serve as a manual of poetic art in the longed-for revival of Italian poetry. And for all this, I reiterate, his library was surely the most natural and convenient place to be in. On the other hand, it is also possible, of course, that in the course of this study, he also actually went down to his garden, perhaps taking a book with him, literally to refresh his mind and spirit in the invigorating air of April and in the midst of the flowering, physical nature. Indeed, it is not at all unlikely that, as he probably paced up and down the paths of his garden, all absorbed in his critical meditation and poetic conception, it was actually the sight of the little *tornalsole* which recalled to his mind the myth of Clytie. It is even beautiful and inspiring, as this comment is intended to be, to imagine that this was how he actually came to conceive this particular sonnet. But, whether this be historical or not[13] it remains that, physically as well as spiritually, he must have done the greater part of this literary research in his metaphorical garden, in the midst of his "literary flowers." And especially, it remains that obviously he found the mythological Clytie, not casually, nor literally in his garden, but after the most diligent research, carried out with rare human "gentilesse," or critical acumen—in his Ovid!

What an interesting revelation is this for the history of the sonnet, and, undoubtedly, for the history of many another in classical Italian literature! Especially, how illuminating is this with reference to the history of the sweet new style, at least according to Lorenzo! For it is evident now that the commentator here reveals incidentally that, as I surmised above, he carried his research on the poetic mystic death into the field of Latin literature. The critic and historian well knew that this *humanistic* principle of education was the principle of the stilnovistic "new life," and he, there-

13. For this supposition to be valid and also consistent with the specification of April in the narrative, the *tornalsole* in Tuscany would have to bloom in April. This is not the case. (Cf. above, n. 2, p. 90.) But, in view of the artificiality connected with the specification of April, and in consideration of the fact that the *tornalsole* is a summer flower, we may infer that the poet's personal and direct observation of this flower in bloom, is at least an indication that this sonnet was composed in summertime.

fore, naturally studied the Latin classics as well, in his effort to
realize himself this principle of the new style. He expected to find
there, too, examples of the poetic mystic death. In fact, as we have
just seen, it was precisely there that he found the example par excellence, the oldest, perhaps, the most elementary, and the most
susceptible of general application. This, moreover, accords with
his philological derivation of the adjective *gentile* used to describe
the *donna* personifying the literary ideal of the stilnovists. It also
shows that in his critical opinion as historian of all *Italian* poetry,
both in Latin and in *volgare,* just as the new poetry in *volgare* was
essentially Roman in character, origin, and excellence, so the
Latin, or old Italian poetry, was essentially "stilnovistic" before the
coining of this term. That is, it conformed with the same principle. And, indeed, in his understanding of the principle of the
stil novo, this style knew no epochs and was always "new," inasmuch as it implied what was for him the true, eternal principle of
a poetic art that continually "renews" itself. Hence, no doubt, the
hoped-for revival of this ideal!

Let us not anticipate, and, especially let us not lose sight of our
present objective.

Philosophical Basis of the Realism with Which the Mystic Death Is Portrayed.

THIS long introduction to the study of the esoteric meaning suspected in the remark that the poet's lady died naturally and fittingly
"on a month of April," has been, I remind the reader, for the purpose of acquiring precise and complete knowledge of the real significance of this curious indication, so specific and yet indefinite;
and this in order that we might perceive more readily now the implied naturalness and appropriateness of that month for that occurrence. Now we are ready, I believe, to expatiate on the glimpse we
got of this naturalness when we first considered the physical environment in which the poet found himself, as he stepped into his
garden all absorbed in the thought of his lady's death.[14] Now, however, we are also cognizant of his real spiritual condition and precise object at the time; we are conscious of the true nature of the

14. Cf. p. 158.

death recalled, as well as of the fact that it was primarily with respect to his own poetic, mystic death; and, finally, we are aware of the psychological character and didactic purpose of his whole experience. We may, therefore, proceed safely with our inferences, keeping in mind all these elements of the complex situation.

But there is one point we may have forgotten in the meantime, a point which is fundamental and essential to the full appreciation of the *real* naturalness here insisted upon by the commentator. We must not forget either the realism of the new style's conceptualism, which required that every expression be a sort of *verbum factum caro,* or the would-be scientific basis, on which the acquisition of all "true" knowledge purported to rest, following the instructive, educative method derived from the very principle of human "gentilesse."[15] The requirement of realism in all poetic conceptions, we should remember, rested on the philosophical principle that "essendo la forma e spezie . . . immortale, di necessità si conviene sempre si muova dalla materia." That is ("species" being the inseparable, outward appearance of the "form"), since form and expression (which are therefore identical) are the indissoluble, vital elements of the immortal spirit, the eternal creative spirit of man (which is his distinctive human prerogative, or "gentilesse") *must always move from matter.*[16] Likewise, the professed scientific foundation for all true knowledge, which supports this realism, also rested on a sort of axiom; namely, the principle that the example of nature substantiating a given concept was the absolute, ultimate test of its veracity.

Very well, these two principles stand at the bottom of the author's reconstruction now of his experience. Apparently, they implied that, since the physical reality of any "thing" is never in life found disconnected from its spiritual essence, the two cannot and must not be dissociated. Or, as in the case in point, since the activity of the human mind ceases with physical death, and, conversely, man's physical existence always accompanies his active, spiritual life, the two must never be dissociated in any psychologi-

15. Cf. pp. 6–7; and my whole discussion of Lorenzo's metaphorical method, pp. 122–134.
16. Cf. Text, p. 24, ll. 12–13; and this study, pp. 63, and 143.

cal study of his mental and affective development. Moreover, by extension, this principle was apparently read also into the life of plants and animals—inasmuch as they, too, are a combination or, better, unity of "body" and "soul," as long as they live. At least, this principle was, I say, also applied poetically to the study of plant and animal life.[17] At any rate, it followed that, since there is no human spiritual activity dissociated from man's physical life, the two must influence each other and presumably be interdependent. Nature, of which man is a part, surely does contribute physically to his spiritual well-being; and, just as the climate, the atmospheric changes, and the seasons, all affect the life of plants, so man, although no longer a plant, is similarly affected by these natural conditions, in so far as he is an animal. Therefore, in any consideration of his spiritual life, bound as this is to his parallel physical existence, they must be not only accounted for, but also counted upon for the proper development of his mind and heart. In fact, that other strictly humanistic saying, *mens sana in corpore sano,* is found side by side with the one significantly cited here by Lorenzo, *nosce te ipsum.* And this explains what I described above as the theoretic, demonstrative, experimental, and experiential character of this wholly psychological process. This is the philosophical, scientific foundation of the mystic death, portrayed here in this peculiar, realistic manner, in the very act of its occurring, and precisely in the way it was actually achieved by the author. And now let us proceed definitely with our inferential conjectures.

17. Recall Dante's understanding of the continuous gradation observable in the proportion of form and matter in all creation, from the lowest or most "material" forms to the highest or purest "forms"; and particularly his concept of an imperceptible line of demarcation between the angelic nature and the human soul, on the one hand, and between the human soul and the most perfect soul of brutes, on the other. *Convivio,* III, vii, 5–7.

CHAPTER IV

Esoteric Meaning of the Month of April: (a) *the*
"Gentilesse" of Spring.

SINCE we are therefore dealing with a purely psychological
process not dissociated from its physiologic elements and
natural factors, since we are dealing with a principle of human education and a method of intellectual development, since
the whole experience is one of mental study and concentration in
a piece of literary research and creative criticism involving the apprehension of the humanistic scope and artistic principle of all
"Italian" literature; in a word, since the phenomenon here called
"death" is in the nature of a spiritual contemplation or intellectual, educative process whereby the student of this literary art arrives at its comprehension, masters it, and becomes imbued with
its spirit: what is there in the natural character of the month of
April that really or theoretically, literally or figuratively, makes
this particular period of the year suitable and especially appropriate to such a simultaneous, mystic death of "lady" and poet?

First with respect to the poet, and taking the specific, natural
virtue of April in its literal implication. Perhaps the following
verses of the aspirant's greatest master have already occurred to us
in this connection:

> Temp'era dal principio del mattino,
>   e 'l sol montava 'n su con quelle stelle
> ch'eran con lui quando l'amor divino
> mosse di prima quelle cose belle;
>   sì ch'*a bene sperar m'era cagione*
>   di quella fera a la gaetta pelle
> *l'ora del tempo e la dolce stagione;*
>
> Dante, *Inferno*, I, 37–43.

Even more apropos, because the additional, further specification of
the early morning hour is lacking,[1] we may have been reminded
also of these verses of his other great master:

---

1. This additional, further specification of *the best hour of the day* for the achievement

Zefiro torna, e 'l bel tempo rimena,
e i fiori e l'erbe, sua dolce famiglia
e garrir Progne, e pianger Filomena,
e primavera candida e vermiglia.
   Ridono i prati, e 'l ciel si rasserena;
Giove s'allegra di mirar sua figlia;
l'aria, e l'acqua, e la terra è d'amor piena;
ogni animal d'amar si riconsiglia.
            Petrarca, *Rime sparse,* Sonnet CCCX, 1–8.

But we do not need either of these citations, or any other similar
poetic reminiscence of a common cognizance registered frequently in all literatures, especially in early Italian poetry, to accept the general consensus of popular and scientific opinion that,
normally, the spring of the year is *naturally* the most suitable and
propitious season for both physical and mental human development. We ourselves have all experienced personally, no doubt, the
natural, beneficent effects on us of the returning spring. A sort of
new energy, mysteriously injected into us, or perhaps accumulated
during the winter months, seems to pervade gradually all our system. It begins to operate, and, arousing us from our torpidness,
awakens also our intellectual and affective organs. There is more
than mere likeness, there is virtual identity, both literally and figuratively, between the sort of renaissance or rejuvenation of nature
in spring and the synchronous reinvigoration of man's body and
spirit. Indeed, there is correspondence, and, undoubtedly, even a
certain intimate relation, in the nature of cause and effect; which
may not determine the spirituality of man, but certainly assists it,
and is essential to his mental as well as physical development.
   Reflect that there is really no time more naturally and spontaneously conducive to man's spiritual communion with Nature herself than early spring; and that in the course of this communion
he, either consciously or unconsciously, observes in nature what is
likewise taking place within himself. In the course of some long
or short walk in the country, which surely everybody at least likes
to take especially in spring, and which everybody probably takes

of the mystic death, which here intrudes slightly, but does not discord, will come up in
connection with a later discussion in which it has a part, and will properly be taken up
there. See pp. 250 and 264–265.

at some time or other during the season, I do not believe that there
is a soul so entirely materialistic, unintelligent, and insensitive to
the glorious renaissance in and about him, who does not stop to
observe it in some specific, concrete form, or in its ensemble, and
who thereupon does not perhaps remark on the beauty of nature.
Others more cultured and refined, or endowed with "gentle
hearts," as the stilnovists said, will instinctively stop to observe perhaps a tiny new leaf working its way out of the stem, or a bud
opening up to give way to the forming blossom, or a bird carrying
material for its nest. And meanwhile they will be thinking, considering, marveling over this truly wonderful miracle of nature.
Meanwhile they are learning, meanwhile they are educating
themselves, meanwhile they are exercising naturally, spontaneously their "human gentilesse," meanwhile, finally, they may become conscious of the fact that they themselves are participating
in this great miracle of all nature. Man, like the plants and flowers,
and like all the animals, is thus responding naturally and instinctively to the periodic call of "new life." And the plants and flowers,
the fresh air and warm sun, all this condition of the earth then, is
assisting him, indeed, contributing to his physical and mental development in preparation for his "new life." Precisely as Lorenzo
implies in his real or realistic portrayal of his own preparation for
this "new life"; when he, too, very likely went literally to his
amenissimi prati, there to *"recreate his soul* with the very pleasant
sight of the varied bloom in April."[2]
  Let us pass to the application of this significance to the kind of
reaction he personally experienced under those favorable natural
circumstances, as the outcome of this very experience later evinces.
This reaction now implies the literal usage, on the authoritative
example of nature, of man's physical and spiritual condition in

2. Lorenzo's use of April, involving his interpretation of the stilnovistic concept of the
"gentilesse" of early spring and his verification of this concept by personal experience, can
be supported by more than simple observation. The *scientific* basis of the concept has recently been brought out by Professor Peter P. Lazarev of the Moscow Institute of Experimental Medicine. In an interview given to the United Press on June 14, 1935, Professor
Lazarev is reported to have said that among the outstanding conclusions reached by him
are the following: "Sensitivity in the brain at birth is nearly zero, after which it increases,
reaching the maximum at the age of twenty. It then declines, but never reaches zero again
because death intervenes. Brain sensitivity varies during the seasons, reaching its high

spring, to carry on, therefore actually in spring, a purely intellectual study which necessitates the use of a metaphorical garden.
(Remember that the poet is not so much interested in the study of
nature and human physiology *per se* as he is concerned with the
scientific method of human education; he is here absorbed in the
purely critical problem of detecting the "soul" of the *gentilissima*
Italian poetry implying such an educative principle.) April, then,
is propitious to the manifestation of the special virtue or talent of
the poet. This literal propitiousness of April can only mean that,
theoretically or in Lorenzo's opinion, nature in spring creates a
favorable environment and a proper condition of man's body and
mind—a situation which is most conducive to the mental activity
and creative criticism in which the poet is now engaged. He has
found it to be so, and, again on the strength of common and scientific experience, no one can deny that, normally at least, this is
so.

On the other hand, it may be observed that, even if, for the sake
of argument, it is granted that the other seasons may be less inspiring, or have perhaps a different charm, which is not applicable to
the poetic concept of spiritual renaissance, neither is spring limited
to April, nor does the beneficent influence of nature cease with the
end of the spring season. Conversely, it may be further observed
that "gentle hearts" at least, do not cease to respond to the environment of physical nature, either during the other months of
spring, or during the other seasons, especially autumn; nor is the
principle of *mens sana in corpore sano* vain and negligible the
other eleven months of the year. The life of man and all animals
and plants goes on without interruption for the duration of its
natural period depending on circumstances, even in winter, when
nature seems relatively dead. The rhythm may be reduced or

points in spring and autumn and low points in winter and summer. *Sensitivity is highest
in April, thus mankind feels best in the spring.* The race has no influence on brain sensitivity, *but climate has,* hence Northern peoples are more sensitive mentally and more
energetic than Southern races." (Cf. the *New York Herald-Tribune,* Saturday, June 15,
1935, p. 1.) The italics are mine, and not all the points thus brought out have bearing on
the detail at present under special consideration, but these conclusions of Professor Lazarev
will be found to bear directly on the stilnovistic theory of springtime as a whole; and so I
quote them all here with the suggestion that the reader keep them in mind in the course of
his reading of all three sections constituting this chapter.

varied during the other months, but it certainly goes on all the year.

Very true. But the essential point of the theory here is that April is *the month par excellence* marking the *principio* of nature's annual revival of the eternal creative spirit, and the resumption of the original rhythm. The point here is that April is a *formative* period, or period of *preparation,* necessary to the actual renaissance, which follows eventually. And the point here is that April is the *normal* period used by nature for this preparation. In fact, May and June mark the blossoming forth of the plants germinated and grown in April, so that, as a Sicilian proverb says significantly, apropos of this fact, *"Aprili fa li sciuri e Maiu n'avi l'onuri."*[3] Later, the summer months present the accomplished fact, or fruit of all this labor, and mark the harvest period. Then autumn follows, the calm and peace of which are marred by the depressing thought of the approaching end. And, finally, comes winter, which closes the cycle with an uncomfortable period of relative inaction, or apparent death of all things. The poet sings:

> Come d'autunno si levan le foglie
> l'una appresso de l'altra, fin che 'l ramo
> vede a la terra tutte le sue spoglie,
> similemente. . . . *etc.*
> *Inferno*, III, 112–115.

And I am here reminded also of Leopardi's *Sabato del villaggio,* in which this most unhappy, modern poet recasts the old theme, and, within the literal as well as figurative span of a week-end, contrasts sadly the joy of Saturday, or spring, or youth, with the melancholy of Sunday, or summer, or mature age, at the thought of the approaching "blue Monday," or sorrowful autumn, or depressing old age.[4] Therefore, April is really the basic, momentous month of the year. It is the most normal, natural period of spiritual preparation and artistic conception. And for this reason it constitutes the perfect month intended to mark the occurrence of the poetic mystic death, or initial stage of the "new life." In fact, in this very experience, its natural *virtus* performs literally its

3. April "makes" the flowers and May gets the credit.
4. Cf. Giacomo Leopardi, *Canti,* in any edition.

function of physical trainer and spiritual inspirer, while figuratively it corresponds to the period of preparation, in the course of which the new poet seeks light and inspiration in the study of the *gentilissima* Italian poetry. Moreover, it constitutes at once the example par excellence furnished by nature, on which the scientific character of this preparation finally rests. And this is its distinction, excellence, or "gentilesse." This is why both "lady" and poet die mystically during this month, without any further specification of day or year.[5]

THE final trend of this discourse has led us now imperceptibly to the discussion of the broader aspect of the esoteric significance of this indefinite specification. For the above discussion has suggested the insensible, natural transition by which the poet himself passes from the literal to the figurative usage of his concept of April—in order to explain now a situation which retains all the elements of the one considered, and differs only in so far as it restricts and also broadens the application of the principle deduced from nature's course. I mean the situation presented by the specific instance of the natural process of human life, whose cycle covers a much longer period than that employed by the earth for its annual revolution. This is really the problem in which the humanist commentator is finally interested, and the critical study of the "gentilesse" of April has all been for the purpose of applying this scientific basis, metaphorically and withal substantially, to the proper regulation, following nature's course, of the true *human* life in the strictest and noblest sense of the word. Therefore, it is not hard to see, especially in view of the now established import and purpose of the mystic death, that what he means to indicate by this poetic, metaphorical usage of his concept of April, is simply the time in the aspirant's natural life which he considers most appropriate to devote to a period of zealous, critical study of the pre-

5. It is hardly necessary to point out that, of course, the above characterization of the month of April applies to the temperate zone of the northern hemisphere, with special reference to Italy; and that, furthermore, it disregards the varying "Aprils" in the lives of the different plants. Lorenzo is here viewing nature in its *ensemble,* as it appears normally around him, and is not concerned with biological variations due either to the special nature of a particular plant, or to different, abnormal climatic conditions. Cf. also the note on p. 180.

vious humanist poets, preparatory to his own proper initiation into
the "new life."

Following nature's course and example, this time corresponds,
of course, to the period of youth, or, more specifically, to the *età
giovenile e tenera,* as he calls it with special reference to himself,
when, in the defense of his subject, he incidentally assigns an approximate, early date to these sonnets of the *principio.*[6] That is, it
corresponds to *the period of adolescence* in the Dantean sense,
when, as the Magnificent now implies, "gentle" human nature, in
the manner of physical nature, awakens to its distinctive, intellectual faculty, or human "gentilesse," and sets it in motion. It corresponds to *the metaphorical springtime in man's natural life,*
which is naturally best suited to mental development, to the formation of character, and to the acquisition of good habits of
thought as well as good taste in all things. It corresponds, I say, to
those *formative years,* when the human mind is more readily open
to all sorts of new and varied concepts, and the heart is also ea-
gerly disposed to entertain noble sentiments and refined feelings.
That is *normally* the time when our natural inclinations and special talent, if we have one, begin to be felt strongly, and when the
creative spirit also begins to manifest itself in us in the form of a
spontaneous desire to translate this potential self into something
concrete embodying our *ego. Then* it is that, having definitely become conscious of the special force or virtue urging us from
within (*nosce te ipsum*), we engage in creative criticism of others'
"finite things," and form our conceptions. Modifying or changing
the "dead" past, revolutionizing or transforming the world about
us, we create our own big or little world of realities and fancies.
Young manhood is, indeed, the age of dreams, of lofty ideals, and
of ambitious undertakings. It is truly man's "April time," marking his spiritual rebirth and the commencement of his really *nuova
vita d'amore.* Finally, it is the period of man's *giovinezza* corresponding to this initiation into the "new life"; a poetic theme
commonly sung especially in Lorenzo's epoch, when it was described as a unique, fleeting opportunity not to be lost, likewise

6. Cf. in this study the whole discussion of the date of Lorenzo's *Commentary* in contradistinction to the date of the sonnets themselves, pp. 35–45, and especially, pp. 42–45.

celebrated by him in a *canto carnascialesco* of very light vein,[7] and handed down to us by tradition in this precise conceptual form of *l'aprile della vita*.[8] This is the real, esoteric significance of the specification of April. It is not little, it is not simple. To recapitulate: this meaning imports the natural principle and natural method of procedure, which apply equally to human education; it reveals the true scope, character, and aim of the poetic, humanistic "new life"; it explains the ideal as well as the art of the stilnovists. Lorenzo's concept of April is very complicated. But when this "conceit," as I might call it, has been divested of its fanciful, poetic dress, it reduces itself to a plain, old-fashioned metaphor of extraordinary simplicity and nicety; and the idea itself loses all notional character to become a respectable, acute observation not devoid of scientific value. I trust, therefore, that even in this prosaic age of ours, this simple, poetic *sovrasenso* is now perfectly clear. And I also hope that it is now plain that, as I have tried to show on every occasion, this sort of figurative language is not precisely allegorical nor symbolical. It is simply poetic, in conformity with the tendency of all human speech to be, by nature, largely metaphorical.[9]

Esoteric Meaning of the Month of April: (b) *the Age of the Poet.*

Now let us see if this same indefinite yet specific remark does not imply also some precise, historical indication, and, as I suspect, a critical opinion. For we should not forget the personal, experiential character of the mystic death thus timed, nor the fact that this

---

7. Cf. Lorenzo, *op. cit.*, II, 249–250, "la canzone di Bacco"; and also "Chi tempo aspetta, assai tempo si strugge," *idem*, p. 201. Cf. Poliziano and others of Lorenzo's circle.

8. Once more, it goes without saying that the author refers to the *normal* age characterized by the youthful spirit. The actual, precise age at which one may "find himself," if ever, varies, of course, with individuals and with the circumstances of their lives. And just as formerly the calendar did not fix generally nor absolutely the month of the year possessing the virtue of "April" required by nature for its rejuvenation; so now, man's spiritual rebirth is not generally, nor absolutely determined by a fixed calendar year or specific period of years in man's natural life, but depends exclusively on the substantial character of the spirit of youth accompanying the activity of the creative spirit. Whence also the idea of eternal *giovinezza,* said to characterize the works of some men, just as before we observed that the beneficent influence of nature does not end with April.

9. Cf. this study, p. 7.

occurrence is thus timed with respect to the "lady" as well, indeed, ostensibly with respect to her alone, while the primary importance of the simultaneous death of the poet remains hidden in the esoteric implication of the *principio as a whole.*

Since April here means "youth": that is, *early spring* with respect to the most suitable season of the year in which to engage naturally in lofty humanistic pursuits, properly under the beneficent influence of nature; and also *young manhood* with respect to the natural cycle of human life, during which, analogously, it is most suitable to undertake intellectual preparation for the poetic "new life"; is it not possible that the commentator here is thus indicating incidentally, both his age at the time he himself made this preparatory study of the previous poets, and the very month of the year in which their precise lofty ideal literally "dawned" upon him? We have already inferred as much, when this point first came up.[10] But now we have all this additional, internal evidence to confirm our suspicion, and the author's own declaration, that he himself went through this spiritual experience actually during his *età giovenile e tenera.* Therefore, it is logical to conclude that, historically, this reference is most likely to the *April of 1465,* or whatever year it was that, presumably, he was at the same time engaged in the preparation of his *Raccolta aragonese,* and was also actually in the period of technical adolescence.[11] Certainly, this appears now to be the real, and a much more appropriate element of reality in the realistic reconstruction of his experience than the date of Simonetta's death.[12]

Moreover, now we see why the year and the exact day of the month could not be included in this otherwise specific indication of the time of the lady's death. The precise day could not be stated because naturally, we now surmise, the ideal involved dawned upon him *gradually* in the course of the said preparation. And the indication of the year also had to be omitted, not only because of

10. Cf. the section on "The date of Lorenzo's *Commentary,*" pp. 35 ff.; also p. 156. And now read the sonnet "Era nel tempo bel, quando Titano," which in Petrarchan fashion gives spring as the date of his falling in love. Lorenzo, *op. cit.,* I, 146.

11. I surmise the spring of 1469. Cf. Appendix B on the date of the *Raccolta aragonese,* pp. 342 ff.

12. Cf. above, "The date of the lady's death," pp. 152 ff.

the generic character given to this experience in view of its intended general application to any aspirant to the poetic "new life," but especially because it is not to be imagined that his own preparation was either confined to the study of the authors and works there included, or limited to that preliminary survey of the previous literature, which perhaps sufficed for the mere compilation of an anthology. Indeed, the presumption now is that his critical studies, especially of Dante, Petrarch, and Boccaccio, must have been *begun then,* or immediately after, but that the penetration of the soul of the *gentilissima* must have occupied him considerably longer than a short month, or even a year. In fact, in our study of the date of the *Commentary*,[13] we observed that the references to his *età giovenile e tenera* tended to become confused with, or to lapse into, references to his *gioventù;* which gave the impression that he began his *nuova vita* in his "adolescence," and continued it for some time at least during his "youth." And this must be our conclusion now, not only because the *Raccolta* (according to *Palatino* 204) included nothing of Dante, except the *Vita Nuova,* and nothing at all of either Petrarch or Boccaccio,[14] but also because his own *nuova vita* extends, as we know, beyond the initial stage of the mere *principio* here portrayed.

We should not imagine that his whole *nuova vita* had to be finished before he could undertake anything entirely original of his own literary production, because this, too, is *nuova vita* in the broader sense. It is a fact that his incomplete *Commentary* already included poems that surely must have been composed much later than this initial preparation imports. Therefore, the presumption is, I repeat, that if it had been completed, it would have comprised *all* his sonnets relative to the "new life"; which, on and off, occupied him most of his life, and this would have taken him pretty close to the end of his days. On the other hand, his own original poetic works (that is, those not involving any creative criticism on his part, or the discussion of any innovation he wished to introduce in the practice of the new style) must, of course, have been

13. Again I refer the reader to secs. *b* and *c* of chap. ii of Pt. I, pp. 34–45, the contents of which are pertinent throughout this discussion.

14. Cf. n. 8, p. 52.

composed side by side with his *nuova vita* or lifelong study of the previous poetry; although, theoretically at least, after the minimum of preparation implied by the *principio* as the absolute requirement for a proper initiation into the "new life." According to the Magnificent, just what constitutes *nuova vita* as a preparatory course, or a series of critical studies in verse, distinct from a stilnovist's original production, which implies the expression of his personality in new forms of art embodying a different concept of things or a new outlook on life? This distinction is a problem for the critic and historian of all his literary production to solve. I may touch upon it later. Here, striking the iron while it is hot, I shall merely call attention to the extraordinarily intelligent understanding we get from his theory and practice of the stilnovistic *nuova vita.* This, on his authority now, can no longer be considered as a sort of vague, juvenile aspiration, or as a mere change from a supposed disorderly life to one of decency and honorable, poetic pursuit. The *nuova vita* should be understood as a life of serious, systematic study and spiritual penetration of the real substance and value of the so-called humanities, ancient and modern, with a view toward renewing them, and perhaps substituting for them similar, new artistic creations, expressive of current thought and more consonant with the prevalent conception of human life. Especially, the "new life" should be understood as a series of what I have just called critical studies in verse. Such an interpretation gives us an entirely new outlook on the preceding *nuove vite, canzonieri,* and the like, and imposes new duties on the historian and literary critic of the whole Renaissance period. It is no small merit of the Magnificent, as such a critic, to have given us through his *principio* this enlightening understanding, and, by his example, an authoritative guide to the study of this literature.

But I must not expatiate and anticipate further. For our immediate purpose here, it suffices to conclude that our previous and present inferences all tally perfectly and thus confirm the high historical probability of the fact already deduced; namely, that Lorenzo veraciously asserts that his "lady" died mystically for him in the course of a critical study of her esoteric significance, such as he now suggests to any other "new Clytie" to undertake under the same favorable conditions—a study which apparently he himself *began,* as a mere youth, *in the spring of 1465* or shortly after, perhaps to satisfy incidentally the desire of his royal friend, and which he then *continued throughout his life,* in the spare moments he could devote to this *nuova vita,* in the narrower sense of the term.

Esoteric Meaning of the Month of April: (c) the Age of the Lady.

CONTINUING our examination of the all-significant indication of the circumstances and time of the lady's death, we come to a new point. What is the historico-critical import of this indication in relation to the *lady's* own mystic death (to which, as I said above, the account, taken literally, ostensibly refers)? We have already concluded that the said indication could not possibly be the specification of any precise year, not to say month, in which the poetic ideal personified by her could be said to have become extinct, or obsolete.[15] But, even if we now realize that her death was primarily mystical, related to the poet's own mystic death, and necessary to his spiritualization of her real essence in his own mind, how could the commentator say *literally* that *she* died in a month of April, unless the literal implication of "April," in its broader metaphorical sense of "youth," applied also to her? The suspicion is therefore justified. And just as the interpretation of the metaphorical April in terms of the poet's age has given us approximately the probable historical date of his actual initiation into the "new life"; so the reading of this esoteric meaning in the life of the *gentilissima* should enlighten us with regard to the commentator's critical opinion relative to her status at the time of her literal death as a body of poetic "finite things," and also give us the historical circumstances attending this death.

But are we then to imagine that the glorious period of Italian literature extending from the Dugento through the Trecento, and comprising, especially, the gigantic literary achievements of a Dante, a Petrarch, and a Boccaccio, whose works, in the opinion of the commentator, are the perfect embodiment of the poetic

15. Cf. above, pp. 155–156.

ideal personified by the *gentilissima* and *eccellentissima* incarnation of the supreme *bellezza e gentilezza umana;* are we to imagine now that this *grande perfezione* was merely the *principio,* or initial stage of a *vero amore* importing perhaps the vigorous rejuvenation of the classic, humanistic spirit and poetic ideal on the fertile, artistic soil of Italy? Are we to imagine that this period of approximately a century and a half, from the first emergence of the Sicilian school to the death of Boccaccio, was only the "April" or "early spring" of a metaphorical new year implying a new era of Italian poetic production? In other words, are we to imagine that this new literary production represented merely the metaphorical sprouting from the old trunk, or body of Latin literature, of a metaphorical *novella fronda* called literature in *volgare,* which was written in a style called significantly "new" and further qualified as "sweet"? Finally, are we to understand that this period of new Italian literature in *volgare* now closed, corresponded to the period of metaphorical adolescence of this *gentilissima,* or to her condition of a *very young* "lady" at the time of her death, when, to revert to the poet's other figure, this "sun" of intellectual light set below the "western" horizon?

Yes, precisely so. At least, this is the historico-critical opinion of the Magnificent. In fact, we may recall that (in his account of the lady's death serving to introduce the comment on the first sonnet, and containing the enumeration of her incomparable virtues to explain the general pity aroused by her demise) he refers to her age at the time as *età molto verde,* or very tender. And he adds that this fact, together with her beauty, which was even greater in her state of death, was the cause of the great compassion and of a most ardent desire left by her in everyone's heart.

E, se bene la vita per le sue degnissime condizioni a tutti la facessi carissima, pure la compassione della morte per la *età molto verde* e per la bellezza, che così morta, più forse che mai alcuna viva, mostrava, lasciò di lei uno ardentissimo desiderio.[16]

Moreover, in the proem, after discussing the four requisites that "lend dignity and perfection to a given tongue" (richness and copiousness, sweetness and harmoniousness, profound importance

16. Cf. Text, bottom of p. 25; and this study, pp. 101–102.

and required effectiveness of the content of its literature to the
purport of human life, and quasi universality); and after exalting
all these qualities, except the last, in the Italian *volgare* and its literature (represented primarily by Dante, Petrarch, Boccaccio, and
also Cavalcanti), it will be recalled that he ends this defense of the
volgare with a special, high commendation of Dante's *Commedia*
and a patriotic, optimistic note regarding the future of this language and literature, saying:

E forse saranno ancora scritte in questa lingua cose sottile ed importanti e
degne d'essere lette; massime insino ad ora si può dire essere *l'adolescenzia*
di questa lingua, perchè ognora più si fa elegante e gentile. E potrebbe facil-
mente *nella gioventù ed adulta età sua* venire ancora in maggiore perfezione;
e tanto più aggiugnendosi qualche prospero successo ed augumento al fiorentino imperio, come si debbe non solamente sperare, ma con tutto l'ingegno e
forze per li buoni cittadini aiutare: pure questo, per essere in potestà della
fortuna e nella volontà dell'infallibile giudicio di Dio, come non è bene affer-
marlo, non è ancora da disperarsene.[17]

This proof of the correctness of our last deduction seems to me
well-nigh indisputable. By the remark that his "lady" died "in a
month of April," the author, then, unquestionably also means that
the new Italian literature in *volgare,* "however beautiful and most
excellent," was still in a primitive stage of development when that
first period of its "new life" closed. Better, in view of the works
he hopes and expects will be written in the future in this language, and in view of the motherly, inspirational function he ascribes to that literature, he undoubtedly means that that first period represented a sort of period of incubation, we may now say,
of these future creations of the eternal Italian spirit.

But this is an extraordinary statement for him to make with respect to that body of literature. This is an astounding critical conception for him to entertain relative to the past and future history
of Italian literature. Especially, for us, this is a strange and most
novel understanding of the true scope, principle, and aim of the
sweet new style. Perhaps, after all that precedes, and after my frequent, indiscreet anticipations in this regard,[18] this view will not

17. Cf. Text, p. 21, and this study, pp. 53–54.
18. Cf. this study: pp. 13–17, 64, 68–69; and especially the whole treatment of
"*gentilezza umana,*" pp. 111–121. Cf. also, pp. 158–165, 174–175, and 188.

surprise the courteous reader who has followed me patiently and attentively so far. But it will almost certainly surprise, and perhaps amaze, the modern historian and critic of that first period who adheres to the current, traditional concept of the *dolce stil novo.* I hope, therefore, that this singular, critical opinion of the Magnificent will at least arouse his curiosity, and lead him to consider it with an open mind.

Recall here (from the commentator's poetic reconstruction of the history of Sonnet I)[19] Lorenzo's vision or conception in the western sky of a "star" symbolizing his own, modern poetic ideal. Recall that he does not very well know whether it be "this" or a "new" star: that is, whether it be either merely the "soul" of the "lady" now dead, or a new, modern concept of poetic art; but concludes that it is

di tanto splendore certamente, che non solamente di gran lunga l'altre stelle superava, ma era tanto lucida che faceva fare qualche ombra a quelli corpi che a tale luce si opponevano, . . . perchè l'anima di quella gentilissima o è trasformata in questa nuova stella o si è congiunta con essa.

Recall also his opinion that this

chiarissima stella . . . ancora potrebbe contendere con Febo e domandargli il suo carro, per essere lei autrice del giorno.

Remember, finally, that this would-be historical reconstruction is in the form of a soliloquy in the course of a probable, or possible, real *conversation* with a real *carissimo amico,* silent but assenting, whom he urges to seek with him light and inspiration from this dazzling splendor.

E, se la vista nostra è debole e frale a tanta luce, preghiamo il nume, cioè la divinità sua, che li fortifichi, levando una parte di tanto splendore, per modo che sanza offensione degli occhi la possiamo alquanto contemplare.

And now consider what all this means in the light of our previous and present deductions. At the risk of some repetition, let us develop these logical consequences.

19. Cf. Text, pp. 26–27; and the esoteric meaning of this account, in this study, pp. 135 ff.

CHAPTER V

Logical Consequences of the Preceding Deductions, and Value of Lorenzo's Critical Implications.

LORENZO implies that the previous literature in *volgare* all came within the scope, principle, and aim of the sweet new style. This is deduced from "the true nature of his subject," and from his inclusion of all his great predecessors in this school. And now, with hope and daring anticipation, he also implies that the outcome of the longed-for revival, already initiated, would most likely be a new poetic production having the identical humanistic scope and aim, and following the same artistic principle, although not presenting necessarily the same outward forms. This is also deduced from his conscious, deliberate, and suggested imitation of the artistic ideal of those same poets.

Moreover, in view of his historico-philological derivation of the adjective *gentile,* and of his philosophical conception and practical definition of *gentilezza,* he now makes further implications. He first implies that the previous literature was indeed *gentilissima* in this respect and according to this principle; for this is indicated in the epithet *gentile* applied to the *donna* personifying the same but individual poetic ideal of those authors; and also clearly demonstrated by his own critical study of the content and form of that literature. And he implies in addition that the new literature would be similarly of Roman excellence, with respect to its humanistic scope, character, and intent, and with respect to its artistic principle of conception and entire *gentilezza.* But the content and outward forms of the new literature might vary again in accordance with the thought and spirit of the new times and the personal talent or fancy of the new poets. Indeed, this new period of humanistic, spiritual activity in all fields—of the arts, letters, and science—would not only mark the revival of the stilnovistic ideal, which the virtue and excellence of the Roman ideal had already inspired during the period of preparation now sometimes called pre-Renaissance or *primo rinascimento,* in the course of which the *novella fronda* had sprouted and begun to bloom, but would also itself be a second Renaissance, or continuation of the operation of the original Roman poetic principle in a new period of fecundity and at the same time ripening of first fruits. The figurative language suggested by the commentator is rich, varied, and complex. But then it could truly be said that the same *gentilissima,* revived, had entered upon a new phase of the poetic "new life," or else that it had either been transformed into or become fused with the *nuova stella* symbolizing the modern, direct derivation of the same ideal and principle from the original, common source of the Latin classics now combined with the Greek. Finally, then it could verily be said that a "new dawn" had appeared on the horizon of western Europe, announcing the return of that same "Sun," which "might well contend now with Phoebus himself," meaning apparently the same metaphorical sun loved by any modern Clytie precisely like that ancient incarnation and personification of man's idealism.

In other words, the Magnificent seems to conceive the Italian humanistic-artistic genius as a form of the eternal creative spirit of man, operating in cycles of many centuries each constituting an era or series of epochs, after the manner of the natural seasons caused by the annual cycle of the earth; and manifesting itself in the form of a corresponding series or aggregate of stilnovistic "new lives" lived in subsequent epochs by great artistic geniuses endowed with broad vision of universal human scope, character, and aim, and prompted by a profound love for the ideal of human perfection.

For him, the first period of Italian literature in *volgare,* coming after a long "winter" of artistic or poetic inactivity, was, therefore, as it were, the "April" of a new "year," represented by the Christian Era as distinguished from the preceding pagan era of Greek and Latin civilization. And the period he anticipates so hopefully because it had already begun, and to which we have ourselves given the name of real "renaissance," was, in his opinion, to be the "May and June," we may say, of this same "spring." This "May and June" should follow the *primizie* of that "year" with a full, general blossoming of human nature, and produce the first "fruits" of the human mind, in further expectation of the full harvest that would come in due course, during the subsequent "seasons" or epochs; namely, the "summer" and "autumn" of the same cycle corresponding to our present era.

This idealistic conception of our author, which is not without analogies to G. B. Vico's *new science* presented more than two centuries later; and this critical survey of Italian literature, which may remind us strangely of De Sanctis' conception of the Phoenix-like nature of the Italian Spirit[1] (similarly substantiated by this critic's own *history* of even more recent date): this idealism and foresight of the Magnificent, I say, are remarkable, but not surprising. For we should not forget that he lived in the very midst of the revival he proposes and anticipates, right in the Quattrocento, which marks the most effervescent, teeming period of the Renaissance he did so much to bring about. Then great conceptions were being thought out, and some of the most daring feats of human genius were planned and achieved; then spirits were bubbling with enthusiasm and fervor to discover, to invent, and to create—aiming at and contributing in one way or another to a higher form of civilization. His was the epoch of Torricelli and Columbus; of Leon Battista Alberti, Donatello, Brunelleschi, and hosts of other daring creative artists; of Poliziano in literature and literary criticism of the ancient classics; of Guido Veronese and Vittorino da Feltre in the field of human education. The art of printing was invented in his day, and the Greek civilization was practically a discovery of his century. Finally, his was the epoch of humanism par excellence, humanism both in the sense of research and study in the field of the ancient humanities, and in the sense of all sorts of enterprises undertaken with the ideal of individual and social human perfection in mind.

1. Tonelli's rendering of De Sanctis' conception reads as follows: "lo spirito italiano, e, per esso, la letteratura italiana, muore per rinascere ben tosto dalle sue ceneri, come l'araba fenice." Cf. Luigi Tonelli, *La Critica letteraria italiana* (Bari, Laterza, 1914), p. 136; and recall especially the last chapter of Francesco De Sanctis' *Storia della letteratura italiana*. In this connection I am reminded also of G. A. Borgese's *Il Senso della letteratura italiana* (Milano, Treves, 1931), where this eminent, modern critic expresses the opinion that Italian literature has always aspired "alla suprema armonia, all'ordine eccelso, all'arte come trasfigurazione dell'uomo e figurazione di Dio." Cf. *op. cit.*, p. 107.

Of course, neither the culmination of this renaissance in the Cinquecento, nor the following epoch produced a greater Dante, or even another Dante. But, without injustice to Petrarch's indisputable merits as poet, literary artist, and humanist, both Poliziano and Pontano were certainly greater than he as humanists and Latin poets, Ariosto as artist of the *volgare,* and Tasso as poet of the human soul. And even if Boccaccio was not surpassed either in his originality as creator of literary *genres* or in his special talent as *novelliere,* the Cinquecento produced innumerable, respectable storytellers, pastoral poets, satirists, and others, not to speak of the epic poets just mentioned. Besides, his century and the following produced a Leonardo, a Michelangelo, a Raphael, who certainly obscured the glory of the Italian primitives. It produced Castiglione and Della Casa in the nice, humanistic science of social refinement. Particularly, it was the epoch of Machiavelli, first modern historian and creator of political science.

This is neither the place nor the occasion for a comparison and contrast of the two epochs referred to by our critic, especially as the Magnificent was not, after all, prophesying, but merely visualizing. Indeed, his remark ends, leaving the future in the hands of God and of Fortune.[2] But this much was necessary, I thought, to make us appreciate the clarity of his intuition and the nicety of his critical judgment. His judgment, on the other hand, had the whole Quattrocento as a basis, or as a sort of promontory from which to observe the immediate and perhaps distant future.

What is truly extraordinary in Lorenzo's comprehensive picture of Italian literature, past, present, and future, is his clear insight into the past. This insight, in the further light of his similarly clear understanding of the humanistic trend of his own times, suggested to him the revival of that poetic ideal. And now, presumably after the achievements of himself, Poliziano, and others, it enabled him to visualize easily at least the immediate future. What is extraordinary is his acute, profound penetration of the "soul" of the *gentilissima.* This revealed to him the true character, principle, and purpose of that literature. He was thus enabled to reconstruct its history; to estimate properly its import and influ-

2. Cf. above, p. 191.

ence with reference to the origin of the humanistic movement then in course; to appreciate its inherent and intended function of inspiration; and therefore to prefigure clearly its natural subsequent development. His study of that literature was undertaken with seriousness of purpose in the thoroughly scientific manner we have noted; and it was carried out with rare critical acumen, with philosophic penetration, with sympathetic zeal, with fine artistic appreciation and infallible good taste, in a word, with the clearest intuition of the qualities that make for the finest human poetry. This study, I say, which is a veritable revelation as he intends that it should be, is also, I believe, our guaranty now that his historical reconstruction and critical valuation of that first period of Italian literature is authoritative and undoubtedly correct. Remember that it was made only a short time after the close of the said period, indeed, while the influence of that literature was still strongly felt. Therefore, even if we did not now have the history of the whole Renaissance, and numerous independent studies on that preliminary or pre-Renaissance period to support his contention, we should still consider it at least substantially correct. It is, then, most interesting to the modern historian to discover it in this hitherto unsuspected work of the Magnificent, which reveals the latter's rôle as a literary critic of the first rank—a rôle never brought out, I believe, except by Flamini, and by him with much minor significance only in connection with the prefatory letter to the *Raccolta aragonese.*

Other Deductions which Reveal Lorenzo's Understanding of the Sweet New Style: the Lady's Degnissime Condizioni *in Relation to the* Vere Laudi *of a Language or* Condizioni *of the Italian* Volgare.

BUT what is particularly remarkable and illuminating in this study of his, is his final implied conclusion, that what thoroughly and really explained that first literature in *volgare,* what informed it all, and what had guided it from Guinizelli until its real or apparent eclipse, was the fundamental, artistic-philosophical principle of the *dolce stil novo!* That literature, in his opinion, was all "new style," from the poets who first began to compose their verses *in volgare,* down to Boccaccio, down to himself and Poliziano now, and all his contemporaries, who were trying to revive that ideal, and looked on this symbolic star for guidance and inspiration in writing their original verses also in *volgare.* Indeed, it was not only "new," but "sweet" as well, from the very beginning; even though at first, he clearly implies, it was not so sweet as Dante, especially, but also Petrarch and Boccaccio had made it, and even Cavalcanti together with others of the same school. What is more, the subsequent production which he fondly expected, would not only be similarly *"sweet new* style," provided the new poets were "modern Clyties" like himself, and adhered strictly to the principle of "newness" and "sweetness," with all that this implied; but, if circumstances favored the further development of the *volgare,* the chances were that this future literature would be even richer, sweeter, and more important in its effect on human life.

This is certainly his thought, derived practically in his own words from the quotations given above, and from all his defense of the *volgare.* This topic now teems with such significance that we must take it up once more. The reader is kindly invited to read it all over again,[3] in order that he may have it present as we now proceed to consider it in relation to our understanding of the origin and development of this literature in *volgare,* and in the light of our interpretation of this *gentilissima* said to incarnate the supreme *bellezza e gentilezza umana.*

Recall first, however, the commentator's basic observation that the adjective *gentile* is a "vocabulo *nuovo* ed al tutto *vulgare."* Remember, not only his historico-philological derivation of this word, but also his definition of *gentilezza,* which implies the natural, scientific method of critical investigation for the acquisition of true knowledge.[4] Then recall our deductions relative to the *bellezza e gentilezza umana* of the *eccellentissima donna* personifying this ideal of human perfection,[5] and connect this humanistic

3. Cf. Text, pp. 18–22; and this study, pp. 47–54.
4. Cf. Text, pp. 57–58; and this study, pp. 111–113.
5. Cf. pp. 120–121.

import with the historico-philosophical conception implied by the connotation of the adjective *gentile*. Note well that the "newness" of this connotation implies the new conception of an original, modern ideal based on the principle (itself new) that the generally recognized virtue and excellence of the ancient Romans was worthy of study and emulation in its sound principle coinciding with the inherent principle of human "gentilesse" itself. The inference immediately is that this "newness" reflects itself on the "newness" of the conception connoted by the *donna gentile*. On the other hand, the inference also is that, just as the new connotation of *gentile* implied an historical derivation of the principle of "gentilesse" from Roman example and Roman teaching, so the modern conception of the *donna gentile* implied the Roman source of the poetic ideal thus recast: In accordance with the rediscovered secret or principle of Roman excellence, now called "gentilesse," the new literature in *volgare* was intended to carry the same humanistic import, now reconceived in the light of modern thought, and recast in new and original forms. Better, perhaps, it was intended to be a sort of creative poetic criticism, generally in verse, of the ancient pagan civilization, in the light of modern Christian morality and conception of human perfection. And naturally, in this process, the language or outward form of this new conception—following the same course—was consciously regarded as being both derived and new. Therefore the commentator says of the *volgare* that "questa lingua . . . ognora più si fa elegante e *gentile*."[6] The idea that the new Italian language and literature were at the same time a continuation and an innovation, was, in other words, congenital with the principle of the new style. The desire to imitate and improve, to emulate and surpass, was the rule and the goal. In a word, progress based on past experience was the keynote of the *volgare* and of the literature inseparable from it: progress in content, and progress in form. And this was the "newness" of this "new style": namely, originality of conception, following the well-established human wisdom of the Ancients, but in the light of modern discoveries, and in response to the trend of modern times; and originality of expression, fol-

6. Cf. the quotation on p. 191.

lowing the natural evolution and artistic development of the *volgare* from classical and vulgar Latin. The ideal, finally, was to advance human culture and refinement beyond the point reached by the Ancients, all in a zealous effort to approach ever nearer to the ideal of human perfection.

Now with reference to the commentator's would-be Dantean apology for poetizing in *volgare:* reflect that this apology not only resolves itself into a defense of the language and literature but this defense concerns more the literature than it does the language itself. In fact, observe that, of the three qualities for which he there exalts his native *volgare* (the fourth not being applicable to it as yet), only the first, he says, may be said to constitute a *vera laude* of this or any given language *per se.* This, I recall again, is the richness and copiousness of its vocabulary, idiomatic expressions, and general syntax. With respect to this richness, as a quality possessed by the *volgare* in a high degree, and with special reference to Dante, Petrarch, and Boccaccio, Lorenzo might indeed have voiced the same opinion contained in the exclamation which Sordello utters in Purgatory upon hearing that the compatriot standing before him is none other than the classic Latin poet, Virgil:

> "O gloria *de' Latin,"* disse, "per cui
> mostrò *ciò che potea* LA LINGUA NOSTRA."[7]

The second, or sweetness and harmoniousness of a given tongue, is and is not a *vera laude* of the language itself. It is in so far as its sounds may in themselves be rich and varied, mellow and sonorous, and commonly susceptible of all sorts of harmonious combinations lending musicalness to the language itself. But it is not in so far as this happy effect depends primarily, on the one hand, on the harmoniousness of the soul of the author, and, on the other, on the harmoniousness of the soul of his reader or listener. That is, the harmoniousness of a language is essentially an internal quality and a product of the spirit of the poet, reflecting itself on the incarnation of his *verbum.* And its appreciation as well as enjoy-

---

7. Cf. Dante, *Purgatorio,* VII, 16–17. I cannot refrain from calling attention here, incidentally but appositely, to the significance of this exclamation put in the mouth of the "Provençal" poet, with respect both to his *Italianity* and Virgil's, and to the continuity, in Dante's opinion, of the Provençal *volgare,* as well as the Italian, from Latin.

ment on the part of the listener depends entirely on the latter's apprehension of this *verbum,* and on the resonance of this expression in his own soul—both of which depend ultimately on the similar harmoniousness of his own spirit. The third quality, on the contrary, is not at all one proper to the language itself. This is its effectiveness, which is wholly due to the content of its literature expressed in that form, or better, to the profound importance and necessity of this content in the shaping of a strictly "human" life in the noblest sense of the word. Finally, this quality affirms the humanistic scope and character of this literature, manifests its didactic intention and inspirational function, and attests its universality. Therefore I say that this apology for the use of the *volgare* is really a defense, indeed, an exaltation of its literature, rather than simply a Dantesque argumentation for the adoption of the mother tongue in preference to Latin.

Moreover, reflect that these "requisites which lend dignity and perfection to a given tongue," or *condizioni,* as he calls them, correspondingly with the *degnissime condizioni* of the young *gentilissima,*[8] are not a criterion independently conceived *a priori* with the idea of demonstrating that the *volgare* measured up to the highest standard. Ostensibly, this is their character and the reason why they are advanced, as a sort of principle to go by, at the beginning of the defense. But this is due merely to the author's stilnovistic method of categorical presentation, which, as usual throughout this Dantesque *Comento,* shows signs of that scholastic influence from which the stilnovists were not free. In reality, it was his study of that very literature that revealed to him those qualities of his mother tongue, and the criterion by which he tests it was supplied by the *volgare* itself. In fact, consider that the qualities for which he exalts it, not only do not all three at once apply in such a high degree to any other literature, ancient or contemporary (I was going to say "modern"), but are almost exclusively the very special qualities of the *gentilissima:* that is, they are the qualities that "characterize" this literature in particular, that "distinguish" it from any other, and that constitute its "excellence" or exclusive "gentilesse." Obviously, what he did in this connection was a bit

8. Cf. the quotation on p. 190.

of stilnovistic, creative criticism of the kind we are now familiar with. First, he applied his own "gentilesse" or critical discernment to the detection of the "gentilesse" or inherent virtue of the literature in *volgare;* and then, after he had extracted these distinctive qualities, he made them his criterion for passing critical judgment on the very language in which that literature was written. We might exclaim,

. . . Quel medesmo
che vuol provarsi, non altri, il ti giura![9]

And, admittedly, his whole argument in this respect is weakened by the prejudice that this literature was not merely *gentilissima,* but *eccellentissima* in the absolute sense. This was presumably the reason why he certainly thought that it might well serve as the example par excellence to supply the principle by which any other language might be judged as to its qualifications to fulfil similarly the noble function of transmitting humanistic conceptions. But that is precisely the point. In his defense, the Magnificent is thinking solely of, and entirely in terms of, the humanistic import of the literature in *volgare,* and hardly of any other literature, nor at all in terms of a linguistic medium conceived as existing apart from the content it conveys. His main, persistent argument is that the outward form or expression of the poet's thought is wholly determined by the content. And this is what he considers. Ultimately, therefore, he is concerned only with the character of that literature, which, I repeat, he regards as supremely humanistic. In other words, he is finally concerned with the qualities of the literature in *volgare,* which are reflected by the richness, sweetness, and effectiveness of the language itself. This is why he seems to measure the *volgare* by its own standard.

This would-be apology for the use of the *volgare* is, then, in reality a defense of its literature which presupposes a previous critical study on his part, and this defense concerns primarily the humanistic value of this literature. Let us now therefore consider in this light the remarks which the commentator makes relative to the authors whose "experience" has given him the criterion by which he judges their "style." We now see that the content and

9. Dante, *Paradiso,* XXIV, 104–105.

form of their *works,* rather than their language *per se,* is the real object of those remarks. I refer to those comments where, passing from the supposed theory to its application, Lorenzo examines their works to see if they come up to the standard set (or to prove that they do). Here, as a matter of fact, he is merely stating his critical opinion regarding their poetic achievement.

Observe first of all who are the poets whose works are taken as the best illustration of the *volgare's* accomplishment. We know them already, for I have recalled them only too frequently on every occasion. They are Dante, Petrarch, Boccaccio, and Cavalcanti, in this precise order of importance. But now consider again, in the light of the commentator's humanistic concern, not so much the significance of their being the only ones mentioned, with Cavalcanti included, as the significance of their being *the ones* taken to illustrate the "dignità e perfezione" of the *volgare* or the medium through which the *bellezza e gentilezza umana* embodied in the *gentilissima* Italian literature have found expression. This, furthermore, in a critical treatise on the sweet new style! Notice again the perfect fusion or identity in the critic's mind, of "humanism" and "new style," and especially the inclusion of both Petrarch and Boccaccio among the supreme stilnovists! For these facts could not be overstressed in an attempt to correct, on the authority of such a critic as the Magnificent, the false traditional opinion that humanism and the *dolce stil novo* were not related, that the latter ended with Dante's juvenile lyrics, or began and ended with him, that Petrarch and Boccaccio were not stilnovists, but the first humanists, and that with them began our modern era, or at least the "humanism" that produced the "renaissance" of the sixteenth century. Lorenzo's historico-critical conception of that epoch is quite the contrary.

Then again observe the terminology used to describe the "style" of those authors' poetic production (Boccaccio's included), which, I say, he regards as supremely humanistic, not only in the sense of its being *gentile* or of Roman derivation and excellence, but primarily also in the sense of its being humanistic in scope and carrying an educational value. The qualities recurring persistently in the critic's mind may be said to fall under two categories, *gravità* and *dolcezza;* which are not easily distinguishable, for, together, they seem to constitute a third, *armonia,* and the three blend one with the other. Moreover, the critic seems to relate them to Dante's three "styles," which, he says, the latter combines *in effetto, in uno solo.* Thus, he remarks that this poet's style is at once (or, I presume, according to the situation) *umile, mediocre ed alto;* which terms correspond, respectively, to Dante's *elegiaco, comico,* and *tragico.*[10] And he adds further that "le canzone e sonetti di Dante sono di tanta *gravità, sottilità* ed *ornato,* che quasi non hanno comparazione in prosa e orazione soluta." Petrarch's style is said to be *grave, lepido e dolce.* Boccaccio, *uomo dottissimo e facundissimo,* is known for his *invenzione, copia,* and *eloquenzia,* for his *materia ora grave, ora mediocre ed ora bassa,* and for his *tante nuove astuzie ed ingegni.* Finally, Cavalcanti has also "combined most happily" *gravità* and *dolcezza,* not only in his celebrated *canzone,* "*Donna mi prega,*" but also in "alcuni sonetti e ballate sue *dolcissime.*"

Observe, moreover, with respect to the spirit of emulation congenital with the principle of the new style, and the consequent desire to improve on and surpass the Ancients, that "*Dante* [in his combination of three styles in one] *ha assai perfettamente assoluto quello che in diversi autori, così greci come latini, si truova";* and that "*queste cose amorose* of Petrarch are *con tanta gravità e venustà trattate, quanta sanza dubbio non si truova in Ovidio, Tibullo, Catullo e Properzio o alcun altro latino.*"

For the moment disregard the critic's apparent tendency to summarize his descriptions of these poets' "styles" by a minimum of three words (except to observe that this seems to be intentional, now with obscure reference to Dante's three styles in one, and now with reference to his criterion concerning the three main requisites applicable to the *volgare*). Notice that the common qualities of these various "styles," and therefore the ones recurring most frequently in these critical summaries, are, as I said above, *gravità* and *dolcezza;* while all the others are practically synonyms of these two, or else they reëcho the requisite of richness and copiousness.

10. Cf. Dante, *De vulgari eloquentia,* II, iv, 5–6.

Gravità refers naturally to "the profound importance and necessity of the *subject-matter* in the shaping of human life," and obviously corresponds to the linguistic requisite of effectiveness for the purpose of human progress. This connotation is reflected in the connotation of *stile alto o tragico,* and, in diminishing degree, of *stile mediocre o comico,* and *stile umile o elegiaco.* It is reflected with similar gradation in the connotation of Boccaccio's matter, now *grave,* now *mediocre,* and now *bassa.* Finally, it is also reflected in the connotation of *sottilità, dottissimo,* and, partly, even *invenzione* (although *invenzione* connotes more the "newness" of the subject matter or concept-image than it does the humanistic quality implied).

Dolcezza, on the other hand, is, of course, the quality in literature called by the same term of "sweet," which is used here to tabulate a requisite of language. Its connotation is implicit in the words *ornato, lepido,* and *venustà.* It is implicit in *facundissimo* and *eloquenzia,* although these perhaps reëcho more the requisite of richness and copiousness expressed by the very word *copia* in the criticism of Boccaccio's production. Finally, it is to be understood, again in proportion, with reference, again, to the three varieties of "styles." For we should not forget that *dolcezza* is coupled with a most significant and clarifying synonym, *armonia.* As I explained above, the latter implies a resonance in the poet's heart of the ideal of human perfection involving the individual and social progress of man in all fields of strictly *human* endeavor. It implies either the original conception on his part of such an ideal, or the sympathetic response of his soul to such a conception, in which case it involves his zealous, faithful reconstruction of it in his mind and heart, all in conformity with his natural inclinations and in harmony with the spirit of the times. Lastly, it implies the absolute conformity of the expression to the poetic intuition, in such a way that it not only renders the concept fully and clearly, but also stirs the chords of the human heart, which respond by vibrating sympathetically. In other words, *dolcezza* is essentially a *figurative* sort of sweetness. It is primarily the internal, sentimental "sweetness" resulting from the harmony (theoretically expected or highly desirable) between the poet's spirit and his universe; between the content of his poetic conception and the artistic form the latter should assume exteriorly and sensorially; finally, between his sensitive, idealistic soul and that of his similarly "gentle" reader or listener. Only secondarily is it a sort of sensory, perceptible "sweetness" resulting from the correspondingly "harmonious" sound of the physical or linguistic expression which embodies the poet's concept and respective sentiment. And, even then, this "sweetness" of the harmonious sound of "words in verse," is a thing more to be felt than heard, or to be felt before it is heard. Consequently, *dolcezza* is really a quality of this very *armonia,* with which it is coupled as an implied connotation more than as a synonym. This sort of spiritual yet perceptible sweetness reflecting the harmoniousness of the content and form applies also with even more propriety to the *gravità* of Italian poetry. This quality of *gravità,* as we remarked above, refers to the profound philosophical importance of its humanistic content; and ultimately it is this *materia,* otherwise called precisely *grave,* that is the real source of all the "sweetness." Verily, the *dolcezza* applies indirectly to the "richness and copiousness" of this literature as well: inasmuch as this quality is in the *volgare* as language merely a reflection of the *essere copiosa e abondante* of the literature itself. And in the *volgare* as literature it is the consequence of the "eloquence" of its *"facundissimi* poeti,*"* who, in turn, owe this faculty chiefly to the nature of their subject and to their enthusiasm for it. Thus, ultimately, the resonance of their eloquence, which is "sweet" indeed, is also due to the humanistic ideal involved. In other words, the *dolcezza* spoken of is the sweetness of the harmoniousness of this literature with respect to all three *condizioni* referred to as making for human *dignità e perfezione* in an ideal language and literature. It is the sweetness of these *condizioni,* or requisites, which harmoniously combined make for a perfect, poetic "new life." It is the sweetness of this humanistic, poetic ideal, which reflects itself in the harmoniousness of the poet's life, and in his art results in the perfect harmony of the *verbum factum caro.* Again, it is the consequent inherent quality of these "conditions" which attests historically and critically the *degnissime condizioni* of the *gentilissima* during her life and her "state" at the time of "death." *Dolcezza,* moreover, is the sentimental-sensorial resonance in "gentle hearts" of the harmony resulting between content and form in any of the three "styles," which in fact are one in principle. Finally, it is the "sweetness" of the sweet new style, inherent in this "style," by principle and practice, like its "newness."

Conclusions Relative to Lorenzo's Critique of the Sweet New Style.

SEVERAL important conclusions may now be drawn from this analysis of Lorenzo's indirect, synthetic criticism of the literature in *volgare.* First of all, as I have already remarked, literature in *volgare* and sweet new style were for him equivalent terms. Indeed, as I have also brought out, the spirit of universal and personal humanism pervading the literature in *volgare* was for him the moving spirit of the very principle nourishing the sweet new style. Not that he ever uses any of these terms to designate either the period, or the spiritual movement, or the poetic ideal. Owing to the peculiar stilnovistic form of *principio di nuova vita* given to his poetic apprenticeship involving the historico-critical study of that body of literature, he never mentions Dante's original definition of his school's *stile,* nor does he ever refer to it directly. But the subject of his discussion is certainly the literature in *volgare;* and his critical penetration of the human scope, character, and educational aim of the *gentilissima* not only implies a clear understanding of the principle of the *dolce stil novo* but is equivalent to his interpretation of the master's definition. In his understanding, the spirit and principle nourishing the sweet new style must have corresponded precisely to the spirit and principle of *bellezza e gentilezza umana* (which, according to him, nourished the literature in *volgare*).[11] In fact, realize again that his historico-critical reconstruction of that period rests entirely on his understanding of the adjective *gentile* and on his consequent definition of *gentilezza,* both with respect to the object, or *cosa gentile,* possessing this quality, and with respect to the subject, or *cuor gentile,* exer-

11. If necessary, see again "the true nature of the lady," pp. 108–121.

cising this preëminently human function.[12] Indeed, realize that the philosophical principle of *bellezza e gentilezza umana,* as understood and esoterically explained by him, is precisely the principle he himself follows, as he proceeds to revive now this same ideal of the sweet new style!

Recall, moreover, our previous conclusion relative to his interpretation, as I then surmised, of Dante's famous definition of this style.[13] Realize now that he must have actually examined most of the literature in *volgare* in the light of that definition, which conformed in every respect with the historico-critical-philosophical principle of "gentilesse." Realize that he himself proceeded accordingly. And, most important, realize that he understood "style," not in the sense of a rhetorical manner signifying the personal mode of self-expression, but in the sense of a school's poetic art which was all one with the literature itself. There is no doubt that, for Lorenzo, what Dante had called *dolce stil novo* had been not only the more-or-less conscious theory and practice of the poets in *volgare* leading up to Dante, but also the program of those who had followed. All he does, therefore, is to substitute his own for Dante's formula. In the light of his critical study of all that literature (including, I say, not only the stilnovists leading up to Dante, but also those who had proceeded from him) he simply replaces Dante's terse esoteric definition of his school's poetic art, with one of his own. Lorenzo gives a critical, clearer, and more comprehensive statement as it must have seemed to him of the truly simple, fundamental principle of the master's school: namely, the principle of *gentilezza.* For Lorenzo, this principle, besides being significant with respect to the historical derivation and philosophical import of all the literature in *volgare* from its inception to its rise and decline, was now no longer the enunciation of a program only partly executed, but was the critical evaluation of an ideal actually achieved.

Bear in mind this identification, now corroborated by the tenor and phraseology of Lorenzo's critical remarks relative to the three styles in one, or the richness, harmoniousness, and effectiveness of the literary production of the poets mentioned. From this we see

---

12. *Ibid.,* pp. 111–113.   13. Cf. pp. 131–134.

that *dolce stil novo,* for the Magnificent, embraced all the literature in *volgare.* In the respective sense explained above, *stile* implied, for him, this harmonious conformity between content and
form; *novo* declared the originality of this content and form; and
dolce described the pleasant resonance in "gentle hearts" of the
noble subject matter expressed harmoniously in noble form. Remembering the spirit of humanism with which this "style" or literature was all imbued; remembering the form it took of a poetic
"new life" strictly humanistic in character, all in an effort to
achieve personally and socially the ideal of human perfection; remembering these things, we may now make the following interesting conclusions.

Stile certainly implied for Lorenzo, first of all, perfect harmony
between the poet's soul and his world of universal human interests; then, perfect harmony between this humanistic content and
the artistic form the poet's conception took in his concrete expression of it; and, finally, perfect harmony between poet's soul and
reader's soul, in order that this content and form might be effective of human progress. Thence, as I said before, the "sweetness,"
in varying degree, of the harmoniousness evinced by any of
Dante's three styles in one. Thence, I add, the "sweetness," not
specified, but certainly implied also with reference to the similar
harmoniousness attained by Boccaccio in his identical three styles
in one, as disclosed by his *materia ora grave, ora mediocre ed ora
bassa.*

Novo, on the other hand, implied sometimes merely originality
in the reconceiving of an old subject matter. Preferably, whenever
possible, it implied the invention of new matter of universal human interest. In this case, this adjective would of course imply not
only the newness of the content but also the originality of the
form resulting from the first conception of this new matter.
Thence, as I also remarked, the "sweetness" of this very "newness," inasmuch as a new discovery in line with the ideal of
human perfection meant a nearer approach to this goal, or the
progress of civilization; and this was "sweet" indeed to anyone
aspiring to this achievement of mankind both for himself and for
the society of which he was part.

It follows that, as I surmised above, these qualities of the *dolce stil novo* were, for the Magnificent, inherent in the literature in *volgare*. They were the natural characteristic properties of the humanistic principle which had determined both the content and form of that literature, in conformity with the spirit that had inspired it. In other words, it was elemental for this "style" to be ideally "sweet" and "new" at once, in the sense described above.

Therefore, if my analysis of Lorenzo's critical concept is correct, and we accept his view, it is wrong to split these indissoluble components of a single conception. It is wrong to speak of precedence of either the element *novo* or the element *dolce*. It is wrong to imagine, as, for instance, Figurelli has recently done, that Dante added the element *novo* to the *dolce stile* already in existence.[14] Dante, no doubt, added enormously both to the newness and the sweetness of the style, or, better, brought these qualities to a supreme degree. Just as Petrarch did, whose very sweet, new *Rime* originated a whole school. Indeed, just as Boccaccio did, who certainly contributed more newness than anyone else. But, according to the Magnificent, neither these poets, nor Cavalcanti, nor even Guinizelli, nor anyone in particular, for that matter, originated either characteristic. These qualities, which as a matter of fact were common, not only to all the Italian literature in *volgare,* but to the other neo-Latin literatures as well, these qualities originated with the new spirit of the time, when all western Europe awoke from the long lethargic sleep in which the Barbaric invasions had plunged her. In Lorenzo's opinion, this was the real beginning of the movement which was to culminate in the Renaissance he foresaw. And, with respect to the *dolce stil novo,* or *gentilissima* Italian literature, these qualities were simply the manifestation of the principle of "gentilesse" operating anew on Italian soil in a spirit of rejuvenation and progress. Certainly they were not the qualities which differentiated it from the other literatures in Romance. The originality and excellence of the sweet new style were entirely due to its universal human import. In other words, the new factor, introduced by Guinizelli, developed by Cavalcanti, and perfected by

14. Cf. Fernando Figurelli, *Il dolce stil novo* (Napoli, Riccardo Ricciardi, 1933), chap. i.

Dante, was the spirit of humanism originated by a clear under-standing of genuine, perfect "gentilesse." And it was this "genti-lesse" that was later developed still further by other writers, especially Petrarch and Boccaccio.

CHAPTER VI

An Attempt To Reconstruct Lorenzo's Interpretation of Dante's Imaginary Dialogue with Bonagiunta da Lucca, Following His Own Critique of the Dolce Stil Novo.

THE foregoing conclusions will become more obvious and convincing if we now proceed to complete our understanding of Lorenzo's undoubted interpretation of Dante's definition and of all those passages in the *Commedia* which refer to this question, applying in this process Lorenzo's own critique as I have deduced it.

We may recall that in *Purgatorio,* XXVI, Dante introduces Guinizelli as

> . . . il padre
> mio e de li altri miei miglior che mai
> rime d'amore usar dolci e leggiadre;[1]

and that, when the latter asks the reason for such a display of affection, he replies:

> . . . Li dolci detti vostri,
> che, quanto durerà l'uso moderno,
> faranno cari ancora i loro incostri.[2]

Guinizelli then remarks:

> O frate, . . . questi ch'io ti cerno
> col dito . . .
> fu miglior fabbro del parlar materno.
> Versi d'amore e prose di romanzi
> soverchiò tutti; e lascia dir li stolti
> che quel di Lemosì credon ch'avanzi.
> A voce più ch'al ver drizzan li volti,
> e così ferman sua oppinione
> prima ch'arte o ragion per lor s'ascolti.
> Così fer molti antichi di Guittone,
> di grido in grido pur lui dando pregio,
> fin che l'ha vinto il ver con più persone.[3]

---

1. *Loc. cit.,* ll. 97–99.   2. *Loc. cit.,* ll. 112–114.   3. *Loc. cit.,* ll. 115–126.

Now, as Figurelli points out, in accord with Rossi on this point, "il dolce stile dunque già esisteva";[4] that is, before Dante. But what neither he nor Rossi seems to realize is that this quality not only does not constitute a Dantesque contribution but, as I say, is not even an exclusive peculiarity of the literature in the Italian *volgare*. As I have already noted in connection with Sordello's apostrophe,[5] the continuity of the Latin language and literature evinced by the development of the Italian *volgare* was not restricted to the latter, but, according to Dante himself, was common to all the *volgari* deriving from Latin. In fact, there he seems to imply that Provençal as a Romance language was as much a *lingua nostra* and had as much claim to the heredity of Virgil's glory, as the Italian *volgare*. This is now corroborated by the qualification *dolci* applied, as we see in the above quotations, not only to the amorous verses of Guinizelli and his followers but also, in varying degree, to the similar verses of the Provençal Arnaut Daniel and the Frenchman Gerard de Brunel. Indeed, the relative inferiority of Gerard de Brunel with respect to Arnaut Daniel, as of Guittone with respect to Guinizelli, does not exclude that their verses, too, were "sweet," though presumably not so much so. In any case, I maintain that this quality was not, therefore, what distinguished the Italian "style" from the other Romance literatures. Nor was it its "newness," either in the superficial sense of a rhetorical mode peculiar to a school of poets, or in the sense of "modern" in contradistinction with the ancient, classical, Latin "style." For the same could be said of the French and Provençal "styles." Rossi is right in maintaining that "tanto la novità quanto la dolcezza dello stile erano già state immesse nella poesia amorosa prima di Dante."[6] And there is no contradiction, as Figurelli seems to think, between this statement of a historical fact and the analysis which Rossi then makes of the *novità* in the *dolce stil novo*. Where Rossi, too, fails, it seems to me, is in not realizing, any more than Figurelli, that, since neither the *novità* nor the *dolcezza* were characteristics introduced by Dante—since, indeed,

4. Figurelli, *op. cit.*, p. 16.   5. Cf. above, p. 200; also the note.
6. For convenience, I quote this opinion of Rossi in Figurelli's rendering, found on p. 18 of his *op. cit.* But see also V. Rossi's own "Il dolce stil novo" in *Scritti di critica Letteraria* (Firenze, Sansoni, 1930).

as we now see, they were qualities common not only to the poetry of the first "stilnovists" but also to the poetry of the previous Italian poets, and even to the literatures of Provence and France—this double qualification of the style of Dante's school, according to himself, does not really sum up nor does it describe further the *ars poetica* just enunciated by him in the preceding cryptic remark. Those adjectives apply merely to the "style" as a literary-artistic production resulting from his procedure, and describe only the result, that is, the "style" or literature itself with respect both to its originality of content and form, and to its effect on the author and reader. They do not refer to the procedure itself, and do not inform us at all as to the method whereby the poet obtained his result. Consequently, it is a mistake to make them the basis for the interpretation of the previous remark, which regards the principle and the procedure. It is a mistake to confuse the cause with the effect, and even to use the effect as a partial elucidation of the cause. In fact, the attempt to interpret Dante's method of procedure, which he implies is that of his school, in the light of those adjectives, or even with their partial assistance, leads inevitably to the reading into these adjectives, and in the whole remark, of connotations conceived more or less arbitrarily.

With all respect to the profound learning of the eminent modern critics just mentioned, may I point out that Lorenzo does not fall into this trap? He, too, makes use of those adjectives to describe the literature in *volgare,* and he, too, is, of course, perfectly aware of the intimate relation between cause and effect. But he is also aware of the fact that neither the *dolce stil novo* in the narrow sense of this phrase (which he does not hold), nor the literature in *volgare* as a whole, had a monopoly of these qualities. And for the penetration of the principle nourishing the Italian literature of the first period, he does not limit himself to an analysis of the finished product depending on a preconceived notion. Rather, as we have seen, he goes straight to the core of the matter, and first of all analyzes primarily the art itself. That is, he investigates first of all the poetic ideal pursued by the various authors, and then the method by which the true stilnovist achieved his *stile* called *dolce* and *novo.* Moreover, not even his point of departure may be said to be from Dante's definition. The latter must have been present in his mind, but he did not allow his possibly imperfect, direct understanding of it to influence him, not only because the master's definition might not apply to the subsequent production, but especially because Dante's theory and practice were part of the object of his investigation. He began by asking himself simply why the *donna* sung by those poets was called *gentile*. He began, I say, by investigating first the philosophical principle involved in the poetic ideal pursued by those poets. And it was this investigation which resulted in his discovery of the principle and ideal of *gentilezza umana*. This principle then enabled him to detect the real implication carried by Dante's esoteric remark, and, since the two principles were identical, he must have felt confirmed in his own independent opinion. Then, and only then, presumably, did he proceed with the task of verification which was to result in his own wonderful synthetic criticism of all that body of literature.

Allow me to quote in full Bonagiunta's discussion with Dante on this point, and, without repetition of Lorenzo's interpretation of the master's remark, as I surmised it before,[7] allow me now to comment on this episode as a whole. The dialogue runs as follows:

Bonagiunta—"Ma di' s'i' veggio qui colui che fore
         trasse le nove rime, cominciando
         '*Donne ch'avete intelletto d'amore.*' "
Dante—E io a lui: "I' mi son un, che quando
         Amor mi spira, noto, e a quel modo
         ch'e' ditta dentro vo significando."
Bonagiunta—"O frate, issa vegg'io" diss'elli "il nodo
         che 'l Notaro e Guittone e me ritenne
         di qua dal dolce stil novo ch'i' odo.
      Io veggio ben come le vostre penne
         di retro al dittator sen vanno strette,
         che de le nostre certo non avvenne;
      e qual più a riguardare oltre si mette,
         non vede più da l'uno a l'altro stilo."
      E, quasi contentato, si tacette.[8]

7. If necessary, see again pp. 131–134.
8. *Purgatorio*, XXIV, ll. 49–63.

The key to this much-disputed passage, the apparent clearness but real obscurity of which has given rise to many misconceptions, which Lorenzo's principle of "gentilesse" will now correct, is to be found in the comprehensive philosophical significance of *Amore.* This word should not be understood superficially and loosely in the ordinary sense of a vague sort of sentimental affection, nor even merely in the primary sense of elemental love according to Dante's own definition.[9] But it should be realized that *Amore* here is a strictly philosophical term connoting the poet's spiritual world; that it stands for the Divine Spirit inspiring his lofty conceptions; and that it is the personification of the poetic ideal he is pursuing. In other words, *Amore* here is that love which Lorenzo considers *quasi necessario* to mankind *ed assai vero argumento di gentilezza e grandezza d'animo.*[10] It is the love which he defines as *appetito di bellezza.* It is that *vero amore* which requires *che si ami una cosa sola . . . e che questa tale cosa si ami sempre.* Finally, it is that love which constitutes the subject of his own verses, and which is equivalent to a *grande perfezione . . . così nello amato come in chi ama.*

It is not entirely clear whether or not, in Lorenzo' opinion, Dante's "Love" came under *quello amore, il quale, secondo Platone, è mezzo a tutte le cose a trovare la loro perfezione e riposarsi ultimamente nella suprema Bellezza, cioè Dio.* For, owing to the fact that, as he says, he limits his subject to *quello amore che s'estende solamente ad mare l'umana creatura*—and this for the now obvious reason that he intends to revive the humanistic poetic ideal of the previous literature and is therefore chiefly concerned with those "human creations," which represented the highest products of the human genius: owing to this fact, I say, his critical remarks do not so much refer to the object of Dante's love as they regard the finished product of the poet's spirit. That is, as critic of that literature as a whole, he does not concern himself with the particular vision of the various poets, so much as he considers the

9. Dante's definition, it will be recalled, is that elemental love is a casual, spontaneous attraction followed by a natural bent toward anything that stirs the soul pleasantly. Cf. *Purgatorio,* XVIII, ll. 19–27.

10. For this and other quotations in this paragraph and the following, see Text, pp. 14–15, and this study, pp. 13–14.

somma perfezione (relatively speaking) of their "human" conceptions and the general *condizioni* of their perfect love as reflected
by their works. Moreover, inasmuch as that literature is now presented as the object of his own love, the *condizioni* he enumerates
for a perfect love really correspond to the characteristics of this
"cosa" amata by him, or to the virtues of the *gentilissima* as a
whole. In fact, *oltre alle naturali bellezze* of this literature, these
"conditions," we should remember, are: *ingegno grande, modi e
costumi ornati e onesti, maniera e gesti eleganti, destrezza d'accorte e dolci parole, amore, constanzia e fede;* which are all qualities of the poets themselves reflected in their works. This is the
reason why he does not precisely reveal the very special, personal
ideal of either Dante or any other of those poets, and, consequently, the reason why he does not bring out the degree of lofti-
ness aimed at, and attained by, each of them.

But, while Lorenzo's own subject, as literary critic, was necessarily limited to the consideration of the "simple" relative *bene*
constituted by the love of those "human creations," so that his poetic creative criticism of those works naturally excluded any original conception on his part regarding the *sommo bene* directly,
there can hardly be any doubt that he regarded the *Divina Commedia* especially as a manifestation of Dante's love for this universal *sommo bene.*

Accordingly, in his opinion, *Amore* here (that is, in the dialogue under consideration) undoubtedly stands for the Platonic
and Christian *sommo bene*—that is, for that composite of divine
and human values which makes for the welfare and happiness of
man in a well-organized civilized society following nature's course
and the universal order of things willed by God. On the other
hand, the inference also is that he certainly regarded the *Commedia* as the most humanistic of those "human creations," and Dante
as the most perfect of the humanists. Which is the point I wish to
make here again: namely, that for the Magnificent the fundamental principle of what has been called *dolce stil novo* was
identical with his own humanistic principle of *gentilezza.* For
him, this principle at once implied the Roman source and inspiration of a progressive continuity; a content of universal human

scope, character, and intent; a natural, scientific method of human education; and a poetic art consonant with this ideal of human perfection. And in his opinion it was this principle that really distinguished the Italian literature from the other literatures in Romance. This was its excellence and immense, incomparable superiority. This was what at once explained and truly entitled it to the appellation of *donna gentile,* indeed *gentilissima.*

Now observe how perfectly all this accords with the tenor and substance of Dante's dialogue with Bonagiunta. Observe the light that Lorenzo's critique of the literature in *volgare* throws on this passage; how at the same time his understanding of the history, import, and real originality of that literature is now confirmed by Dante's declaration of the true principle nourishing the *dolce stil novo* of Guinizelli's school in contradistinction to the common foreign type of "sweet new style" produced by those poets who had either preceded or remained extraneous to this important fundamental reform.

Bonagiunta remarks: "Are you not the poet who extricated the new Italian poetry from the tangles of imitation and superficiality, brought out the principle that newly informed it, and raised it to a high level of distinction and excellence, beginning his own new verses with the *canzone 'Donne ch'avete intelletto d'amore'?"* And Dante replies simply, modestly: "I was not the originator of the new principle you refer to, for this was introduced by Guinizelli,

> 'il padre
> mio e de li altri miei miglior che mai
> rime d'amore usar dolci e leggiadre.'

Nor was I the first to compose original verses in accordance with this new principle; for, although Guinizelli was not himself such an expert *fabbro del parlar materno* as Arnaut Daniel was of his, so much so that Cavalcanti soon deprived him of *la gloria de la lingua,*[11] I myself was preceded by both of them, in this respect. But I am a member of this new school, and 'perhaps' the one who now *l'uno e l'altro caccerà del nido.*[11] Indeed, I hope that,

11. *Purgatorio,* XI, ll. 97–99.

se mai continga che 'l poema sacro
al quale ha posto mano e cielo e terra,
sì che m'ha fatto per più anni macro,
vinca la crudeltà che fuor mi serra
del bello ovile ov'io dormi' agnello
nimico ai lupi che li danno guerra:
con altra voce omai, con altro vello
ritornerò poeta; ed in sul fonte
del mio battesmo prenderò 'l cappello;
però che ne la fede, che fa conte
l'anime a Dio, quivi intra' io, e poi
Pietro per lei sì mi girò la fronte.[12]

Now, if you wish to know the essence of my own contribution to this new style, I tell you simply that I adore the *suprema Bellezza, cioè Dio,* and in my practice merely adhere to the good old Roman principle of *gentilezza umana.* I love the *Sommo Bene,* and this *Amore,* which as Guinizelli said evinces a *cuor gentile* with which it is all one, corresponds therefore to my natural disposition to seek the light which illumines mankind and thus effects its welfare and happiness. In other words, I am a *humanist* of the good old Roman type, but a *Christian* one, who, thinking in terms of universal human values, strives to advance human civilization in the new light of the now current Christian faith to which I adhere. And my poetic ideal is to achieve my own degree of human perfection, while contributing to this general human progress. This *Amore,* or my conception of the *Sommo Bene* corresponding to my humanistic ideal, is the whole source of my inspiration. It is my personal guide in my poetic 'new life.' It is the real *dittatore* of my 'new verses.' I bide my time, and when an inspiration comes to me spontaneously from this source, I register it carefully in my mind and heart, or 'note it down'; and then merely proceed to express it faithfully, sincerely, in a sort of *verbum factum caro.* This, to be perfect, should not only reproduce my new conception, the state of my soul in harmony with the Spirit, and all the sweetness that comes from the effect of this content on my spirit. It should also produce in turn the same effect on the soul of my reader. That is, the concrete objective expression of the humanistic

12. *Paradiso,* XXV, ll. 1-12.

content, which was subjective in me, should in turn be capable of inspiring others similarly. And in becoming subjective again in other 'gentle hearts' it should originate in them a similar harmonious response accompanied by the same sweet affection. Therefore, I have no other rule but this: an original content of universal human scope, character, and effectiveness; and a corresponding form harmoniously new, sweet, and effective. And that is all there is to the style of my *nove rime.* On the other hand, this implies the closest adherence to the philosophical scientific principle of human 'gentilesse'—a principle which has the merit of being typically Latin (or Italian) and which in the past produced the great ness and glory of Rome. Finally, this is the 'newness' and the 'sweetness' of my *dolce stil novo.*"

The effect of Dante's cryptic remark has all been lost now in my elucidation of it with the aid of other related passages, all interpreted in the light of Lorenzo's critique. But Bonagiunta is illumined, convinced, and impressed by his concise, clear-cut, and precise description of the new ideal and poetic principle. There is no question as to his perfect understanding of all its esoteric meaning; and he must have considered the form in which the new concept was signified as exceedingly appropriate to express both the simplicity of the principle involved and the profound philosophical import of the ideal. Perhaps he regarded the statement as an example of the very style thus described. At any rate, he exclaims thereon what we may reword thus: "Now I see the difference between your sweet new style and ours. Now I see the *knot,* or crux of the argument, whereby the Notary, Guittone, and myself may truly be said not to have qualified as poets of the *dolce stil novo ch' i' odo.* The *point,* then, is that you poets of this new school entertain a Platonic, philosophical conception of Love; you pursue the ideal of human perfection; and in your poetic art you adhere strictly to the Roman principle of 'gentilesse' both as a human ideal and a natural scientific method of procedure. This is why you insist so much on the question of the real human noblesse, maintain that *Amore e 'l cor gentil sono una cosa,* and have made this principle the foundation and guide of your poetic 'new lives.' Moreover, the point is that you in particular now mean to revive, emulate, and possibly surpass the ancient learning of the Gentiles. You wish to resume, maintain, and transmit the noble tradition of their humanism and universality. You hope to advance human culture and refinement beyond the point reached by them. Finally, you imply that you mean to imitate no one unintelligently, slavishly, or superficially; rather, you mean to be armed with this past experience, and following the best examples of Roman poetic art, you believe that all inspirations should be derived from the philosophical, theologic conception of the supreme Beauty and fountain of all true knowledge.

"Verily, it cannot be said that this was our ideal and practice. Neither Giacomo da Lentini, standing for all the Sicilian School, nor Guittone d'Arezzo, who headed the Tuscan school of learned *provenzaleggianti,* nor I (to whom you have reserved the honor of this realization now, perhaps because my own ideal came the closest to Guinizelli's): none of us visualized all this. We did not conceive such a grand and inspiring program, which is, indeed, sweet and new in a supreme degree. We were merely content to follow the trend of the French, and especially the Provençal school of modern poetry, and to this foreign content and form we contributed no originality of our own. Therefore, in truth, our *nove rime* were 'new' and 'sweet' only in the sense in which all that current literature in any of the new *volgari* might be so described. That is, they were 'new' only in the sense that they were modern, both in content and form, with respect to the old type of Latin poetry, and modern was also the language in which they were written. And they were 'sweet' only in the sense that this modern and common subject matter was generally romantic, sentimental, light, and pleasant; and delicate was also the prosody—pleasant especially the softness of the new *volgare* in comparison with the Latin *gramatica.* We had no idea of the profound, intimate, and real 'sweetness' you speak of in connection with your humanistic content. We never conceived the real originality you contemplate with reference to the invention of new subject matter of universal human import, which calls of course for a first conception and therefore a truly original form.

"Therefore, now I see how in reality

. . . le vostre penne
di retro al dittator sen vanno strette,
che de le nostre certo non avvenne.

The subject and object of your verses, is, in fact, as you imply, the Platonic and Christian Love, and I fully realize now that this *Amore* is truly the inspirer of all your poetic activity. This was *certainly* not the case with us, who had the common, ordinary conception of terrestrial human love, and did not visualize the *Sommo Bene,* nor aimed at all at the ideal of human perfection. Moreover, now I can see how in your poetic art you actually adhere strictly to the principle of 'gentilesse.' For you mean that ideally your expression is always equivalent to or identical with your intuition. You mean that, in the process of materializing your response to the inspirations of the *Sommo Bene* (and the concepts that these inspirations originate in your mind), you strive to reproduce faithfully both your intuition in the natural form in which it comes to you and the affection that your humanistic ideal and the new discovery produce in your heart. You mean that you attune your soul to the harmony of the Universe with the ideal of human perfection in mind. You apply the principle of 'gentilesse' to the study of human nature and human values. And, when the revelation or inspiration confidently awaited comes to you, you merely reproduce your new conception in the form in which it has come, together with all the elements of your spiritual experience. Finally, you mean that you always strive to attain perfect harmony between the content of your concept and the external form of its expression—in order that it may produce in others the same affection. Wherefore your style may, in fact, be *aspro* on occasion, or otherwise virile, but is always suitable to the matter in hand. And this, you maintain, is also 'sweetness.' I see. It is the sweetness of all this harmoniousness you strive for: harmony between your natural disposition and the object of your pursuit; harmony between the content and the form of the subject matter treated; and harmony between the effectiveness of your verses and the response expected from other 'gentle hearts.'

"This is, indeed, a great, a tremendous difference. It is a profound, substantial difference. But it is all internal. Externally and superficially, there is no obvious difference between your style and ours. For, outwardly, you too have fashioned your ideal after the manner of the French and Provençal poets. I mean that you have conceived your new poetic ideal as a *donna gentile,* who, as *donna,* does not differ apparently from any of the numerous *donne* (real or symbolical) sung by us and all the previous poets of our modern age. Moreover, you sing your love for this ideal as if it were a common human love between man and woman, precisely as we did our own *amori* more or less idealistic. Thus there is no external evidence that you are singing the lofty humanistic ideal you say. Nor is your principle of 'gentilesse' at all obvious. Your general manner and attitude appear to be the same as ours. Your sentiments and feelings seem to be the same. Even the qualities you exalt are identical with or resemble very closely the qualities praised by us. Indeed, your language is none other than our dear common *volgare,* sweet and new, and all your images, your very phraseology, are all exactly like ours. Verily, anyone who tries to see any other difference than the one just brought out by you, so simply and modestly, so clearly and effectively, will not find it."

E, quasi contentato, si tacette.

CHAPTER VII

Summary of the Esoteric Meaning of Sonnet II and of the Author's Comment on It.

THE preceding long elucidations—the first concerning the author's would-be apology for his use of the *volgare,* and the second regarding his presumable understanding of Dante's principle informing his *dolce stil novo*—have probably diverted the reader's attention from the main line of my argumentation. But they were both necessary, in order that we might comprehend fully the import of Lorenzo's critique of the literature in *volgare,* which, in turn, we needed in order to detect the historical implications we suspected in his remark that his "lady" as well as himself died mystically (and withal literally) "in a month of April." On the other hand, the fact that they have been made in the light of this very critique, resulting from his own application of the principle which, according to him, informed all that literature, has permitted us to point out the said implications and to consider them in the very course of making these elucidations. Thus all we need to do now is to recapitulate our findings and draw our conclusions.

We were saying:[1] Just as the interpretation of the metaphorical April in terms of the poet's age has given us approximately the probable historical date of his actual initiation into the "new life"; so the reading of this esoteric meaning in the life of the *gentilissima* should enlighten us with regard to the commentator's critical opinion relative to her status at the time of her literal death as a body of poetic "finite things," and also give us the historical circumstances attending this death. We have not been disappointed in our expectation. For I believe we now have a fairly clear idea of the truly *degnissime condizioni* of the *eccellentissima "donna"* incarnating the supreme *bellezza e gentilezza umana* when her "death" occurred historically. Now we know all the *bellezza* of

1. Cf. above, p. 189.

that truly *gentilissima* Italian literature; we appreciate her apparently greater beauty when its ideal, alas, seemed spent; and we understand the nature as well as the naturalness of the *ardentissimo desiderio* left by her in every *cor gentile*. We realize also the splendor of this literature's *bellezza,* notwithstanding the *età molto verde* at the time of its decline. We understand the fond hope of our "new Clytie," who worked for the revival of its ideal, and prophesied even greater "things" for it *nella gioventù ed adulta età sua.* Finally, we, too, visualize now the poet's *chiarissima stella:* the star whose splendor was truly such that it outshone by far every other "star" or literary ideal of western Europe, the star that even obscured, or "cast a shadow" on all materialistic aims opposing this lofty illuminating conception of the true ideal of human perfection (faceva far ombra a quelli corpi che a tale luce si opponevono).

Verily, as we look back upon that whole period of actual revival called the Renaissance, we see that it was not so much the revival of the ancient humanistic spirit and learning, as it was the revival of the Italian ideal of arts and letters originated by the "stilnovists" (in Dante's sense of this word later extended by the Magnificent). We cannot but agree that "either the soul of that *gentilissima* had become transformed into this new 'star,' or else it had been fused with it." We cannot but agree that it might truly be said that this "star," in either case, could well contend with Phoebus himself then *e domandargli il suo carro, per essere lei autrice del giorno.* For it was in fact the new bearer of the intellectual light illumining all mankind; it was the artificer of our modern civilization.

From the remark that his lady died in a month of April we make the following final deductions. Lorenzo implies that he himself was very young when he began the systematic critical study of the new Italian literature in *volgare,* a study which was to mark his initiation into the "new life" of the stilnovists. Further, he implies that, in his opinion, that literature, too, had not yet advanced then beyond the primitive stage, or period of adolescence. On one hand, he means that he was a mere youth when in the course of that study he first realized all the import of that literature (a realization which involved his mystic death coincidently with that of this "lady" for him). And, on the other, he implies that the poetic ideal, proposed and exemplified by that literature, had declined by then; in fact, it had been dead for nearly a century, and had spent itself at the height of its fecundity, just when that first period of splendid *primizie* promised a more abundant harvest.

Moreover, remembering our conclusions relative to the theoretico-philosophic import of this remark about April, and remembering the didactic purpose of the whole *principio,* as well as the exemplary character of the author's personal experience, we conclude this: Lorenzo means not only that he himself engaged in this preparatory study (indispensable for a proper initiation into the "new life") naturally and properly in his early youth, indeed auspiciously *del mese d'aprile,* but also that, in his opinion, the period of adolescence, or formative years of one's life, is naturally the period best suited to such a zealous, intensive study of the humanities here represented by the *gentilissima;* and that early spring is naturally the season of the year most conducive to the spiritual elevation necessary to pierce the literal veil of that literature, realize its philosophic import, detect its artistic principle, and become imbued with its humanistic spirit.

Keep in mind all this esoteric significance of the initial remark; and, without forgetting the intent of the *principio* as a whole, recall also the various other points made: relative to Lorenzo's respectful but independent approach to that body of literature, relative to the original, "creative" nature of his criticism, relative to the newness of his own style resulting from his strict adherence to the maxim *nosce te ipsum,* and, especially, relative to his immediate task here of finding a suitable embodiment of the mystic death to illustrate the present status of the *gentilissima* and his own condition in relation to her. Remembering all this, we may now recast for the last time, in the following form, the comment as a whole, in order to bring out all its historico-critical import.

Says the Magnificent, in my recast of his comment on Sonnet II many years after it was written: "My initiation into the poetic 'new life' of the stilnovists, which as I said in the proem forms the subject of the first four sonnets of my *nuova vita* therefore called the *principio,* my initiation occurred naturally, spontaneously, and auspiciously in a month of April. Then, like nature in the first of its annual cycle of seasons, I, too, was in a state of adolescence, and, like nature in spring, I also felt an internal urge to put forth shoots and flowers in new manifestations of my potential self. As I said in the preceding comment on the first of those sonnets, it began with that very sonnet; or, more precisely, with the conversation I happened to have with a dear friend of mine on the subject of the *gentilissima* Italian poetry and its sad, premature decline. This reflection gave rise to that sonnet. In fact, it was in the course of this conversation, or literary discussion, while we were both deeply regretting the *commune iattura* of this great loss to humanity, that I suddenly developed the desire to revive the spirit of that great literature. I spontaneously conceived the idea of making the poetic ideal of those first authors our own. The idea was to make a thorough and systematic critical study of all the poets of the period now closed, especially of the most significant ones, for the purpose of discovering the secret of their excellence, or the poetic ideal and artistic principle followed by them. Then we would be able to look up to this 'soul' of the *gentilissima* as to a *chiarissima stella,* which should illumine and guide our poetic lives, inspire our own original production, and generally influence, if not actually nourish, all the literature of the new epoch.

"Accordingly, in my youthful enthusiasm, I decided there and then to become a stilnovist, resolved for myself too to live as well as to write a *nuova vita;* and I began my own initiation precisely by registering my first experience. In fact, in the first sonnet, I voice the above sentiments: I point to the new ideal, which in principle was intended to be substantially the original ideal of the great masters; and I pray to the 'divinity' of the brilliant star I had just conceived to mitigate its splendor, that we might not be dazzled by it. That is, I hope that the splendor of this 'divine' ideal conceived by me shall not impede our critical task of deriving from the literature itself the very ideal and principle we meant to revive. For, while that first experience proved the 'gentle' nature of my own heart and marked the initial stage of my personal initiation into the 'new life,' the reader should not assume that the mere conception on my part of a new ideal which involved the old implied necessarily that either I or my friend had then a clear understanding of the original ideal we had decided to adopt. Then we had only a vague intuition of the humanistic import and Roman derivation of that literature, and we were deeply impressed mainly by its manifest beauty and effectiveness. We did not realize as yet either the principle on which those authors had conceived their poetic ideal, or the ideal itself, or the principle of their art. In other words, we had no idea as yet of the principle of 'gentilesse' informing both their ideal and their style, which I discovered later. Still, we divined enough to make us feel that the decline and consequent obscuring of their basic principle was equivalent to the setting of a sun of intellectual light. And, in the ensuing darkness, or in my ignorance of that principle, I wondered when, if ever, a new dawn of enlightenment would announce the return of this sun to the world. That is, I wondered when some new genius would resume the spirit and ideal of that poetic art. I personally despaired of ever detecting the secret we were looking for, although I knew that it might be sought in the 'finite things' those poets had left us.

"I felt, therefore, that, under favorable conditions of mind and body, of age and environment, by a zealous effort to rise to their level of spiritual contemplation, and by constant, profound meditation on those works, one could at least hope to realize finally all their import and discover the principle underlying them all. Even then, this would be no guaranty that we ourselves should produce works of similar value and perfection. But it seemed to me that the definite knowledge of that principle would at least enlighten us as to their real poetic ideal and the secret of their art. Their works then would be a real source of inspiration to us. They would give us guidance without hampering our personality. And we could then emulate them without imitating them either slavishly or unintelligently.

"But meanwhile our immediate task was precisely the sort of critical investigation I suggested. Only, I did not realize what this meant, until after more mature reflection. The difficulty of penetrating into the heart of that literature, of detecting both singly and collectively the real significance of the major works at least, and, finally, of extracting the soul of the *gentilissima*—the arduousness and indispensableness of this task now tempered my enthusiasm. But this consideration also clarified the project. It defined my position with respect to that literature, which, obviously now, was to be at the start one of historian and creative critic. It brought out the necessity of a period of apprenticeship. And, above all, it made me realize the indispensableness of my own mystic death coincidently with that of the *donna* of my imagination. That is, in order to grasp first the principle of the poetic ideal I had decided to adopt, it was necessary, as I suggested, to rise to the high level of spiritual contemplation reached by those poets. And, if ultimately I wished to qualify fully as a stilnovist, it was essential that I also attune my soul to the spirit which had dictated their noble works. The difficulty of this undertaking did not deter me, but I feared lest my capacity might prove unequal to it.

"I was, therefore, dejected, disconsolate, and felt like an ardent lover, who wishing to revive his dear beloved lying dead before him, gazes upon her countenance helplessly and yet longingly, hoping against hope that his love may bring her back to life again, and thus remains in a state of vague expectancy. This condition of my spirit was piteous, but poetically beautiful, and also gave promise of future success. For I felt that I was even then undergoing the necessary process of mystic death, which was fundamental to the successful execution of my immediate task.

"Indeed, I now realized that my spiritual elevation had commenced with the first consideration of the excellence and sudden decline of the Italian poetry. But now the realization of the preliminary task revealed to me my real position with respect to my lady 'dead'; and the spiritual condition, which this consciousness created in me, was clearly indicative of the spiritualization I was undergoing consciously, since I was aware of this condition and pitied my lot. Accordingly, it seemed to me that the full consciousness of my arduous, indispensable task; the consequent fearful state of my mind and heart; and my zeal and determination despite everything—these all marked a step forward in the direction of my immediate and ultimate goal.

"This might be said to correspond to the second stage of my initiation, and so I decided to register it in another of those sonnets which should constitute the *principio* of my *nuova vita*. The idea was to compose a sonnet which for one thing would portray my present condition of ardent lover in almost hopeless expectancy before the beautiful body of his beloved apparently dead; and which would depict my longing for the light I sought in order to interpret correctly that body of literature and later attempt to revive its spirit, ideal, and principle; but one which would also depict the state of mystic death I was then attaining not unlike the poets I took to be my masters. Finally, I sought to compose a sonnet which might stand as the example par excellence of man's eternal love for the intellectual light. In other words, I wanted this sonnet to be a practical demonstration of *my* experience of the mystic death in connection with my particular problem, and also serve as a model of *any* instance of mystic death past or future.

"With this idea in mind, I went therefore to my library, and, seeking inspiration, began to review all the recorded cases of mystic death I could think of, both ancient and modern. There was Petrarch's, there was Dante's, there was Cavalcanti's, there was Guinizelli's, and many others. I picked out some of these texts, and, with them, went out into the garden to meditate. For it was a beautiful day, and, as I say, we were in the month of April. The garden was all a-bloom, and it was most refreshing to feast my eyes and recreate my soul in the midst of that variety of natural and literary flowers. Meanwhile I was waiting for an inspiration. I wanted especially a metaphor that would incarnate my concept, and picture my present condition in relation to the state of Italian poetry at that time. But, while almost any one of the various suggestions offered by the masters seemed to lend itself to such treatment, and I even read my thought in the numberless suggestions offered by nature all about me, none of them met with all my requirements and satisfied me completely.

"Then I happened to cast my eye on the humble *tornalsole* and had a flash of inspiration. For this little flower, called in Latin

clitia, reminded me of the myth Clytie related by Ovid. It reminded me of the nymph Clytie, first recorded example of man's
natural aspiration to unite with the supreme Beauty, that is, God,
as Plato puts it; of Clytie, thereafter symbol of this aspiration,
whose name had been immortalized by being given to the little
flower resembling her in nature. The aspiration of the ancient leg-
endary Clytie was so identical with my own, and her image on
earth in the evening was such a perfect reflection of my own situation then, that I felt at once: there was my sonnet. In fact I only
needed to compare myself to her in order to depict briefly and
pointedly my longing for the light I sought, my discouragement
at the time, and my attitude toward that earlier literature. To be
sure, there appeared to be a difference: The grief of the *tornalsole*
might be said to be all the greater because the vision denied to it
at night is even then enjoyed on the other side of the terrestrial
globe; and by this, in my simile, I could imply that the sun of intellectual light which had set for us was even then perhaps shining
on other parts of the world. Nevertheless the flower is sure of the
return of the sun the next morning, just as the human genius may
always expect at intervals a divine inspiration of some kind or
other; whereas I knew not when, if ever, a new dawn would announce the return of our 'Sun,' or the particular ideal and principle nourishing the previous Italian poetry. I felt, however, that
the comparison of myself to the ancient Clytie would imply that I
was reaching that level of pure spiritual contemplation which I
deemed necessary in order to pierce the veil of fiction around
those poetic works and to penetrate the secret of their art. I decided, therefore, to adopt this simile, and did so all the more
readily because of the way in which I had come to conceive it. For
it had come to me in the act of the very mystic death I was even
then myself achieving and which I wished to portray. This is how
I came to compose this sonnet, this is its esoteric meaning, and this
is how it, too, like the first, is *principio di nuova vita.*"

Transitional Remarks.

HERE I end this long third part of my treatise. But I am aware of the fact that, notwithstanding its prolixity and repetitiousness, I have not yet drawn many of the inferences to which I have hinted on various occasions, besides the ones which demanded immediate attention. In view of the larger scope of my work, it is now desirable that, before I proceed with the exposition of the comments on the third and fourth sonnets, I take up at this point some of the matters left for later consideration. For my study is not limited to the mere understanding of Lorenzo's *principio,* but is intended to bring out finally the value of his *Comento* as a guide to the thorough understanding and proper appreciation of the literature embodying his poetic ideal. Consequently, I shall postpone the treatment of the second half of the *principio,* and insert here a section or part which will be in the nature of a long digression pertinent, however, to the subject at hand. The reader who is anxious to apprehend the esoteric meaning of Sonnets III and IV, may skip this part for the time being, and pass directly to Part V.

This extra section—which perhaps intrudes here, but which I feel should not be relegated to the end of the book as if it were an appendix—will deal with Lorenzo as a *continuatore insieme e novatore* of the theory and practice of the stilnovists. This rôle, which he assumed with full consciousness, involves his derivation and modification of both his theory of springtime and his concept of the poetic mystic death; and therefore its study has a proper place here. Besides, the study of Lorenzo's sources is important, not only to demonstrate the correctness of my interpretation of his comments, but also to bring out the innovations introduced by him in his borrowed *principio.* This study, moreover, will afford us a double opportunity, because Lorenzo's derivations and modifications in connections with the *principio* of the poetic *nuova vita* reveal two things: first, his penetration of this *principio,* and, second, his assumption (shared by his contemporaries) that such a *principio* existed in the minds of his predecessors. We shall be able to appreciate better the critical acumen of the Magnificent, which will strengthen his authority as a critic and historian of the pre-

Renaissance period. And we shall begin to apply his "key" to the interpretation of the previous poets; this test, if successful, will demonstrate the veracity of his principle and its value for us, and will also illuminate his concept further.

Furthermore, our inferences will reveal the historical and critical significance of his adoption of the myth of Clytie to represent the attitude of the modern stilnovist. And this will enable us, both to visualize fully and correctly the ideal pursued and proposed by him, and to realize the continuity of this ideal in the history of Italian arts and letters. Finally, these inferences will not only bring out his own innovations in the theory and practice of "gentilesse" —innovations which constitute his originality as a critic of the previous literature—but will also clarify for us his historico-critical concept of that literature. As we have seen already and shall see better anon, he regarded the great masters especially as poetic critics like himself, or *continuatori insieme e novatori* of the ancient classical poetry. This is most significant in connection with the vast scope, true character, and whole purpose of the Renaissance in its various manifestations. Of course, I shall only touch upon the various questions involved, and shall limit myself to a bare outline of the vast critical field they reveal. For an adequate treatment of them, or even any one of them, would take me too far afield, would exceed the proportions of this work, and might easily lead me to anticipate its later use. On the other hand, I shall insist properly on the new point of view the Magnificent reveals for the study of Italian literature through the centuries, and especially from its inception throughout the Renaissance.

PART IV

LORENZO, *CONTINUATORE INSIEME E NOVATORE*

CHAPTER I

*Introduction to the Study of Lorenzo's Sources for His
Theoretic Principle.*

LORENZO'S sources for his *principio* as a theoretic principle of
the stilnovistic *nuova vita* must have been the very poets he
exalted in the proem. Cavalcanti, Dante, Petrarch, and Boccaccio, whom he presented there as the greatest masters of the
dolce stil novo or new Italian literature in *volgare,* are also regarded by him, we well remember, as the highest authorities on
the subject of stilnovistic or humanistic love, which is the subject
of his own *nuova vita*—as he explains most carefully and emphatically. Indeed, his own ideal, as we have now deduced, was precisely the revival of the spirit and poetic art of those masters. Consequently, it was both natural and necessary for him to resort to
their works. And, since he intended that these initiatory sonnets
should incarnate their principle, we should have been surprised if,
on the contrary, we had not found them imbued with their spirit
and doctrine. They are; and that Dantean and Petrarchan flavor
especially, which we sensed in our first perusal of them,[1] now becomes the very substance of these sonnets, as we penetrate them in
the light of his own comments.

The elements advisedly chosen and fused together to form the
principle, are, to be sure, common to all those poets—a circumstance which shows the critic's acumen and judicious discrimination in selecting and combining the essentials. Nevertheless, we
are frequently able to recognize, now a concept first contributed
by a certain one of them, and now the particular form given to
it by another; now the special doctrine or general practice of still
another, and now the peculiar style of any one of them. Thus, for
instance, the form of the first sonnet seems to me modeled more
after Dante than after Petrarch; although this is difficult to say, inasmuch as this sonnet is the most original, and perhaps naturally

1. Cf. p. 94.

so, since Lorenzo there presents his own modified modern conception of the old ideal. In contrast, the doctrine of the third and fourth sonnets, as we shall see in the chapters dealing with them, was derived primarily from Cavalcanti's *canzone* following the comments of Egidio Colonna and Dino del Garbo; although their form, especially that of the fourth, is all Petrarchan. Finally, I shall bring out presently the contribution of both Dante and Petrarch, and probably also Boccaccio, to the composition of Sonnet II just expounded. All of this seems to leave very little to their author. But this method is in keeping both with his profession of being a *continuatore insieme e novatore* and with the derivative nature of his *principio,* which was what he sought in the works of the masters and what they alone could best give to him. The result is precisely what I believe he wanted it to be. For the reader is thus made aware of what each poet has contributed to the *principio* presented, and finally realizes that, by his own intention, the critic constitutes a sort of least common denominator to those poets. Still further, in the light of this remarkably poetic and creative criticism, the reader can do even more than arrive at a clear and true understanding of those poets' original concepts. He can also realize the common essentials of their doctrine, and perceive finally Lorenzo's own contribution or innovations.

With this expectation, let us proceed, then, with our investigation of the sources relative to the elements entering especially in the composition of Sonnet II. These are the concept of the mystic death, the theory of springtime, and the simile of Clytie.

I have already quoted intentionally part of a sonnet of Petrarch's and certain verses of Dante's,[2] in which these poets undoubtedly voice the same sentiments regarding spring which are also implied by the Magnificent as our deduction has shown us. Petrarch recalls the general state of nature during this season, and implies its normal, beneficent effect on man, as well as on all animals, by contrast with his own condition at the moment. Dante implies as much, and bases his hope of success on this same influence. Then I observed that Dante in those verses referred also to *l'ora del tempo,* which was *dal principio del mattino,* and spoke of

2. Cf. pp. 178–179.

this circumstance as also propitious. Now, before I comment on this additional factor, we need to collect other data, which all together will constitute the material for our discussion.

We may remember that Dante stages his ultramundane voyage in spring, and precisely during Holy Week. He descends into Hell on the eve of Good Friday, reaches the summit of Purgatory, or the Terrestrial Paradise, where he meets his symbolic Beatrice, at dawn on Resurrection Sunday, and begins his ascension to Heaven at noon of the same day. This, in the year 1300, occurred in April. And the *Commedia* is full of similar references to appropriate circumstances, now natural, now spiritual, and now both. Dante does not specify the precise time and place when his first and second meeting with his lady occurred, because, as we know, he was apparently interested in other significances on those occasions.[3] But it is relevant here to recall that the incident which resulted in his adoption of a so-called *donna della "difesa"* or *donna dello "schermo"* took place in a church during a religious service likewise attended by Beatrice.[4] Finally, we should remember this: Dante's lady does not die in April, but historically on June 8, 1290, and he apparently does not connect this date with his first initiation into the "new life"; but, nevertheless, he goes out of his way and calls into play all his rare ingenuity to demonstrate, with the aid of three calendars, that Beatrice died on the ninth day of the month, on the ninth month of the year, and on the ninth decade of the century. He does all this in order to prove that the symbolic number nine was *in tanto amico di lei.*[5]

We need to recall these various points, which are part of the ground investigated by the pupil in his analysis and synthesis of the master's doctrine, because later Petrarch too enveloped his amorous experience in a significant veil of poetic mysticism. And, in order to see what the critic selected from his authorities in the process of establishing their principle, in order to see the relation he perceived in their several, varying concepts, finally, in order to realize his own critical innovations—we need to cover approximately the same ground.

3. Cf. *Vita Nuova*, II and III.   4. *Idem*, V.
5. *Idem*, XXIX.

Proceeding: In a well-known sonnet, which I shall presently quote, Petrarch signifies that he first saw his Laura in church during a Good Friday service. And from a famous, hitherto mystifying, note, which I shall also quote—a note found written in his own handwriting on the flyleaf of his dear, inseparable Virgil (now preserved in the *Biblioteca Ambrosiana* of Milan), we learn that this church was the Church of Saint Claire in Avignon, and that the date was the first hour, or early morning, of April 6, 1327. Moreover, this note informs us that Laura later died on the precise anniversary of this commencement of his amorous passion, namely, on the first hour of April 6, 1348. Skeptic critics usually smile upon all this, and pass it on without explanation. But, as we shall see, in the light of Lorenzo's creative criticism, these circumstances set forth by Petrarch as facts all acquire a significance which is hard to dismiss lightly. In fact, the esoteric implication of the circumstances attending the various stages of the poet's amorous experience, and especially the significance of the precise correspondence established by him in the said note called by Scherillo a sort of *chiave storica del "Canzoniere"*:[6] these implications seem to be confirmed by a passage from his *Epistula Posteritati*. In this, after alluding presumably to his love for the mother of his illegitimate children—an *amore acerrimo sed unico et honesto,* from which a *mors acerba sed utilis* had freed him, he recalls his final victory over the senses amounting to a veritable Laurentian mystic death. This passage, too, I shall quote in full and discuss in turn.

Now I shall end this brief suggestive list of Lorenzo's probable sources by recalling finally that, while Cavalcanti apparently has left no record of any such mysterious happenings and miraculous coincidences in connection with his amorous experience, on the contrary Boccaccio, too—like Dante and Petrarch—gives at least a hint of wishing to imply something similar. He also connects the beginning of his amorous passion with an anniversary of Christ's passion, declaring, in turn, that he first met his Fiammetta in the Church of San Lorenzo in Naples on Resurrection Saturday![7] It is

6. Cf. Michele Scherillo, *Le origini e lo svolgimento della letteratura italiana* (Milano, Hoepli, 1919), I, 257.

7. *Idem,* p. 404; and Scherillo's source for this account: Boccaccio, *Filocolo,* I.

true that he does not elaborate this "fact": probably either because Holy Saturday in 1336 recurred on *March* 30 (not in *April*), or because he personally did not attach much importance to the date of his "commencement" and the circumstances attending it. This last supposition is more likely, but it is obvious that his recording in turn such a detail is at least an indication of his desire to imitate his predecessors in this respect, especially Petrarch. Moreover, it is relevant in this connection to remember that the young men and women of the *Decameron* meet in a church (the Church of Santa Maria Novella in Florence), and that the setting for their *novelle* are presumably the beautiful hills of Fiesole in late spring or early summer while in the city below the plague is raging and people are dying of the "black death" by the thousands.[8]

This is the sort of "fact" from which the Magnificent obviously derived his masters' doctrine and the substance of his *principio*. To him, such real or realistic circumstances were significant, and he attached considerable importance to them. For, as critic of the previous literature, he evidently regarded such "facts" either as allusions to theories and philosophical concepts held by those poets on the basic principle of the stilnovistic new life, or as contrivances excogitated by them to present in poetic form the real or supposed factors which, on analysis, they discovered to have determined theoretically their respective "new life." At least, this is the conclusion we must come to when we consider the use he made of them and what he discarded in his reconstruction, or creative criticism, of their theoretic principle. Perhaps we begin to see already what each contributed to this reconstruction. At any rate, now we realize that Lorenzo's main authorities for the concept of the mystic death and the theory of springtime must have been Dante and Petrarch, while Boccaccio probably taught him especially ancient mythology, and particularly the use he could make of the myth of Clytie. Moreover, since, of those poets, Petrarch alone had placed the death of his lady specifically within the month of April, and since Petrarch alone had established unequivocally a definite relation between this death and the commencement of his amorous passion, it follows, I believe, that Petrarch was his direct source

8. Cf. Boccaccio, *Decamerone,* the introduction to the first day.

and main authority for the content and form of his own *principio*.[9] So, let us review first this poet's initiation into the "new life."

9. This reasoning is especially based on the authenticity of the note on the Ambrosiana "Virgil" (cf. above, p. 240), which, however much it may have been questioned in the sixteenth century, is yet accepted by the majority of modern scholars. For a discussion of this authenticity, cf. Gustav Gröber, "Von Petrarca's Laura," in *Miscellanea di studi critici edita in onore di Arturo Graf* (Bergamo, 1903), pp. 53–76.

CHAPTER II

Petrarch's Sonnet on His Initiation into the "New Life."

PETRARCH'S sonnet referred to above reads as follows:

> Era il giorno ch'al sol si scoloraro
> per la pietà del suo fattore i rai,
> quando i' fui preso, e non me ne guardai,
> chè i be' vostr'occhi, donna, mi legaro.
> Tempo non mi parea da far riparo
> contr' a' colpi d'Amor; però m'andai
> secur, senza sospetto: onde i miei guai
> nel commune dolor s'incominciaro.
> Trovommi Amor del tutto disarmato,
> et aperta la via per gli occhi al core,
> che di lagrime son fatti uscio e varco.
> Però, al mio parer, non li fu onore
> ferir me de saetta in quello stato,
> a voi armata non mostrar pur l'arco.[1]

Let us examine it rather closely. As I said above, the implication is that it was Good Friday when the poet first saw his Laura. We are not told here which Good Friday it was, nor the month in which it fell that year, nor the hour of day. These details are specified minutely in the note to which I referred, which was written many years later, on the occurrence of his lady's death. Here, very properly, they were not included in a poetic account; instead, all the attention was centered upon the most significant circumstance in connection with the crucial moment described. The importance of this circumstance was that, accordingly, the commencement of his amorous passion coincided with the annual reënactment of the passion of Christ: which, of course, symbolizes the mystic death of humanity for its spiritual redemption. Wherefore he says that his troubles began in the midst of the general sorrow for the death of the Lord, implying by this the common painful effort, on that occasion, to rise above the purely materialistic aspect of things,

1. Cf. Petrarca, *Le rime sparse, ed. cit.,* p. 4, Sonnet III.

and, discarding the pleasures of the senses, elevate one's spirit to the consideration of true human life.

In the light of Lorenzo's interpretation of the terms *morte* and *donna* in stilnovistic literature, the meaning therefore is that Petrarch's initial mystic death and simultaneous first conception of his poetic ideal occurred under those circumstances. Indeed, the elevation of his spirit and first manifestation of his "gentle" nature did not merely happen to occur then, but were brought about by those circumstances. It was the mournful reënactment of Christ's sacrifice, before a doleful congregation in a gloomy atmosphere, that first drew Petrarch's attention to the profound, anagogic significance of that sacrifice. It was this circumstance that led him to meditate over the theological concept of the mystic death. And thereupon "the eyes of his lady bound him." That is, the very act of his realizing the significance, or "gentilesse," of Christ's death was, as it were, a ray of light coming from the eyes of the *donna gentile* sung by the stilnovists; and his visualization of this poetic ideal meant at once his devotion to it ever after. In other words, it was the principle of human "gentilesse," involving the state of mystic death for "lady" and poet, that illuminated his mind the moment his spirit was attuned to the "judicious distinction" of the "thing" called Christ's death. It was this "light" emanating from the intellectual eyes of the stilnovists' metaphorical lady that gave him the true intelligence of Christ's death. Or else, the two concepts simply illumined each other, and they were found identical; with this difference, that Christ's example now seemed to him the supreme incarnation and indisputable proof of the veracity and excellence of the principle held by the stilnovists.

The dual nature of Christ pointed to the human and divine nature of man as well, especially the seer or humanist-poet. His death symbolized the elevation of the spirit above matter, the redemption of the human soul from the slavery of the senses; in a word, it implied the commencement of the kind of "new life" which the stilnovists idealized and practiced. In any case, the immediate effect of this double realization was that, given his natural disposition, he inclined at once toward this kind of poetic life, or was captivated by it. This was natural and inevitable. For, as

Dante had said, quoting and interpreting Guinizelli, "Amore e 'l cor gentil sono una cosa."[2] Accordingly, the future poet was bound forever to follow this ideal, for he had now seen the "light" in his "lady's" eyes. Indeed, his initiation into this "new life" began at that very moment, with this first clear realization of the principle of the mystic death; which implies presumably a first vague visualization of his special poetic ideal, or, at least, the potential expectation of "finding himself." But the application of the maxim, *nosce te ipsum,* was by no means easy. Wherefore he remarks somewhat bitterly, "i miei guai / nel commune dolor s'incominciaro."

The solemn occasion of a Good Friday service was indeed no time in which to expect either the revelation of the ideal pursued by a school of poets, or the manifestation of a natural disposition to adopt their course. Consequently, the future stilnovist was, as he says, unprepared to withstand the onslaught of Love, and went to the service unaware of what was in store for him. This surely implies the spontaneity of his conception and the sincerity of his whole experience. Perhaps it is a sign that the account is historically true. In any case, the effect is the same, whether true or ingeniously devised in order to substantiate by means of a real or realistic personal experience the veracity of the concept involved and of the theory thereby propounded. The poet means to demonstrate how he himself came to join the school of the stilnovists and first attained a clear conception of both their principle of the mystic death and the poetic ideal pursued by them. There is nothing improbable in this account. Whereas, whether or not we accept his testimony, that is, whether or not this all happened in church on a Good Friday, it is very significant to the historian and critic that Petrarch connects his initiation into the stilnovistic new life with the passion and death of Christ. For, in the light of Lorenzo's *principio di nuova vita,* this reveals the real nature and purpose of Petrarch's *rime,* manifests the intimate connection between these and the rest of his poetic production, explains all his literary activity and the real intent of his noble humanism, and thus confirms the critical opinion of the Magnificent regarding the value

2. Cf. *Vita Nuova,* XX.

of his works and his proper place in Italian literature. We shall conclude later that nothing is true in this account, except the connection I have mentioned and the intent of exemplary character given to the death of Christ. But this will merely prove that Lorenzo's similar contrivance had an authoritative precedent in Petrarch's *principio,* as we shall see in a later investigation.

Writing this sonnet many years after the occurrence of the event, indeed after Laura's death when he decided to collect his *rime sparse* and arrange them in order, the poet now plays with his recollection of this initial step in his career as a poet-humanist. Elaborating on it, he envelops his simple original experience in a conceit which is as suitably juvenile as it seems reminiscent of the primitive type of stilnovistic content and form. He pictures Love classically as a youthful archer, remarks sportively that this last feat of his has certainly brought him no honor, and complains lightly that he has been wounded unfairly. He was all absorbed in religious meditation, and was therefore completely disarmed. Indeed, owing to the sense of security afforded by the circumstances, he was all too unsuspecting of any imminent danger. And Love had taken unfair advantage of this situation. Finding through his eyes—which now have become an outlet for many tears—the way open to his heart, he had shot an arrow into it, and had thus inflicted on him presumably a "mortal" wound; whereas to his "lady" fully armed he had not even displayed his bow.

If we discard the playful tone of this reminiscence, which may be due to its fanciful character at a time when the poet, already laureate and fully mature, had long outgrown the forms of primitive stilnovism, and especially if we center our attention on the content, we shall see that all this implies a number of significant things. It continues, first of all, to signify the sincerity and spontaneity of the initiate's vocation for the stilnovistic *nuova vita d'amore.* Then it also implies that in that instant he was "penetrated" by the spirit of Christian and Platonic love, and became all imbued with religious, poetic fervor to pursue this ideal of human perfection. Moreover, since the concept of perfection was none other than the poetic ideal of the stilnovists, it means that his pursuit of this ideal began precisely with his realization and verification of their principle of the mystic death. In other words, this realization was at once two things: his first conscious experience of this kind of death; and his ascertainment as well as demonstration of the veracity of this principle on the highest possible authority, or by the example par excellence furnished by the death of Christ. His own mystic death, therefore, occurred, or at least began, at that instant. And this was also the beginning of his "new life."

Naturally, at this time he had presumably no conception either of his eventual personal ideal within the general scope of the *dolce stil novo,* or of his particular poetic "style" in Lorenzo's understanding of this term. Then, his love was simply for the kind of life idealized by the stilnovists: a life of study and meditation over the factors of a truly human life; namely, the pursuit of the ideal of human perfection and the application to oneself of the maxim, *nosce te ipsum.* Indeed, the presumption is that at the time he had no clear understanding of either the ideal or the poetic art of the stilnovists. Finally, the implication is also that this ideal, personified by the *donna gentile,* was naturally unconcerned with his pangs and tears. These were his strenuous, painful efforts to "find himself" and master that poetic art, to give adequate expression to the self stored potentially in his "gentle" heart, and to achieve thus his full measure of human perfection. The *donna gentile,* or the poetic conception of the stilnovists, was not concerned with the occasion or the manner in which Love had struck him, nor did his subsequent plight interest her in the least. Love did not so much as threaten her with his bow. For she had as yet no reason either to pity him or love him. On the contrary, she already had to her credit many a splendid poetic achievement, and was, as it were, "fully armed." She possessed the ideal and principle first propounded by Guinizelli, the doctrine of love expounded by Cavalcanti, all the "new lives" of his predecessors—including the sweet verses of his literary father, Cino da Pistoia, and especially all the power of Dante. Consequently, she was ready to defend this glorious patrimony against the wanton encroachment of his new, incipient love. In fact, her love for him was long in coming. Before she showed any interest in his constant efforts to obtain her love, before she began to be pleased with his contribution to her praises and glory, in other words, before he could imply that he had been accepted in *la bella scuola* of the new Italian poets, many years were to pass. It was not until he had been crowned poet laureate, not until more than half of his *rime* had been written, especially not until his Laura was *dead* that he began to give signs of self-satisfaction. Then he was persuaded to gather these scattered fragments of his *nuova vita.* Then Laura, in whom meanwhile he had embodied his conception of *la donna gentile,* his own poetic ideal, and even his worldly ambitions, began to smile upon him. She prayed for him in Heaven, she drew him up to her in his dreams, she guided him from Heaven and awaited his death in turn to be perfectly happy. Then at last he could imply that the new Muse of Italian poetry truly loved him. He had done her honor and deserved well of her.

Space and convenience do not permit me to elaborate further the ramification of this elucidation of Petrarch's initial poetic experience. For this would involve a study of his entire *canzoniere,* which is out of place here and unnecessary for my immediate purpose. I conclude that the sonnet "Era il giorno ch'al sol si scoloraro" might then be entitled "Petrarch's Mystic Death" or, in Dantean fashion, "Incipit Vita Nova." Moreover, it is now obvious, I believe, that Lorenzo's initial experience of the mystic death, simultaneous with and equivalent to his initiation into the "new life," was all conceived by him exactly in the manner in which it had previously been conceived by the master. Observe, in fact, that, *mutatis mutandis,* their first amorous experiences are substantially identical, not only in every theoretic respect, but in the very mode in which they were conceived as having taken place. Leaving out for the moment the "April" element, observe that both Petrarch and Lorenzo describe certain suitable attendant circumstances, both present an example par excellence of the mystic death, both experience and at once demonstrate the veracity of this principle. Observe especially that, with both, this personal experience is equivalent to their realization of the principle of mystic death, which in turn may be said to occur simultaneously with their respective initiation into the "new life."

On the other hand, there is a difference, a very real, significant difference, which only proves my contention. The more medieval, religious Petrarch had recourse to theology to illustrate the philosophical principle and poetic ideal of the stilnovists. He chose the very incarnation of the mystic death, or the indisputable example of the passion and death of Christ, to represent both their concept of the "new life" and their humanistic aim. Lorenzo, on the contrary, being more modern and probably skeptical, and seeking moreover a different example, resorted to natural science and pagan philosophy. He staged his experience in Nature's laboratory, and selected the ancient Clytie, whose example was not perhaps so patent nor so forceful, but was no less authoritative. Besides, the simile of Clytie—in contrast with the simile of Christ—had the literary advantage in a poetic *principio* of being already a poetized concept involving the poet's mystic death; indeed, *clitia* (both as flower and as nymph) was the oldest known symbol of the noblest human aspiration. No doubt the character of this difference was due to almost two centuries (from Dante to Lorenzo) of novel research in the field of the ancient humanities, and in particular to the influence of Boccaccio, who in his critical approach toward ancient mythology was, to be sure, preceded by both Dante and Petrarch—especially by Dante—but who was the first to undertake a systematic critical study of the subject, a veritable *fatica d'amore,* as he calls it.[3]

Petrarch's Note on the Death of Laura, and a Passage from His "Letter to Posterity."

LET us now turn to the note on Laura's death, which, for convenience, I transcribe from Scherillo's edited copy, contained in his manual of Italian literature and including certain explanatory notes by this eminent scholar.[4] It runs as follows:

Laurea, propriis virtutibus illustris et meis longum celebrata carminibus, primum oculis meis apparuit sub primum adolescentiae meae tempus, anno Domini M° III° XXVII° die VI° mensis Aprilis in ecclesia sanctae Clarae

3. Cf. Boccaccio, *De genealogiis deorum gentilium.*
4. Cf. Scherillo, *op. cit.,* I, 257-258. For a discussion as to whether or not Lorenzo knew this entry of Petrarch, cf. below, p. 256.

Avin. (= *Avinionensis*) hora matutina; et in eadem civitate, eodem mense Aprilis, eodem die sexto, eadem hora prima, anno autem Mº IIIº XLVIIIº, ab hac luce lux illa subtracta est, cum ego forte tunc Veronae essem, heu! fati mei nescius. Rumor autem infelix per literas Ludovici mei (= *Lodovico del Brabante, ch'ei chiamava Socrate:* Fam. IX, 2) me Parmae repperit, anno eodem, mense Maio, die XIXº, mane. Corpus illud castissimum ac pulcerrimum in locum Fratrum Minorum repositum est, ipso die mortis, ad vesperam. Animam quidem eius, ut de Africano (= *Scipione*) ait Seneca, in coelum, unde erat, rediisse mihi persuadeo. Haec autem ad acerbam rei memoriam, amara quadam dulcedine, scribere visum est hoc potissimum loco qui saepe sub oculis meis redit, ut scilicet cogitem nihil esse debere quod amplius mihi placeat in hac vita, et, effracto maiori laqueo, tempus esse de Babilone fugiendi crebra horum inspectione ac fugacissimae aetatis existimatione commonear, quod, praevia Dei gratia, facile erit praeteriti temporis curas supervacuas, spes inanes et inexpectatos exitus acriter ac viriliter cogitanti.

With our minds full of stilnovistic doctrine following Lorenzo's mode of conceiving, experiencing, and depicting his initiation into the "new life," it is impossible to read this note, especially after the preceding interpretation of the sonnet with which it is bound, without suspecting at once that in these two compositions, the sonnet and the Latin note, we have perhaps the principal sources of all his data for the conception of his own *principio*. Here the month of April figures prominently, by name. Indeed, here, as in Dante's passage quoted above,[5] emphasis is likewise put on the morning hour, to which Lorenzo evidently attached little or no importance, since he apparently discards it. Here Petrarch, too, establishes an intimate relation between his realization of the principle of the mystic death—equivalent to the commencement of his amorous passion—and the death of his lady. To be sure, this realization, with him, is in the nature of a relation of cause-and-effect established only by means of an *anniversary* recurrence. This causative relation, however precise, is still not a simultaneous occurrence, but we shall see that, esoterically, it, too, amounts to an absolute "simultaneity." Finally, here we have Petrarch's great resolution consigned to a place of highest honor, significantly on the flyleaf of his inseparable Virgil, and therefore constantly before his eyes. He resolves to escape from the turmoil of fleeting,

5. Cf. p. 178.

worldly considerations, and to consecrate his life thereafter to the bitter yet sweet memory of his lady's death, away from the vanity of worldly cares and hopes.

This resolution, made in 1348, is strikingly in keeping with the confession he makes in that passage of his *Epistula Posteritati* to which I referred above, and which I now quote:

Amore acerrimo, sed unico et honesto, in adolescentia laboravi, et diutius laborassem, nisi iam tepescentem ignem mors acerba, sed utilis, extinxisset. Libidinum me prorsus expertem dicere posse optarem quidem: sed, si dicam, mentiar; hoc secure dixerim, me, quamquam fervore aetatis et complexionis ad id raptum, vilitatem illam tamen semper animo execratum. Mox vero ad quadragesimum annum appropinquans, dum adhuc et caloris satis esset et virium, non solum factum illum obscaenum, sed eius memoriam omnem sic abieci, quasi nunquam feminam aspexissem: quod inter primas felicitates meas memoro, Deo gratias agens, qui me adhuc integrum et vigentem, tam vili et mihi semper odioso servitio liberavit.[6]

As I said before, the reference here is probably to his love for the mother of his illegitimate children. For the year in which he says to have at last achieved a final victory over the senses, and to have attained a state of perfect purity, of body as well as mind: this year, being nearly his fortieth, takes us back to 1343. Thus the death of which he speaks must be one which occurred sometime before this date, and cannot possibly refer to Laura's, even if other reasons did not militate against this supposition. But, in view of the stilnovistic principle of the mystic death, which implied such a state of purity for the proper development of one's natural talent and the attainment of one's measure of human perfection,[7] the passage is relevant here. Indeed, it is most significant in connection with this theory, which is the subject of Lorenzo's treatise and of our own discussion.

Observe that Petrarch considers such a confession proper subject matter for inclusion in a carefully prepared brief of his life, a brief which is destined to posterity as a kind of example for it to

6. Cf. Angelo Solerti, *Le vite di Dante, Petrarca e Boccaccio* (Milano, Vallardi), pp. 241–242. (This is a volume of the "*Storia letteraria d'Italia scritta da una Società di Professori.*")
7. In this connection remember that Dante does not reach the presence of Beatrice until he has reached the summit of Mount Purgatory, or the terrestrial paradise of a pure, innocent humanity; and that he is not *puro e disposto a salire a le stelle* until he has undergone a final process of purification.

follow. The place assigned to the confession, toward the beginning of the *Epistula,* suggests perhaps the importance that he attached to such a fundamental matter for the education of future generations. At any rate, observe the studied candor with which he speaks of such a delicate matter, the emphasis he puts on the naturalness and potency of his instinct, and the care he takes to bring out not only that this irresistible love was an experience of his early youth but also that it was his only one, and it was "honest." Observe how he stresses his execration at all times of *factum illum obscaenum,* notwithstanding the vigor of his age and of his natural "complexion." Observe especially that he speaks even of this death—which, as I say, does not refer to Laura's, and which extinguished the fire of his passion "when it was already cooling" —as "acerba sed *utilis.*" Then, toward his fortieth year, although still in possession of his manly powers, he had finally succeeded in abstaining completely from carnal passion. In fact he had succeeded in dismissing from his mind even the memory of such relations, and was as pure "as if he had never cast his eyes on woman." Finally, looking back now upon this experience, he considers his liberation from the vile, odious slavery of the senses, while still unimpaired and robust, as one of his greatest blessings.

The educational intent of this confession is obvious, it seems to me; because of this, we should not perhaps take the author too literally. At the same time, the veracity of the story can hardly be doubted in the main, owing to the specific character of the account, the likelihood of the experience, and the earnestness of the letter in which it is found. Moreover, if it were false, its value for us would, if anything, be enhanced. For that would prove its theoretical character, which would in itself be a proof of the existence of the theory perceived and maintained by the Magnificent. It would show the importance attached by the humanists, or stilnovists, to the condition of physical as well as spiritual purity for the proper development of one's natural talent and the attainment of one's spiritual goal. And the connection between such a condition and the concept of the mystic death would then be self-evident. The fact is, I believe, that Petrarch's experience described in this passage is, as usual and as required, stilnovistically real or realistic and at the same time also theoretical, that is, exemplary. Substantially, it has the force of truth.

Accordingly, although the letter to posterity was written much later than the note on Laura's death, since the passage quoted from it refers to a condition already attained four or five years before this occurrence, the inference is that now the note confirms, as it were, the import of the passage. Indeed, the inference is that the effect of Laura's death on the poet was a natural, final consequence of the spiritual condition described in the passage. That is, the poet's mystic death, which began, as we have concluded, with his apprehension of the stilnovistic principle in the example furnished by the death of Christ, was a slow, gradual process of spiritual development. Around his fortieth year, this process culminated in his achievement of the state of perfect purity required for the proper pursuit of his poetic ideal; and this condition was indeed essential to his full realization of his natural vocation. This vocation had originally manifested itself with his first perception of the *donna gentile;* the presumption then is that it had grown on him *pari passu* with this spiritual evolution. But his final decision did not come at that time, just as later his state of physical and mental purity did not produce immediately a perfect condition of mystical death. This came with his final definite conversion to the stilnovistic *vita d'amore* produced by Laura's physical death. It was this decease that made him realize fully and perfectly both the holiness of the stilnovistic humanistic ideal and his definite propensity toward this *nuova vita;* then, and only then, could he be said to be truly "dead." Then, we might say with Dante, Petrarch was really *puro e disposto a salire a le stelle.* Consequently, this is the function of the mysterious and mystifying note. In it Petrarch solemnly records his final, complete achievement of the mystic death and his definite decision to pursue thereafter only the humanistic ideal of the poet-stilnovist. He would relinquish all worldly pleasures and ambitions, and either in the peace and solitude of his Vaucluse, or traveling about in search of precious ancient manuscripts, he would devote the rest of his life to the study of the humanities, in pursuit of that ideal which his *donna angelicata* personified.

This interpretation seems so obvious in the light of Lorenzo's *principio,* and is so consonant with all the facts, as we know them, of Petrarch's biography and poetic life, that, in my opinion, it is entirely plausible. Recall here his three dialogues *De contemptu mundi,* inspired by Saint Augustine and intended to remain a *Secretum;* which Scherillo asserts to have been "meditati e distesi a Valchiusa tra il 1342 e il '43."[8] Recall his *De vita solitaria,* "incominciato a Valchiusa nella *quaresima* del 1346," says Scherillo again.[9] Recall especially the sonnets in commemoration of his first falling in love;[10] the one signifying his flight from Avignon, called there too *Babilonia;*[11] and the ones on the anniversary of Laura's death.[12] Consider, incidentally, that in the custom of commemorating such anniversaries in verse he had been preceded by Dante.[13] And realize finally the true scope, nature, and intent of his *Rime sparse,* or *nuova vita.* Need I clarify the obvious import of the relation established by the poet between his initiatory sonnet and the death of his "lady"? Need I bring out the implication of this intimate connection in what must be his theory of the mystic death? And need I point to the significance of all this with reference to Lorenzo's creative criticism of the stilnovistic *principio di nuova vita?*

After all, what has made Petrarch's famous note appear mysterious, fanciful, or false? It is the remarkable and strange "simultaneity" which he embroiders around the simple statement of the date of Laura's death. It is his puzzling, careful observation that this lady died, as it were miraculously, on the precise anniversary, down to the very hour, of her first appearance before his eyes. It is the great care with which he registers these two dates; the repetition with which he emphasizes the month of the year, the day of the month, and the hour of the day; and the esoteric significance that he apparently attached to this coincidence. Otherwise, it must be admitted that the facts there exposed, or, better, registered there

---

8. Cf. Scherillo, *op. cit.,* I, 389. 9. Cf. *idem,* p. 390.
10. Cf. Petrarca, *Rime, ed. cit.,* p. 54, Sonnet LXII; p. 100, Sonnet CXXII; and p. 208, Sonnet CCLXXI.
11. Cf. *idem,* p. 93, Sonnet CXIV.
12. Cf. *idem,* p. 211, Sonnet CCLXXVIII; and p. 269, Sonnet CCCLXIV.
13. Cf. *Vita Nuova,* XXXIV.

—apparently for his own personal and private benefit, those facts are neither incredible, nor whimsical, nor unintelligible. On the contrary, they seem so real, or are so realistic, that they invite verification.

There is nothing suspicious in the assertion that a certain Laura, loved and sung by the poet, died early in the morning of April 6, 1348, while he was in Verona. It is not at all unlikely that this news reached him by letter sent to him by his friend, Lodovico del Brabante, and that this letter was delivered to him in Parma on the morning of May 19 of the same year. It is entirely possible, indeed most likely, that, as he says, Laura was buried—somewhere or other—"that same evening," since the year 1348 was a year of plague. Finally, even the indication that he saw her for the first time in the Church of Saint Claire in Avignon, in the early morning of April 6, 1327—even this unverifiable "fact" is not in itself dubious. The others, I repeat, are, or seem, verifiable. And the rest of the note is pure sentiment, personal reaction, all so natural and so consonant with the spirit and the subject matter of his *Rime in vita di Madonna* that this effect of the news of his lady's death was almost to be expected. If anything, it is precisely all this wealth of "facts," all this precision, the likelihood of it all, and the solemn tone of the whole composition—it is the combination of these veracious factors that arouses our suspicion.

On the other hand, these "facts" may well have been as the poet states them. And if they interested us, that is, if they were relevant here, except the very one which is ingeniously unverifiable, we might be tempted to investigate them. As it is, we are only mildly interested in the author's veracity, or the historicity of his "facts." For, discussing the passage from his letter to posterity, I predicted we might discover that the facts presented here, as well as in the initiatory sonnet, were not historical, but merely based on reality, and that they had been manipulated or skilfully conceived in order to incarnate a real or theoretical state of mind in conformity with a principle of human education. But, as I said with reference to the "facts" exposed in the said passage, even this discovery would be no proof that the poet's spiritual development did not take place exactly in the manner described and precisely in connection with the occasions recalled. Moreover, again I say that, even if we discovered that this too were false—though in fact it is at least supported by the poet's whole literary life and poetic production—even then, this artificiality would nowise weaken the veracity of the principle maintained and thus presented in its essential elements.

For, while his principle would be confirmed by the poet's personal experience, it does not depend on the reality of the particular circumstances attending his development, but on the nature of those circumstances, whether these be real or simply based on reality. In other words, the principle is a concept which—as it were—stands apart, waiting to be verified by a personal experience. The poet's efforts to picture his own realization of this principle in a manner that is at once its demonstration and a true account of his experience—these efforts should not be confused with the veracity and the value of the principle as a theoretic concept.

Indeed, let us suppose that the combination of material, external facts presented by Petrarch in his dubious "simultaneity" is all a grand contrivance on the order of that concocted by the Magnificent for his representation of his own realization of the principle of the mystic death. This will simply prove, I maintain again, first the existence of the principle substantially as perceived and adopted by Lorenzo; second, the latter's critical acumen and direct derivation from Petrarch; and, third, the extent to which the pupil felt that he also could take liberties with historical facts.

The real question is, was Lorenzo familiar with the material I am presenting as his probable Petrarchan sources? There is no doubt that, of course, he was thoroughly familiar and imbued with both the spirit and the substance of the *Rime*. There can hardly be any doubt that he was equally familiar with the widely known *Letter to Posterity*. In fact, a Petrarchist of his caliber must have studied all the writings of the master. I do not know whether or not he had read the kind of epitaph with which we are concerned at this moment. But I believe he had. I base this opinion on his imitation of various elements contained in Petrarch's note—an imitation which will now become obvious. In his own contrivance to adapt the death of Simonetta Cattaneo to the intents and purposes of his *principio,* he even imitated Petrarch's license with historical facts. In this respect, the evidence will, I think, speak for itself. And, in any case, even without the assistance of Petrarch's note, he had many precedents to guide him, in and outside of Petrarch's works, for the construction of his *principio,* including the mode of such fabrications. As I said before, Lorenzo combined his various sources; or, better, his task as creative critic of the stilnovistic *principio* was to select and combine. That is how he was a *continuatore insieme e novatore.* Consequently, it is not always possible to point to any one source certainly or exclusively. But the material I present contains certainly the doctrine and the kind of facts on which he bases both the substance and the form of his own *principio.*

CHAPTER III

Critique of Petrarch's Initiatory Sonnet and of His Note on Laura's Death.

LET us scrutinize the mysterious, incredible "simultaneous occurrence" registered by Petrarch with reference to the date of his lady's death. This is the key to the whole note and to Petrarch's conception of his own mystic death. Besides, it involves a technical difference, a point of contention we might say, between master and pupil; which is perhaps evidence, therefore, that this note was at least one of Lorenzo's sources.

Observe that the simultaneity remarked or devised by Petrarch, in connection with the date of his lady's death, does not concern directly the date of his first view of her, but the anniversary of this crucial moment twenty-one years later. In other words, Laura's death is merely said to have coincided with another of those anniversaries which he had already commemorated in verse at least twice before that date,[1] and which he was to commemorate again a third time indirectly in his sonnet on the anniversary of this death.[2] It is obvious, therefore, that Petrarch either saw a connection between the beginning of his amorous passion and the death of his lady, or he meant to establish one theoretically. Truly or artificially, the death of his lady was intimately connected with his initiation into the "new life"; and this fact or theoretic principle is emphasized by the repeated commemoration of his initial step. Therefore, as the Magnificent well saw, Petrarch also meant to expound a theory in his *Rime;* he also meant to incarnate a *principio* in his personal experience of the *nuova vita.* And the key to his *principio,* to this note, and to all his *canzoniere* must, of course, be the initiatory sonnet, to which he undoubtedly refers in the anniversary sonnets and here emphatically as well as clearly. Otherwise, what would be the purpose of his bringing out this

---

1. Cf. above, n. 10, p. 254. 2. Cf. above, n. 12, p. 254.

significant, miraculous coincidence? Unless the import of that sonnet were implicitly involved in the sonnets celebrating the most memorable event of his poetic life; especially, unless it were carried over by the anniversary which coincided with his lady's death, there would be no point in either noticing or establishing such a coincidence. Consequently, the importance of this coincidence lies entirely in the import of the anniversary. This takes us back to the significance of the initiatory sonnet.

The significance of this sonnet has already been deduced.[3] But what is its import in relation to Laura's death? Presumably, it is the following. In that sonnet Petrarch had practically said that his realization of the stilnovistic principle of the mystic death, which marked the beginning of his amorous pursuit of those poets' humanistic ideal, coincided with the anniversary of the death of Christ. Now, any reënactment of this death is, theologically and anagogically speaking, an actual repetition of Christ's exemplary sacrifice. Consequently, Petrarch has practically said that the beginning of his amorous passion—which implies the apprehension of the principle and at least the beginning of his own mystic death—coincided with the passion and death of Christ. Indeed, as I said before, his spiritual elevation and lofty thinking were started by this circumstance; and then his poetic nature—in view of Christ's divine example, which confirmed the principle and the ideal of the new poetic school—immediately revealed itself. This determined the course of his poetic career. It follows, therefore, that, although Laura actually died twenty-one years after this event, since her death coincided precisely with the anniversary of this initiation, and since this initiation in turn coincided with the death of Christ: it follows I say, that Laura too died on an anniversary of Christ's death, or on a Good Friday. This means that, accordingly, her death, too, coincided with the death of Christ—speaking again theologically and anagogically. In other words, the upshot of all this reasoning is that the poet's mystic death coincided finally with the physical death of his lady, and that both these deaths, the one mystical and the other physical, occurred in

3. Cf. above, pp. 243–249.

conjunction with the death of Christ which was at once both physical and mystical.

Is this dialectics or downright sophistry? Whatever it is, it is not mine, but Petrarch's, who, following apparently the medieval mode of *trobare oscuro* and adhering to the stilnovistic belief that the principle and doctrine of the school were intended only for the initiates—namely, those who had *intelletto d'amore*—chose to involve his simple theory in contrivances and conceits of this kind. For, obviously now, a poetic ideal and a principle of human education are involved in his "simultaneous occurrence" or "coincidence"—a principle, moreover, or a conception which, in the light of Lorenzo's *principio,* will not now be difficult for us to understand and elucidate.

It follows from the conclusion just reached that the value of Petrarch's "simultaneous occurrence" lies wholly in the fact that, as it were, the poet found his Laura significantly on a Good Friday and, in the physical sense lost her significantly on the recurrence of the identical occasion. Indeed, since, as I have just remarked, all reënactments of Christ's sacrifice are theologically and anagogically speaking actual repetitions of His death, the implication is that he did not merely find her first, and then, in the physical sense, lose her under the same circumstances, but that he both found her and lost her physically in the same instant. In other words, the anagoge of Christ's death seems to eliminate the time intervening between his first glimpse of her and her literal death. This period of twenty-one years becomes thereby, theoretically as well as practically, a single continuous process of mystical and literal dying. In fact, the significance of the identity of the circumstances under which first she appeared to him and later she died literally, the significance is this: His spiritualization in the manner of Christ, or his own mystic death to the end that he might "know himself" and develop his genius along the lines of strictly *human* perfection, in a word, his initiation into the "new life," this occurred from beginning to end under the influence of Christ's example. That is, his process of physical and mental purification and the simultaneous evolution of his poetic ideal—all in conformity with the stilnovistic principle of human education, and consonant with his own nature—this spiritual experience, I say, followed a definite process. It began at the instant of his first clear perception of, and conversion to, the stilnovistic principle and ideal, and continued uninterruptedly until the *esser verace* who had kindled his imagination and aroused his dormant "gentle heart" died literally. It was all one single process, or a prolongation of the original spiritual elevation brought about by the occasion described, whereby the lady called Laura first appeared to him as the personification of the *donna gentile* and then gradually became the incarnation of all his noble aspirations and of his particular poetic ideal. In other words, the experience which involved his own mystic death for the detection and proper pursuit of his natural human goal, this experience was a process of idealization which imported the contemporaneous mystic death for him of his lady as well. It necessitated the severance from the very beginning of the soul from the body of the *esser verace* who was withal the source of his inspiration. Consequently, in this sense, his Laura began to die literally for him the very instant he began to idealize her. But her mystic death in his mind was not, and could not, be perfect until she had actually died physically. For, as long as she remained in the flesh, there was always some vestige of sensuousness in her and possibly of sensuality in him. Her physical death was indeed necessary to the perfection of both his own and her mystic death. And it was this perfect mystic death of Laura, or the poet's perfect and definite visualization of his ideal, which, following her death, coincided with his own perfect mystic death. This involved the absolute purification of his mind *and body* correlatively to Laura's physical death. It was this double process of spiritualization which, beginning naturally and auspiciously on a Good Friday, was achieved perfectly on the same occasion. In its progressive stages, the mystic death of the lady and the poet was, theoretically, always an accomplished fact. But practically, it lasted twenty-one years, indeed, throughout the course of Petrarch's "new life" covered by his *Rime*. His *canzoniere* was a continuous "dying" in the flesh in order to live in the spirit of Christ and of the *donna gentile*. This process culminated in Petrarch's perfect conception and realization of his humanistic poetic ideal within the general scope and aim of the *dolce stil novo*.

Finally, as I hinted above, all this means that Petrarch's *Rime* were at once a *principio di nuova vita* and *nuova vita* itself, precisely as Lorenzo maintains with reference to his own *principio*. It means that, in the opinion of Petrarch himself, his apprenticeship in the school of the sweet new style began substantially in the manner described and at the time specified; it progressed gradually in the way narrated in the *Rime;* and it ended, technically at least, no less than twenty-one years later, namely, with Laura's death in 1348.

AFTER this analysis of the sonnet in its relation to the note, turn back to the note itself.[4] Observe how masterly it was conceived and composed so as to imply all this and epitomize at once both the history of the author's poetic apprenticeship and his doctrine of the "new life." Every significant word or phrase was advisedly chosen, carefully weighed, and nicely placed so as to convey exactly the esoteric meaning hidden under the veil of an apparently common simple memento. The note was so phrased that the frequent reading of it would constantly keep alive in his mind and heart both the thoughts and the feelings that had prompted his resolution at the news of Laura's death. In fact, this note was to be thereafter Petrarch's *vade mecum*. Presumably, this was why it was inscribed in such a *potissimum loco* as the flyleaf of his Virgil, chief source of his poetic inspirations.

This note sounds like a solemn epitaph on his lady's tombstone. And in a way, it is that. But observe that all his remarks concerning her death and burial are related to himself. As we have seen, the date and the occasion of her death are made to coincide miraculously with the anniversary of her "first appearance before his eyes," which occurred under the identical circumstances; and this remark is accompanied by the reminder that he was then still in the period of technical "adolescence." There is no reference to the Good Friday factor. But this is certainly understood in the connec-

4. Cf. above, pp. 249–250.

tion made between this occasion and the occasion of his initiatory sonnet, where it is predominant. Besides, as we shall see, he had good reason for not bringing it out here. Then follows his most significant esoteric remark; namely, that *illa lux,* or his Laura, who was his denomination of the *donna gentile* and at the same time the personification of his personal poetic ideal—*illa lux* was, as it were, "drawn from beneath" (*subtracta est*) or deduced from *hac luce,* which presumably emanated from the volume of Virgil's works then beneath his hand! Virgil, the representative of the ancient classical civilization and poetic art, was the source of his enlightenment! It follows that for him, too, as for Dante, Virgil was his *maestro* and his *autore!* But let us not digress. Accordingly, this remark also is related to himself. Again, Laura's death occurred while he was in Verona, "unaware, alas, of his fate!" This probably means that the final revelation of the true scope and aim of the stilnovistic ideal, or the critical conviction that the new Italian literature should be of classical inspiration, this perfect consciousness of his destiny to be a poet-humanist came to him while he happened to be in Verona. In this case, it is not only plausible but most likely that the news of this "death," or the confirmation of his own *constatation* was actually contained in a letter from his "Socrates," Lodovico del Brabante, which he may well have received in Parma the following month—perhaps in reply to one of his own asking for an expression of opinion on the subject.[5]

I cannot undertake here the verification of all these deductions or, shall I say, "suppositions" of mine. I offer them for whatever they may be worth, which may indeed be very little. Returning to the note, observe that even the reference to Laura's *propriis virtutibus illustris* (notice this recognition perhaps of the inherent merits of the *donna gentile* or Italian poetry of his time) is made with reference to his own *carminibus* in praise of her. Finally, *corpus illud castissimum ac pulcerrimum* (consider the moral and æsthetic value of these qualities of the "body" of Italian poetry when the phrase is interpreted esoterically) was laid to rest, no doubt also significantly, in a mystical "place" par excellence; namely,

5. Does anyone know of any such correspondence? I do not. But what a fascinating topic is this for the biographer of Petrarch and the historian of Italian literature!

the church or convent of the "mystic" lay brothers of Saint Francis.[6] But he was convinced that her soul, like that of his "Scipio" (namely, his *Africa*), had returned to Heaven "whence it was."[7]

The rest of the note is taken up with his resolution in conjunction with his reaction to this "death." Indeed, the whole note, we may now say, concerns him more than it does his "lady." The thought of her death pervades it all, but it is really a note on how this thought affected him and hovered over him ever after. It affected him precisely as the thought of his "lady," being dead, later engrossed the mind of his disciple in the course of his initiation in turn.[8] Notice that we even have here "the bitter memory of this thing" suffused with "a certain pungent sweetness," which, in Lorenzo's *principio,* becomes the special subject of Sonnet IV.

Finally, observe now the emphasis laid on the month of the year and the hour of the day in which the poet's initiation is said to have begun in 1327 and later to have been achieved in 1348. These favorable natural conditions were not brought out in the initiatory sonnet; there, all the emphasis was laid on the spiritual circumstance attending his rebirth. They are brought out here; and now we realize that in the sonnet they were contained implicitly in the recurrence of Good Friday in April and in the early hour of the Mass presumably attended by the poet. The esoteric theoretic implication of the April factor is not made any too obvious here, either. This may be for the simple reason that, while the natural virtue of this month as a seasonal factor was always in order and could be said to have contributed to this experience, the wider implication of April as the spring of life did not apply here to Petrarch, who was no longer a youth at the time of his perfect mystic death. But the repetition of the name of the month seems to stress the fact that it was April, and no other month, both when his mystic death began and when he achieved it perfectly.

6. The mysticism of Dante and all the stilnovists who preceded Petrarch, indeed of Petrarch himself, is well known, I believe.

7. The heavenly origin of the *donna gentile,* called by the historians of Italian literature also *donna angelicata,* is a common stilnovistic concept. Recall, for instance, the last strophe of Guinizelli's *canzone,* "Al cor gentil ripara sempre Amore," and Dante's *canzone,* "Donne ch'avete intelletto d'amore," as well as the latter's sonnet, "Tanto gentile e tanto onesta pare" (ll. 7–8).

8. Cf. this study, pp. 149 and 158.

In other words, by calling his own attention sharply to the
month of the year, and this by repeating the name twice, Petrarch
seems to say to himself: "Realize that it was significantly the
month of April when you first perceived *illam lucem,* that it was
both the spring of the year and the spring of your life corresponding to the period of your adolescence; and realize that it was again
the spring of the year when, no longer 'adolescent' but a mature
'youth' (in the medieval technical sense), you finally visualized
clearly your poetic ideal and decided definitely on the course to
follow." At any rate, this interpretation is plausible in the light of
Lorenzo's *principio.* And it is supported, not only by Dante's belief regarding *l'ora del tempo e la dolce stagione* and by Petrarch's
own sonnet on spring, both recalled by me before,[9] but also and
especially by the similar emphasis put at the same time, in this
very juncture, on the *hora matutina,* in which Laura first appeared to him, and on the *eadem hora prima,* in which later she
died. Indeed, he even feels the need of specifying in such a concise
note that the news of this death also reached him *mane.* Laura, on
the other hand, was buried naturally and, I add, conveniently
from a theoretical point of view, *ad vesperam.* All this is undoubtedly conventional, and it is therefore evidence, I think, that Petrarch, before Lorenzo, had implied substantially the same theory
and principle of human education that the disciple later implied
in his creative criticism of the master's *principio.*

9. Cf. pp. 178–179.

CHAPTER IV

*A Reconstruction of Lorenzo's Criticism of Petrarch's and
Dante's Princìpi, and the Purely Technical Nature
of His Simple Innovations.*

IRRESPECTIVE of the merits of the esoteric conventionalism
brought out in the previous chapter, Lorenzo's derivation from
Petrarch in this connection is now quite obvious. We even begin to see just what he accepted and what he discarded, not only
from Petrarch, but also from Dante. Perhaps now we realize both
the nature and the extent of his own modifications, and observe
that these were not substantial, but merely formal. Obviously, he
meant to systematize, clarify, simplify, and correct but slightly a
principle which seemed to him none too plain nor well organized,
but on the contrary, rather vaguely suggested and somewhat exaggerated, indeed, inexact in some respects. Moreover, he apparently wanted to modernize this principle by ridding it of its religious character—which perhaps was not to his taste nor consonant
with growing religious skepticism—and by bringing out and
stressing its would-be scientific basis and value. Finally, he wanted
to secularize it, generalize it, and—by making it clearly applicable
to all the arts and letters—present it as a standard principle of education and higher culture in any field of human endeavor. But he
wanted to do all this remaining withal within the conventional
forms already established by his predecessors. This he wished to
do either because he approved of their *trobare oscuro* intended for
the initiates only, or because he sought to expound their concepts
in the same figurative language in which they were found expressed in their exemplary "new lives." It may also be that he
simply meant to be what Flamini has so aptly called him, namely,
a *continuatore insieme e novatore.*[1] In any case, the result was the

1. The reader may have observed that I have appropriated this denomination of Lorenzo
by Flamini, and used it continually without reference to its "paternity." I find it very expressive of my own concept of Lorenzo as a poet. But I referred to its source the first time
it came up in my treatise. Cf. p. 2.

principio with which now we are to a large extent already familiar.

There was considerable confusion in both Dante and Petrarch, a confusion which had required a good deal of philosophical insight and critical acumen on his part to disentangle, and which, though more apparent than real, was no less objectionable in the kind of "primer" or "manual of human education" he himself thought a *principio di nuova vita* should be. There was confusion between the technical term *morte*, which implied the mystical death of both "lady" and poet as a principle of the "new life," and the literal meaning of *morte* used to indicate the actual physical death of the *esser verace* who served as the poet's source of inspiration and as the personification of his ideal. Indeed, there was confusion in the use of the term *morte* in its technical sense of mystical death. For at times it was employed to indicate the spiritual elevation of the poet necessary and equivalent to his initiation into the *nuova vita;* at other times it connoted the mystical death of the lady coincident with her physical death and equivalent to the poet's clear conception of his personal ideal; and still at other times it seemed to mark the final goal aimed at by the poet, and then it was equivalent to his achievement of the highest degree of perfection within the scope of the ideal he had conceived and had set out to attain. Finally, there was confusion between the *principio di nuova vita* and the *nuova vita* itself: inasmuch as, on the one hand, *principio* was understood as the "beginning" of the "new life," which involved both the apprehension of the principle of mystic death and the embodiment of this conception in the very first poetic composition; and, on the other hand, by *principio* was also meant the "principle" of the mystic death itself, or the condition of spiritualization of both "lady" and poet, which naturally underlay the whole *nuova vita* and therefore embraced the entire poetic production of a given author.

Thus, in Petrarch's *canzoniere* it was difficult if not impossible to say just where his initiation ended and his real *nuova vita* began. Admittedly, the *principio* in the sense of "beginning" was already *nuova vita,* as I have just observed, and as the Magnificent himself later insisted.[2] But this was not saying that all *nuova vita* was *principio* in the sense of mere "initiation" into the new life; it was not, notwithstanding the fact that the same philosophical principle obtained throughout.

Petrarch's *rime* all seemed to remain within the scope and purpose of a mere apprenticeship. There was no *nuova vita,* at least, not in the sense of a separate and distinct poetic production which, going beyond this stage, could be said to contain—even in the intention of the author himself—the fruit of his artistic maturity, or the subsequent manifestation of his poetic originality. There was none, unless one took for *nuova vita* his insipid and insignificant *Trionfi d'Amore;* which, besides being a great disappointment after the most promising *principio,* were a Dantean imitation in more ways than one. Nor was there any, unless one took his *Africa;* which, besides being a comparatively early work, was written in Latin, and was another disappointing imitation. There was none, finally, unless one took his other works in Latin, including his "Letters"; which were *nuova vita* in the true sense of the word, but were not exactly modern poetry in *volgare.* Indeed, from this point of view, Petrarch might be said to have been a *poeta mancato.*

Moreover, from Petrarch's *Rime,* it was not clear when his mystical death had truly occurred. It was not clear even if one were acquainted with his note on the death of Laura. For, although this note seemed to fix the date of his final achievement of the perfect mystical death, the fact that Laura's death implying this was made to coincide anagogically with the occasion of his first view of her—this apparent confusion puzzled the reader. Again, his *canzoniere* was formally divisible into *Rime in Vita di Madonna* and *Rime in Morte di Madonna,* which seemed to confirm the import of the note. But in the second part of this volume he had continued to long for "death," and also complained that it was long in coming, quite as much as in the first part. Indeed, his *canzoniere,* or formal *nuova vita,* was all *principio.* Worse than this, the student who attempted to derive his poetic principle from those *rime* ran the risk of either not grasping it at all or of being

2. Cf. this study, p. 7.

misled; he would surely end by losing himself in the superficial intricacies of the beautiful external form. In fact, this is precisely what happened to many a Petrarchist before and after Lorenzo. For Petrarch remained what he was by natural disposition, an eternal seeker after the purity of form and the perfection of style in our sense of this word. This was his originality, this his contribution to the school of the *dolce stil novo*. He was hardly a poet in the sense of being a seer or of stimulating deep human emotions. He was primarily a stylist or literary artist. As a humanist, he was only a scholar, not an apostle like Dante; and this is how and why he was the "father of humanism" in our modern, narrow sense of the word. His *Rime,* therefore, were his only real *nuova vita d'amore;* and they were all *principio* because the artistic "principle" of the *stil novo* was all the scope and purpose of his stilnovistic "new life." In other words, his Laura stood for his concept of a perfect style, which he apparently identified with the external form of the expression. And this was his ideal within the general scope of the poetic ideal of the stilnovists. For this reason, finally, his *principio,* or "beginning," or "initiation," had no subsequent *nuova vita.* It needed none, since it was an end in itself. His *canzoniere* was at once both his *principio* and his truly original poetic production.

Dante, on the contrary, had composed two distinct and separate works, one embodying primarily his *principio,* and the other being the crowning achievement of his *nuova vita.* Dante's literary production comprised on the one hand a *Vita Nuova* and other minor works of an initiatory character, and on the other a *Commedia* which was truly the embodiment of his wholly original poetic "new life." To be sure, just as his *Vita Nuova*—which was called so precisely because it was *"principio* di nuova vita"—was already "new life," so his *Commedia*—which was the continuation of this initial "new life" and the realization of his ideal—was withal "principle" from beginning to end, or the continuous application of the *principio* propounded in the *Vita Nuova.* But, both theoretically and practically, Dante had substantially distinguished his apprenticeship in the art of the new school of poetry from the original manifestation of his own poetic genius. Indeed, two other separate works—the *Convivio* and the *De vulgari eloquentia*—both of which had contributed to his preparation, had intervened between his *principio* and his distinctly *nuova vita d'amore.* These, too, involved both the principle and the actual leading of the "new life"; indeed, their contents continued to develop or found perfect poetic expression in the body of the *Commedia,* just as did the elements and factors of the "new life" which had been only primitively set forth in the *Vita Nuova.* But, I repeat, in theory and in practice both, Dante had clearly implied the sharpest distinction between the poet's *initiation* into the "new life" and his subsequent pursuit of his own poetic ideal manifested by his *original artistic production.*

On the other hand, there was some apparent confusion in Dante's *principio* as well. For his *Vita Nuova* also contained poems which might be entitled *in vita di madonna,* and others which might be said to be *in morte* of her. His *libello* was not divided formally in two such parts, as was Petrarch's *canzoniere.*[3] But the central position in the *Vita Nuova* was occupied by the *canzone,* "Donna pietosa e di novella etate," in which Dante also established an absolute simultaneity between his "lady's" mystic death and his own. In fact, this canzone is the second of the three which, like pillars, support the little "temple," as the *Vita Nuova* has been called. Moreover, the first of these is the canzone, "Donne ch'avete intelletto d'amore," in which the poet portrays his first visualization of his ideal; and the third, the canzone, "Li occhi dolenti per pietà del core," in which he narrates Beatrice's physical death. Finally, as everybody knows, Dante's *Vita Nuova* ends with his *mirabile visione* of his "lady" in Heaven.

I cannot undertake to expound here the central canzone, which is undoubtedly the key to Dante's *principio,* for this would take me too far afield and would distract the reader from the present argument. But some idea at least of its content is necessary at this juncture, and so I quote it in full; with no other comment, however, than that furnished by my bringing into relief those words and phrases to which I wish to call special attention.

3. At least by later editors, in the sixteenth century.

1   Donna *pietosa* e di *novella etate,*
     adorna assai di *gentilezze umane,*
     ch'era là 'v'io *chiamava spesso Morte,*
     veggendo li occhi miei pien di pietate
5   e ascoltando le parole vane,
     si mosse con paura a pianger forte.
     E altre donne, che si fuoro accorte
     di me per quella che meco piangia,
     fecer lei partir via,
10   e appressarsi per farmi sentire.
     Qual dicea: *"Non dormire,"*
     e qual dicea: *"Perchè sì ti sconforte?"*
     Allor lassai la nova fantasia,
     chiamando *il nome de la donna mia.*
15 Era la voce mia sì dolorosa
     e rotta sì da l'angoscia del pianto,
     ch'*io solo intesi il nome nel mio core;*
     e con tutta la vista vergognosa
     ch'era nel viso mio giunta cotanto,
20   mi fece verso lor volgere Amore.
     Elli era tale a veder mio colore,
     che facea ragionar di morte altrui:
     "Deh, consoliam costui"
     pregava l'una l'altra umilemente;
25   e dicevan sovente:
     "Che vedestù, che tu non hai valore?"
     E quando un poco confortato fui,
     io dissi: "Donne, dicerollo a vui.
     Mentr'io pensava la mia frale vita,
30   *e vedea 'l suo durar com'è leggiero,*
     piansemi Amor nel core, ove dimora;
     per che l'anima mia fu sì smarrita,
     che sospirando dicea nel pensero:
     —*Ben converrà che la mia donna mora*—.
35   Io presi tanto smarrimento allora,
     ch'io chiusi li occhi vilmente gravati,
     e furon sì smagati
     li spirti miei, che ciascun giva errando;
     e poscia imaginando,
40   di caunoscenza e *di verità fora,*
     visi di donne m'apparver crucciati,
     che mi dicean pur:—*Morra'ti, morra'ti*—.

Poi vidi cose dubitose molto,
nel vano imaginare ov'io entrai;
45   ed esser mi parea non so in qual loco,
e veder donne andar per via disciolte,
qual lagrimando, e qual traendo guai,
che *di tristizia* saettavan foco.

Poi mi parve vedere a poco a poco
50   turbar lo sole e apparir la stella,
e pianger elli ed ella;
cader li augelli volando per l'are,
e la terra tremare;
ed omo apparve scolorito e fioco,
55   *dicendomi:—Che fai? non sai novella?*
morta è la donna tua, ch'era sì bella—.

Levava li occhi miei bagnati in pianti,
e vedea, che parean pioggia di manna,
li angeli che tornavan suso in cielo,
60   e una nuvoletta avean davanti,
dopo la qual gridavan tutti: OSANNA;
e s'altro avesser detto, a voi dire'lo.
Allor diceva Amor:—Più nol ti celo;
vieni a veder nostra donna che giace—.

65   Lo imaginar fallace
mi condusse a veder *madonna morta;*
e quand'io l'avea scorta,
vedea che donne *la covrian d'un velo;*
ed avea seco umilità verace,
70   che parea che dicesse:—Io sono in pace—.

Io divenia nel dolor sì umile,
veggendo in lei tanta umiltà formata,
ch'io dicea:—*Morte, assai dolce ti tegno;*
tu dei omai esser cosa gentile,
75   *poi che tu se' ne la mia donna stata,*
e dei aver pietate e non disdegno.
Vedi che sì desideroso vegno
d'esser de' tuoi, ch'io ti somiglio in fede.
Vieni, chè 'l cor te chiede.—

80   Poi mi partia, consumato ogne duolo;
e quand'io era solo,
dicea, guardando verso l'alto regno:
—Beato, *anima* bella, chi te vede!—
Voi mi chiamaste allor, vostra merzede."[4]

4. Cf. *Vita Nuova* in Dante's *Opere, ed. cit.,* pp. 30–32.

What a flood of light Lorenzo's *principio* throws on this canzone! And how it, in turn, illuminates his *principio* and also confirms our interpretation! Unfortunately, the continually growing size of my modest treatise prevents me from bringing out the wealth of stilnovistic doctrine contained in this poem. Besides, I must not anticipate the proposed later use of this manual. It will suffice here, for the purpose of the present argument, to point to this additional source of Lorenzo's *principio,* and to declare that with this canzone Dante had undoubtedly meant to establish by theory and personal experience the perfect simultaneity of his own mystic death and that of his "lady." This is not only deducible from the nature of the content and the general drift of the thought, from the dreamy character of the experience involving the expectation of his own death (see ll. 3, 21–22, 29–30, and 42), as well as that of his "lady" (see ll. 34, 56, and 66), and especially from the effect produced on him by the vision of his "lady" lying dead (see ll. 73–79); but it is actually brought out, I think, by the poet himself in his comment in prose preceding this poem.[5] There he clearly intimates that the *pur morra'ti, morra'ti* of line 42, means *tu pur morrai,* indeed, *tu se' morto.*[6] That is, taking up first the first of these two versions, "you *too* will die," or, if we prefer, "you *alone* will die." For, whether we take the *pur* of this phrase in the sense of "also" or in the sense of "only," the esoteric import of the remark remains substantially the same. In fact, the meaning "you too will die" will then imply that Dante also was expected to die, and, inasmuch as his death could not be physical without this putting an end to all his poetic activity, the inference is that he is talking of "mystic death" both with respect to himself and to his "lady." And, if we prefer the meaning "you alone will die," the implication will be not only that for the same reason his death was intended to be merely mystical but also that his own mystical death involved the simultaneous mystical death of his "lady" as well. In other words, the inference then will be, not only that he is talking of mystical

5. *Idem,* XXIII, pp. 28–30.
6. *Loc. cit.,* 4, running from p. 28 to p. 29. On the strength of this comment of Dante, it seems to me that Barbi has punctuated wrongly l. 42 of the canzone. Without any further authority, I decide in favor of the following punctuation:
"che mi dicean:—Pur morra'ti, morra'ti—."

death, but also that the psychological process of his own spiritual elevation—which, of course, took place *in his own mind only*—involved the simultaneous spiritualization *on his part* of his "lady" as well. This is the reason why, in further explanation of his textual remark in the body of the canzone, and, as it were, riveting this point, he adds significantly, *tu se' morto:* as if he had meant, "you are mystically dead already," or "in fact, you are mystically dead even now, and your own mystic death, conjointly with that of your 'lady,' occurred in the course of your present fanciful dream."

On the strength of this elucidation of Dante's own comment on the mysterious remark which is, as it were, the key to the esoteric meaning of the entire canzone (this may be indicated also by the central position it occupies, on line 42 of a poem eighty-four lines long), and on the strength of the obvious import of this whole poem (obvious to anyone who has followed me in my exposition of Lorenzo's *principio*), I believe that, even more than Petrarch's note on Laura's death, this canzone of Dante on the simultaneity of the mystical death for "lady" and poet, was Lorenzo's authority for this point of contention in his own *principio*. And my belief is further strengthened by other evidences of direct derivation found in this same poem. Observe, in lines 1 and 2, the *novella etate* and the *gentilezze umane* of the *donna pietosa* standing presumably for the new Italian poetry in *volgare*, at least according to Lorenzo's *principio*. Notice especially the newly acquired "gentilesse" of death, in lines 73-75, whence no doubt Lorenzo derived verbatim the identical concept, saying in his third sonnet: *ma morte è sì gentile oggi e sì bella,* and again, *Morte è gentil, poich'è stata in colei.*

And, while we are on the subject of origins and derivations, consider the import of the whole fourth stanza. The vision there described reminds one of the turbulent condition of nature and humanity, which accompanied the death of Christ; it reminds us of the earthquake which caused the three *ruine* in Dante's *inferno.* Realize that a similar circumstance accompanied the poet's mystical death, according to this canzone. This in turn reminds us that Petrarch's mystical death, too, occurred during the reënactment of the passion and death of Christ. Notice, moreover, the subsequent apparition of an *omo scolorito e fioco,* which incident reminds us immediately of *Inferno,* I, lines 61–67, where later Virgil's apparition to the poet in the "valley of death" is described as that of "chi per lungo silenzio parea *fioco,*" and then was no longer *omo,* but *ombra!*

This is all very significant in relation to, and in the light of, Lorenzo's *principio.* Moreover, there is evidence of Dante's sources in Virgil, and of derivations from himself, as it were. There is perhaps evidence of Petrarch's derivation from Dante, or at least of Dante's influence on Petrarch. Above all, the theoretical and historical implications involved in the esoteric meaning of this source of the Magnificent show not only his direct derivation from Dante, as well as from Petrarch, but also his profound penetration of the thought of the supreme master.

But the doctrine of the masters and of all the stilnovists was not obvious to the uninitiate. Indeed, it was intentionally hidden under a veil of fiction. Dante, for instance, had declared repeatedly, in various ways and on different occasions, what he implies in this very canzone with regard to *madonna morta;* namely, that he "vedea che donne *la covrian d'un velo*" (l. 68). This means that each poet's *donna,* or his personal concept of the stilnovistic ideal, and therefore *the poet himself,* enveloped his pursuit of his particular poetic ideal in a veil of mystery which was effected by means of a fictitious personification and a fictitious narrative.

This practice was itself a kind of corollary of the stilnovistic principle of human "gentilesse." It was based on the belief or the principle of what might be called the natural aristocracy of the intellect. In other words, the lofty concepts of the poet humanists and their artistic creations were, on principle, intended only for those who by nature had "gentle hearts" and who, therefore, according to Guinizelli—the father of this theory—had "intelligence of Love." I have made this point before, but here I wish to remark again what I observed when this matter was first discussed in the study of Lorenzo's *proemio;* namely, that, while the Magnificent obviously accepted this theory and practice, he himself was not intransigent in this regard. In fact, while even his own *Comento* remains on the allegorical plane required by his Dantean model, the *Vita Nuova*, neither is his *trobare* so *oscuro* as that of the primitive stilnovists, nor is his *Comento* beyond the possibilities of an ordinary intelligence and higher learning. Indeed, judging from his desire to clarify every possible misunderstanding in connection with his own *principio*, judging from his very attempt to present a creative criticism of the stilnovistic principle itself, it would seem that he wished to appeal to a wider circle of readers. Perhaps by his time higher education and culture had become more democratic.

Lorenzo's exception to the masters' *princìpi* was not, then, to the practice of concealing the true meaning under a veil of poetic fiction, although he himself probably felt that the concealment was frequently so effective that not even the initiate sometimes succeeded in penetrating the veil to get to the *sovrasenso*. His main objections seem to have been of a purely technical nature. He found their doctrine too widely scattered and fragmentary. Moreover, apparently their practice, or the application of the principle of mystic death to which they in reality adhered strictly, was not entirely consistent with the theory they propounded. We have already noted the long interval of time and space intervening in Petrarch's *canzoniere* between his first initiation into the "new life," which theoretically implied his experience of the mystical death at the same time, and his final achievement of the perfect mystical death. On the strength of his note on the date of Laura's death we concluded then that this final achievement did not occur until 1348 or fully twenty-one years after his first initiation, which in the body of the *Rime* corresponded to a point well beyond the middle of the volume. That is, according to himself, he did not achieve the perfect mystical death until he had written more than half of his *rime*. Indeed, as we also remarked then, there was evidence in the second part of his *canzoniere* of his having continued to long for death and of his having despaired of ever achieving it, even after he had solemnly recorded the fact that he had already fully achieved it at the time specified, namely on the early morning of April 6, 1348. To Lorenzo, this seemed inconsistent with a strict adherence to the principle of the mystic death or with the concept of the mystic death as he understood it; or, better, he perhaps feared that the student of Petrarch might not appreciate the poet's nice distinction between the initial stage of a state of mystical death, its perfect achievement, and the final achievement of the poetic ideal.

The same criticism applied to Dante's *Vita Nuova*. As we have observed already, in Dante's *libello*, too, there was the same confusion between poems *in vita* and poems *in morte di madonna*. There too, as in Petrarch's *canzoniere*, there was the same apparent inconsistency in the application of the principle of the mystic death. This was not surprising, notwithstanding the fact that Dante, in the central *canzone* which we have just considered briefly, maintained and demonstrated not only the perfect simultaneity of his own mystical death and that of his "lady" but also the nonessentialness of his lady's physical death to his and her perfect spiritualization. (Remember that the canzone on the death of Beatrice Portinari comes after, and is the last of the three embodying his complete mystical death.) It was not surprising because, as we now see, Dante too, before Petrarch, had conceived his *principio* as a unit—with this important difference: that Dante's *principio* prefigured and was followed by the *Commedia*, whereas Petrarch's, as I said above, was and remained an end in itself. Finally, this confusion or inconsistency was not surprising to the initiate who had a nice sense of values and realized that the inconsistency was only apparent. In reality, the apparent confusion was the result of a nice distinction, and the Magnificent well appreciated this fact.

But, I remark, all this was not obvious even to the initiate. Besides, this nicety of distinctions and the consequent obscurity of the esoteric meaning of *morte* gave rise to real if only technical contradictions. Both in Dante's *Vita Nuova* and in Petrarch's *canzoniere*, exactly or approximately one half of the poems preceded in their arrangement the one containing the account or lament of the lady's physical death: in Dante in the form of a premonition, and in Petrarch in reality. Indeed, again I recall, in the *Vita Nuova*, the *canzone* on the actual death of Beatrice Portinari is the last of the three and is placed toward the end. This *apparently* proved—contrary to the principle upheld and demonstrated especially by Dante in his central canzone—that the decease of the lady used as model was not really necessary to the poet's mental abstraction of her qualities in the course of his own mystical death. There was contradiction, I say—even if it was not real but only apparent—in the fact that Dante on the one hand maintained the nonessentialness of the lady's physical death, and on the other clearly indicated that his final *mirabile visione* did not come to him until after Beatrice's actual physical death, indeed, only as climax to his whole *principio.* Just as, again apparently, there was contradiction in Petrarch, if one regarded the arrangement of his *rime.* Judging only by this order, Petrarch on the one hand seemed to say that his mystical death occurred under the circumstances described in the initiatory sonnet and at the time later specified in the note; and on the other hand—by this note, by the distinction of his *rime "in vita"* and *"in morte di madonna,"* and by the position of his canzone on the death of Laura—he seemed to show that he did not really achieve it until his Laura had actually died. Indeed, as I said before, apparently he never achieved it in the sense of his achieving his poetic ideal perfectly, at least not in his own estimation or to his complete satisfaction.

Consequently, in accordance with the experience of both Dante and Petrarch, one might say that, both theoretically and practically, the physical death of the lady was at the same time considered necessary and yet not essential. Of course, this was precisely the point. For, as I said in connection with Petrarch's experience, the theoretic implication of the principle of the mystic death was that the lady, or *esser verace,* or "model," died actually for the artist—in the real physical sense, though only technically—in every point of his and her spiritual elevation equivalent to their common and simultaneous mystical death. This "death" was merely the poet's own mental process, by which he abstracted her qualities, and in the course of which he at once conceived his poetic ideal based on those qualities and also realized the idealistic character of his conception or artistic creation. Therefore, in the course of this process, he actually severed, as it were, her soul from her body; and the implication is that naturally this process ended only with her physical death or when she ceased to be a direct source of inspiration. That is, it was complete or it simply ended when the artist either was through with his "model" or had to stop, owing to the intervening physical death of his *donna angelicata.*

This was so, and the Magnificent understood it perfectly. But if I interpret correctly his intention in bringing out what for all intents and purposes is a modern revised edition of the poetic art of his illustrious predecessors, Lorenzo, as critic and expounder of their doctrine, was disturbed by the difficulty of penetrating this nicety of the stilnovistic principle. He was disturbed by the complexity it caused in the masters' "new lives," by the confusion that all this intricacy was bound to create in the mind of the modern student of that principle, and especially by the fear that, on account of this intricacy and apparent confusion, the effectiveness of the principle itself might be lost on future generations. In his attempt to present it clearly, concisely, and scientifically revised, Lorenzo decided therefore to simplify it by reducing it to its minimum scientific import and humanistic value, and to avoid the possible confusion simply by removing its cause, at the risk of making the *principio* itself too rational and inflexible for varied poetic treatment. He probably reasoned something like this:

"The real scientific import of the mystic death is the poet's spiritual elevation and the simultaneous spiritualization by him of the *esser verace* constituting his source of inspiration. Further, this purification of the poet's spirit and his idealization of the object of his love are the *sine qua non* and the beginning of all *nuova vita.* And this mental process of the poet-artist, requiring a state of purity both of his mind and body, is possible not only *in morte di madonna* but also *in vita di madonna.* Indeed, while it may continue after her death, it begins presumably—if not necessarily— while she is alive, and then, throughout her earthly existence, she dies physically in the artist's mind, either continuously or at intervals; so that her actual death merely intensifies or refines this process, making it absolutely perfect.

"It follows from these premises that all *rime* embodying the poet's *nuova vita* are, theoretically speaking, really *in morte di ma-*

donna, whether she was alive at the time of their composition, or actually dead. Therefore, for practical purposes, the factor of her being physically dead or alive may be discarded. Indeed, this is an unnecessary, false, and confusing element in the artist's poetic life. For, if the *esser verace* were not a human being, but if on the contrary the object of the poet's love happened to be the qualities of a natural subject—let us say, a beautiful landscape, or a glorious day in May, or the 'gentilesse' of a work of art—then the factor of its being dead or alive could not be said to exist at all; which shows that it is wholly irrelevant.

"Besides, the poet or other kind of artist who during the earthly existence of his lady cannot entirely free his spirit from the sensual influence of this 'model' or actual personification of the ideal he loves, shows thereby that he has not really fulfilled the truly essential condition required for a *vera vita d'amore.* (Such a one may be said to resemble Orpheus, who failed to bring his Eurydice back to spiritual life because he was not truly mystically dead.) And, accordingly, his artistic creations *in vita di madonna* will not be, strictly speaking, true *nuova vita.* Indeed, if the same sensual influence or the memory of that sensuality continues to pursue him after her death, even those *in morte di madonna* will not be true *nuova vita.*

"Again, it cannot be presumed that, after the realization of the principle accompanied by the first experience in creative art, every moment of the poet's natural life is spent in this kind of trance or state of artistic fervor, but, naturally, only the more-or-less-long periods of his poetic activity, which normally occur at intervals. The time spent in other occupations or in worldly pleasures is not *vera vita.* It is true that a *vero amore* is characterized by singleness of purpose, constancy, and faith, and that therefore a great poet-humanist with a true and strong vocation may devote every moment of his life to his ideal and also conform his life to his ideal; but such 'perfection' is very rare and cannot be expected of ordinary mortals. At any rate, any verses which do not conform or deal with the poet's *vera vita d'amore* cannot be said to constitute part of his *nuova vita* and therefore do not properly belong in such a collection. On the other hand, those which do and are

therefore comprised in it should all be regarded as having naturally been composed *in morte di madonna,* as in fact they were,
either literally and metaphorically speaking, or only metaphorically.

"In conclusion, it may be said that for all practical purposes the
requirement of a state of mystical death is either met completely
by the poet on his first initiation into the 'new life,' or not at all.
Either his *nuova vita* is *vera vita* from the very beginning, or any
part of it which is not *vera vita* is not *nuova vita* and should be
excluded from it. Therefore, following this principle, the poet
should begin logically with *Morte,* or with his poetic portrayal of
his personal experience of the stilnovistic principle of the mystic
death. For this underlies and nourishes all his *nuova vita.* His
nuova vita should contain only poems which portray 'moments' of
his *vera vita d'amore,* however long or short these may have been,
and however near or far apart from each other. For the intervals
do not count. Finally, the *principio* should be brief and be followed by a much longer, more specifically termed *nuova vita.*
This, technically, should comprise the *principio* but not be confused with it. The *principio* should precede the *nuova vita* and
although part of the *nuova vita* should be regarded as distinct
from it."

This reconstruction of Lorenzo's criticism of Dante's and Petrarch's *princìpi* accounts, I believe, for the form given to his own.
Especially it accounts for the main innovation announced by him
toward the end of his *proemio* and there defended by him on
philosophical grounds.[7] Our critical analysis of his sources made
in the light of his own *principio* now confirms my previous intuition. As I said when we first reflected on the probable character of
his modification,[8] and as I have just concluded, all he means is
that, contrary to the custom established by the first stilnovists and
especially by Petrarch, he himself would have no poems *in vita di
madonna,* but his own *nuova vita* would consist of a brief *principio* and of verses all in *morte di madonna,* without, however, entitling them so. His choice of the sonnet form exclusively, on the

7. Cf. Text, bottom of p. 23 to the top of p. 25; and this study, pp. 62–64.
8. Cf. this study, pp. 67–68.

other hand, is accounted for by his preference of this form shown in his own discussion of the current Italian prosody, found also in the *proemio*.[9] I conclude that Lorenzo's very modest innovations are of a purely technical nature, and made apparently for the purpose of clarification, simplification, and modern revision.

On the other hand, Lorenzo's reduction of the principle of mystic death to its minimum theoretic import as an absolute requirement of the *vera vita d'amore,* this simplification which accounts for his main innovation had a kind of corollary, which produced in turn another technical modification. He does not announce this change in the *proemio,* nor does he bring it out particularly anywhere; indeed, he does not even mention it. He merely introduces it in the organism of his *nuova vita* as a logical consequence, we may say, of his new revised conception of the *principio,* and again obviously only for purposes of clarification and coherence. But it is so interesting in itself and so important, I think, in view of its critico-historical significance, that I on the contrary feel that it should be given prominence.

This additional, technical but significant innovation was to the effect that in the case of each stilnovist in turn his borrowed *donna gentile* should be distinguished from his own *gentilissima.* That is, the source of his inspiration should not be confused with the result of this inspiration, namely, his own original poetic production. The *principio di nuova vita,* importing first the apprehension of the principle of mystic death and then a period of apprenticeship in the poetic art of the stilnovists, this inseparable combination of *principio* and *nuova vita* was one thing; and the subsequent "new life" par excellence, or the original works of art produced by the new "master" poet in the same *dolce stil novo* during the years of his maturity, this product of his then properly trained mind was another. In other words, the "studies" of the young poet, or his compositions in imitation of the masters' *nuove vite* and embodying his own apprenticeship in their school; those "copies," as it were, of their "studies" in turn, which had been made in the same spirit and for the same purpose of training;

9. Cf. Text, pp. 22–23; and this study, pp. 55–61.

finally, the youthful stilnovistic efforts of any poet of that school, these should not be confused with the mature products of his own genius which involved the mastery of the stilnovistic art and his originality.

The previous poets—Lorenzo found—had generally fused and therefore confused their conception of the *donna gentile* personifying the poetic ideal called *dolce stil novo,* with their own *gentilissima* or personification of their particular ideal within the same scope. Even Dante, who was the originator of this poetic denomination implying a nice distinction, and who therefore was certainly conscious of the difference involved, at least in degree if not in quality—even he had not succeeded in avoiding a certain amount of at least apparent confusion. His *Commedia,* which was the embodiment of his "new life" par excellence during the years of his maturity, and which was his most original artistic creation, indeed, the perfect incarnation both of his ideal as a poet-artist and his ideal as a humanist—the *Commedia* had been conceived apart by him and, especially outwardly, had been kept separate and distinct from his minor works, including the *Convivio* and even the *Vita Nuova,* which had prefigured it. But his Beatrice in the *Commedia* was by name and qualification the identical Beatrice of the *Vita Nuova;* and this *gentilissima,* whether viewed from the *Commedia* or the *Vita Nuova,* was not easily distinguishable from his *donna pietosa* or *donna gentile* found in both the *Vita Nuova* and the *Convivio.* This real or apparent confusion was certainly a cause of great confusion in the mind of anyone, incipient poet or literary critic, who attempted to reconstruct Dante's poetic principle.

Petrarch, on the other hand, seemed to have made no distinction at all between *donna gentile* and *gentilissima.* His Laura, at first and especially in his initiatory sonnet, appeared as his denomination of the *donna gentile* and certainly signified his first conception of the principle and ideal of the *dolce stil novo.* But Laura soon lost this character in the course of his *rime;* she became almost immediately identified with Petrarch's own particular ideal of poetic art. Indeed, his Laura might be said to be all *gentilissima* and at the same time viewed as the perfect representation of his gradually changing and developing original concept of the *donna gentile*. His *canzoniere* portrayed his apprenticeship in the art of the *dolce stil novo* and at the same time the progress he was making in the evolution of his own poetic ideal in conformity both with the principle of the *donna gentile* and his own poetic genius. For this reason, Petrarch's Laura was a continuous modification of his original concept of the sweet new style, or a gradual transfiguration of his *donna gentile* into his *gentilissima*. But this continuous identification of the two "ladies" in the poet's mind, indicated at least apparently a certain confusion on his part between the subject of his study and the object of his apprenticeship. And this real or only apparent confusion in the case of Petrarch as well was also a source of possible confusion and misunderstanding to anyone attempting to reconstruct his principle of poetic art in order to form his own style in his school.

To be sure, Lorenzo must have thought, the fusion of the two "ladies," or the gradual transfiguration of the *donna gentile* into the new poet's own *gentilissima,* this is implied in, and required by, the fundamental principle of "gentilesse" underlying all stilnovistic poetic production. For the conception, on the part of any incipient stilnovist, of his own *gentilissima* involves his absorption of the poetic ideal and artistic principle which have guided the previous stilnovists in their production of what in his time constitutes the Italian literature in *volgare*. It implies, moreover, his subsequent or contemporaneous idealization of the concept thus derived, which he does in conformity with his own poetic genius. In other words, each stilnovist in turn begins his apprenticeship with a critical reconstruction of the ideal and principle nourishing all previous poetry written in the *dolce stil novo,* and this conception on his part is symbolized by his *donna gentile*. (Accordingly, his *donna gentile* is a kind of composite "lady" made up of elements taken from all the various *gentilissime* who have preceded his time; she is the growing Italian literature.) At the same time, however, he gradually forms his own ideal both in conformity with this *donna gentile* and his poetic genius; and this conception in turn is symbolized by his particular *gentilissima*.

This being so, it follows that the fusion of the *donna gentile* with the *gentilissima* in the poetic production of the stilnovist, is theoretical. It is therefore inevitable, indeed desirable. But fusion does not mean confusion, Lorenzo contended; and especially in a *nuova vita*, which purports to be the apprentice's critical reconstruction of the masters' *principio* and of their theoretico-critical studies in turn of the previous stilnovistic poetry which had been their source of inspiration; in such a work particularly they should be kept separate and distinct. That is, the apprentice should differentiate carefully, on the one hand between the absolute, fundamental principle of the *dolce stil novo* common to all stilnovists of any generation, and his own concept of the *donna gentile* or Italian poetry in its historical evolution; and on the other hand he should also distinguish sharply his own *gentilissima* from this *donna gentile* who was the source of his inspiration and enlightenment. In other words, as I said before, the combination of *principio* and *nuova vita*, in the sense of initiation and period of training, was one thing; and this same *nuova vita* or apprenticeship, which at the same time gradually produced the new poet's *gentilissima*, was another. As Petrarch especially had indicated, the latter originated and developed *pari passu* with the apprentice's better and better understanding of the principle of the sweet new style and also of the poetry which followed this principle. But Lorenzo, the critic and expounder of the theory of the *dolce stil novo*, undoubtedly thought that, critically speaking, they were nevertheless two separate and distinct products of the poet's mind. The *donna gentile*, we might say briefly, was the *subject* of the poet's study; she was a concept which thereafter remained stationary and passive in his mind, except in so far as it might become clearer or more precise with further study, and except in so far as it was continually a source of inspiration for him. His *gentilissima* on the contrary was the *object* of this study; she was the object of his poetic ambition and artistic aspiration; finally, she was, as it were, an active or growing concept, which, vague at first and indefinite, gradually became clearer until it assumed a definite form corresponding to the final ideal of the then mature poet.

As such, his *gentilissima* still waited to be incarnated in an original work of art; but when the poet had achieved his ideal he had also produced his masterpiece.

Therefore, concluded the *continuatore insieme e novatore* of this poetic form of creative literary criticism, since the "ladies" involved in a *nuova vita* are really two—one personifying the poet's initiatory realization of the principle of the sweet new style and also his conception of the historical development of the literature embodying this concept of poetic art, and the other signifying his own stilnovistic ideal in the act and process of its formation—let us therefore have two distinct "models" for their proper artistic portrayal. Let us have one model for the *donna gentile* and another for the *gentilissima*. This is logical, critically more consonant with the principle of "gentilesse" itself, and, besides, the future student of such *nuove vite* will not have to contend with the difficulty caused by the confusion of the two symbols. On the contrary, by this "material" distinction between the two most important factors in the making of a true stilnovist, he will be assisted in his own penetration of the veil which envelops both the *donna gentile* and the *gentilissime* of the early Italian poets, and he will also be guided perhaps in the formation of his own *gentilissima*.

Moreover, by this simple means it is hoped that the future critic and historian of the early Italian poets will no longer confuse, for instance, a *Laura* with a *monna Vanna,* or a *monna Lagia,* or a *Beatrice,* or a *Selvaggia,* all of whom preceded her as the *gentilissime* of Guido Cavalcanti, Lapo Gianni, Dante, and Cino da Pistoia, respectively, and all of whom no doubt contributed to Petrarch's concept of the *donna gentile;* nor, on the other hand, will he confuse her, again for instance, with Boccaccio's *Fiammetta,* who followed her, and to whose formation she no doubt contributed, entering as an element, together with the others, in this poet's conception in turn of the *donna gentile.* On the contrary, it is hoped that he will apply his "gentilesse" to the differentiation of these various *gentilissime,* and that he will appreciate not only their derivation and special originality but also their influence on the subsequent and all later *gentilissime.*

In a surprising and remarkable manner this accounts, I believe, for Lorenzo's unequivocal introduction, in the organic structure of his revised edition of a typical *nuova vita,* of two separate and distinct ladies, instead of the customary one or, as in the case of Dante, of an obscure combination of several. In fact, he has one for the *principio* in the sense of initation into the "new life," and an entirely different one, unmistakably distinct from the first, for his *nuova vita* in the sense of a subsequent period of apprenticeship. The first, as we have seen, stands for his personification of the poetic ideal embodied in the early Italian poetry, which was based on the philosophical principle of the mystic death equivalent to the historico-critical principle of human "gentilesse"; she symbolizes his achievement of the mystic death and at the same time stands for his historico-critical concept of the previous Italian literature in *volgare* obtained through this process; finally, she is his *donna gentile,* who, however, with respect to herself, was *gentile* both in the superlative degree and in the absolute sense, indeed, she was *gentilissima.* The second, on the other hand, will undoubtedly stand for his own *gentilissima* in process of evolution throughout his period of apprenticeship; she will symbolize the constant application during this process of the principle of "gentilesse," which in this connection will be equivalent to the application to himself of the ancient maxim, *nosce te ipsum;* finally, after the completion of this apprenticeship, when if ever he will have incarnated his own poetic ideal in some original work of art, then she will personify this original poetic production.

The place where he introduces this second lady is naturally at the beginning of his *nuova vita* distinct from the *principio,* philosophically speaking. There, after the usual transitional paragraph, in which he repeats the contention *che la morte sia stata conveniente principio a questa nuova vita,* it seems necessary to him *per maggior delucidazione far prima un nuovo argumento, il quale sia comune a tutti li seguenti sonetti.* And in the course of this long preamble, after recalling man's *naturale appetito di felicità,* after touching also on the origin and desirability of *la varietà degli studi umani,* he says textually as follows:

Fu adunque *la vita e morte di colei* che abbiamo detto *notizia universale*

*d'amore e cognizione in confuso che cosa fussi amorosa passione; per la quale
universale cognizione divenni poi alla cognizione particulare della mia dol-
cissima ed amorosa pena,* come diremo appresso. Imperocchè, essendo morta
la donna che disopra abbiamo detto, fu da me e laudata e deplorata nelli
precedenti sonetti come *publico danno e iattura comune,* e fui mosso da un
dolore e compassione che *molti e molti altri mosse alla città nostra,* perchè
fu dolore molto universale e comune. E se bene nelli precedenti versi sono
scritte alcune cose che più tosto paiono da privata e grande passione dettate,
mi sforzai, per meglio satisfare a me medesimo ed a quelli che grandissima e
privata passione avevono della sua morte, *propormi innanzi agli occhi d'avere
ancora io perduto una carissima cosa, e introdurre nella mia fantasia tutti gli
effetti che fussino atti a muovere me medesimo, per poter meglio muovere
altri.* E, stando in questa immaginazione, cominciai meco medesimo a pen-
sare quanto fussi dura la sorte più di quelli che assai avevono amato questa
donna, e *cercare con la mente se alcuna altra ne fussi nella città degna di tanto
amore e laude.* E, stimando che grandissima felicità e dolcezza fussi quella di
colui, il quale o per ingegno o per fortuna avessi grazia di servire una tale
donna, *stetti qualche spazio di tempo cercando sempre e non trovando cosa
che al giudicio mio fussi degna d'un vero e costantissimo amore.* Ed essendo
già quasi fuora d'ogni speranza di poterla trovare, fece in un punto più il caso,
che in tanto tempo non aveva fatto la esquisita diligenzia mia; e forse Amore
per mostrare meglio a me la sua potenza, volle manifestarmi tanto bene in
quel tempo, quando al tutto me ne pareva essere disperato.

Facevasi nella nostra città *una publica festa,* dove concorsono molti uomini
e *quasi tutte le giovane nobile e belle.* A questa festa quasi contro a mia voglia,
credo per mio destino, mi condussi con alcuni compagni ed amici miei,
perchè *ero stato per qualche tempo assai alieno da simili feste,* e, se pure qualche volta mi erono piaciute, procedeva più presto da *una certa voglia ordi-
naria di fare come gli altri giovani,* che da grande piacere che ne traessi. Era,
tra l'altre donne, una agli occhi miei di somma bellezza e di sì dolci ed attrat-
tivi sembianti, che cominciai, veggendola, a dire:—*Se questa fussi di quella
delicatezza, ingegno e modi che fu quella morta che abbiamo detta, certo in
costei e la bellezza e la vaghezza e forza degli occhi è molto maggiore.*—Di
poi, *parlando con alcuno che di lei aveva qualche notizia,* trovai molto bene
rispondere gli effetti, non così comuni ciascuno a quelli che la bellezza sua e
massime gli occhi mostravano, *nelli quali si verificava molto quello che dice
Dante* in una sua canzona parlando degli occhi della donna sua:

"*Ella vi reca Amor como a suo loco.*"[10]

There follow some irrelevant remarks on how he began to love
quell'apparente bellezza, indeed, how his admiration grew at the
sight of *una donna che tanto eccedesse la bellezza e grazia della*

10. Cf. Text, p. 34, l. 29, to p. 36, l. 5. Also Dante, *Convivio,* Canzone Seconda, 58.

sopradetta morta; and then comes a full and minute though summary description of the beauty of this "lady." This description being all significant, I shall not bring into special relief any parts of it but consider it all as most pertinent to the matter in hand. It reads as follows:

Era la sua bellezza, come abbiamo detto, mirabile: di bella e conveniente grandezza; il colore delle carni bianco e non ismorto, vivo e non acceso; l'aspetto suo grave e non superbo, dolce e piacevole, sanza leggerezza o viltà alcuna; gli occhi vivi e non mobili, sanza alcun segno o d'alterigia o di levità. Tutto il corpo sì bene proporzionato, che tra l'altre mostrava dignità sanza alcuna cosa rozza o inetta; e nondimeno, nell'andare e nel ballare e nelle cose che è lecito alle donne adoperare il corpo, ed in effetto in tutti li suoi moti, era elegante ed avvenente. Le mani sopra tutte le altre, che mai facessi natura, bellissime, come diremo sopra alcuni sonetti, alli quali le sue mani hanno dato materia; nell'abito e portamenti suoi molto pulita e bene a proposito ornata, fuggendo però tutte quelle fogge che a nobile e gentile donne non si convengono, e servando la gravità e dignità. Il parlare dolcissimo veramente, pieno d'acute e buone sentenzie, come faremo intendere nel processo, perchè alcune parole e sottili inquisizioni sue hanno fatto argomento a certi delli miei sonetti. Parlava a tempo, breve e conciso, nè si poteva nelle sue parole o desiderare o levare; li motti e facezie sue erono argute e salse, sanza offensione però d'alcuno dolcemente mordere. L'ingegno veramente meraviglioso assai più che a donne non si conviene; e questo però sanza fasto o presunzione, e fuggendo un certo vizio che si suole trovare nella maggior parte delle donne, alle quali parendo d'intendere assai, diventano insopportabili, volendo giudicare ogni cosa, che vulgarmente le chiamano "saccenti." Era prontissima d'ingegno, tanto che molte volte o per una sola parola o per un piccolo cenno comprendeva l'animo altrui; nelli modi suoi dolce e piacevole oltra modo, non vi mescolando però alcuna cosa molle o che provocassi altri ad alcun poco laudabile effetto; in qualunque sua cosa saggia ed accorta e circonspetta, fuggendo però ogni segno di callidità o duplicità, nè dando alcuna sospezione di poca constanzia o fede. Sarebbe più lunga la narrazione di tutte le sue eccellentissime parti che il presente comento; e però con una parola concluderemo il tutto, e veramente affermeremo nessuna cosa potersi in una bella e gentil donna desiderare, che in lei copiosamente non fussi.[11]

I have quoted these passages *in extenso,* not with the intention of expounding them at this juncture, but merely in order to bring out how much more beautiful and graceful is this "lady" supposed to be than the "lady" of the *principio.* Of course, those are the

11. Cf. Text, p. 36, l. 22, to p. 37, l. 23.

qualities constituting Lorenzo's humanistic ideal, or his concept of the perfect man; and those are also the qualities he proposes to incarnate stilnovistically in his own original and effective poetic production. In a word, this "lady" now, in contradistinction to his *donna gentile,* is his particular *gentilissima.*

Moreover, I wish to bring out especially how distinct and separate she stands in the mind of the commentator of his own verses and critic of the previous poetry, from his concept of that first incarnation of the supreme *bellezza e gentilezza umana* which was withal his source of enlightenment and inspiration. His *gentilissima* is unequivocally a different personality, indeed, an entirely different "person." At the same time, obviously, she is substantially the identical *gentilissima* of the *principio;* she is the same in principle and humanistic import, the same in her general characteristics, the same in the effectiveness of her qualities. The principal difference seems to be only one of degree and explicitness.

No doubt a careful analysis of this preamble to Lorenzo's *nuova vita,* accompanied by a faithful interpretation of its esoteric meaning, and especially the further critique of the *nuova vita* itself; such a study would bring out the particular "gentilesse" of this Laurentian *gentilissima.* But such a complete and profound penetration of the factitious veil enveloping her, must not concern us for the present. That task is properly reserved for the expounder of Lorenzo's *nuova vita;* it is one which I plan to do myself in a separate volume.

Here, merely in the light of the *principio,* it will suffice to say that Lorenzo evidently means to pass from the abstract to the concrete and from the generic to the particular. He visualizes a change in the character and form of the subsequent Italian poetry, which may be radical, but is certainly not substantial. He proposes to alter the generic and universal character of the Italian poetic ideal in such a way that the new works of art instead of appearing to be mere theories and generalizations on the principle of the *dolce stil novo* will now present the actual application of that principle. Further, he wants the application of the same principle to all walks of life, in all fields of human endeavor; and even more he wants the consideration of details. He implies that the individual seeking to carry out the stilnovistic principle will find his happiness in the variety of human studies and in any of the applied arts and sciences. Especially, the modern stilnovist should conform his habits of personal conduct, speech, and general behavior to an ideal of human refinement and culture even higher than the one formerly conceived and not generally achieved. Finally, from this rapid, superficial, and tentative interpretation of the passages quoted above, it would seem that Lorenzo's personal humanistic ideal was at once broader and narrower, more liberal but more exacting, less universal and more specific; but above all clearer, definite, and concrete, especially with respect to its apprehension and practical execution on the part of any individual member of society. In a word, his *gentilissima* was apparently the ideal, or program, I may say, of the Italian *High* Renaissance. No wonder it was a totally different "thing" from the excellent but primitive form of the same ideal current during the period called *Pre*-Renaissance!

I may seem to exaggerate, and perhaps I do. But, whether or not my own later study of Lorenzo's *nuova vita* will support the present view, the point of the argument here is that, as I have just said, his *gentilissima* was in reality, or at least technically, an entirely different and distinct "thing" from his *donna gentile*. Moreover, the point is that, theoretically at least, she was intended to be different. In fact, she was or was meant to be so different that, when many years later the poet decided to comment on his youthful *nuova vita,* he felt the need of an entirely different "model" for the framework of these sonnets from the one he had used for the four initiatory ones. And just as the model chosen for the realistic and vivid representation of his *principio* was an artificial adaptation of a well-known, striking decease, so the model chosen for the portrayal of his *nuova vita d'amore* was essentially a happy adaptation of his own *servitù d'amore cavalleresco e poetico,*[12] similarly well known. In other words, once the death of *la bella Simonetta* had served him well as a model for the forcible depiction of his own mystic death and that of his *donna gentile,* he had

12. The phrase is not mine, but Rossi's. Cf. Vittorio Rossi, *Il Quattrocento* (1933), p. 347.

to find another model likewise specially suitable for the graphic representation of his *servitù d'amore neoplatonico ed artistico.* And this, not simply because he had just said that the Simonetta was now dead, nor because it was well known that this lady had been the object of his brother's attentions; the main reason was that both logically and technically the "lady" of the *nuova vita* was not and could not be the same "lady" of the *principio,* nor a confused modification of her.

It is generally believed that the lady referred to by the commentator in the preamble quoted above, was in life a certain Lucrezia Donati, whom Lorenzo courted for a long time: it is said as far back as 1465.[13] I accept this belief readily but with indifference. For, as I have indicated already, personally I am only mildly interested in the historical identity of the models used either by poets or other artists. As a rule I am mainly concerned with the poetic reality of a work of art. But this one interests me. It interests me, however, not because it matters one iota who the lady was in real life; nor because I for one moment believe that the description of the lady contained in the said preamble is a literal or even a literary portrait of Lucrezia Donati. It interests me precisely because the poetic reality of Lorenzo's *nuova vita* seems to have been affected by the reality of his courtship of this lady, and especially by its quality. It is charming to think that his love for the poetic ideal and the "new life" of the stilnovists had an actual counterpart in his simultaneous *servitù d'amore cavalleresco e poetico* for a definite lady of distinction, who actually personified in her the very virtues and qualities of refinement and culture which he exalted. This factor may also have contributed to the realism of the feelings and sentiments expressed in the verses. At any rate, it seems to me that he could not have chosen a better model for the portrayal of his poetic life.

Thus, I agree with Rossi that Lucrezia Donati, or, better the poet's courtship of this lady, "sarà stata ispiratrice al giovinetto mediceo di sonetti e canzoni."[14] On the other hand, observe the

---

13. Cf. Rossi, *loc. cit.*

14. *Idem.* In this connection, Rossi refers to the study of Isidoro del Lungo, *Gli amori del Magnifico Lorenzo,* already mentioned by me.

artificiality of this second "adaptation," again to the framework of the *Comento*. Just as the death of Simonetta Cattaneo surely did not inspire originally the sonnets of the *principio,* but her death was an excellent model for the subsequent exposition of the principle of mystic death involved in those sonnets; so the *servitù d'amore cavalleresco e poetico* cannot be said to have supplied more than a mere *spunto* to the sonnets of the *nuova vita.* For, as Rossi again says, "con essa non può aver a che vedere la storia d'amore ch'egli narra nel commento. . . ."[15] In fact, as we perhaps realize already, the purely doctrinal character of the subject matter excludes all possibility of any connection other than one merely formal.

Observe, moreover, that, if we accept the supposed historical identity of both the lady of the *principio* and the lady of the *nuova vita,* if we accept also literally the supposed veracity of the episodes with which these ladies are connected, and especially if we then naturally link these two episodes together; in short, if we attempt to reconstruct historically the commentator's narrative on the basis of these identifications taken literally both as to time and the persons involved, we fall immediately upon the most obvious inconsistency. The poet is first inspired by the death of *la bella Simonetta* in 1476, and writes four sonnets in her honor, which are said to be the beginning of his poetic career and the first of the series commented on. Then sometime later he comes upon his real and longer source of inspiration; he meets casually Lucrezia Donati, already married to Niccolò Ardinghelli, and makes her the subject of his chivalrous and poetic love. Meanwhile, we know all the time that his courtship of Lucrezia had been going on since 1465; we know that he was not even in Florence when the Simonetta died; finally, we know that the four sonnets of the *principio* and at least one of the *nuova vita*[16] had already been comprised in

15. *Idem.* But Rossi's reference to the date of the *Comento* in the same sentence in which he expresses this opinion is misleading. The date of the *Comento* has nothing to do with this question. (Cf. Appendix B, at the end of this study.) The real, sound basis for this conclusion, in which I concur, is the character of the sonnets, which he explains immediately after.

16. This is the sonnet, "Occhi, voi siete pur dentro al mio core," which is the seventh in the *Comento,* and the third among those coming under the strict specification of *nuova vita.*

the *Raccolta aragonese* as early as approximately 1469 or 1470.[17] I omit other considerations, and conclude that, taken literally, the author's narrative, historically, is simply untenable.

It follows, I believe, that the artificiality of the two adaptations in the framework of the *Comento* was conscious and wilful. And if it was wilful it must have had a purpose. This purpose, in a critically revised edition of the masters' *principio* and *nuova vita d'amore,* could not have been other, in my opinion, than one of method and clarification. Moreover, in view of the principal innovation introduced by the author in the organic structure of his *nuova vita;* in view of the critico-theoretical value of this technical change; finally, in view of the methodological character and practical value of the distinction made between *donna gentile* and *gentilissima:* in view of all this, it seems reasonable to infer that the introduction of two distinct models to portray these "ladies" was actually for the purpose I surmised, and also a logical consequence of beginning with *Morte.* I so conclude.

17. Cf. Appendix B, at the end of this study.

CHAPTER V

Contrivances by Masters and Pupil: the Probable Historicalness of the Date of Laura's Death, and the Artificiality of the "Simultaneity" Built Around It by the Poet-Stilnovist.

WE must now return again to Petrarch's note on the death of Laura for one last consideration.[1] This further analysis will bring out that, apparently, Lorenzo's contrivance to adapt the death of Simonetta to his *principio,* this contrivance also was at least in conformity with the ingenious scheming of the master.

Who was Laura? We do not know. At least, the historians are not agreed on her identity, and we do not need to satisfy now this minor literary curiosity. For, since we are concerned chiefly with her poetic reality, we cannot lay weight, in our discussion, on her identity, which is that of a "model." To gratify the positivists, it is sufficient to grant to them that the artistic reality of this "lady" —like that of any *donna gentile* or *gentilissima*—must have had a counterpart in physical life. And this, not merely because in the case of Laura, the poet himself testified emphatically to her real existence,[2] but also because of the deeper reason which I have already indicated. The stilnovistic principle of strict realism in all factors of the "new life" called for an actual *esser verace* that would serve at once as a source of inspiration and as the incarnation of the ideal pursued.

The point I wish to make is that the very fact that there was a Laura of flesh and blood is in itself a sign that the date of her death, as registered by Petrarch, is very likely historical and precise. Indeed, everything points to this historical accuracy: the private character of the note, apparently intended to be primarily for personal use; the precision of the language in which it was couched; the conspicuous place of honor to which it was con-

---

1. Cf. chap. ii of this section, pp. 249–250, 254–255; also chap. iii, pp. 258–265.
2. Cf. the passage from *Lettere familiari,* II, 9, quoted by Scherillo, *op. cit.,* I, 206–207.

signed; the wealth of external details, most of which were readily verifiable then.

Especially significant is the fact that, as I have hinted before and shall show presently, the causative relation established by the poet between the death of his lady and the commencement of his love—this relation is all a contrivance for the purpose of giving realistic consistency to his *principio;* it all revolves around this date. That is, the date of Laura's death is a fixed point or a point of departure for an ingenious contrivance to make this death coincide significantly, in the manner we have seen, with his initiation into the "new life."

This contrivance reminds us again of Dante's similar ingenuity to fit the date of Beatrice's death into the symbolic number nine;[3] and the inference is that, just as such an effort on Dante's part is a fair indication of the historicalness of the date of Beatrice's death deduced from an analysis of his scheme, so this fabrication of Petrarch testifies, we may say, to the veracity of his statement regarding the date of Laura's death. I conclude therefore that this lady, whoever she was, actually died on April 6, 1348.

At the same time, there can be no doubt that the famous simultaneous occurrence, presumably "remarked" by Petrarch, was, I maintain, all a fabrication to the intent and purpose of his *principio*. In fact, remember that the miraculousness of this simultaneity, its esoteric significance and the connection thus established between the initiatory sonnet and the note, finally, the coherence of all this depends entirely on the assumption that both April 6, 1327, and April 6, 1348, were recurrences of Good Friday. And now realize that on neither of those years did Good Friday fall on April 6. According to Augustus de Morgan's *Book of Almanacs* (London, 1851), Good Friday in 1327 fell on April 10, and in 1348 on April 18!

Consequently, either Laura died on April 6, 1348, and it was not then Good Friday, or she did die on Good Friday of that year, and the date of her death was not then April 6, but April 18. Either Petrarch fell in love with her on Good Friday of the year 1327, and this recurrence (April 10) then coincided neither with

3. Cf. above p. 239.

April 6 of that year (the date given) nor with April 6, 1348 (the date of Laura's death); or he did fall in love with her as he says on April 6, 1327, and this date then coincided neither with Good Friday in 1327 (which fell on April 10) nor with Good Friday in 1348 (which fell on April 18).[4] Both dates cannot be true, and since we have already concluded that the date of Laura's death recorded by him is probably historical, the inference is now clear: Either the miraculous simultaneity remarked by him lacked the very element which made it significant, namely, the recurrence of Good Friday; or else there never was any such coincidence, and this was imagined by him merely for the purpose of his realistic, theoretic *principio*. Inasmuch as, in view of the general character and import of the note, the latter is the more plausible inference of the two, I decide in favor of it.

On the other hand, it may also be that he actually saw Laura for the first time on the morning of Good Friday, 1327. In this case, it is possible that he later thought the date April 10 sufficiently near to April 6 to permit him to establish realistically the simultaneity he desired for poetic and theoretical reasons. But in this case then, he had to make an even bigger allowance at the other end as well; he had to imagine that April 18, 1348, was sufficiently near to April 6 of that year to permit him to imply that Laura had died on *Good Friday* of that year.

Such an adjustment saves both the veracity of the date given in the note with respect to Laura's death and the veracity of the occasion recalled in the initiatory sonnet with reference to the poet's first view of her. It does not save the "simultaneity," but this only proves my contention that the *perfect* coincidence was artificial and established only for theoretical purposes.

I believe that the adjustment I have suggested represents precisely what took place in Petrarch's mind when he composed the note and, perhaps at the same time, also the initiatory sonnet. This is shown by the following consideration. As I said before, Petrarch must have composed his initiatory sonnet after Laura's death, precisely when he had decided to collect and arrange his *rime sparse,*

4. Indeed, on the strength of this contradiction alone, we might also infer that the note is a forgery.

and felt the need of this and several other sonnets as an introduction to these "scattered fragments" of his *nuova vita*. This means that, while he probably composed the initiatory sonnet shortly after he had written the note, the two conceptions were undoubtedly present in his mind on both occasions. Indeed, while writing the note he must not only have been thinking already of what form to give his initiation but the note itself must have been conceived in view of this sonnet. Similarly, no doubt, when he composed the sonnet he had the note well in mind. In other words, both compositions were the product of the identical intention to give to his *nuova vita* a suitable real or realistic beginning—a beginning which would at the same time be both theoretical and in accordance with his actual experience.

Now observe that in the note he could not mention the "Good Friday" factor without going counter to the calendar specification and thus revealing the fanciful character of his theoretical "coincidence." Accordingly, he omitted it, probably feeling, I repeat, that for the purpose of a theoretic simultaneity, the date April 6, 1327, was sufficiently near the actual date (only four days apart) to satisfy both his conscience and the theory. In the note, he was content to establish it merely on the basis of the calendar date, enriched, however, by the additional specification of the early-morning hour and by the repeated specification of the month of April. This is a strong indication that, as I said above, his date of Laura's death is historical.

In the sonnet, on the contrary, where the whole point was that his initiation had coincided with the recurrence of Good Friday, he could not specify the day of the month without again going counter to the calendar and thus destroying the reality or realism of his experience. Therefore, inasmuch as this realism was necessary to the effectiveness of the "Good Friday" factor, here he did just the reverse, and left out the date. This in turn is a strong indication that this factor was actually responsible for his poetic initiation. That is, the inference is that, whenever it did happen—either actually on Good Friday of 1327 or at any other time—the realization of the stilnovistic principle of the mystic death came to him in conjunction with his consideration of the death of Christ.

And, since it is both natural and plausible that this consideration should have occurred to him on a Good Friday during his youth, it is fair to deduce that his amorous passion actually began on the occasion of the recurrence implied in the sonnet and in the year specified in the note.

Recall the repeated, formal commemoration of this date, which before Laura's death was made directly, and after it indirectly. Observe it in this very note, and remember also the continuous reference made to this crucial moment of his poetic life throughout the *canzoniere*. All this certainly lends veracity to his statement as but slightly corrected by me. In any case, it is perfectly obvious now that the two compositions balance each other nicely, and also complete each other. Each supplies what the other lacks to make it fully significant both with respect to the theoretical import of the principle and with respect to Petrarch's actual experience of this *principio di nuova vita*.

In conclusion of what has just been considered and deduced, I trust we are now convinced of both the character and the purpose of Petrarch's contrivance. Now we see the influence on Lorenzo of this precedent established both by Petrarch and Dante. Now we realize all the extent of the masters' influence on the pupil. And, with reference to my whole analysis of his various sources, I trust we are now willing to recognize them as obviously direct, and also perceive just what interested Lorenzo in those sources: just what he discarded, modified, or accepted; and just how he came to conceive his own *principio* in the manner we have seen with respect to content and form. Finally, I feel confident that now we are ready to acknowledge the great critical acumen of the Magnificent; his deep, intelligent penetration of the whole scope, character, and intent of the previous poetry; and the light that his *principio* both throws upon the poetic life of his predecessors, and in turn receives from an analysis of their works carried out under his guidance. His *principio* is truly a key, I may now say, both to his own *nuova vita* and to the *nuove vite* of his great masters.

PART V

THE *PRINCIPIO:* SONNETS III AND IV

FOREWORD

THANKS to the consciousness we have acquired of the rich content of the first two sonnets, the esoteric meaning of Sonnets III and IV will now be visible at a glance. Better, the author's own comments ought to suffice, provided we continue to read between the lines and apply our former deductions to the further development of his theoretic concept. For now he passes to the application of the principle expounded, and portrays the initiate's "new life" in the course of achieving mystic death.

Accordingly, my own elucidations will now be in the nature of very brief comments intended to bring out, first the direct significance of the commentator's new implications, second the progression of his poetic initiation, and, finally, such conclusions of critical and historical importance as may be derived from his additional information. In taking up these sonnets in order, I shall first reproduce for convenient reference the sonnet itself in the original Italian, then I shall give the barest translation of the author's own comment, and, finally, I shall add my exposition of both. The reader who may not recall the textual meaning of these and the preceding sonnets, nor their relation, may refresh his memory by turning back to my preliminary literal rendering of the *principio*, given on pages 89–91.

CHAPTER I

Sonnet III

Di vita il dolce lume fuggirei
a quella vita, ch'altri "morte" appella;
ma morte è sì gentile oggi e sì bella,
ch'io credo che morir vorran gli dèi.

Morte è gentil, poich'è stata in colei
ch'è or del ciel la più lucente stella;
io, che gustar non vo' dolce, poich'ella
è morta, seguirò quest'anni rei.

Piangeran sempre gli occhi, e 'l tristo core
sospirerà del suo bel sol l'occaso,
lor di lui privi, e 'l cor d'ogni sua speme.

Piangerà meco dolcemente Amore,
le Grazie e le sorelle di Parnaso;
e chi non piangerà con questi insieme?

Translation of the Author's Own Comment.

THIS sonnet is thus commented upon by Lorenzo: "It is the nature of lovers commonly to indulge in sad thoughts and melancholy, which, amid tears and sighs, are food to their amorous hunger; and this commonly while they experience withal the greatest joy and sense of sweetness. I believe the reason for this is because the love which is single and constant[1] proceeds from a strong imagination, and this process can hardly originate unless the melancholy humor prevails in the lover. For the nature of the latter is to be always suspicious and prone to turn every event, whether favorable or adverse, into sorrow and passion.

"If this is the peculiar nature of lovers, their grief must certainly be greater than that of other men, when to this natural characteristic is added some accident which is in itself dolorous and lamentable. And, since nothing could happen to the lover more worthy of sorrow and tears than for him to be deprived for-

---

1. *Solo e diuturno,* says the text; and these adjectives of course reëcho the two conditions of a *vero amore,* namely, *che si ami una cosa sola* and *che questa tale cosa si ami sempre.* Cf. Text, p. 14; and this study, p. 13.

ever of the object of his love, one may well imagine the immensity of the grief caused by the death of that "lady" [colei] to those who most loved her. It is fair to assume that it was greater than any ordinary man could feel.

"Moreover, it is the nature of such melancholy people as I have said lovers to be, to seek no remedy for their grief other than an accumulation of more grief. They hate and flee from anything soothing and consoling. Therefore, when at times death presented itself to me as a remedy for the very bitter sorrow I felt, I hated it, since it meant the end of my dolorous passion. And it was to be hated: indeed all the more, because after it had been in the eyes of *colei* it might be deemed sweeter and more *gentile*. In fact, since it had been communicated to a *cosa gentilissima,* it partook necessarily of the quality which there it had found in great abundance. Verily, considering how *gentile* death had thereby become, I thought the immortal gods ought to change their fate and they, too, wish to taste of the 'gentilesse' of death.

"This being so, since in accord with my nature I sought only grief and wished to taste of nothing sweet—in order to suffer more I chose to follow the course of my natural life. And this, in order that my grief, abiding daily with me, might be more constant, that my eyes might weep for a longer period, and that my heart also might sigh longer, lamenting the setting, or death, of my sun. With my eyes deprived of their exceedingly sweet vision, and my heart bereft of all its hope and consolation, I would spend the years of my life weeping and sighing in the company of Love, the Graces, and the Muses.

"The latter may weep and grieve just as properly as my eyes and heart. For, just as my eyes and heart have lost the purpose for which Love had ordained and destined them, so Love has lost the sway and purpose which he had placed in the eyes of *costei*. Therefore, he too must weep. Likewise the Graces, who had entrusted all their gifts and virtues to her beauty. And likewise the Muses, who had committed the glory of their chorus to the singing of her most worthy praises. Accordingly, the attribution of tears to them and to everyone is entirely proper. For anyone who would not weep with them must needs be a man without a trace of either love or grace. Verily, everyone should weep, those who are not indifferent, as well as those who at least do not wish to appear indifferent to so much 'gentilesse.'

"These are the affections which I should have liked to express in the present sonnet."

Now let us reconsider the sonnet in the light of this comment, which we laid aside in our preliminary study of the literal meaning of the *principio* and of its most obvious esoteric implication.[2] Let us interpret both the sonnet and the comment in the light of our deductions so far. Perhaps this penetration of Lorenzo's real and full intention with respect to both will lead to other inferences and conclusions of an historico-critical nature.

We are faced immediately with the usual difficulty of the triple point of view maintained consistently by the author throughout his *principio*. First he takes the point of view of the literary critic who is concerned with the discernment and presentation of the principle and poetic ideal that he exalts. Then he adopts the point of view of the incipient stilnovist who wishes to evolve his own ideal in conformity with this principle and also model it after the same ideal. Finally, he takes the point of view of the poet-humanist and pedagogue who intends that his personal experience should be at once an example and a kind of scientific demonstration of the truth of his principle and the excellence of his ideal. Moreover, this is all involved as usual, not only in the composition of the sonnet itself, but also in its exposition, which remains largely on the same allegorical plane. But now clearly and according to the point of view, this sonnet and relative comment might be entitled either: "The 'Gentilesse' of Mystic Death," or "The Poet's Fervor and Enthusiasm in the Pursuit of His Ideal," or, again, "The Physiological and Psychological Basis of the Joys and Sorrows of the 'New Life.'" Indeed, all three titles apply at once. And now we see how this sonnet is related to the preceding ones and marks a progression in the *principio* of the author—critic, poet, and teacher in one.[3]

2. Cf. pp. 89–99.
3. Recall the various titles suggested for the first and second sonnets. Cf. above, p. 151.

The "Gentilesse" of Mystic Death.

WE already know what he means by the "gentilesse" now acquired by Death. He is not merely imitating or repeating Dante.
He is realizing for himself and bringing out for future stilnovists
the truth of the master's beautiful concept. It was this concept
which involved the nice "distinction" made by Dante and all the
stilnovists, between death in the literal sense and death in the
metaphorical sense of "mystic" death. Indeed, Lorenzo goes one
step forward. In his own " 'gentilesse' *newly* acquired by Death"
he first includes the "gentilesse" of the mystic death whereby his
predecessors, each in turn, had made this distinction in connection
with their individual realization of their respective *donna gentile*
and had become initiated into the "new life." Then he goes on to
include the "gentilesse" of this death whereby he himself has
come to the realization of the ideal embodied in the now *gentilissima* Italian poetry, and whereby he is likewise becoming initiated
into the same "new life."

As I said before, he means the "gentilesse" of his own mental
abstraction. Through it he has, as it were, severed the "soul" of
the "thing" called Death from its "body" constituted by its physical reality. And by it he has thus brought out the true essence and
excellence of the poetic mystic death, distinguishing it from the
literal meaning of physical death. In his own words, he means the
distinctively *human* "gentilesse" of the mental process whereby
the poet, "distinguishing judiciously" between the inward form of
"things" and their outward, sensuous manifestation, expresses
their inherent virtue and peculiar excellence, and thus substantially elevates them to the world of pure spirit.

Finally, he points to the "gentilesse" of this distinctively human
faculty which had been possessed in a supreme degree by the ancient Roman poets. He indicates it as a principle or instrument
whereby the previous stilnovists, elevating their souls and the pure
form of their varying subject matter, had come to "know themselves," had attained their measure of human perfection, and had
reversed the process to embody their humanistic principle and
ideal in their respective poetic works.

The "gentilesse" of *Morte* is therefore: the mystic character of the poetic death, and this "communion" of the mystic death with the *donna gentile,* as the cause, the means, and the substance of her very being.

Of course, in this sense, it is not only conceivable, but also natural and predictable *che morir vorran gli dèi.* For the gods, too, are "things" which human "gentilesse" "will want" to explore in order to detect their true essence, inherent *virtù,* excellence, and human import. As the commentator himself paraphrases this remark taken from his sonnet: indeed, the immortal gods *ought,* or *must,* or *are expected*[4] to change their fate; in order that they, too, may wish to taste of the "gentilesse" of death—as they certainly will want to (vorran), first they must be considered mortal in the mystical sense.

And this is not a facetious conceit, but a serious, profound "belief."[5] For this opinion shows his deep appreciation of Boccaccio's *De genealogiis deorum gentilium.* It shows the importance he attached to such a study, which was preëminently humanistic and *gentile* in every sense of the word. It shows that he thoroughly appreciated both the intended scientific approach of the master to the art of expression and the thought of the ancients, and the human importance of such investigations. Finally, his remark voices a recommendation to future stilnovists not to neglect the ancient humanities, but to pursue this research and continue the master's *fatica d'amore.*

This is in the interest of their own "new lives" and for the progress of civilization. Even the "immortal" Greek and Roman gods had to undergo mystical death in the mind of the incipient poet-humanist. Then those ancient concepts could be understood, and their virtual cause and effect could operate again for the benefit of humanity in its continuous march toward human perfection. The gods of mythology had to follow the nymph Clytie, who obviously dies of such a death in the course of the author's own initiation, and thereby is really revived in his reincarnation of her ancient spirit.

4. The textual phrase in the comment is, *"dover* mutare sorte." Cf. Text, p. 31, l. 2.
5. He says *credo* in the sonnet, and *credevo* in the comment.

It follows then that the god and goddesses mentioned directly after are the ones who here are especially expected to "die." Indeed, Love, the Muses, and the Graces are the ones in whom the humanistic poet is immediately and chiefly concerned. Thus, if he would begin his *nuova vita* properly and methodically, they are the ones who must "die" first in his mind, in the course of his own mystic death.

He should begin by realizing that they are poetic personifications: *Love* personifies a definite lofty concept of human aspiration to the divine; the *Muses* personify various fields of human interest and culture primarily standardized by the Greeks; and the *Graces* personify certain qualities in which the ancient classical arts excelled, especially poetry which typified them all. He should interpret them, too, esoterically, like the *donna gentile* of the modern Italian poets. Finally, he should understand that the god Love, as understood and employed by the previous stilnovists, was a Christian modification of the Platonic concept of God: a fusion of the ancient concept of God as the *Suprema Bellezza* of the world of pure spirit, with the Christian concept of God as the *Sommo Bene* of humanity. He should realize that probably "the sisters of Parnassus" were originally real personages: either poets who had excelled in the various types of poetry and had thus set the standard for those *genres,* or other artists who had similarly originated the various gentle arts and had likewise excelled in them. He should observe that the Graces, as sister goddesses and beautiful maidens intimate with the Muses, had always represented imaginary persons symbolizing artistic merits: charm, easy elegance, effectiveness, propriety of form, et cetera. In other words, he should realize immediately the metaphorical character of such poetic terminology, and begin at once a systematic study of the concepts hidden under the veil of those rhetorical figures. He should approach the classical figures as he would similar creations by the stilnovists.

The Poet's Fervor and Enthusiasm in the Pursuit of His Ideal.

SINCE this is the sense in which the gods, too, "ought" and "will surely want" to die, there is no contradiction or surprise in the subsequent remark that he, the prospective *continuatore insieme e novatore* of ancient and modern Italian poetry, will spend the natural span of his life "weeping and sighing in the company of Love, the Graces, and the Muses." For he draws an interesting parallel. On the one hand, the decline and present obscurity of the stilnovistic ideal and principle meant the loss for him of this guiding spirit and illuminating, consoling vision, and in consequence the loss of his purpose in life, or the nullification of his natural poetic inclination and humanistic bent. On the other hand, the decline of that poetic art meant for Love, that is, for the Spirit animating the concept of Supreme Beauty and the ideal of human perfection (the *Sommo Bene* of humanity), the loss of his rule on earth, or of the beneficent influence over mankind which he had previously exercised through the enlightening volumes of the *gentilissima* Italian literature.

Love, too, had thereby lost his very *raison d'être*. And so had the Muses; their melodious chorus in worthy praise of that ideal remained unheard and ineffective within the verses of that now *passée* poetry, which was no longer comprehended nor appreciated. The same was true of the Graces, who had similarly lost the gifts and virtues generously but vainly bestowed upon the beauty of the *gentilissima* Italian literature. Truly, these various personifications might well weep and sigh with him. Poetically speaking, they, too, might well lament with him the extinction of such an ideal of gentle and ennobling poetic art. And this in the interest of humanity, which had thus lost a powerful instrument of human refinement and civilization.

Indeed, anyone who would not join him and them in this lamentation "must needs be a man without a trace of either love or grace." Let such a one "at least not appear to be indifferent to so much 'gentilesse.' "

The fervor of the initiate for this kind of death is now explicable and legitimate. Indeed, his youthful enthusiasm in connection with the twofold mystic death of himself and his "lady," is worthy of encomium. It is undoubtedly genuine.

But, indirectly, it is also a recommendation, a fervent exhortation, almost an injunction to the prospective stilnovist. For this all means the delightful but difficult study of the great classical authors, both ancient and modern. It means the sweet communion with their noble spirits and generous souls, the reliving of their poetic "new lives," with all their passions, their joys, and their sorrows. But this also means the arduous penetration and appreciation of their lofty but intricate concepts, of their beautiful but fanciful images, and of their refined feelings; in a word, the critical analysis of their whole poetic art. Finally, it means drinking at the fountain of true love and knowledge; but this involves great sacrifices, both physical and spiritual. And all this occurs in conjunction with one's own spiritual elevation, one's own intellectual culture and refinement, and the manifestation of one's own gentle nature; which is all "new life." This also is difficult.

The Physiological and Psychological Basis of the Joys and Sorrows of the "New Life."

IT is no easy task to "know oneself," to form one's own "sweet new style," and to produce similar, yet original works. It is especially difficult if one does not possess either the principle or a clear visualization of those poets' ideal now decadent and no longer understood. Truly, the "new life" of the prospective stilnovist, especially during the period of his initiation and apprenticeship, is all a mixture of joy and sorrow.

As the commentator says, "it is the nature of lovers commonly to indulge in sad thoughts and melancholy, which, amid tears and sighs, are food to their amorous hunger; and this commonly while they experience withal the greatest joy and sense of sweetness." They are melancholy by nature because, being by nature inclined to pursue the same ideal of poetic art, they naturally regret its disappearance. And they weep and sigh because of the difficulty of detecting its basic principle and then applying it to their own creations. But at the same time, what joy and sweetness there is in the course of this creative criticism! What great satisfaction this study and poetizing afford! The zealous student of that poetry, the disciple of those masters, the new expounder of the same ideal and principle, in a word, the prospective humanistic poet will gladly spend his natural life in such a fruitful and happy enterprise, "weeping and sighing in the company of Love, the Graces, and the Muses."[6]

This is why *a vero amore* requires *che si ami una cosa sola e che questa tale cosa si ami sempre*. This is why this true love of the stilnovist, *solo e diuturno*, "proceeds from a strong imagination, and this process can hardly originate unless the melancholy humor prevails in the lover." This is why lovers are said to be melancholy by nature, and, also by nature, "to seek no remedy for their grief other than an accumulation of more grief." This is why "they hate and flee from anything soothing and consoling." Finally, this is why the poet hates death, that is, physical death, or *the death of his spirit* if he should indulge in worldly pleasures while engaged in his noble pursuit. Such a relief from his arduous task would be spiritual suicide, or at least an impediment to his purpose in life.

Accordingly, the commentator means that the business of the creative critic and artist in the school of the *dolce stil novo* calls for constancy and singleness of purpose. His love for this poetic ideal must be genuine, fervid, and everlasting; his discipline in this art a "daily" training. He must not resent the difficulty and the irksomeness of the task, but bear it patiently, courageously. As Virgil says to Dante before the wall of fire in the seventh cornice of Purgatory: *"Or vedi, figlio: / tra Beatrice e te è questo muro."*[7] Let him discipline his mind and heart. Let him ascend gradually the mountain of his purgatory, and go through the fire of final purification. And there must be no weakening of the flesh. On the contrary, he should wish to suffer more, for this will be the true remedy for all his grief. This will finally bring him into the presence of his *gentilissima*.

6. I am reminded of Machiavelli's "gentle" custom of attiring himself properly before retiring to his study in the evening to commune with the great spirits of antiquity, preparatory to his own original works of a critical and historical nature. I quote from his *Lettera a Francesco Vettori, ambasciatore fiorentino a Roma:* "Venuta la sera, mi ritorno a casa, e entro nel mio scrittoio; e in sull'uscio mi spoglio quella veste cotidiana, piena di fango e di loto, e mi metto panni reali e curiali; e rivestito condecentemente entro nelle antique corti degli antiqui uomini, dove, da loro ricevuto amorevolmente, mi pasco di quel cibo, che *solum* è mio, e ch'io nacqui per lui; dove io non mi vergogno parlare con loro; e domandoli della ragione delle loro actioni, e quelli per loro umanità mi rispondono; e non sento per quattro ore di tempo alcuna noia, sdimentico ogni affanno, non temo la povertà, non mi sbigottisce la morte; e tutto mi trasferisco in loro."

7. *Purgatorio*, XXVII, 35–36.

There is nothing trifling, nonsensical, or incoherent in this sonnet, as it seemed to us when we first considered it. Nor is the author's comment at all involved, as it first seemed to be, though it is certainly rather vague and mysterious like the sonnet itself. We smile perhaps a little at his attempt to explain "scientifically" what he calls the "nature" of lovers, or of the stilnovist. But neither his attempt as such, nor his explanation of this "nature" is to be belittled. For such an attempt is in itself significant, as evidence of the usual preoccupation of the stilnovist to explain his amorous experience on real or realistic grounds, as far as possible scientifically ascertained. Besides, his primitive hypotheses in the field of experimental educational psychology should not be confused with our modern realizations resulting from such studies, which have now long become commonplaces.

The explanation itself is at least plausible, notwithstanding its primitiveness. Indeed, I doubt if modern psychologists could suggest a better one, using different terms. At any rate, his meaning is simple: The art of poetic creative criticism involved in the experience of a new *nuova vita,* requires primarily a resourceful imagination, or the capacity to divine and visualize the original intricate concept-images of the previous poets, in order to grasp their real philosophical intent. This is undeniable. And it is also a fact that this psychological process imports a certain sadness and even physical discomfort, due to the difficulty of the task and to the natural anxiety of the critic and "lover" to ascertain the truth hidden *sotto il velame de li versi strani.*[8] This actually leads to utter discouragement at times, even to despair, especially when one lacks the "key" to the poet's style. As the commentator says, it calls for great constancy and for real devotion and daily effort, all supported by a great intuitive power.

Lorenzo's *principio* will be the "key" to all that poetry. And this is the substance of his physiological and psychological basis for the "nature of lovers"; this is the value of his "scientific" explanation of the character of the "new life." It savors of medieval pseudo-science, and it reminds one especially of Cavalcanti's *canzone,* "Donna mi prega."

8. Dante, *Inferno,* IX, 1. 63.

As the author says, these are the affections he meant to express in the present sonnet. This sonnet therefore indicates a period of severe discipline joyfully endured, and a "night of darkness" spent groping in search of the principle of the *dolce stil novo*. All this will presumably be portrayed poetically in the fourth and last sonnet of his *principio*. But this will all end in the "dawn" of his poetic *nuova vita*. Before we comment further on this anticipation of joy and sorrow, let us now take up the fourth sonnet.

CHAPTER II

Sonnet IV

In qual parte andrò io ch'io non ti truovi,
trista memoria? in quale oscuro speco
fuggirò io, che sempre non sie meco,
trista memoria, che al mio mal sol giovi?
 Se in prato, lo qual germini fior nuovi,
se all'ombra d'arbuscei verdi m'arreco,
veggo un corrente rivo, io piango seco:
che cosa è, ch'e' miei pianti non rinnuovi?
 S'io torno all'infelice patrio nido,
tra mille cure questa in mezzo siede
del cor che, come suo, consuma e rode.
 Che debb'io far omai? a che mi fido?
Lasso! che sol sperar posso merzede
da morte, che oramai troppo tardi ode.

Translation of the Author's Own Comment.

THE author's comment is as follows:
 "No one whose heart was ever inflamed by the fire of
love will be surprised to find in these verses of mine diverse
passions and affections which are quite the opposite of one another. For, since love is only a *gentile passione,* one should sooner
be surprised to find that lovers led a uniform life or ever had any
rest at all. Accordingly, if my amorous verses, as well as those of
others, evince this variety and contradiction, one should reflect
that *this is the privilege of lovers, who are freed of all human
qualities.*[1] It is their privilege because no reason can be given for
those things which are ruled by passion alone, nor can any mode
or counsel be found for them.

 "The present sonnet seems to be very contrary to the preceding
one: The previous one shuns anything producing consolation, and
seems to feed on present sorrow as well as on the hope of its in-
creasing; but this one, on the contrary, shows that various grounds

---

1. Cf. Petrarca, *Rime sparse, ed. cit.,* p. 10, Sonnet XV, 13–14.

for consolation were sought, and that, although vainly, many things were attempted to make the very bitter memory of that lady's death vanish from my mind. Moreover, in the end, this one shows some desire for death, a note which is entirely extraneous to the preceding one.

"He who is in the throes of excessive grief commonly tries to mitigate it in two ways: either by something light, sweet, and pleasant, which may soothe it, or by some grave momentous consideration, which may drive it away. Moreover, one commonly chooses the easier, sweeter remedy first. Therefore, feeling the bitterness of this memory, I went about, either in search of a shady or lonely spot, or sought the pleasantness of some green meadow, as the second sonnet testifies, or, again, sat down by some clear, flowing water or in the shade of a bush.

"But I underwent thereby the experience of one afflicted by some malady. Such a one, having his taste corrupted, even though various kinds of dainty food may be served to him, finds that these all taste alike to him; this fact turns the sweetness of those foods into bitterness. The same happened to me. My taste was corrupted and my soul disposed to weep. Consequently, the greater the gladness that these diverse and pleasant things should have afforded my heart, the more they all multiplied my grief. Furthermore, the memory of *colei,* which was present everywhere, seemed to display those things before me with a feeling of bitterness on my part much greater than usual. On the other hand, although this memory was extremely vexatious and hard to bear, nevertheless: just as the patient referred to above is nourished and kept alive by those very foods which all taste bitter to him, so was my life sustained by this extremely bitter food consisting of her memory. In fact, to counteract this ill, there was no better antidote or remedy than the ill itself; nor could that thought be overcome otherwise than by the thought itself. My heart had no other sweetness left than this most bitter memory, and so this alone availed my illness.

"Since it was therefore necessary to have recourse to the second remedy, I fled from these delightful places into the mind-absorbing labyrinth and storm of civil occupations. But this remedy too proved insufficient, because, with that *gentilissima* in possession of and ruling over my heart, the thought and memory of her, in the midst of all my other thoughts, stood in the very center of my heart. And she, notwithstanding all my other cares, consumed my heart as a thing belonging to her. For *cura* means merely 'that which burns and consumes the heart.'[2]

"Consequently, since I could not get relief from so much bitterness and acerbity by either means, death was the only remedy left and my only hope: Death, who hears too late (as the sonnet says). This remark is susceptible of two interpretations at the same time. It means that Death had previously refused to listen to the prayers of countless persons who wished that lady to live. And now, after the lady's death, since the affliction caused by her death could not be overcome otherwise than by dying, this affliction was so great that the smallest delay and procrastination of death seemed unbearable."

The Apparent Contradiction and True Continuity of Sonnets III and IV.

AT the beginning of this comment, Lorenzo notes a diversity of passions and contrariety of affections. Is this not the apparent inconsistency and incoherence which we too observed, especially in this sonnet and the preceding one, when we considered the literal meaning of the *principio* without the aid of the commentary?[3] Thus the author's own present admission confirms our former critical judgment, and would seem to bear out our first reading. But it is a satisfaction of short duration.

This *contradizione di cose*, the commentator warns us, is more apparent than real. He says, immediately after, *"pare,"* that is, "it seems so, but in reality there is no contradiction." In fact, as the reader may have realized already, the diversity and contrariety of the passions and affections portrayed in the two sonnets are due to the conflicting emotions prevailing at once in the poet's soul. But

---

2. I suspect that Lorenzo's source for this definition was Varro, who says: "Curare a cura dictum. *Cura quod cor urat.*" Cf. Varro, *De lingua latina,* 6.46.

3. Cf. above, "The literal meaning of the *principio,*" pp. 89–99, especially pp. 91–93.

the very contradiction between the two sonnets is superficial and formal rather than inherent and substantial. I mean that this pertains to the literal meaning of the sonnets, and does not affect in the least their esoteric meaning; nor does it weaken at all the true link connecting the one to the other. This link marks the passage to the final step in the process of mystic death; and it is the literal contradiction which, interpreted esoterically, reveals on the contrary this true connection and the cause of the real conflict. The discord is not really between the two sonnets; rather, it is due to the diversity and complexity of the same emotions prompted in both by a single desire.

On the other hand, the commentator now exploits this literal contradiction ably and skilfully. He ascribes to the sonnets the contrariety, which, I say, is really in the conflict of their emotional content. By this simple transfer of epithet, he indicates forcibly and clearly, both the distinction between them, and the continuous progression now marked by this final stage of his initiation. This can be expressed in the concept I phrased at the end of my elucidation of the third sonnet. There I noted, first, the eager anticipation of the "gentle" but painful mystic death; and, second, the sorrowful expectation of the grievous yet joyful lamentation over the passing away of the *gentilissima* (both depicted in the preceding sonnet as a single emotional complex). Now these two look forward to the delightful but difficult execution of the implicit program of study, and to the period of pleasant but hard apprenticeship signified by this initiation into the "new life." It is this *fatica d'amore* that is now portrayed in the fourth sonnet, which is truly a joyful and yet painful "labor of love": joyful because it involves the charming perusal of so many gems of Italian poetry, and painful because it involves strenuous study and the grievous regret that this ideal of poetic art no longer prevails.

Accordingly, there is no inconsistence between the content of this sonnet and that of the preceding one. On the contrary, there is the most remarkable continuity of thought, while the poet's initiation proceeds naturally, uninterruptedly. Indeed, the fourth sonnet presents the same emotional content, transferred now from the conceptual stage to the terrain of practical application.

But, as the commentator explains: *Apparently* the preceding sonnet said that the initiate shuns consolation and feeds more and more on sorrow, while the present one, on the contrary, says that he tries at least two common remedies to find relief and rid himself of his oppressive thought. The present one finally indicates at least some desire for death, whereas the other excluded such a desire entirely. And this is the main contradiction. Let us see how this comes about.

The Labor of Love, or the Joys and Sorrows of the Apprentice in the Art of "Gentle" Poetry.

As the author says, what else is love but a *"gentile* passione"? And do we not know what this adjective implies? First, this qualification of the amorous passion makes the new description a corollary of his previous definition of love as *appetito di bellezza*.[4] Next, it is also the logical epithet to apply to the amorous passion in view of his understanding of *gentilezza umana,* both as a human ideal and an ideal of human education. This accounts for the peculiar nature he attributes to "lovers"; for their "strong imagination," or superior intuitive faculty; for the sentimental character of their amorous lives; and for all their emotional complex, superficially so erratic. All this makes for the "artistic" temperament. The epithet *gentile* also accounts for the purely spiritual character and critical nature of their passionate, fascinating research; although this involves a truly strenuous physical effort as well as a mental strain. Hence, finally, comes the peculiar character of the "remedies" tried in order to obtain relief from this continuous reaching toward the principle and ideal of human perfection. Hence the sweetness and discomfort of it all. Hence the inadequacy of those remedies, and the only hope left, the hope of the mystic death.

What are those "remedies," and what does all this mean? As I said before, the inference is that the prospective stilnovist is now actually engaged in his delightful but difficult study of the masters' works. He is now ascertaining the lofty poetic ideal embodied in them. He is now in search of the principle of that art.

4. Cf. Text, p. 14, l. 9; and this study, p. 13.

And all this pleasant, but sad and irksome task is undertaken for the purpose of self-education, in order that his own poetic art may conform in principle and ideal with that of those authors. It is therefore natural that, as a remedy for his "malady," he should turn first of all precisely to their works. Lorenzo expected to derive from them both the enlightenment and the inspiration necessary for pursuing the same course, and thus to attempt at least a continuation of their glorious art.

As an example for this study, he naturally takes the most perfect model of this stilnovistic procedure. He takes his study of Petrarch's *Rime,* which are all *principio,* as I deduced from an examination of sources. And what does he do? He portrays how he himself proceeded in order to interpret properly and appreciate thoroughly the master's lyrics. He tried to relive in himself Petrarch's *nuova vita* as depicted in his *canzoniere.* Indeed, he reenacted, as it were, the most typical manifestations of the master's amorous experience, through which the latter had himself become initiated into the *dolce stil novo.* That was how Petrarch had come to realize the stilnovistic principle. That was how he had created his own, perfect "sweet new style." That was, therefore, the way he, too, was to proceed. Finally, that is the way any prospective stilnovist should proceed.

On the other hand, it is not necessary to presume that Lorenzo actually went in search of what we might call typical Petrarchan environment to study and enjoy the master's *rime.* I do not for one moment imagine that he did, although such a suggestion is apparently made. If it were established that he actually went in search of shady nooks, blossoming fields, or babbling brooks—this would be another proof of the realism of the new style, or, at least, of his understanding of the theoretical principle. This would indicate that he interpreted Petrarch literally in this respect, that he accepted the doctrine of nature's beneficent influence, and that he both followed it himself and now recommends it to others. But let us not digress.

The comparison of himself to the patient who has lost the sense of taste, and to whom all kinds of exquisite food are equally disagreeable, is most appropriate here. It clarifies his own æsthetic sense in this initial stage of his poetic training, as well as that of his contemporaries. Perhaps it is a reminiscence and a variation of Dante's metaphorical "banquet" or intellectual feast, the *vivanda* of which was to consist of fourteen *"maniere . . ., cioè . . . canzoni."*[5] But this is not important. The historico-critical import of this comparison is that he himself, as a novice in the study of Italian poetry, and his contemporaries, as unintelligent imitators of it, were all "sick men" in their critical understanding and æsthetic appreciation of this most excellent and truly exquisite poetry. We do not even have to change the wording to apprehend its figurative meaning. His and their taste was literally *corrotto.* Those choice, sweet "foods," which Petrarch and the other "doctors" served, all seemed to taste the same; they were all equally bitter. That is, he did not distinguish one poem from the other as to their inner import. He did not appreciate the nicety and delicacy of the thoughts and feelings embodied in them, which was what differentiated one from the other. In a word, he neither truly understood them nor appreciated the author's art. He realized neither the ideal pursued by the poet nor his artistic principle.[6]

Yet such poems were the intellectual food that sustained his own spiritual life and that of every poet of his time. They were the means with which to work out one's poetic destiny and attain the true poetic goal. They were nourishing food to the mind and soul. They were educative and inspiring. And this is why they tasted all the more bitter in proportion to their sweetness. This is why these pleasant "excursions" multiplied his grief instead of mitigating it. Finally, this is why the memory of *colei* who now was dead, pursuing him everywhere, made him feel this bitterness all the more. The anxious novice, as he struggled to detect the principle and ideal of that poetic art, perhaps feared his own incapacity and that of others to produce anything like those perfect gems, and became especially discouraged at the thought that perhaps that art was irreparably lost. But at the same time, naturally, this thought, or fear, or preoccupation was truly the best "anti-

5. Cf. *Convivio*, I, i, 14.
6. This is eloquent comment on the opinion of those who think that after you have read a dozen or so of Petrarch's poems you may lay him aside.

dote" or "remedy" to counteract his grief. Thinking of it, or concentrating his mind and heart on his critical research, was surely the most sensible way in which to attempt to resuscitate that art.

Lorenzo's Gentile Passione, *or His Poetic Avocation.*

THIS remedy, however, did not suffice. This critical reconstruction would not make him a poet like the masters. It might make a critic and a historian of him, but not a creative critic of their art, not an original stilnovist. For this he needed the spark of genius, which is innate and cannot be acquired. Feeling or fearing that he did not have it, he turned therefore to the second common "remedy." Presumably, in his discouragement he merely abandoned his studies and tried to forget his genuine sorrow over the decline of Italian poetry. He probably decided to give up his hobby and, with it, all idea of becoming a poet. As he says, he fled from the bitterness of his pleasant but irksome studies, even from the memory of that poetic art now spent, and engulfed in the turbulent, intricate network of civil occupations. That is, he plunged into the all-absorbing, stormy sea of political machinations and domestic problems.[7]

But this remedy also was inadequate. For, in the very midst of his heavy responsibilities, his "poetic" grief, as we may call it, did not leave him. Indeed, the thought of his favorite avocation and the sorrowful memory of the passing away of that poetic ideal, both stood, as it were, in the center of his heart. In other words, his natural inclination toward that poetic art, and his great desire to continue it, had the upper hand, and all his civil worries did not avail to make him forget or neglect entirely the promptings of his heart. Indeed, notwithstanding all his other "cares," the thought of the *gentilissima* was his greatest *cura.* As he says, apparently on Varro's authority, *cura* means "that which burns and consumes the heart." So that we might well say that the *gentilis-*

---

7. This, of course, is historical, although it would have been more exact to say just the reverse; namely, that he was led away from his natural inclination by those very duties in which, on the contrary, he says to have taken refuge. In fact, only at intervals did those preoccupations allow him to devote himself to his favorite literary occupation. But we must grant the poet some license in the construction of his realistic, theoretic *principio.*

sima was literally consuming his heart; she ate it, as it were, "as if it were a thing belonging to her."[8]

This means that his natural bent for the stilnovistic "new life" was genuine and all-powerful over him. It means that his love for the *gentilissima* had the qualities of a *vero amore,* which was *solo e diuturno.* In fact, he says that the latter literally possessed and dominated his heart (avendo quella gentilissima preso il dominio del mio cuore e . . . fattolo suo). Finally, this means that he was determined to pursue his natural goal and develop his poetic talent in the face of all obstacles. Indeed, he could not resist the urge which he felt naturally within him. And all this, of course, is at the same time meant to be exemplary, or suggestive of the strict fundamental requirement for a *vera vita d'amore.*

Accordingly, it is no wonder that death was then "the only remedy left and his only hope." Death in the literal sense had been "slow of hearing" before, when it had refused to listen to the prayers of all lovers of the stilnovistic ideal and had allowed the ideal's extinction. Death, in the sense of mystic death, now was again "slow of hearing" in apparently refusing to bring about, in him and in all novices in the "new life," that perfect spiritual elevation and poetic inspiration, essential for detecting the principle of that poetic art, and for creating new works of art in conformity with it.[9] Finally, this is why "the smallest delay and procrastination of death seemed unbearable." This is why "in the end, this sonnet shows some desire for death, a note which is entirely extraneous to the preceding one." As we now see, there is really no contradiction between the two, not even in this respect. For he is thinking all the time of the mystic death, and this is the death which he exalted in the preceding sonnet, and now hopes for in this. In other words, in the two sonnets he is really holding to his concept of the *principio di nuova vita* by insisting all the time on the essential-

8. The reminiscence and influence of Dante's first sonnet, "A ciascun'alma presa e gentil core," are patent here. Cf. *Vita Nuova,* III. And, of course, this must be his interpretation of the master's significant dream portrayed in that sonnet. Indeed, we may regard this portion of his comment as another of the various versions made of Dante's mysterious sonnet in answer to the poet's intentional request.

9. Now we see the import of the double connotation ingeniously and purposely involved by the poet in the sonnet's phrase, *troppo tardi ode,* and the reason why the commentator later was so careful to bring it out.

ness of the spiritualization of "lady" and poet for a true and effective "new life of love."

It follows that we may now entitle this sonnet, in a manner analogous with the titles suggested for the others, either: "The Labor of Love Implied by the Mystic Death," or "The Period of Hard Apprenticeship in the Art of 'Gentle' Poetry," or, if we prefer, "The *Gentile Passione* of the Poet-Stilnovist." And this is all as we had expected.

DEDUCTIONS AND CONCLUSIONS

DEDUCTIONS AND CONCLUSIONS

A Glance Forward at Lorenzo's Nuova Vita.

NOW that we have a thorough and comprehensive grasp of all the elements entering into the poet's *principio,* we may perhaps imagine what his *nuova vita* is going to be. At least, we may anticipate the purported character and object of those sonnets in turn.

As I had occasion to infer when we discussed Lorenzo's second main innovation, which involved a sharp distinction on his part, as commentator of his own verses, between the generic *donna gentile* and his particular *gentilissima,*[1] this "new life" of his will undoubtedly be the constant pursuit of the masters' ideal through a critical study of their works, and at the same time the gradual manifestation of his own poetic genius. It will be a continuation of his spiritual preparation and technical training already begun so promisingly in the *principio;* but at the same time it will consist of his first efforts to imitate their art following both their principle and technique in proportion to his grasp and mastery of these. Finally, it will be a kind of poetic autobiography dealing with his apprenticeship in the school of the *dolce stil novo.*

For the reasons given in the proem,[2] he will not include in his *nuova vita* exercises in various forms of versification, as the masters had done, but will prefer throughout the sonnet form. And now we appreciate this preference. Apparently he intends to treat neatly and concisely, as well as separately, a number of distinct points which seemed to him significant or especially important in the poetic art of the masters. These sonnets of his formal apprenticeship, both those comprised in his incomplete *Comento* and all the others destined to be included, accompanied by similar comments, will be successive bits of poetic training and elucidation of their technique. They will be exemplary "copies" or "models" or "studies" of one detail or another of the masters' *chefs d'oeuvre.*

1. Cf. above, pp. 282–294.
2. Cf. Text, pp. 22–23; and this study, pp. 55–61.

Finally, they will be original examples of creative criticism in verse, executed in the spirit and style of his *maestri* and *autori,* and with the sole intent of illustrating concretely now one point of their doctrine and now another.

Perhaps my present assertion may be disproved in some detail by my eventual study of the love life of the Magnificent, to which I have already alluded. But I make the assertion with absolute confidence in this study of his *principio,* and base my anticipation on his clear implication that the sonnets constituting his formal *nuova vita* are precisely critical studies of the masters' works, and exercises in the art of "gentle" poetry.

Therefore, they were all, admittedly, imitated. Indeed, they were intended to be imitations, and were proffered as such. To say that they are Dantean, or Petrarchan, or otherwise stilnovistic, is, of course, nothing new. But to point out that this was precisely their whole purpose, is, if I may be permitted to say so, a respectable contribution to our knowledge of this particular portion of Lorenzo's poetic production. Indeed, this fact, already demonstrated by his *principio,* presents an entirely new point of view, which illuminates his whole literary career. And this is perhaps my most important deduction of an historico-critical nature with reference to the Magnificent himself.

Final Words on the Historico-Critical Value of the Principio:

Its Humanistic Educational Import.

THE pedagogical scope and intent of the *principio* as a whole and the methodological character of the last two sonnets in particular ought to be evident now. For, as I have repeatedly shown, Lorenzo's *principio* implies a threefold purpose: first, it seeks to reveal the humanistic character and æsthetic principle of Italian poetry, in Latin and especially in *volgare*. Next, it wishes to present stilnovistically Lorenzo's own initiation into the same poetic "new life." Finally, it seeks to suggest indirectly to any prospective stilnovist both the ideal he should pursue and the training he should undergo. That is, it contains both the principle and the method for successfully pursuing the true poetic ideal, according to Lorenzo. Therefore, his *principio* and all his *nuova vita* enter into the category of the educational treatises so common during the Italian Renaissance, following the pedagogical principle that the study of the humanities would form an excellent character and would suggest noble ideals. Indeed, one might say that his *principio* is a veritable outline of such a study, especially in the field of Italian poetry.

In other words, it enters the category of such works as Giambattista Alberti's *Libri della famiglia,* of Castiglione's *Il cortegiano,* of Della Casa's *Il galateo*—although these were in prose and their scope varied considerably from that of his work. Moreover, it involves the same kind of interest which led to the teaching activity of such men as Guarino Veronese and his pupil, Vittorino da Feltre, who created the science of pedagogy. Recall Vittorino's *Casa zoiosa,* which may well be called the first prototype of the English residential college, in view of his humanistic ideal and the principles of physical as well as intellectual education which he had evolved and then applied in his *Casa.* Recall Guarino's fame as a maker of poets and of literary men of high repute. Finally, realize that this was the modest but all-important beginning of our modern science of education. This also perhaps explains the true character and purpose of the "courtesy books" in English literature.

Its Use as a Key to the Dolce Stil Novo.

WITHOUT repeating my progressive and comprehensive deductions made in the course of this analytico-synthetical study of Lorenzo's *principio,* let me now merely summarize its critical value for us. Our expectations, voiced at the end of my exposition of the *proemio,*[3] have been more than justified. As I said then, this *principio* is not precisely the open sesame to the *dolce stil novo,* but, *mutatis mutandis,* it is at least a most excellent guide. The real key, I expect, will be the continuation of this *principio* in Lorenzo's following *nuova vita.* That is, Lorenzo's *principio* is substantially a recasting of the principle followed, according to him, by all the stilnovists in their respective "new life"—whether they called it *Vita Nuova* like Dante, or *Rime Sparse* like Petrarch, or by no special name at all. On the other hand, it is much more than a mere introduction to the poetry of the sweet new style in the narrow sense of the term. It is actually the key, we might say, to the Italian literature of the whole Renaissance period.

Gentilezza, *the Renaissance, and Modern Culture.*

BETTER perhaps, it supplies the proper approach for a correct and comprehensive understanding of all the intellectual and artistic activity of Italy, at least, during those centuries. From our previous observations, we might say that indeed there is no phase of intellectual activity and artistic refinement in all western Europe since the fourteenth century which is not substantially and fundamentally related to the *principio* set forth by the Magnificent. The stilnovistic principle of *gentilezza umana* was responsible for the direction given to all modern culture and civilization. And, indisputably, Renaissance Italy can best be interpreted through this principle of *gentilezza umana* first detected and expounded by the Magnificent. Indeed, this is his greatest glory as a literary critic. And it is so true, moreover, and so illuminating of all that period, that, I believe, it establishes his authoritativeness beyond a doubt.

3. Cf. above, pp. 80–81.

APPENDICES

APPENDIX A

INFERENCES AND SUPPOSITIONS

Preamble.

THIS appendix contains certain vague inferences and other partial deductions of an historico-critical nature which have been suggested to me by this interpretation. Inasmuch as, in addition to being summary and provisional, these inferences are rather surprising, I have been in doubt whether I should include them in this volume, or wait until I could determine better their value for publication, after I had gone farther into the study of Lorenzo's *nuova vita* and presumably had accumulated more evidence.

I felt that I have surprised the reader—who may be a critic or historian of Italian literature—too many times already with certain unexpected results of my investigation; and feared lest their inclusion here, without the necessary documentation or at least an ampler clarification of my concepts, might detract from the value of the interpretation itself. This might jeopardize my main thesis.

On the other hand, I also thought that their inclusion in this volume would enable me to demonstrate concretely, though only summarily, the value of Lorenzo's *principio* as an aid to the study of Renaissance literature. It would give me an excellent opportunity to present already the new vista which his point of view discloses before our critical eyes. I should be able at least to mention some of the problems which now arise with respect to the history and real import of the Renaissance movement in Italy. Finally, I could also indicate some of the numerous studies which this interpretation suggests, and which I think might be undertaken profitably in view of the *principio's* critical import.

Naturally, I could not elaborate nor substantiate these hypotheses, except as I attempt to do, by the barest outline in the form of suggestive references. For, an adequate treatment of the questions involved would have entailed the presentation of a mass of material which was obviously out of place here and impossible at this time; practically, it would have amounted to actually doing the critical studies which here I only mean to suggest. In other words, this would have exceeded both the limits and the purpose of this work. Still I wished to give some idea at least of the way in which, in my opinion, Lorenzo's *principio* might be applied to research similar to his own, and also of the variety of subjects to which it does apply. And this, on the contrary, was required by my thesis.

Accordingly, I have finally decided to include these "suggestions" in this appendix. But I do so, not without specifying that they are mere suggestions, and not without this preamble which I trust will now prevent their being mistaken for conclusions.

It is understood that here I address myself primarily to my colleagues and other mature students of Italian literature. I may therefore assume that such readers are thoroughly familiar both with the content and spirit of the works referred to and with the importance of the contribution made to Italian literature by the various authors mentioned. In any case, believing that the main object in publishing a study of this character is the exchange of ideas and the stimulation of discussion, I shall welcome any criticism, either public or private, of any part of my treatise.

Medieval Æsthetics: the "Privilege of Lovers," or the Independence of Art.

WITH reference to the apparent *contradizione di cose* presented by the third and fourth sonnets, the commentator remarks that the same contradiction may similarly be suspected "often" *negli altrui amorosi versi* as well. He adds somewhat unconvincingly that *questo è privilegio degli amanti sciolti da tutte qualitadi umane.*[1] But this is the close of a sonnet by Petrarch.[2] Moreover, this is a new point he makes regarding "the nature of lovers," and it is a significant point notwithstanding the fact that it is made incidentally and is covered by a thin veil of mystery. It is important critically and historically because it suggests his interpretation of this particular sonnet of the master, and also because it doubtless represents his personal experience in the course of his own perusal of the various masters' works.

This observation made with reference to the verses of other poets (read especially Petrarch) shows that he appreciated this difficulty in the penetration of their thought. But now the inference is also that, like his own "contradiction," the contradiction often observable in the amorous verses of others is not real but only superficial. Just as we found none in his own sonnets when we realized their real import, so he must have found none in theirs after he had understood them thoroughly. This is a lesson to the student of the poets to whom the commentator has reference, including the great triad and all the stilnovists.

On the other hand, the reason he gives for this apparent and only "literal" contradiction is especially significant of his and their attitude toward art in general. Apparently, a clear and definite concept of the independence of art, on the part of Lorenzo and of all the stilnovists, is implied in the "privilege" accorded to the poets. It is especially implied in their prerogative of being "freed of all human qualities," that is, of being superior men or *divini,* as

1. Cf. Text, p. 32; and this study, p. 316.
2. Cf. the sonnet "Io mi rivolgo in dietro a ciascun passo," vv. 13–14.

Dante had said, following Aristotle.[3] In fact, he explains this privilege or liberty of "lovers" on the ground that "no *reason* can be given for those things which are ruled by *passion* alone, nor can any mode or counsel be found for them" (perchè alcuna *ragione* nè se ne può dare, nè trovar modo o consiglio in quelle cose che solo la *passione* regge).[4] That is, *art is intuition,* as the modern philosopher Croce would say, or the intuitive faculty is independent of the rational faculty.[5] And this "modern" æsthetic principle is implied by a *quattrocentista,* obviously expressing what to his critical mind must have been a principle clearly realized, adhered to, indeed maintained by all stil-novists!

One may therefore wonder precisely how much influence this concept and practice of the early Italian poets had on the founder of the modern science of æsthetics, on Giambattista Vico, who was a zealous student of those poets. One may perhaps imagine the rôle played by them, in this and other respects, in his conception of the *Scienza nuova.* In another connection, I shall hint at a definite proof, as it seems to me, of Dante's direct influence, for example. Here I do not wish to digress.

As Croce says, there is no treatise on æsthetics which does not point out this independence of the intuitive knowledge from the rational. Indeed, the ancient poets and philosophers, too, made this distinction in their way. But the point here is, Who were the primitive founders of this science in modern times? Does this not show that the principle of the *dolce stil novo* (in this respect, for the present) anticipated Vico's "New Science" by several centuries? Especially, does this not show the correct foundation of my suspicion about the Dantean problem, which started me on this study, and at whose solution I hinted in the preface? Does this not explain the conflict between the Beatrice of the *Vita Nuova* and the Lady Philosophy of the *Convivio?* And does this not likewise resolve the fusion of these two "ladies" in the Beatrice of the *Paradiso,* symbol of the complete and divine *Sapienza Santa?* I do not affirm all this. I merely suspect it, and suggest that the matter be studied.

The Identity of Stilnovism and Humanism: Seen in the Metaphor of Clytie. The Influence of Boccaccio.

I SAID when we were discussing Lorenzo's adaptation of the myth of Clytie to represent his attitude toward the previous Italian poetry,[6] that he obviously derived this myth, either directly or indirectly, from Ovid. This is evinced by the fact that, as we remember, at the beginning of his comment on the second sonnet, he quotes Ovid as if he were the source of his information regarding

3. Cf. *Convivio,* III, vii, 6–7.   4. Cf. Text, p. 32; and this study, p. 316.
5. Cf. Benedetto Croce, *Estetica* (Laterza, Bari), chap. i.
6. Cf. above, the section on "The choice of the metaphor of Clytie," pp. 171–175.

clitia, the *tornalsole*.[7] But his intellectual approach to ancient mythology is striking. He interprets Clytie, the nymph, as the symbol in antiquity of the highest and noblest human aspiration: namely, man's constant love of the *Sapienza Santa,* or his natural longing for the intellectual light which emanates from the "Sun," symbol of the supreme *Bellezza* that is God. Lorenzo understands the nymph Clytie as a personification of this aspiration or human ideal, and as a real personage, probably, who in antiquity had actually incarnated in herself to a supreme degree this lofty, human love for the divine knowledge, and who remained thereafter the prototype of this kind of lover. Finally, he adapted this myth to the intent and purpose of his *principio,* in such a way that he did not merely compare himself to the ancient Clytie, but represented himself as a "new," modern Clytie with respect to the Sun of intellectual light that was the new Italian poetry in *volgare;* he was one pursuing the same ideal.

This method of handling the myth savors of stilnovistic doctrine. This identification of the modern ideal of the stilnovists with the ideal pursued by the ancient poets, and this incarnation in himself of the spirit and aim of the ancient Clytie, these concepts point especially to Boccaccio as his *maestro* and his *autore.* Of course, Dante's works (especially the *Commedia*) were full of instances of such an approach, such an understanding, and such a modernization. And Petrarch, too, presented numerous corresponding instances. But Boccaccio alone had turned his mythological doctrine into a kind of primitive form of Giambattista Vico's *Scienza nuova.*

As I have remarked before, Boccaccio had spent the best years of his maturity in a veritable *fatica d'amore* entitled *De genealogiis deorum gentilium.* This is a vast repertory of ancient mythology and a mine of profound, intelligent penetration of ancient thought, even though at times it may seem, or be somewhat fanciful. Boccaccio had also himself conceived two similar myths, as though he had meant to show how the ancient poets used to create them out of raw material, as it were, and out of even the crudest *esser verace.* Truly, his *Ninfale fiesolano* and *Ninfale d'Ameto* are nothing else but such artificial, poetic creations and such a demonstration. This is evidence of his attitude toward this ancient form of poetic, human expression; this is evidence of his undoubted implication that all such works, ancient or modern, should be approached in a similar manner—with a view toward detecting their esoteric content and the author's real intent.

The influence of Boccaccio on Lorenzo's *principio* is not always so patent as that of either Dante or Petrarch, because it was much more subtle, and because Boccaccio was unquestionably the most original of these three *eccellentissimi* stilnovists. Boccaccio spent very little time, apparently, on his formal stilnovistic *principio,* which, nevertheless, may be looked for, presumably, in his *rime* of ordinary stilnovistic character. Contrary to the experience of

7. Cf. above, p. 149.

Petrarch, and more like Dante's, his literary production was mostly "new life" par excellence, as I have called the strictly original works of a poet-stilnovist. Consequently, his influence, always substantial rather than formal, will, I expect, come out more clearly in my eventual study of Lorenzo's *nuova vita d'amore.* But meanwhile, observe that no better example could be found of the application of Lorenzo's definition of *gentilezza umana* than Boccaccio's acute research of the genealogy of the Greek and Roman "gods." This much will suffice to show that Boccaccio, too, is illumined by our critic's *principio,* and that this enlightenment, in turn, confirms our deductions.

My main concern now is to bring out the historico-critical value for us of Lorenzo's choice and use of the myth of Clytie. And this will be merely a *suggestion* (I say again) of the new angle he gives us for the proper approach to all the poetry, arts, letters, and other humanistic activity, not only of the *Pre-*Renaissance period, but also of the period which is differentiated from that by the term *High* Renaissance. (All the same, remember what I said at the end of the section on the *proemio,* with reference to the narrow conception of the *dolce stil novo:* I do not mean to imply that Lorenzo's *principio* is precisely and mechanically the open sesame to all Italian intellectual and artistic activity.)

In connection with this clarification of the true character, scope, and intent of Boccaccio's *whole* literary production, consider now, from Lorenzo's point of view, Poliziano's *Praelectiones,* his *Silvae,* and his *Miscellanea* at the side of his *Orfeo,* his *Rime,* and his *Stanze.* Why should this precocious "Homeric youth," who was a consummate "humanist" in the commonly accepted sense of the word and who later revealed himself a remarkable modern critic of classical poetry, why should he have thought at all of recasting the ancient myth of Orpheus, if he had not thus meant to interpret it esoterically in the manner of Boccaccio? Did he not mean to embody this interpretation in the new artistic form he gave to it, precisely like Lorenzo in his adaptation of the myth of Clytie? Try also to explain why in his *Stanze,* which ostensibly were in celebration of Giuliano's athletic prowess, why there the historical Simonetta is soon forgotten in favor of a complete transfiguration of her being into a "nymph" and a *donna angelicata* not unlike Petrarch's Laura or any other stilnovistic *donna.* Finally, recall the distinctively stilnovistic character of most of his *Rime.* And, in connection with this apparently double literary interest of Poliziano, recall Lorenzo's own humanistic studies, embodied, no doubt, in his original and varied artistic production. Try especially to explain the true, natural motive of his noble and generous patronage of the arts and letters.

We cannot explain the apparent double personality of the same author, now humanist and now stilnovist-poet or other kind of artist, unless we grant that for Lorenzo and Poliziano (and for everyone in the *Trecento* and *Quattrocento*) humanism and stilnovism were identical. We must understand that the stilnovistic principle of spiritual education and the new poetic art implied the interpretation of the past in the form of an eternally recurring human experience. This involved the presentation of modern ideals in terms of a "gentle" reconception of the same ideals in ancient times. We must assume that this was the prime and true motive of all "humanistic" studies, and that this was the way in which the principle of Roman "gentilesse" generated the new artistic creations. This simple assumption shows naturally, clearly, and wonderfully the continuity in the history of Italian arts and letters.

The identification of humanism and stilnovism in their true sense, seems so enlightening of all mythological or metaphorical works in Italian literature, arts, and science, that it is easily superior to the mechanical superficial "positivism" of the "positivistic" critics.

Take Pontano, whom I shall call without the slightest sense of contradiction "the stilnovist in Latin" or the perfect reincarnation of, as it were, "a Latin stilnovist." Are we to deny him all intention of saying anything new in his numerous new presentations of ancient myths and even more numerous creations of new myths? Should we deny him originality merely because we do not generally perceive his esoteric implications? Think of his *Urania* and his *Meteora;* and remember that he was a contemporary of the cosmographer Torricelli and the discoverer Columbus. Perhaps in his way he was a precursor of Galileo. Think of his *Amorum libri, Lepidina, Lyra, Hendecasyllabi, De amore coniugali, Naeniae, Quinquennius,* and other works. And realize that his innumerable "nymphs" are personifications of the hills, the islands, or the villas in and around Naples; or of the waters forming the perpetually enchanting bay; or, again, of the starry constellations in the clear sky above. Surely, he is saying concrete "things" in his mythological language: things which are perhaps an early form of the new science of the heavens soon to follow in the wake of the poetico-artistic Renaissance. His conceptions may be poetically and artistically fanciful, but he is surely expressing real feelings and thoughts; and his style as well as his attitude toward the ancient world are those of Boccaccio.

Now take his disciple and a member of the same *Accademia* which goes by his name. Take Sannazzaro, and recall his similar poetic production, his eclogues and elegies in Latin. Think especially of his famous *Arcadia,* which, as Scherillo showed, is entirely modeled upon Boccaccio's similar works, particularly the *Ameto.*[8] We can now explain the tremendous popularity of the *Arcadia,* its long renown and wide influence in and outside of Italy, hitherto baffling to modern critics. It is only necessary to consider it as a *nuova vita* and to study it in the light of Lorenzo's *principio.*

I omit all references to the numerous artists who, like Botticelli, were inspired by ancient mythology and chose this medium, closely allied to allegory

8. Cf. the Introduction to Michele Scherillo's edition of Sannazzaro's *Arcadia* (Milano, Hoepli).

in general, to express their understanding of antiquity and their modern conceptions. But with the example of Sannazzaro we are already in the *Cinquecento*, although his *Arcadia* is *quattrocentesca*. And I do not need to recall the rôle of mythology in the poetry, the arts, and even the science of sixteenth- or seventeenth-century Italy, throughout the history of Italian classical literature, down to Vico's time and to the modern epoch of the *Risorgimento*. I do not wish to lay unnecessary emphasis by accumulating excessive proof on this point which is merely incidental to my demonstration of the historico-critical value of Lorenzo's stilnovistic attitude toward ancient mythology. But I wish to show that for centuries before the appearance of Vico's philosophical treatise, his "new science," or better, his intelligent approach to ancient mythology had been the common practice of poets, artists, and even scientists. Perhaps crude and fanciful, it was still the same point of view. And this point of view was none other than that implied by the Laurentian definition of *gentilezza umana!*

Vico himself seemingly supplies the proof of this surprisingly significant fact. Prefixed to his *Scienza nuova*,[9] there is an allegorical picture intended to illustrate the content of his work and serve as a prospectus. And this picture, I might say, is a revised, scientific edition of Dante's poetic conception of Lady Philosophy, indeed, of his Beatrice of the *Paradiso!* In fact, it represents Providence, or God, as an eye within an equilateral triangle, itself inscribed within a circle representing a "sun." The wisdom of God, in the form of a ray of light coming from the eye within the triangle, illumines the figure of a *donna* symbolizing metaphysics; and from a mirror on her chest, it is reflected on humanity symbolized by a statue of the poet Homer standing below her on one side. The woman stands on a globe, which, in turn, rests on the edge of a symbolical altar. On this altar, as well as around it and at the feet of Homer's statue, all in proper juxtaposition, are various symbolical articles of a mythological character. This is all explained later by the author in his introduction, and, as I say, serves as prospectus to his entire subject matter.

This rapid sketch of sources and influences relative to the import of Lorenzo's metaphor of Clytie may aptly conclude with this striking discovery of Vico's apparent derivation, and with the suggestion that innumerable studies might profitably be undertaken from the new critical angle revealed by the *principio* we have now apprehended.

9. Cf. Giambattista Vico, *La scienza nuova, giusta l'edizione del 1744, a cura di Fausto Nicolini* (Laterza, Bari, 1928), I, 4.

APPENDIX B

CONCERNING THE DATE OF THE
RACCOLTA ARAGONESE

WORKING from original sources, independently of any study I had read on the subject of the relation between the death of Simonetta Cattaneo and Lorenzo's sonnets on Death, I had reached a conclusion contrary to current critical opinion, at least in part. Basing my arguments largely on internal evidence derived from the author's own comments, but also on the date of the *Raccolta aragonese,* I had concluded that the death of Simonetta had not originally inspired the composition of those sonnets, but her death had served the "commentator" well later as a model for his realistic portrayal of his concept of the mystic death involved in those sonnets. Indeed, I had finished my entire treatise on this Laurentian *principio* of the poetic life, when a comment of Professor Fletcher's on the history of the *Raccolta aragonese*[1] revealed to me the doubtfulness of the date 1465–66 usually assigned to this anthology. Mr. Fletcher referred to a critical study of this date by Michele Barbi,[2] and, on the strength of the arguments adduced by this eminent scholar, which he summarized, he agreed that this traditional date should now be discarded in favor of the one proposed by Barbi, namely, 1476. Moreover, he called attention to the fact that another eminent Italian scholar, Vittorio Rossi, accepted this later date in a new edition of his *Quattrocento* (1933).

This disturbed me a little because I had used the earlier date in partial support of my contention that, precisely as Lorenzo maintains in his commentary on his *nuova vita,* at least the sonnets of the *principio* were very youthful compositions which could not have been inspired by the death of the Simonetta occurring in 1476. In fact—I had remarked—they were all to be found among the author's own lyrics included in the famous *Raccolta,* which, as I thought, had been compiled ten years before. To be sure, the date now assigned so authoritatively to this anthology, although later by a decade and coinciding with the year in which the Simonetta died, did not invalidate my contention that this lady's death served at best only as a "model" for the poet's portrayal of the mystic death. For this contention was based entirely on internal evidence furnished by my analysis of the author's *Comento* and of the

1. Contained in his recent chapter on Lorenzo de' Medici. Cf. Jefferson B. Fletcher, *Literature of the Italian Renaissance* (New York, The Macmillan Company, 1934), pp. 117–118.
2. To be found among the latter's *Studi sul canzoniere di Dante* (Firenze, 1915), pp. 220 ff.

sonnets themselves. Nor did it affect the early date of these sonnets, which, as I say, was vouched for by the author himself, who, it will be remembered, declares repeatedly in the *proemio* that the love sonnets he is about to expound were written during his *età giovenile e tenera*. In fact, even if the anthology was compiled soon after September, 1476, as now supposed, this was no proof that those of Lorenzo's own poems, which were included therein, were composed that very year. The presumption was still that they constituted a selection, if not a collection, of what the compiler had himself written up to that time; so that, if any of them could then be said to be relatively old (as one may assume), these must certainly have been the sonnets of the *principio*. Accordingly, these sonnets on Death preceded in any case the death of Simonetta Cattaneo, which occurred only at the end of the preceding April. My point had been that, notwithstanding the relation later apparently established, for the purpose of his exposition, by Lorenzo the "commentator," remember, and not by Lorenzo the "poet," the death of this lady was not the true, original source of inspiration for those sonnets.

The thought may intrude here again that, if not her death, then the death of someone else must have inspired the poet. This does not follow necessarily, especially in view of the philosophical import and the whole esoteric meaning of those sonnets. This is another question, which I believe is solved by my explanation, on various occasions in the course of my treatise, of the principle of realism involved in the theory of the *dolce stil novo*. Here I am concerned with the falseness of the purely imagined, would-be historical fact that the death of Simonetta Cattaneo inspired the composition of Lorenzo's sonnets on Death, and that, consequently, the presence of these sonnets in the *Raccolta aragonese* is another argument in favor of the later date now proposed for this *Raccolta*. This is not so because the premise of this syllogism is arbitrary, or, better, it is a false assumption based on a superficial reading of Lorenzo's own misleading indications.

My main thesis, then, would not be affected by this new date, even if it were definitely established on indisputable historical grounds. This reassured me, and now I was even pleased that the earlier, traditional date had been questioned and found wanting in historical validity. I was pleased because I, too, had felt all along, as Mr. Fletcher now did, and as Barbi and Bianca Maria Scanferla, working independently of each other, had felt before us both,[3] that for a youth of seventeen going on eighteen, such as Lorenzo was in 1465, and a boy of thirteen, such as Prince Frederick was at the same time, they were both too young, the latter to have had the "laudable desire" to see all the early Tuscan poets assembled in one volume, and the former to have satisfied this wish so notably. It is true that this same *principino* was even then either on his way to, or returning from, Milan, formally entrusted with

3. Cf. B. M. Scanferla, "Per la data della *Raccolta aragonese*," in *Rass. bibl. della lett. ital*, August 31, 1913, XXI, 244–250.

no less a mission than to escort in state to Naples the bride of his elder brother Don Alfonso, Duke of Calabria and heir to the throne; namely, the Duchess Ippolita Maria, daughter of Francesco Sforza, Duke of Milan.[4] This surely means that he was a mere figurehead as leader of such a formal diplomatic mission. It means that at least all his official acts in the course of this voyage, indeed, all his desirable "desires" were most likely prompted and directed by some high dignitary, a mature person, who was really in charge of the mission, of the numerous party, and of the young Prince himself. Accordingly, the learned suggestion to the brilliant, scholarly son of the then potentate of Florence may have really come originally from some tutor or learned diplomat in his suite. Scanferla suggests that the Prince's "laudable desire" may even be simply *una gentile invenzione dell'estensor dell'epistola,* which would not be unlike similar "inventions" found in the author's *Comento.*

However this may be, the more important point is that Lorenzo himself was really too young then to have executed such a task so ably. He, too, may have received assistance. Indeed, this is suspected by Barbi even with respect to the later date he assigns to the *Raccolta.* On the other hand, I wish to remind the reader that, as Professor Fletcher puts it moderately, Poliziano at fifteen was already translating the *Iliad* "into creditable Latin hexameters." Lorenzo, in an age of general intellectual precocity perhaps due to the humanistic method of education, was scarcely less precocious, not only in the political arena, but in the literary field as well. Indeed, quoting again from Professor Fletcher, by 1469 when he succeeded his father, "he had been given an education such as few royal princes have enjoyed." First at the hands of his private tutor, the learned Gentile Becchi, and later also in the intimacy of his constant association with such humanists as Marsilio Ficino and Cristoforo Landino, he undoubtedly received early the most ample training for a thorough understanding and a nice appreciation of the previous Italian poets in *volgare.* Therefore, he was well qualified early in life to compile such an anthology, though not perhaps so early as 1465.

The youth of the two *dramatis personae* in the gentle episode referred to in the prefatory letter was not, then, a strong objection to the validity of the early date hitherto attributed to this anthology. But, I confess, it had seemed to me, too, a little too marvelous to picture, as Mr. Fletcher says, "these two princely youths so earnestly concerned with high things." Moreover, I had marveled even more at the profundity of the philosophical thought and at the grandeur of the literary conception, which I found implied in Lorenzo's sonnets on Death: too profound, indeed, and too grand to ascribe them to a youth of seventeen. It is true that this philosophy and this conception were deducible from the much later *Comento,* rather than obvious from a first

---

4. Cf. Allegretti, "Diarium senense," in Muratori's *Rerum ital. script.,* XXIII, 771–772; "Giorn. nap.," *idem,* XXI, 1135; Ammirato, *Istorie fiorentine* (Firenze, 1641), III, 93–94; C. Cipolla, *Storia delle signorie italiane* (Milano, 1881), p. 455.

reading of the sonnets; but, after all, even if only hazily, they were implicit in the original poems, and this significance (which I, too, now detected in them) was vouched for by the author himself. Many a time, therefore, I had vaguely wished that the date of the *Raccolta,* in which they were found—I was about to say "unfortunately"—would permit the addition of at least a few years to the author's extreme youth at the time of their composition. Agreeing only partly with Barbi, it had seemed to me also that, as he says, *a conceder molto al comporre di maniera* common at the time, all the wisdom, critical acumen, excellent taste, and lofty poetic conception, which I found in those sonnets, was really too much to attribute to so young a scholar, however precocious and excellently trained. In other words, I had felt all along the need of a date for the *Raccolta,* which, falling well within the technical period of the poet's "adolescence," to conform with his declaration that he was in his "tender" age when he composed at least the *principio* of his *nuova vita,* would at the same time advance his age reasonably beyond that incredible seventeenth year. But, somehow, it never occurred to me to doubt the date I found assigned to it, as I thought, on good authority.

Now, therefore, I welcomed the rejection of the traditional date, and was grateful to Professor Fletcher for calling attention to Barbi's research on this, to me, important point. Barbi, in turn, referred with commendation to the study by Scanferla, already cited, which had preceded his own independent research by two years. And I also found in Rossi's note on the *Raccolta aragonese*[5] a reference to a later study on this same question by Lucile Wood Ferguson.[6] The latter, while concurring with Barbi and Scanferla in favor of the date 1476, did not seem to reject altogether the earlier, 1465 date. Indeed, she gave a list of other years in which Frederick appears to have at least stopped at Pisa, namely, 1467, 1474, 1478, 1479, 1482, and with respect to each of these she referred to the evidence for and against the possibility of a meeting there with the Magnificent.

As I say, for the reasons given, I was only too glad that the research of these scholars now permitted the postponement of the *Raccolta's* date, but I was not ready to accept the new date they proposed in its stead. Although, I maintain, my thesis was not affected, I feared that the coincidence of the new date with the year in which the Simonetta died might seem to cast some doubt on my absolute exclusion of her death as the original source of inspiration for Lorenzo's sonnets on the subject of the mystic death. Not that this would itself have made any difference with regard to the esoteric meaning of those sonnets, but I had found that it was not historically true. Moreover, the date 1476 placed the poet well within the technical period of his *gioventù,* and again I feared that at least this might seem to contradict the commentator's statement that he was in his "adolescence" when he became interested in the

5. Cf. V. Rossi, *Il Quattrocento* (Milano, Vallardi, 1933), p. 400, n. 43.
6. Cf. *Modern Philology,* XXIII (1925–26), 43–45.

subject of Platonic love and began to write his own *nuova vita* in imitation or in emulation of the poets represented in the *Raccolta*. Therefore, I decided to review the evidence that had been brought forth, especially with reference to the years 1465 and 1476; and this all the more because now my scientific curiosity had been thoroughly aroused, and, if possible, I wished to establish the truth.

Some of my reflections in the course of my reading of the studies mentioned have already been incorporated in the foregoing exposition of my perplexity. Without now repeating all the arguments pro and con, which have been adduced especially with reference to the traditional date and the new one, and admitting that the case for 1465 is, indeed, weak, I do not find that the arguments in favor of 1476 are all so strong as they have been felt to be. For one thing, it seems that, once the earlier date had to be discarded, it became necessary, or desirable, to discover one at least more likely. This was well, but this also led to an accumulation of reasons in favor of the substitute, which are more or less weak, to say the least. The higher probability conceded to the date 1476 is not a certainty. It rests almost entirely on a remark found in a letter of Luigi Pulci, dated September 20, 1476, and addressed to Lorenzo, then apparently at Pisa. This remark is as follows: "Harai riavuto il nostro messer Johanfrancesco; che l'ò caro, dipo' la partita di don Federigo *tutto gentile,* habbi ancora qualche *gentile* compagno."[7] This is obviously proof that Lorenzo and Frederick were both at Pisa in 1476, and this historical fact, which other sources confirm, is not disputed. But, while the reference to the *gentilezza* of both Frederick and his successor in the company of the Magnificent may indicate the nature of the conversations, indeed, suggests literary studies, there is nothing in the whole remark which indicates that this was the occasion in which the Prince expressed the "laudable desire." This inference is a conjecture, and on the basis of this remark alone we cannot exclude the possibility that the gentle episode may have taken place in the course of some other meeting either preceding or following this particular one. In the absence of more complete information, however, Pulci's remark certainly gives to this date a high degree of probability.

On the other hand, I notice that, while Barbi shows complete familiarity with Palermo's considerations regarding this question,[8] he does not pay the slightest attention to a strong argument advanced by the latter in favor of an early date for the *Raccolta*. Palermo does not exactly defend the 1465 date; indeed, without excluding it, he mentions several other occasions in which the episode may have taken place, merely to show that this date is not at all certain. It was originally advanced by Apostolo Zeno, who had even thought that the occasion he referred to had taken place in 1464. But Palermo observes that the MS. examined by him (*Codice 204,* which is the famous Palatin

7. Cf. L. Pulci, *Lettere,* ed. S. Bongi (Lucca, 1886), pp. 151–152; the italics are mine.
8. Cf. F. Palermo, *I manoscritti palatini di Firenze* (1853), I, 363–367

MS. containing this first anthology of Italian literature) does not contain any *rime del soave Poliziano; sopra ogni altro caro al Magnifico, e salito in grido di poesia fin dalla giovinezza.* And then he remarks: *questa mancanza non persuade egli che la Raccolta sia stata fatta in tempo che il Poliziano era fanciullo?*[9] It seems so to me, too, because it is verily inconceivable that, if it had been made as late as 1476, Lorenzo would have included some of his own lyrics and not a single one by his favorite contemporary poet, who, by that time had not only equaled him in the gentle art of poetry but surpassed him. Now, as Del Lungo points out,[10] Poliziano, who was born in 1454, was not taken under Lorenzo's wing until 1470, when he was barely sixteen and had just begun to attract attention by his remarkable translations of parts of the *Iliad* from the Greek into Latin hexameters. In fact, he was not taken regularly into the Medici household until 1473. By 1470, as it seems, he had not yet written anything in Italian, whereas by 1476 he had surely composed many a lovely lyric in the neo-Platonic, stilnovistic style of his patron, such as the *Raccolta* seems to have called for, and worthy of being comprised therein. Indeed, by the summer of 1476, when this anthology is now said to have been conceived, he had already begun to write his famous *stanze.* Therefore, as Palermo says, on the strength of this otherwise truly inexplicable omission, it would seem that the compilation of the *Raccolta* must antedate both Poliziano's Italian production and his friendship with Lorenzo (which, incidentally, was not wholly disinterested, but was also based on sincere, mutual admiration). To be sure, the anthology does not contain any poems of Luigi Pulci either, or by any other immediate contemporary, for that matter. But the *Morgante* and the rest of Pulci's verse could hardly be characterized as neo-Platonic and stilnovistic; and at the time there were no other "contemporaries" worthy of being included, except perhaps Boiardo, whose *canzoniere,* similarly, does not antedate 1469.

Barbi thinks that the introductory letter to Frederick preceding the *Raccolta* is *scrittura del Poliziano,* and bases his belief, not only on the authority of *Riccardiano 2773,* which attributes it clearly to "M. Angelo Politiano," but also on points of style and signs of erudition, which, in his opinion, support his contention. Now, of course, having once accepted the year 1476 for the date of the *Raccolta,* he finds that the position then occupied by Poliziano in the library of the Magnificent confirms this belief. But, apart from *le somiglianze nei pensieri e nella forma notate dal Palermo tra l'Epistola e il Commento del Magnifico* (*op. cit.,* I, 364 ff.; I quote from his own note on page 222 of his study), which he dismisses with a simple *non valgono davvero a provare che l'Epistola sia di Lorenzo:* if this letter were really by Poliziano, would not the omission from the anthology of any of his own lyrics be all the more striking? Can anyone imagine the *soave* but consummate artist, great

9. *Op. cit.,* p. 367.
10. Cf. his *Florentia,* pp. 222 ff., cited by Barbi.

humanist and *continuatore insieme e novatore* of the Italian poetry in *volgare,* writing enthusiastically a most appreciative and acute critical treatise on the very subject of the previous Italian poetry, such as the *Epistola* is, and not wishing to include in that *Raccolta* at least some of his own *stanze,* which he was even then composing? I for one cannot, and so I agree with Palermo that the absence from the anthology of any poems by Poliziano, not only points to an early date, but also excludes the possibility of his authorship of the prefatory letter. Incidentally, I may add that Rossi in the note already referred to, while inclined to accept now this false attribution, is influenced, not so much by the authority of the only MS. which attributes it to Poliziano, but apparently by this new date which Scanferla and Barbi have assigned to the *Raccolta.* In other words, he seems to discard Barbi's arguments based on points of style and on the erudition evinced by the author, and, without committing himself otherwise, says simply that the later date of the *Raccolta* now makes Poliziano's authorship of the prefatory letter *molto probabile.*

In conclusion, the case for 1476 seems to me only a little less weak than the case for 1465. On internal evidence, the earlier date seems too early and the later date too late. Historically, the former does not seem to be justified and the latter is not sufficiently documented. While waiting for further light on this matter, I incline toward a middle course. That is, I suspect a date which, without making Lorenzo technically a "youth," would allow him to be reasonably mature enough to have executed such a pretentious task so admirably, and would also exclude Poliziano's active collaboration. This would be a date close to 1469, and preferably preceding Lorenzo's accession to the dictatorship of Florence: which would make him about twenty-one at the time, and also conform with the assumption that he probably undertook this task in connection with his educational studies toward the end of his formal training when he had relative peace and quiet. But any date falling roughly between 1468 and 1472 would seem to me much more probable than either 1465 or 1476.

Since the proposed date, 1476, is doubtful after all—and, anyway, it would not affect the substance of my thesis—since, moreover, I believe that the correct date must antedate this year considerably, I have not thought it advisable to modify that part of my argumentation which conforms literally with the earlier date, 1465, now discarded. On the other hand, those of my arguments which may have seemed weak because of Lorenzo's extreme youth at the time of his poetic initiation are now enhanced as to their validity by this rejection of the earlier date and assumption of a somewhat later one.

DATE DUE

Demco, Inc. 38-293